Microsoft®

Introducing Microsoft® ASP.NET 2.0

Dino Esposito

Wintellect

PUBLISHED BY
Microsoft Press
A Division of Microsoft Corporation
One Microsoft Way
Redmond, Washington 98052-6399

Library of Congress Cataloging-in-Publication Data
Esposito, Dino, 1965-
Introducing Microsoft ASP.NET 2.0 / Dino Esposito.
p. cm.
Includes index.
ISBN 0-7356-2024-5
1. Active server pages. 2. Web sites--Design. 3. Microsoft .NET. I. Title.

TK5105.8885.A26E875 2004
005.2'76--dc22 2004044898

Printed and bound in the United States of America.

4 5 6 7 8 9 QWE 9 8 7 6 5

Distributed in Canada by H.B. Fenn and Company Ltd.

A CIP catalogue record for this book is available from the British Library.

Microsoft Press books are available through booksellers and distributors worldwide. For further information about international editions, contact your local Microsoft Corporation office or contact Microsoft Press International directly at fax (425) 936-7329. Visit our Web site at www.microsoft.com/learning/. Send comments to *mspinput@microsoft.com*.

Acquisitions Editors: Danielle Bird Voeller and Ben Ryan
Project Editor: Kathleen Atkins
Copy Editor: Ina Chang
Indexer: Lynn Armstrong

Body Part No. X10-46133

To Silvia, Francesco, and Michela

"I never let schooling interfere with my education."
—Mark Twain

Table of Contents

Part II Data Access

Part IV Advanced Topics

Acknowledgments

Introducing ASP.NET 2.0 was actually written twice. I started it in the summer of 2003 and worked hard on it around the PDC 2003 timeframe, finishing up a few hours before New Year's Eve. But then it became clear that the public beta program would not begin until summer 2004, so I had to rework it. The result is a book written over four seasons. I hope you enjoy it as much as I enjoy four-seasons pizza. (If you don't have four-seasons pizza in your country, come to Italy and try it!)

A fine ensemble of people at Microsoft Press helped make this book happen: Danielle Bird Voeller, Ben Ryan, and Kathleen Atkins. You will also see the results of Ina Chang's excellent copy editing of my pretty messy drafts. Christoph Wille, who reviewed the contents from a technical perspective, was one of the most attentive and insightful reviewers I have ever had (and I have written quite a few books).

Writing an introductory book on a new technology is a challenge, and I made it through by taking advantage of all the available tools—decompilers, e-mails, conference slides, sample code, and all sorts of papers that crossed my path. All in all, I'm proud of the result and want to thank everyone who shared ideas (or, more often, hunches) with me on how "the darned thing" would work eventually. The list (not in any specific order) includes Stephen Toub, Jeff Prosise, Bill Vaughn, Gert Drapers, Fernando Guerrero, Juwal Lowy, and Jason Clark. Rob Howard, Brad Millington, Joe Croney, and Shanku Niyogi from the Microsoft ASP.NET team also provided significant assistance and helped transform my own conjectures into accurate statements.

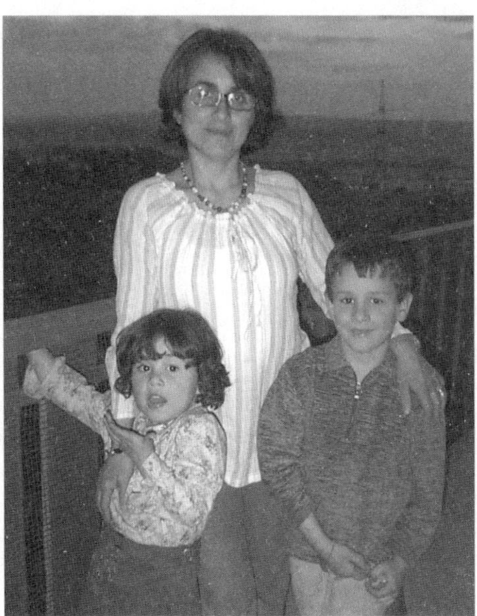

Thanks to you all,
Dino Esposito

P.S. I wrote this book while continuing many other activities, such as writing, speaking, training, consulting, traveling, swimming, and watching soccer games. However, I managed to have lunch at home almost every day (when I was in Rome), to sleep at least six hours every night (when I was at home), and to eat enough vegetables and fruits (to be a good example to my kids). I also took the kids to school every day at 8:30 (except when I was traveling in the States). Does this mean that I'll be voted MVP? (And I don't mean that nice award that Microsoft grants to valuable professionals—I'm interested in another kind of award—for Most Valuable Parent.) Kids, please vote for your dad!

Introduction

What's a Web application? Basically, it's a set of publicly accessible pages bound to a well-known URL. No matter which direction Web-related technologies take in the future, this basic fact will never change. The reason is the underlying transport protocol, HTTP. If we were to change the underlying protocol, we would end up with a different type of application. Period.

For all practical purposes, Web development began 10 years ago. Since then, we've seen numerous technologies emerge, from short-lived ones such as Microsoft ActiveX documents to watershed technologies such as Microsoft Active Server Pages (ASP). The arrival of ASP in 1997 made it clear that real-world Web development would be possible only through a rich and powerful server-side programming model.

Much as Microsoft Visual Basic did for Windows development, ASP provided a set of server tools for building dynamic Web applications quickly and effectively. More important, it pointed the way ahead. ASP wasn't perfect (or, more accurately, not yet perfected), so vendors improved the model by adding object orientation and dynamic code compilation. Java Server Pages (JSP) introduced key concepts such as compilation, components, tag customization, and a first-class programming language. (This was a different company, different platform, different programming paradigm, and different underlying technology—but the underlying idea was the same.)

ASP.NET took five years to materialize—an entire geological era in Web development terms—finally arriving in 2002. It was the next step in the evolutionary process that started with ASP and found an excellent next version in JSP. ASP.NET 2.0 is a major upgrade from there.

ASP.NET 2.0 features a new set of controls that simplify Web-based data access and includes functionality that facilitates user interaction, code reuse, and design-time development and even improves the aesthetic experience.

What This Book Covers

This book is based on Beta 1 of ASP.NET 2.0 and covers the vast majority of the features you'll find in the final release (expected in the first half of 2005). While it is not meant to be a full programmer's reference, it introduces key aspects of the new Web platform by using more than 70 fully functional examples. You'll also find concise explanations of important concepts and features.

Articulated in four parts, the book covers page essentials, data access, application services, and more advanced stuff like configuration and compilation models. Master pages, Web parts, personalization, themes, rich controls, and data source objects are explained and demonstrated through numerous examples. In the first part ("ASP.NET Essentials"), you'll learn about the Microsoft Visual Studio 2005 environment, the Page class, master pages and Web Parts. A look at personalization and themes completes the part. Next, the book moves on to tackle data access and present changes in ADO.NET 2.0, data binding, and the newest data source components and related server controls. Part III is about Application Services, including rich controls (wizard, dynamic images, site counters), state management, and security. Finally, Part IV covers the ASP.NET HTTP runtime environment, the compilation model, and the configuration API.

System Requirements

This book is designed to be used with the following software:

- One of the following Microsoft Windows versions with Microsoft Internet Information Services (IIS) installed:
  - Windows 2000
  - Windows XP Professional
  - Windows Server 2003
- Visual Studio 2005 (Beta 1 or the March Community Tech Preview [build 2.0.40301])
- Microsoft SQL Server 2000

The book doesn't specifically require a beta version of SQL Server 2005 (code-named Yukon).

Notice that most examples that use SQL Server assume a blank *sa* password, although the use of a blank password is strongly discouraged in any serious development environment. If you don't use a blank *sa* password in your SQL Server installation, you must add your own password to the connection strings or add the ASP.NET user to the login of the Northwind database. In the latter case, you can use *TRUSTED_CONNECTION=true* in the connection strings in place of the *sa* user and the blank password.

Code Samples

This book doesn't have a companion CD; all of the code samples are available on the Web at *http://www.microsoft.com/learning/books/products/6962*. Click the Companion Content link in the More Information box on the right side of the page.

The language used in the book is C#, and sample code is available only in C#. All of the examples are wrapped up in a single Visual Studio 2005 application and can be easily run from a central console, as shown here:

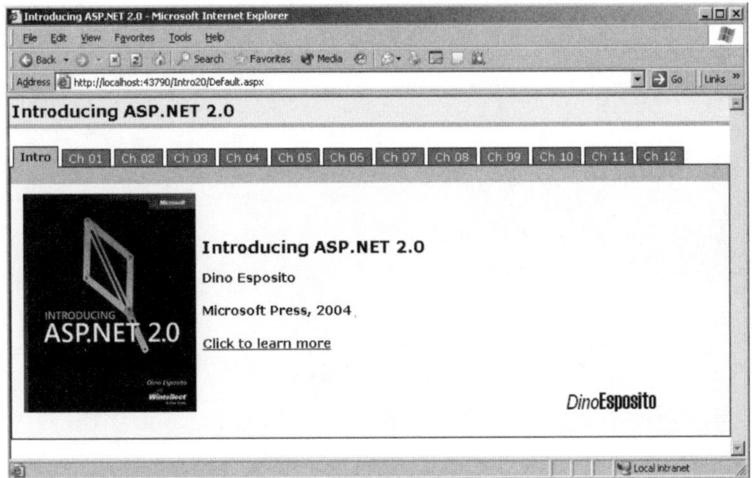

Support

Every effort has been made to ensure the accuracy of this book and the companion content. Microsoft Press provides corrections for books through the World Wide Web at the following address:

http://www.microsoft.com/learning/support/

Contact Information

Feel free to send questions about the book directly to the author at either of these addresses:

- dinoes@wintellect.com
- desposito@vb2themax.com

For additional information and resources, check out the following Web sites: Wintellect (*http://www.wintellect.com*) and the newest addition to the 2-The-Max family of Web sites, .NET-2-the-Max (*http://www.dotnet2themax.com*).

Part I
ASP.NET Essentials

1

Creating an ASP.NET 2.0 Application

No matter how you design and implement a Web application, at the end of the day it always consists of a number of pages bound to a public URL. The inexorable progress of Web-related technologies has not changed this basic fact, for the simple reason that it is the natural outcome of the simplicity of the HTTP protocol. As long as HTTP remains the underlying transportation protocol, a Web application can't be anything radically different from a number of publicly accessible pages. So what's the role of Microsoft ASP.NET?

ASP.NET provides an abstraction layer on top of HTTP with which developers build Web sites. Thanks to ASP.NET, developers use high-level entities such as classes and components within the object-oriented paradigm. Development tools assist developers during the work and make programming with the ASP.NET framework as seamless and quick as possible. Development tools are ultimately responsible for the application being created and deployed to users. They offer a programming paradigm and force developers to play by the rules of that paradigm.

The key development tool for building ASP.NET 2.0 applications is Microsoft Visual Studio 2005—the successor to Visual Studio .NET 2003. It has a lot of new features and goodies expressly designed for Web developers to overcome some of the limitations that surfaced from using Visual Studio .NET 2003.

In this chapter, we'll cover the three basic elements of an ASP.NET application—the IDE you use to build it, the page, and the core controls that make it run. We'll start with Visual Studio 2005.

Getting Started with Visual Studio 2005

Visual Studio 2005 is a container environment that integrates the functionality of multiple visual designers. You have a designer for building Windows Forms applications, one for building ASP.NET sites, one for building Web services, and so on. Visual Studio .NET 2003 has a single model for designing applications: the project-based approach. Real-world experience has shown that this is not the best approach—at least as far as ASP.NET and Web applications are concerned.

Drawbacks of Visual Studio .NET 2003

Visual Studio .NET 2003 designs applications around the concept of the *project*, which is the logical entity that originates any application—be it Windows Forms, Web, console, or Web service. Developers build an application by creating a new project, configuring it, and then adding pages, Web services, classes, and controls. In terms of implementation, the project is an XML file that links together some other files and directories. As far as Web applications are concerned, a Visual Studio .NET project requires a Microsoft Internet Information Services (IIS) virtual directory and also has a few other key drawbacks. Although developers do successfully use Visual Studio .NET for real-world applications, the tool isn't ideal for simpler projects.

> **Note** Microsoft also offers Web Matrix, a community-supported, free tool designed for ASP.NET applications. Web Matrix provides most of the features of cutting-edge code editors, such as syntax coloring, WYSIWYG designers, and different views of the code. Unlike Visual Studio .NET, Web Matrix is designed around the standalone ASP.NET page. It supports only pages with inline code and lets you develop applications as a set of standalone pages and resources.

For one thing, Visual Studio .NET requires Microsoft FrontPage Server Extensions (FPSE) and doesn't support FTP, local file system, or direct IIS access. In addition, it is dependent on IIS, which must be installed on the development machine or on a development server. These limitations have much greater impact on the development process than one might think at first. Debugging configurations and scenarios is quite difficult, developers need administrative privileges to create new projects, and effective corporate security policies for developer machines should be defined.

In Visual Studio .NET 2003, the project file is the single point of management for the constituent elements of the application. As a result, to make a file part of the project, you must explicitly add it into the project file and configure it—you can't just point at an existing virtual directory and go. The information coded in the project file counts more than the actual contents of the directory, and useless files are often forgotten and left around the site. Synchronizing hundreds of files in large applications is not easy; deploying projects onto other machines can be even more annoying. In addition, Visual Studio .NET has no interaction with IIS and doesn't let you browse and edit virtual roots.

However, the number-one issue with Visual Studio .NET–driven Web development is the inability to open a single page outside of a project. You can open and edit a page, but IntelliSense won't work; the same happens with other key features, such as running and debugging the page. Frankly, in this type of scenario, Visual Studio .NET offers only one advantage over Notepad—HTML syntax coloring.

Highlights of Visual Studio 2005

Visual Studio 2005 provides a simpler and friendlier way to create Web Forms applications. The key improvements address all the shortcomings detailed earlier. Let's review these features briefly.

Visual Studio 2005 supports multiple ways to open Web sites. In addition to using FrontPage Server Extensions, you can access your source files using FTP or a direct file system path. You can also directly access the local installation of IIS, browse the existing hierarchy of virtual directories, and access existing virtual roots or create new ones. IIS is not a strict requirement for the development tool to work. Like Web Matrix, Visual Studio 2005 ships with a local Web server that makes IIS optional, at least for testing and debugging purposes. Figure 1-1 shows the user interface of the embedded Web server.

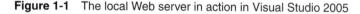

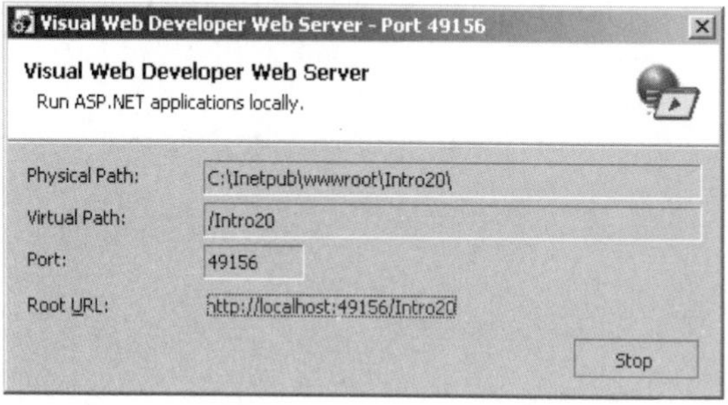

Figure 1-1 The local Web server in action in Visual Studio 2005

The local Web server is a revised version of Cassini, the free mini–Web server that originally shipped with Web Matrix. The local Web server is the default option unless you explicitly open the project from an existing IIS virtual directory. As Figure 1-2 demonstrates, you can open your Web site using a file system path or an IIS virtual directory. In the former case, the local Web server is used to test the site.

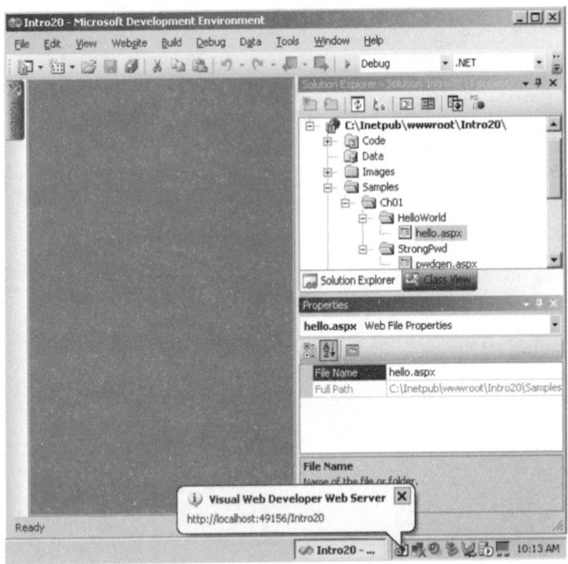

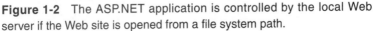

Figure 1-2 The ASP.NET application is controlled by the local Web server if the Web site is opened from a file system path.

The interaction with IIS is greatly simplified, as Figure 1-3 shows. When you try to open a Web site, you are given a few options to choose from. You can locate a project by using a file system path, using the IIS hierarchy of virtual directories (only the local IIS), using FTP, or by just typing the URL of the site configured with FrontPage Server Extensions. The IIS tab also contains buttons to create new virtual roots and applications.

Visual Studio 2005 does not compile everything in the site into an assembly, as Visual Studio .NET 2003 does. Instead, it uses the ASP.NET dynamic compilation engine. In this way, not only are changes to .aspx files immediately caught, but so are those made to .cs or .vb files. This results in a sort of dynamic compilation for code-behind classes.

Another long-awaited feature worth mentioning is the Copy Web site feature. Basically, by selecting a menu item you can copy your current Web site to another local or remote location. Figure 1-4 shows a glimpse of the feature.

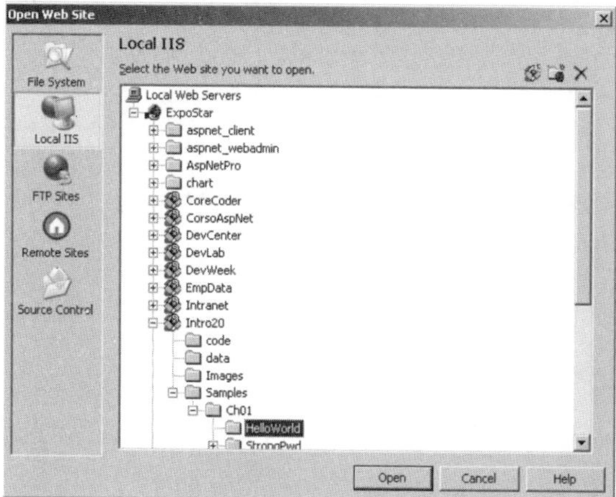

Figure 1-3 Navigating the IIS hierarchy to locate the existing virtual directory to open

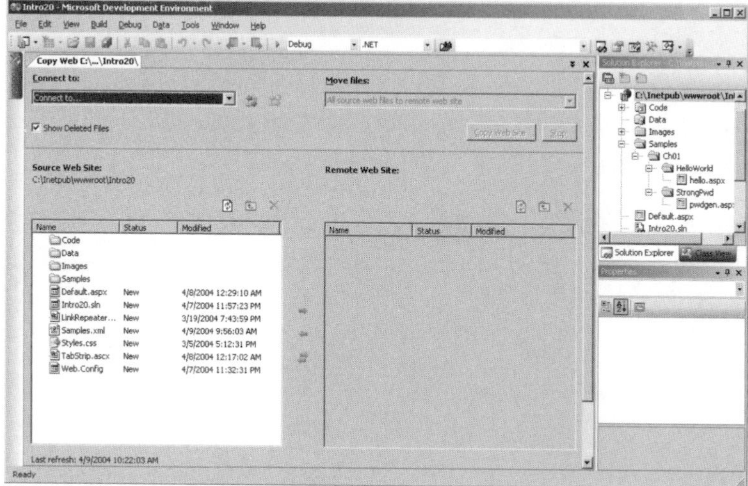

Figure 1-4 The Copy Web Site feature in action

Last but not least, if you double-click an.aspx file in Windows Explorer, Visual Studio 2005 starts up and lets you edit the source code. As it does not in Visual Studio .NET 2003, IntelliSense works great and the page can be viewed in the embedded browser through the local Web server. IntelliSense works everywhere, including within data binding expressions and page directives.

Creating a Sample Web Site

Let's create a sample Web site using Visual Studio 2005. You first create a new Web site by choosing File | New and choosing Web Site. The dialog box that appears prompts you for the type of site you want to create. You'll notice a couple of similar-looking options—ASP.NET Web site and ASP.NET Internet site, as shown in Figure 1-5.

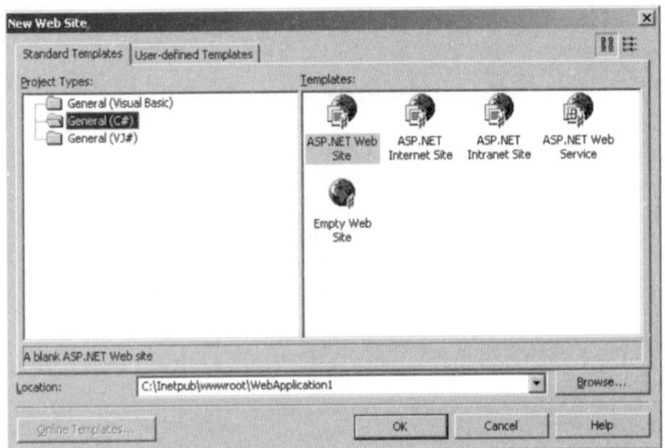

Figure 1-5 The options available to create a new Web site with Visual Studio 2005

If you select the Web Site option, Visual Studio generates the minimum number of files for a Web site to build. Basically, it creates a default.aspx page and an empty Data directory. If you opt for an Internet site, an ASP.NET starter kit is used to give you a functional Web site with several standard features built in. Let's go for a Web site.

> **Important** Visual Studio 2005 creates a project file but doesn't use it to track all the files that form an application. The root directory of the site implicitly defines a Web project. To add a new file to the project, you just copy or create that file to the directory, and it is in the project. If it isn't, right-click in Solution Explorer and click Refresh Folder.

To edit a Web page, you can choose from three views—Design, Source, and Server Code. The Design view displays the HTML layout, lets you select and edit controls and static elements, and provides a graphical preview of the page. The Source view shows the HTML markup along with the inline code. The markup is syntax-colored and enriched by features such as IntelliSense, tips, and autocompletion. The Server Code view shows only the inline code, if any. The good news is that Visual Studio also applies syntax coloring to the inline code.

You choose the template of the item to add to the site from the menu shown in Figure 1-6.

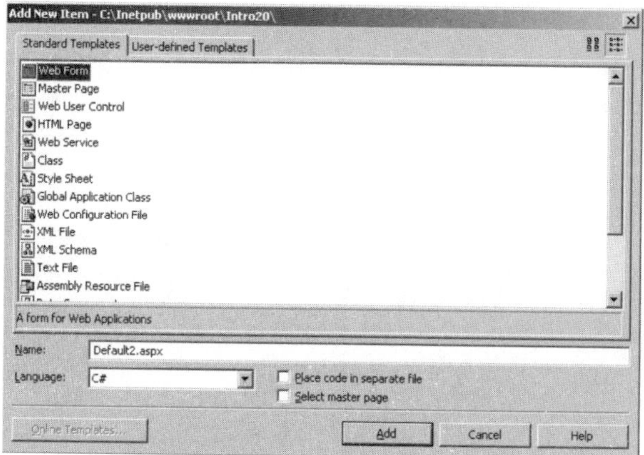

Figure 1-6 Item templates supported by Visual Studio 2005

Note the two check boxes that appear at the bottom of the window. You can choose to keep the code of the page in a separate file (similar to the code-behind model of Visual Studio .NET 2003), and you can associate the current page with a master page. (Master pages are a cool new feature of ASP.NET 2.0 that we'll discuss thoroughly in the next chapter.) The code-behind schema touted by Visual Studio .NET 2003 has been revised and restructured. As a result, pages built with Visual Studio 2005 are not forced to use code separation (page separated into .aspx and .cs files). Code separation is fully supported but is now optional.

Let's add some HTML markup to make it a Hello, World page. At a minimum, we need a text box to take the message and a button to send it to the world. The following HTML code renders the page shown in Figure 1-7:

```
<% @Page language="C#" %>
<script runat="server">
void Send_Click(object sender, EventArgs e)
{
    MsgSent.Text = Msg.Text;
}
</script>
```

```
<html>
<head runat="server">
    <title>Hello, World</title>
</head>
<body>
    <form runat="server" id="MainForm">
        <h1>Send a message to the world</h1>
        <asp:textbox runat="server" id="Msg" text="Hello, ASP.NET 2.0" />
        <asp:button runat="server" id="Send" text="Send"
                    onclick="Send_Click" />
        <hr />
        <b>Last message sent: </b>
        <asp:label runat="server" id="MsgSent" Font-Italic="True" />
        <hr />
    </form>
</body>
</html>
```

Send a message to the world

Hello, ASP.NET 2.0 Send

Last message sent: *Hello, ASP.NET 2.0*

Figure 1-7 The sample page used to take and display a welcome message

> **Note** As mentioned, you can open existing Web sites using the FTP protocol and then create and edit files. You must have access to the FTP server and read and write permissions for a particular FTP directory. The directory must already exist because Visual Studio 2005 cannot create a new Web site via FTP.

Designing Web Forms

Filling a Web Forms page is easy, too. You drag and drop controls from the toolbox onto the form, move elements around, and configure their properties. If you need to, you can switch to the Source view and manually type the HTML markup the way you want it to be. A pleasant surprise for many developers is that you can drag and drop controls from the toolbox directly into the Source code view; instead of viewing the control graphically rendered, you see the corresponding HTML. Similarly, you can edit the properties of a server control by selecting it the design view or highlighting the related HTML in the Source code view.

One of the first things you'll notice is that Visual Studio 2005 preserves the formatting of your HTML edits as you switch between views. Any edits in the design view affect only the changed elements. The Visual Studio .NET 2003 autoformatting features that kick in on view switching are now turned off.

Visual Studio 2005 enhances the HTML validation mechanism found in earlier tools. The HTML validation ensures that the HTML you are writing is suitable for the current target browser. The current target is visible at the bottom of the edit window and is set to Microsoft Internet Explorer 6.0 by default. When you type an invalid or malformed tag, the IDE detects the incompatibility and warns you about it. The tool leaves you free to enter the bad text anyway.

The number of client targets is significantly larger in ASP.NET 2.0 and ranges from Internet Explorer 6.0 to HTML 3.2 (covering Internet Explorer 3.x and Netscape Navigator 3.x). Other validation targets are mobile schemas (Compact HTML 1.0 and mobile HTML 3.2), Netscape 4.0, and the XHTML 1.0 Transitional schema. The latter schema covers browsers such as Netscape 7.0 and Opera 7.0.

Adding Code to Web Forms

How do you attach server code to the various HTML elements in an .aspx page? To try it out, place a button on a form and double-click. Visual Studio switches to the Server Code view and creates an empty event handler for the control's default event. For a button control, it is the *Click* event.

```
void Send_Click(object sender, EventArgs e)
{
    ⋮
}
```

The HTML markup is automatically modified to contain an additional *onclick* attribute:

```
<asp:button runat="server" id="Send"
     text="Send"
     onclick="Send_Click" />
```

Notice that in a difference from Visual Studio .NET 2003, the new version doesn't inject code in the page for automatic event wireup. Event binding is always done declaratively in the .aspx page. Recall that in Visual Studio .NET 2003, double-clicking a button adds the following code to the code-behind class:

```
// VS.NET injects this code in the code-behind class of a page
// when you double-click a button to handle its default event
Send.Click += new EventHandler(this.Send_Click);
```

The first time the page is compiled for use, ASP.NET performs the dynamic binding and the *onclick* attribute is expanded to the code shown above. Note that the *onclick* attribute is also used when you work with a page with code separation—the old code-behind schema. The only difference is that in this case, the event handler is defined in the code-behind class instead of being placed inline.

We now have the page layout and some significant code to play with. Testing the page is as easy as pressing F5. Visual Studio 2005 might complain about a missing web.config file, which is necessary if you want to debug the code. If you want to run the page without debugging it, click Run. Otherwise, you can let Visual Studio generate a proper web.config file for you. If you create your own web.config file, make sure it contains the following string:

```
<compilation debug="true" />
```

Once this is done, you can commence your debugging session.

The Local Web Server

The embedded Web server is a small executable; it can't replace all of the features of a full-blown Web server such as IIS, of course. It works only with individual pages and doesn't include any of the extra features of IIS such as the metabase or the ability to work as a Simple Mail Transfer Protocol (SMTP) mail server. As a result, an application that has to send e-mail messages should be tested under IIS because the local Web server can't handle e-mail messages. However, if you install the SMTP service, the embedded Web server can send e-mails, too.

Another point to consider about the embedded Web server concerns the security context. When run under IIS 5.0, an ASP.NET application ends up being served by a worker process—a separate Win32 executable whose name and features depend on the process model in use for ASP.NET applications on that server machine. No matter what the internal implementation, both aspnet_wp.exe (the worker process of the ASP.NET classic process model) and w3wp.exe (the worker process when the IIS 6.0 process model is used) run under a highly restricted account. In the former case, the account is ASPNET; in the latter case, the account is named NETWORK SERVICE.

In contrast, the embedded Web server takes the security token of the currently logged on user—that is, you. This means that if the developer is currently logged as an administrator—a much more common scenario than it should be—the application receives administrative privileges. The problem here is not a risk of being attacked; the real problem is that you are actually testing the application in a scenario significantly different from the real one. Things that work great under the local Web server might fail miserably under IIS.

For simple applications that only read and run ASP.NET pages, this problem is not that relevant. However, the results of your testing under the local server will become less reliable if you access files other than Web pages, files located on other machines, the Windows registry, or a local or remote database. In all these cases, you must make sure that the real ASP.NET account has sufficient permissions to work with those resources.

The bottom line is that even though you can use the local Web server to test pages, it sometimes doesn't offer a realistic test scenario.

Special Folders in ASP.NET 2.0 Applications

In Visual Studio 2005, any files found in the subtree of the application are implicitly part of the site. Any file that is copied to one of the existing directories, and any directory that is created, is reflected in Solution Explorer. But some of the folders have a special meaning to ASP.NET 2.0; others are named only by convention in a certain way. Table 1-1 details some of the special folders in the structure of an ASP.NET 2.0 application.

Table 1-1 Special Folders in ASP.NET Applications

Folder	Description
Bin	Contains all precompiled assemblies the application needs.
Code	Contains source class files (.vb or .cs) that the ASP.NET runtime engine dynamically compiles to assemblies.
Resources	Contains resource files (.jpg, .resx, .xsd) that the ASP.NET run-time engine dynamically compiles to resource assemblies.
Themes	Contains the definition of the themes supported by the application. The contents of this folder are compiled to a dynamic assembly. (More on ASP.NET themes in Chapter 4.)

The folder names are case insensitive. Folders such as Images and Data are also frequently used, but unlike the other two they have no role in the ASP.NET runtime architecture. They are simply named by convention to store images and local data files (e.g., Access databases, XML files), respectively.

As in ASP.NET 1.x, the Bin folder is where custom precompiled assemblies should be stored. Another key folder in the structure of an ASP.NET 2.0 application is Code. It is designed to contain reusable components that are automatically compiled and linked to the page code. Visual Studio 2005 constantly monitors the Code directory, and when new class files are added, it compiles them. The components in the Code subdirectory are compiled by default into a single assembly. The assembly is then referenced in the project and made available to all pages in the site. (More on this in a moment.)

The Code-Beside Model

Inline code is not exactly a best practice, though I'll be the first to say that in some situations it can be more practical than other techniques. Inline code doesn't make the page run slower, nor does it affect critical parameters of a site such as throughput and scalability. Nothing bad can happen to your application if you use inline code. The only one who might suffer from the use of inline code is you, the programmer. Real-world pages need a good amount of server code, and appending all that code to the *<script>* tag of the .aspx file makes the file significantly hard to read, edit, and maintain.

In ASP.NET 1.x, the alternative to inline code is code-behind classes. Code-behind and inline code are two functionally equivalent ways of attaching code to pages for the ASP.NET runtime engine, but not for Visual Studio .NET 2003.

Evolving from Code-Behind

Visual Studio .NET 2003 doesn't support inline code; if you try to use it anyway, things can get tricky. For one thing, you no longer get IntelliSense support and a fair number of other useful features. For real-world projects, in Visual Studio .NET 2003 you simply have to play by the rules and resort to pages with code-behind classes.

Code-behind is based on the idea that each Web Forms page is bound to a separate class file. This class ends up being the basis of the dynamically generated page class that the ASP.NET runtime creates for each requested .aspx resource. All the server code you need to associate with the .aspx resource flows into the code-behind class. This is neat and elegant in theory, but it's not very practical in the Visual Studio .NET 2003 implementation. A Visual Studio project always compiles down to an assembly in which all the constituent classes, including code-behind classes, are packed together. This approach comes with at least three drawbacks, as you have probably experienced:

- It requires an explicit compile step to deploy or run. The code-behind classes are automatically compiled by ASP.NET only if they are referenced in the pages through the *Src* attribute. For some reason, another attribute is used in Visual Studio .NET 2003 projects—*CodeBehind*—which is unknown to the ASP.NET runtime.
- The AppDomain that hosts the application is restarted on every change. To apply changes to the production machine, you must copy the new assembly to the Bin directory. The timestamp of the directory is modified, and when this happens, the ASP.NET runtime restarts the application.
- If you have large Web projects, the compile step is quite expensive. Even more expensive for users is the dynamic compilation step that ASP.NET needs to perform on all pages as required.

ASP.NET 2.0 has a new and improved compilation model that extends the compile-on-demand feature to class files and eliminates the need for Visual Studio .NET to require IDE compilation for Web application projects.

Compile-on-Demand for All Resources

ASP.NET 1.x supports the dynamic compilation of a few file types: ASP.NET pages (.aspx), Web services (.asmx), user controls (.ascx), HTTP handlers (.ashx), and global.asax. These files are automatically compiled on demand when first required by a Web application. The compiled copy is invalidated as soon as a change to the dependent source file is detected. This system enables programmers to quickly develop applications with a minimum of process overhead—you just hit Save and go.

In ASP.NET 2.0, the compile-on-demand feature is extended to various file types, typically class files (.vb and .cs), resource files (.resx), Web service discovery files (.wsdl), and typed *DataSet* schema files (.xsd). Once the ASP.NET runtime ensures that all changes to certain file types are promptly detected, there's no need for a development tool to force a compile step. The changes to the ASP.NET runtime make it possible to refine the whole code-behind mechanism. The ASP.NET 2.0 build system is also backward-compatible with the code-behind schema of older ASP.NET applications.

> **Note** That ASP.NET 2.0 compiles class files (.cs and .vb) on demand is a fact. That ASP.NET 1.x doesn't do the same is debatable. ASP.NET 1.x does have the ability to compile on demand class files that are explicitly bound to .aspx pages through the *Src* attribute of the *@Page* directive. Unfortunately, this code model is not supported by Visual Studio .NET 2002 and 2003, and therefore it often passes unnoticed.

Code-Beside vs. Code-Behind

There's nothing wrong with the code-behind model. It promotes object-orientation, leads to modular code, and supports code and layout separation. The only problem with code-behind is in the implementation provided by Visual Studio .NET 2003. The newest version of Visual Studio comes with a revised model for page/class association. The new code model, code-beside, looks like the code-behind model, but each uses a different set of keywords and behaviors. The following code shows the header of ASP.NET 1.x code-behind pages created with and without Visual Studio:

```
<%@ Page Language="C#" Inherits="Company.MyClass"
         Codebehind="MyPage.aspx.cs" %>
<%@ Page Language="C#" Src="MyPage.aspx.cs" %>
```

The following code shows the page/class binding as it can be coded in ASP.NET 2.0 using code-beside. Note the use of the new keyword *CompileWith*.

```
<%@ Page Language="C#" CompileWith="MyPage.aspx.cs"
         ClassName="Company.MyClass" %>
```

By default, Visual Studio 2005 creates pages that store their code inline. To design your site using code separation, you choose the appropriate template by choosing Add New Item from the Website menu. When you edit a page with code separation, Visual Studio stores any code in the class file specified through the *CompileWith* attribute. Pages and projects do not have to be built to run. Instead, ASP.NET compiles the page when it is first requested.

Partial Classes

The compilation models of ASP.NET 1.x and ASP.NET 2.0 differ significantly because they are built on completely different underpinnings. Pages that use code separation take advantage of a feature known as partial classes. When the page runs, the compiler uses the *CompileWith* attribute in the *@Page* directive to find the file containing the code. It then dynamically merges the .aspx page and code page into a single class that inherits the base *Page* class. The class is then compiled into an assembly for execution.

Once you add a Web form with code separation, the top *@Page* directive in the page looks like this:

```
<%@ page language="C#" compilewith="HelloBeside.aspx.cs"
         classname="ASP.HelloBeside_aspx" %>
```

When the page runs, ASP.NET 2.0 dynamically creates and instantiates a class representing the page. The *CompileWith* attribute identifies the code file for this page. The *ClassName* attribute defines the name for the class that will be created. By default, Visual Studio 2005 uses the page name as the basis for the class name.

By default, the code in the code-beside file is rooted in the ASP namespace and contains only a class definition. The class definition is incomplete (partial) and contains only a portion of the complete class that will make up the run-time page. Specifically, the partial class defined in the code file contains the event handlers and other custom code that you write. The ASP.NET 2.0 runtime parses the .aspx layout file and combines this information with the contents of the partial code-beside class. The resulting class inherits from *Page* and is compiled and used to serve the request. The following code shows the sample code for the code-beside version of the aforementioned Hello, World example.

```
using System;

namespace ASP
{
   public partial class HelloBeside_aspx
   {
      void Send_Click(object sender, EventArgs e)
      {
            MsgSent.Text = Msg.Text;
      }
   }
}
```

We'll discuss the ASP.NET 2.0 compilation model in more detail in Chapter 11.

Sharing Source Components

The code-beside model extends the compile-on-demand feature to the classes bound to a Web page. What about other class files (i.e., helper components and business objects) that your application might be using and reusing? Should they always be precompiled and deployed to the Bin folder? Well, not exactly.

The *Code* Subdirectory

You can keep your helper classes and business objects in the Code subdirectory. As mentioned, Visual Studio 2005 monitors the directory and compiles any new class file that is added or edited. The resulting assembly is automatically referenced in the application and shared between all pages participating in the site.

You should put only components into the Code subdirectory. Do not put pages, Web user controls, or other noncode files containing noncode elements into it. All the files in the Code subdirectory are dynamically compiled to a single assembly, named code.dll. The assembly has application scope and is created in the Temporary ASP.NET Files folder—well outside the Web application space.

Building a Sample Shared Class

To experience the advantages of reusable source components, let's design a page that uses a fairly complex and large component that would be annoying to insert inline in each page that needs it.

Many products and services available over the Web require a strong password. The definition of a "strong password" is specific to the service, but normally it is at least eight characters long and has at least one character from each of the following groups: uppercase, lowercase, digits, and special characters. We'll use that definition here. The sample page you will build asks the user for the desired length of the password and suggests one built according to the preceding rules. You create a new file named StrongPassword.cs and place it in the newly created Code subdirectory. The class outline is shown here:

```
public class StrongPassword
{
    public StrongPassword()
    {...}
    public StrongPassword(string password)
    {...}

    public bool Validate()
    {...}
    public bool Validate(string password)
    {...}

    public string Generate()
    {...}
    public string Generate(int passwordLength)
    {...}
}
```

The class features two methods—one to check the robustness of a given password and one to generate a new strong password. Of course, the definition of a "strong password" is arbitrary. Once placed in the Code directory, this class is compiled on demand and made available to all pages. In the sample page, the code to generate and validate a password becomes simpler and more readable.

```
void buttonGenerate_Click(Object sender, EventArgs e) {
    StrongPassword pswd = new StrongPassword();
    // Use the minimum length
    labelPassword.Text = pswd.Generate();
}

void buttonValidate_Click(Object sender, EventArgs e) {
    StrongPassword pswd = new StrongPassword(TestPassword.Text);
    labelResult.Text = pswd.Validate().ToString();
}
```

Figure 1-8 shows the page in action. The same functionality can also be achieved placing the code inline. However, a savvy use of the Code directory enhances the readability and the modularity—in other words, the quality—of the code you write.

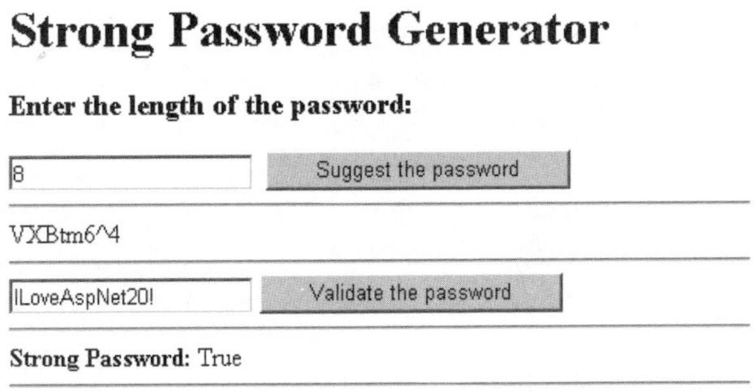

Strong Password Generator

Enter the length of the password:

8 | Suggest the password

VXBtm6^4

ILoveAspNet20! | Validate the password

Strong Password: True

Figure 1-8 Although it doesn't show up in the overall user interface, the page has a more logical and maintainable internal design.

The Page Object Model

In the .NET Framework, the *Page* class represents an .aspx file—a Web page—and provides the basic behavior for all pages. The contents of the .aspx file are parsed at run time and a class is dynamically created (in C# or Visual Basic .NET, according to the page's language setting). This dynamically created class inherits from the base class *Page*. Unlike in ASP.NET 1.x, in ASP.NET 2.0 the page's base class doesn't change if code separation is used. (In ASP.NET 1.x, when you use code-behind, the code-behind class becomes the parent of the dynamically generated page class.)

The *Page* class is a built-in HTTP handler that the ASP.NET runtime invokes through the methods of the *IHttpHandler* interface to finalize the request processing. Furthermore, the class represents a special type of control because it inherits from *TemplateControl*. In ASP.NET 2.0, the *Page* class also implements the *IPaginationContainer* interface, which allows the page (and any container control) to be paginated by the new *Pager* control. (More on this later.)

```
public class Page : TemplateControl, IHttpHandler, IPaginationContainer
```

The behavior of each page can be declaratively controlled through the attributes of the *@Page* directive. To get the most out of the *Page* class, though, you must become familiar with properties, methods, and events of the *Page* class and have a clear idea of the page life cycle in the ASP.NET runtime. Overall, the structure of the page has not been revolutionized in the transition from ASP.NET 1.x to ASP.NET 2.0. However, quite a few new features have been added. Some are related to the page as an object; some are inherited from the surrounding runtime environment.

What's New in the *Page* Class

In ASP.NET 2.0, a page supports some new features such as personalization, master pages, theming, and site counting. You can control, enable, and disable these features through new methods, properties, and directive attributes. Let's start our exploration from the very beginning of a page—that is, from the *@Page* directive. In this section, we'll mostly focus on changes and improvements in the programming interface of the *Page* class. All the members the class features in ASP.NET 1.x are supported in version 2.0. For a detailed explanation of ASP.NET 1.x members, please refer to my book *Programming Microsoft ASP.NET* (Microsoft Press, 2003). Infrastructure features such as theming and site counters will be covered in detail in Chapter 4 and Chapter 8, respectively.

The *@Page* Directive

ASP.NET 2.0 adds some new attributes to the *@Page* directive to give developers control over new framework features such the aforementioned personalization and theming. Table 1-2 lists the new attributes of the directive.

Table 1-2 New Attributes in the *@Page* Directive

Attribute	Description
Async	If set to *true*, the generated page class from derives from *IHttpAsyncHandler* rather than *IHttpHandler* and adds some built-in asynchronous capabilities to the page.
CompileWith	Specifies the name of the referenced code-beside file to use for the page.
EnablePersonalization	Indicates whether any profile information should be used to build the page.
MasterPageFile	Specifies the path of the master to use for building the current page.
PersonalizationProvider	Specifies a valid provider defined in the application's configuration file.
Theme	Specifies the name of the theme to use for the page.

You met the *CompileWith* attribute earlier in this chapter, and I will cover master pages in depth in Chapter 2. Personalization and theming are the subject of Chapter 4. Personalization concerns the automatic use of the profile information associated with the page. Theming has to do with the page's ability to change the visual appearance (skin) while maintaining all of its functions.

Note The use of the Boolean *Async* directive (false by default) forces the ASP.NET runtime to generate code that serves the page request in an asynchronous way. In ASP.NET 1.x, you can build asynchronous applications but you must be very familiar with the concepts involved and you have to write a fair amount of code. The model has been integrated with the ASP.NET 2.0 runtime and can be enabled using the *Async* page directive.

The page executes its custom code asynchronously while the runtime progresses on the page life cycle. A single unwind point on the page is set between the *PreRender* and *PreRenderComplete* events to synchronize the request threads and generate the output for the browser.

Properties of the *Page* Class

The properties of the *Page* object fall into two distinct groups: intrinsic objects and page-specific properties. Intrinsic objects include references to environmental standalone objects such as *Cache*, *User*, and *Trace*, plus all the classic intrinsic object that form the HTTP context—*Session*, *Application*, *Request*, and the like. Page-specific properties are all the properties that affect or describe the state of the page—for example, *IsPostBack*, *EnableViewState*, and *SmartNavigation*.

The new properties of the *Page* class can also be categorized into either of the preceding groups. Table 1-3 lists the new intrinsic objects of ASP.NET 2.0.

Table 1-3 New Intrinsic Objects in the *Page* Class

Property	Description
ClientScript	Instance of the *ClientScriptManager* class that represents a separate object that groups all the methods that work with client-side scripts.
Header	Instance of the *HtmlHead* class that represents the contents of the page's *<head>* block if this is marked as *runat=server*.
Master	Gets the master page that determines the overall look of the page.
Pager	Instance of the *Pager* control (if any) that paginates the contents of the current page.
SiteCounters	Instance of the *SiteCounters* class that represents the built-in service to track page usage within the application. You'll learn more about site counters in Chapter 8.

The *ClientScript* property returns the manager object of all methods that inject JavaScript code in the page. The object returned by the *ClientScript* property acts as a centralized console to invoke script-related methods such as *RegisterHiddenField* and *RegisterStartupScript*. Note that the script-related methods of the class are now marked as obsolete and are implemented through a call to the corresponding methods of the *ClientScript* object. The following code snippet shows an example:

```
[Obsolete("...", false)]
public void RegisterHiddenField(string fieldName, string field value)
{
   this.ClientScript.RegisterHiddenField(fieldName, fieldValue);
}
```

The false value in the *[Obsolete]* attribute indicates that the use of the obsolete element isn't considered an error.

Table 1-4 lists the other new properties of the *Page* class.

Table 1-4 Other New Properties of the *Page* Class

Property	Description
EnablePersonalization	Gets and sets whether any profile information should be used to build the page.
EnableTheming	Lets you configure the page to ignore themes. This is useful when the page has a predefined look that you do not want an external theme to override.
IsAsync	Indicates whether the page is processed asynchronously.
IsCrossPagePostBack	Indicates whether the page is being loaded in response to a client postback requested by a different page.
IsPagePersonalized	Indicates whether the page contains profile information and whether this information is currently used.
MasterPageFile	Gets or sets the filename of the master page for the current page.
MaximumWeight	Gets and sets the maximum size of each page of content when a *Pager* control is used to paginate this .aspx page. The default is 4000 bytes. (More on this in a moment.)
PersonalizationMode	Specifies the personalization mode by using a value taken from the *PersonalizationMode* enumeration.
PreviousPage	Returns an object that represents the previously visited *Page* object when a cross-page posting is done.
Title	Gets and sets the string that represents the title of the page.

A couple of these properties—*IsCrossPagePostBack* and *PreviousPage*—deserve a few more words. In ASP.NET 2.0, pages are no longer forced to always post to themselves. Pages can automatically post the contents of their unique HTML form to other pages. How can the target page distinguish between a page and a cross-page postback? By simply using the *IsPostBack* and *IsCrossPagePostBack* properties. In the case of a cross-page postback, the target knows about the posting page and can retrieve the values of the original controls because a reference to the posting page is returned by the *PreviousPage* property. In the upcoming section "Programming the Page," you'll see an example of this feature.

Methods of the *Page* Class

The *Page* class features a handful of new methods, most of which are simply inherited from the base *Control* class. Table 1-5 lists them all.

Table 1-5 New Methods of the *Page* Class

Method	Description
EnsureID	Inherited from *Control* and not especially useful for a page, this method ensures that the current object gets a unique ID.
Focus	Inherited from *Control* and not especially useful for a page, this method ensures that the page gets the input focus.
GetCallbackEventReference	Returns the prototype of a client-side JavaScript function that posts back to the server using a callback function to implement a form of remote scripting.
GetValidators	Returns the collection of all validator controls that belong to the specified group.
GetWebResourceUrl	Returns a valid URL that serves up a file (i.e., a GIF file) that was embedded in the page as a named resource.
RegisterRequiresControlState	Registers the specified control as one that requires control state management. (More on control state later.)
SetFocus	Sets the input focus to a particular control contained in the page.
TestDeviceFilter	Checks whether the current browser is of the specified type.

The methods listed in the table address some interesting new types of functionality, such as the control state (as opposed to the control view state), validation groups, and an enhanced script object model.

Events of the *Page* Class

The life cycle of a page in the ASP.NET runtime is marked by a series of events. By wiring their code up to these events, developers can dynamically modify the page output and the state of constituent controls. In ASP.NET 1.x, a page fires events such as *Init*, *Load*, *PreRender*, and *Unload* that punctuate the key moments in the life of the page. ASP.NET 2.0 adds quite a few new events to allow you to follow the request processing more closely and precisely. The new events are listed in Table 1-6. The order is alphabetical; we'll discuss the order in which they are fired in just a moment.

Table 1-6 New Events of the *Page* Class

Event	Description
InitComplete	Occurs when the page initialization step is completed.
LoadComplete	Occurs at the end of the load stage of the page's life cycle.
PreInit	Fires before the page begins its initialization step. This is the first event in the life of an ASP.NET 2.0 page.
PreLoad	Fires just before the page begins loading the state information, immediately after initialization.
PreRenderComplete	Occurs when the prerendering phase is completed and all child controls have been created. After this event, the personalization data and the view state are saved and the page renders to HTML.

Let's review the full life cycle of an ASP.NET 2.0 page.

The Page Life Cycle

An ASP.NET page springs to life when the ASP.NET runtime invokes the *IHttpHandler::ProcessRequest* method on the dynamic class created to wrap the source code of the requested .aspx resource. The method sets the intrinsics for the page, such as the HTTP context and the *Request* and *Response* objects. Next it builds the tree of controls that were declared in the .aspx source and determines whether the page is being run in postback mode, callback mode, or cross-page postback. (I'll say more about callback mode later.) The first chance that developers have to get into the game is when the *PreInit* event occurs.

- **Page preinitialization** When the *PreInit* event handler returns, the page loads any personalization data and initializes any themes. This is the right time to intervene if you want to programmatically set the page theme.
- **Page initialization** Each control in the page is recursively given a chance to initialize and configure its state. Child controls have their *Init* event fired before the *Init* event on the container page.
- **End of page initialization** The *InitComplete* event occurs at the end of the loop that initializes all child controls. In between *Init* and *InitComplete*, only one thing happens—the view state of controls is set up for tracking. Each control has its *TrackViewState* method called. By default, this method sets a flag that instructs the control to track its view state for changes.

- **Loading the control state and the view state** In ASP.NET 2.0, the control state is a sort of private view state that each control is responsible for maintaining. Unlike the view state, the control state can't be modified programmatically outside the control and can't be turned off. The control state is loaded before the view state. Both steps fire no events but can be customized, overriding a couple of protected methods.
- **Loading postback data** The posted values are processed and their ID matched against the ID of all declared controls. If a match is found, the posted value updates the state of the control. (How this happens for a specific control depends on the control's implementation of the *IPostBackDataHandler* interface.)
- **Page preloading** The *PreLoad* event occurs when the page is finished processing any posted values. You handle this event if you need to perform any operation before the page loading phase begins.
- **Page loading** The *Load* event is fired recursively for all constituent controls and then for the page. Before the loading stage ends, a number of interesting actions take place. The page makes a second attempt to find a match between posted values and page controls. This attempt is designed to load any available state into dynamic controls created or restored in the *Load* event. If the page has a callback event handler, the event is raised at this time. Finally, if the posted values modify the properties of some child controls that require notification of changes, the related postback change notification events are fired. For example, if the posted values modify the *Text* property of a *TextBox* control, the *TextChanged* server event is fired.
- **Postback events** The page executes the server-side code associated with the client-side event (i.e., a click) that caused the page to post back. This step is the core of the ASP.NET event model.
- **End of page loading** The *LoadComplete* occurs to mark the end of the preliminaries. From now on, the page enters its rendering phase.
- **Prerendering** Before the page fires the *PreRender* event, it ensures that all needed child controls have been created. The *PreRender* event is first fired for the page and then recursively for all children. At the end of the loop, the page fires the *PreRenderComplete* event and saves personalization data, control, and view state.

- **Rendering** Generates the markup to be rendered to the client. The default implementation can be customized, overriding the *Render* method. No user event is associated with this phase.
- **Page unload** Performs any final cleanup before the page object is released. The event you need to hook up from your code is *Unload*. Child controls are unloaded before the page is unloaded. The *Unload* event is followed by the *Dispose* event, which indicates that the page object is being destroyed.

> **Important** Notice that the *xxxComplete* events are fired only for the page. Contained controls never receive it. The *xxxComplete* events signal that a certain operation is complete. For this reason, they make sense only at the page level.

Programming the Page

Compared to its implementation in ASP.NET 1.x, the *Page* class in ASP.NET 2.0 provides a few new capabilities, such cross-page posting, content pagination, and personalization. In this section, we'll take a closer look at cross-page posting and pagination, saving personalization for Chapter 4. Cross-page posting is a feature that the community of ASP.NET developers loudly demanded. Pagination is the offspring of the tight level of integration achieved between ASP.NET and Mobile ASP.NET. We'll start this quick overview of new page functions with another feature that was widely requested—the ability to program the *<head>* tag of a Web page.

The *HtmlHead* Control

The *HtmlHead* control belongs to the *System.Web.UI.HtmlControls* namespace. An instance of this control is automatically created if the page contains a *<head>* tag marked with the *runat=server* attribute. Note that this setting is the default when you add a new page to a Visual Studio 2005 Web project, as shown in the following snippet:

```
<head runat="server">
    <title>Untitled Page</title>
</head>
```

The header of the page is returned through the new *Header* property of the *Page* class. The property returns null if the *<head>* tag is missing or if it is present but lacks the *runat* attribute.

The control implements the *IPageHeader* interface, which consists of three collection properties—*Metadata*, *LinkedStylesheet*, *Stylesheet*, and a string property—*Title*. The *Metadata* property is a dictionary that collects all the desired child *<meta>* tags of the header:

```
Header.Metadata.Add("CODE-LANGUAGE", "C#");
```

The code results in the following markup:

```
<meta name="CODE-LANGUAGE" content="C#" />
```

To express other common metadata such as *Http-Equiv*, you can resort to adding literal controls to the *Controls* collection of the header. Notice that you must explicitly cast the *Header* object to *Control* because the *Header* property is declared of type *IPageHeader*, which has no *Controls* property defined.

```
LiteralControl equiv;
equiv = new LiteralControl ("<meta http-equiv='refresh' content='3' />")
((Control) Header).Controls.Add(equiv);
```

To link a stylesheet file, you use the following code:

```
Header.LinkedStyleSheets.Add("MyStyles.css");
```

Finally, the *HtmlHead* control features the *Title* property, through which you can retrieve and set the title of the page.

```
Header.Title = "This is the title";
```

Note that this property returns the correct page title only if the *<title>* tag is correctly placed within the *<head>* tag. Some browsers are quite forgiving on this point and allow developers to define the title outside the header.

Cross-Page Postbacks

Implementing cross-page postbacks requires only a couple of steps. First you set the *PostBackUrl* property on buttons and server controls that can cause postback. When the *PostBackUrl* property is set, the ASP.NET runtime binds the corresponding HTML element to a new JavaScript function. Instead of our old acquaintance *__doPostback*, it uses the new *WebForm_DoPostBackWithOptions* function:

```
<form runat="server">
   <asp:textbox runat="server" id="Data" />
   <asp:button runat="server" id="buttonPost"
            Text="Click"
            PostBackUrl="~/target.aspx" />
</form>
```

The button declaration renders the following markup:

```
<input type="submit" name="buttonPost" id="buttonPost"
     value="Click"
     onclick="javascript:WebForm_DoPostBackWithOptions(
        new WebForm_PostBackOptions(&quot;buttonPost&quot;,
                                    &quot;&quot;,
                                    false,
                                    &quot;&quot;,
                                    &quot;target.aspx&quot;,
                                    false,
                                    false))" />
```

As a result, when the user clicks the button, the current form posts its content to the specified target page. What about the view state? When the page contains a control that does cross-page posting, a new hidden field is created—*__PREVIOUSPAGE*. The field contains the view state information to be used to serve the request. This view state information is transparently used in lieu of the original view state of the page being posted to.

You use the *PreviousPage* property to reference the posting page and all of its controls. Here's a sample page that can access the content of the text box defined in the server form presented a moment ago:

```
<%@ page language="C#" %>
<script runat="server">
    void Page_Load(object sender, EventArgs e)
    {
        if (PreviousPage == null)
        {
            Response.Write("Invoke me only through cross-page posting.");
            Response.End();
            return;
        }

        // Retrieves the data textbox
        TextBox txt = (TextBox) PreviousPage.FindControl("Data");
        Response.Write("<b>You passed:</b> " + txt.Text);
    }
</script>
<html>
<head runat="server">
    <title>Target page</title>
</head>
<body>
</body>
</html>
```

Paging the Page

If you have ever played with ASP.NET mobile controls, you should know about pagination. Pagination is a mobile page's ability to automatically display the contents of a form in pages according to the characteristics of the target device. The individual page to display is composed by dividing the overall markup into blocks of approximately the same size.

ASP.NET 2.0 comes with a new control named *Pager* that adds similar functionality to all server controls, including mobile controls. The pager is capable of paginating container controls based on their weight or the number of items to display per page. The *Pager* control also displays its own user interface to let you move around the pages. Figure 1-9 shows a page with 50 text boxes that a pager displays a few at a time.

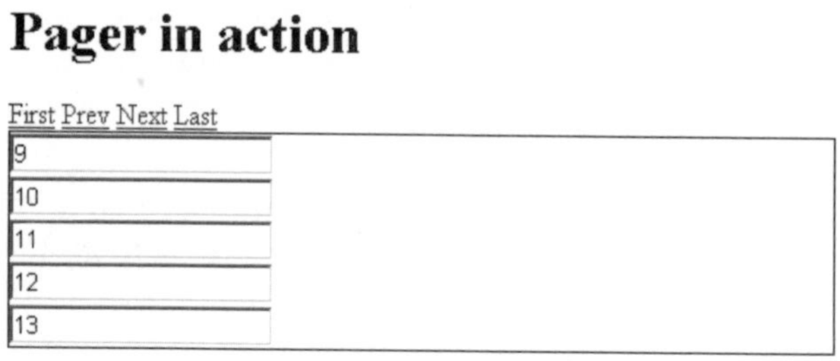

Figure 1-9 Several controls are contained in a panel and are paginated by means of a *Pager* control.

The source code of the page is shown here:

```
<%@ Page Language="C#" %>

<html>
<script runat="server">
    void Page_Load (Object sender, EventArgs e)
    {
        for (int i=0; i<50; i++) {
            TextBox txt = new TextBox ();
            txt.Text = i.ToString();
            panelSample.Controls.Add (txt);
            panelSample.Controls.Add (new LiteralControl("<br>"));
        }
    }
</script>
<body>
<form runat="server">
<h1>Pager in action</h1>
<asp:contentpager runat="server" id="pagerPanel"
```

```
    Mode="NextPreviousFirstLast"
    ControlToPaginate="panelSample"
    ItemsPerPage="9" />
<asp:panel runat="server" id="panelSample" borderwidth="1" />
</form>
</body>
</html>
```

The *ContentPager* control paginates the contents of a container control based on one of two algorithms—weight-based or item-based. The algorithm used depends on the *ItemsPerPage* property. If the property is set, the item-based algorithm is used; otherwise, the weight-based algorithm is used. The two algorithms work in a similar manner, but the weight-based algorithm allows finer control over the elements that go in each page. Basically, the item-based algorithm attempts to place in each page exactly the number of controls indicated by *ItemsPerPage*. The weight-based algorithm assigns each container a maximum weight that can't be exceeded when paginating. For example, the *Page* class has a maximum weight of 4000. Each control is also given a default weight (100). As you can see, in the default case the two algorithms are nearly identical, but the weight of each control can be overridden, thus allowing for a customized form of pagination.

The Page Scripting Object Model

The great news about the scripting object model in ASP.NET 2.0 is that it allows calls to server events from client code without causing the page to post back and refresh. This sort of remote scripting engine is implemented through a callback mechanism that offers a clear advantage to developers. When you use script callbacks, the results of the execution of a server-side method are passed directly to a JavaScript function that can then update the user interface via Dynamic HTML. A roundtrip still occurs, but the page is not fully refreshed.

Script callbacks are not the only good news. The overall scripting model has been enhanced. As a result, setting the input focus to a particular control is now as easy as calling the *SetFocus* method.

Script Callbacks

Script callbacks allow you to execute out-of-band calls back to the server. These calls are special postbacks, so a roundtrip always occurs; however, unlike classic postbacks, script callbacks don't redraw the whole page and give users the illusion that everything is taking place on the client. You can use callbacks to update individual elements of a page, such as a chart or a panel, provide different views of the same data, download additional information on demand, or autofilling one or more fields. In particular, the ASP.NET 2.0 *TreeView* control uses script callbacks extensively to implement its expand/collapse features and the *GridView* control (see Chapter 7) uses callbacks to page and sort without explicit postbacks.

A script callback begins with a client-side event (typically a click) that triggers a built-in JavaScript function named *WebForm_DoCallback*. If you use a push button to trigger the function, avoid using the *<asp:button>* tag. This tag renders through a submit button that would refresh the whole page anyway. Use a link button or a client-side button such as the HTML 4.0 *<button>* tag. The *WebForm_DoCallback* script function requires a few arguments, as shown here:

```
WebForm_DoCallback(
   pageID,            // ID of the page that makes the call
   argument,          // string argument to pass to the server-side code
   returnCallback,    // JavaScript code invoked when the callback returns
   context,           // value the caller needs to pass to return callback
   errorCallback);    // JavaScript code invoked in case of errors
```

The first argument represents the ID of the page and can't be omitted. When the server-side code returns, the ASP.NET 2.0 infrastructure invokes the specified *returnCallback* function and passes the return value (always a string) obtained from the server-side code plus any context information. The *returnCallback* function is responsible for processing the return value, thus updating the user interface via Dynamic HTML.

Let's consider an example. A page that wants to support out-of-band calls must implement the *ICallbackEventHandler* interface. This requires the use of the *@Implements* directive:

```
<%@ Implements Interface="System.Web.UI.ICallbackEventHandler" %>
```

The *ICallbackEventHandler* interface has only one method, *RaiseCallbackEvent*:

```
public virtual string RaiseCallbackEvent(string eventArgument)
{
    // eventArgument indicates the parameter(s) passed
    // TO DO: retrieve the server-side values based on the
    //        parameter(s) and pack everything into a return string
}
```

The following page provides a full demonstration of script callbacks. The page shows a drop-down list populated with employee names taken from the Northwind database. The More Info button triggers a piece of JavaScript code that retrieves the currently selected employee and passes that ID to the server-side code.

```
<%@ page language="C#" %>
<%@ import namespace="System.Data" %>
<%@ implements interface="System.Web.UI.ICallbackEventHandler" %>

<script language="javascript">
    function UpdateEmployeeViewHandler(result, context) {
        // The result is presented as a comma-separated string
        var obj = result.split(",");
        e_ID.innerHTML = obj[0];
        e_FName.innerHTML = obj[1];
        e_LName.innerHTML = obj[2];
        e_Title.innerHTML = obj[3];
        e_Country.innerHTML = obj[4];
        e_Notes.innerHTML = obj[5];
    }
</script>

<script runat="server">
    public virtual string RaiseCallbackEvent(string eventArgument) {
        // Get more info about the specified employee
        int empID = Convert.ToInt32 (eventArgument);
        EmployeesManager empMan = new EmployeesManager();
        EmployeeInfo emp = empMan.GetEmployeeDetails(empID);

        // Pack the data into a string
        string[] buf = new string[6];
        buf[0] = emp.ID.ToString ();
        buf[1] = emp.FirstName;
        buf[2] = emp.LastName;
        buf[3] = emp.Title;
        buf[4] = emp.Country;
        buf[5] = emp.Notes;
        return String.Join(",", buf);
    }

    void Page_Load (Object sender, EventArgs e) {
        // Populate the drop-down list
        EmployeesManager empMan = new EmployeesManager();
        DataTable dt = empMan.GetListOfNames();
        cboEmployees.DataSource = dt;
        cboEmployees.DataTextField = "lastname";
        cboEmployees.DataValueField = "employeeid";
        cboEmployees.DataBind();

        // Prepare the Javascript function to call
        string callbackRef = GetCallbackEventReference(this,
                "document.all['cboEmployees'].value",
                "UpdateEmployeeViewHandler", "null", "null");

        // Bind the callback to a client button
        buttonTrigger.Attributes["onclick"] =
```

```
                String.Format("javascript:{0}", callbackRef);
    }
</script>
<html>
<body>
    <form runat="server">
        <asp:dropdownlist id="cboEmployees" runat="server" />
        <button runat="server" id="buttonTrigger">More Info</button><br>
        <table>
        <tr><td><b>ID</b></td><td><span id="e_ID" /></td></tr>
        <tr><td><b>Name</b></td><td><span id="e_FName" /></td></tr>
        <tr><td><b>Last Name</b></td><td><span id="e_LName" /></td></tr>
        <tr><td><b>Title</b></td><td><span id="e_Title" /></td></tr>
        <tr><td><b>Country</b></td><td><span id="e_Country" /></td></tr>
        <tr><td><b>Notes</b></td><td><i><span id="e_Notes" /></i></td></tr>
        </table>
    </form>
</body>
</html>
```

The page posts back to the server and gets initialized as usual. The *Init* and *Load* events are fired, and the *IsCallback* property is set to *true*. *RaiseCallbackEvent* is invoked when the load phase is completed. After that, the request ends without entering the rendering phase. A client-side system component—the Callback Manager—controls the interaction between the page and the server. The Callback Manager is a script library sent to the client by ASP.NET. It is responsible for creating a request to the server, and will fire the appropriate server-side event. It also parses the response and passes the appropriate data to the specified JavaScript return callback.

> **Note** Should you write the call to *WebForm_DoCallback* yourself? Should you know about its details? Not necessarily. The *GetCallbackEventReference* method on the *Page* class returns the script string that starts the callback. You prefix this string with *javascript:* and attach it to the *onclick* attribute of a client button. Alternatively, you can wrap the string in another JavaScript function and inject it into the page. The whole process of generating the client script code for starting the callback is a bit more complicated if you have parameters to pass. In this case, it's easier if you use *WebForm_DoCallback* directly. However, a runtime error occurs if no call to *GetCallbackEventReference* is made. To ensure that all required references are inserted, you insert a fake call to the method for initialization purposes.
>
> GetCallbackEventReference(this, “arg", “callback", “null", “null");

Setting the Focus

A useful feature that ASP.NET 1.x lacks is the ability to assign the input focus to a particular control when the page is displayed. In ASP.NET 2.0, the *Page* class is purposely endowed with the *SetFocus* method. The following code shows how to set the focus to a *TextBox* control named *txtLastName*:

```
void Page_Load(object sender, EventArgs e) {
    if (!IsPostBack)
        SetFocus("txtLastName");
}
```

The *SetFocus* method caches the ID of the control and forces the *Page* class to generate ad hoc script code when the page is rendered. The following code shows an alternative approach to setting the input focus:

```
<form runat="server" defaultfocus="txtLastName">
  ⋮
</form>
```

You can set the *DefaultFocus* property on a form to denote which control should receive the focus. This is equivalent to calling *SetFocus*. The difference is that if one control at a time requests the focus through *SetFocus*, the default focus is ignored.

Overview of Server Controls

ASP.NET 1.x has two distinct but similar-looking families of controls—standard ASP.NET controls and mobile controls. A key goal of ASP.NET 2.0 is to let developers build Web applications for a range of devices without knowing the specific device semantics. ASP.NET 2.0 defines a common architecture for Web controls and adapters and unifies functionality expressed in Mobile ASP.NET with the desktop model expressed in ASP.NET 1.x.

The unified model for controls is not the silver bullet that lets you build applications that successfully respond to every device in any situation. In simple scenarios, this might be the case, but in more realistic situations you must write extra code to adapt the application to a particular family of devices. The amount of extra code can range from simple customization to account for a different set of capabilities to a supplementary application to deal with a significantly different interaction and usability model. But in this case, the unified programming model still guarantees that there's no new programming technique or API to learn.

The adaptive rendering of ASP.NET mobile controls is extended to ASP.NET controls, blurring any difference between mobile and Web applications, at least at the API level. It is worth noting, though, that mobile and Web applications remain quite different in terms of the required semantics and the usability model.

New Control Features

ASP.NET 2.0 controls provide 100 percent backward compatibility with ASP.NET 1.x controls, with the same or better performance. The controls also reflect some of the new features found in the platform, such as personalization, theming, the data binding model, and control state. All controls have the same *<asp:>* prefix, whereas in ASP.NET 1.x mobile controls have a custom *<mobile:>* prefix by default.

Adaptive Rendering

Adaptive rendering is the process of creating different markup and layout for various devices. Adaptive rendering applies first and foremost to controls, but it is also extended to container elements such as forms and pages. Although such a flexible rendering engine reduces the code needed to write multidevice applications, it is conceptually different from the somewhat seductive "write once, render everywhere" paradigm.

The write-once option is based on the idea of a least-common denominator used to generate the markup. This is not the case in ASP.NET 2.0, where controls always try to render in the best possible way for each device. Adaptive rendering is better described using another slogan: design once, render everywhere. The functionality is designed once and can be rendered on virtually any device, but the physical code adaptation might require some additional code. The extra code adapts the output of a control to the device so that no functions get lost in the transition.

Adapters are components that override life-cycle stages of controls to allow for device-specific handling. ASP.NET 2.0 maps a single adapter to a control for each served request. Of course, the selected adapter depends on the current device. A control holds a reference to the mapped adapter instance through the *Adapter* (protected) property. Each control has an associated adapter unless it is a composite control that defers to its children for rendering. Custom controls might not have a direct adapter mapping; in this case, ASP.NET 2.0 walks the inheritance tree of the control to find an adapter.

Adaptive rendering is thus a part of the internal process of generating a Web page. There are two ways to extend adaptive rendering—custom adapters and device filtering. You can construct your own adapters to extend the built-in adapter classes to modify the appearance of controls on a given device.

Alternatively, you can use device-filtering expressions to declaratively or programmatically override specific properties, as shown here:

```
<asp:label runat="server"
          text="This book is the best in its genre."
          IsWml:text="Great book" />
```

For example, you can specify that the *Text* property of a control display a short string for a mobile phone but a longer string for a device that supports a larger viewing area.

Control State

Some ASP.NET controls require that some state be kept across requests. Examples of this type of state information include the current page of a paged control and the current sort order of a sortable data control. In ASP.NET 1.x, there is only one container in which this data can be stored—the view state. However, the view state is mainly designed to maintain settings set by the application, and more important, it can be turned off. What would happen to control-specific state in this case? So ASP.NET 2.0 introduces the notion of the *control state* and keeps it separate from the view state to make clear that control state is a vital piece of the control infrastructure.

Control state is a collection of critical view state data that controls need to function. Because of its critical role, control state data is contained in a separate collection from normal view state and is not affected when view state is disabled. Unlike view state, control state requires extra implementation steps to use. A control that needs this private state signals it to the page by calling the *RegisterRequiresControlState* method of the *Page* class:

```
// This code is part of the control's implementation
protected override void OnInit(EventArgs e)
{
Page.RegisterRequiresControlState(this);
   base.OnInit(e);
}
```

The storage medium for control state is any object you want. In general, simple arrays or collections are a good choice. Each control persists and loads its control state using a pair of overridable methods, as shown here:

```
protected override object SaveControlState()
protected override void LoadControlState(object state)
```

Control state works similarly to view state and is saved and loaded at the same stage of the pipeline that view state is processed. Controls should make limited use of control state except for critical, private state information.

> **Note** As a control developer, you're responsible for serializing and deserializing the control state. You can do that only through the pair of aforementioned methods—*SaveControlState* and *LoadControlState*. It's important to consider that all objects that form the control state must be of serializable types.

New Core Controls

Although ASP.NET 2.0 is 100 percent backward compatible with ASP.NET 1.x, only a handful of components have not significantly changed. The new and revised controls can be grouped into six main categories—container, button, text, image, list, and data controls. Chapter 7 covers new data and view controls in detail.

Let's get familiar with some of the new controls, starting with an existing control—the *Panel* control—which in ASP.NET 2.0 provides an interesting new capability.

The *Panel* Control

The *Panel* control groups controls in a *<div>* tag. It allows developers to add and remove controls and supports style information. In ASP.NET 2.0, panels support horizontal and vertical scrollbars implemented through the *overflow* CSS style. Here's an example that demonstrates two nested panels, the outermost of which is vertically scrollable:

```
<asp:panel runat="server" scrollbars="Vertical" height="105px"
           style="border:solid 1px;">
           0<br />1<br />2<br />3<br />4<br />5<br />6
</asp:panel>
```

The Figure 1-10 shows the page in action.

Scrollable Panel

Figure 1-10 A page that uses a scrollable panel

The *MultiView* Control

The *MultiView* control defines a group of views in which only one can be defined as active and be rendered to the client. The active view is a *View* object.

```
<asp:MultiView runat="server" id="Tables">
   <asp:View runat="server" id="Employees">
      ⋮
   </asp:View>
   <asp:View runat="server" id="Products">
      ⋮
   </asp:View>
   <asp:View runat="server" id="Customers">
      ⋮
   </asp:View>
</asp:MultiView>
```

You change the active view through postback events when the user clicks button or links embedded in the current view. To indicate the new view, you can either set the *ActiveViewIndex* property or pass the view object to the *SetActiveView* method.

The Figure 1-11 shows a sample page in action. You select the page from the Views drop-down list and then refresh the view.

```
void Page_Load(object sender, EventArgs e)
{
   // Views is a drop-down list
   Tables.ActiveViewIndex = Views.SelectedIndex;
}
```

Figure 1-11 A multi-view control in action

The *Wizard* Control

Similar to the *MultiView* control but more specialized is the *Wizard* control. It is a composite control that uses the *MultiView* control internally to display and hide the panels that form the steps of the wizard. Here's an example of the wizard:

```
<asp:wizard runat="server" id="BookWizard"
    style="border:solid 1px" width="300" height="100"
    onfinishbuttonclick="Finished">
<WizardSteps>
```

```
    <asp:WizardStep steptype="Start">
        <h3>Thanks for choosing this book.
        Please, proceed with payment!</h3>
    </asp:WizardStep>
    <asp:WizardStep steptype="Step">
        <h3>Enter your credit card number:</h3>
        <asp:textbox runat="server" id="CreditCard" text="" />
    </asp:WizardStep>
    <asp:WizardStep steptype="Finish">
       <h3>You're all set. Click and your credit card
       will be charged. Thank you!</h3>
    </asp:WizardStep>
    <asp:WizardStep steptype="Complete">
       <asp:label runat="server" id="FinalMsg" />
    </asp:WizardStep>
</WizardSteps>
</asp:wizard>
```

The control provides navigation buttons and fires server-side events whenever the user clicks to change the page. The navigation can be both linear and nonlinear—you can jump from one page to the next as well as randomly to any listed page. When the Finish button is clicked, you typically collect all the data and proceed with the final step. Since all the controls are part of the page, you can access them codewise using their ID. Figure 1-12 shows the steps of a sample wizard to make a payment.

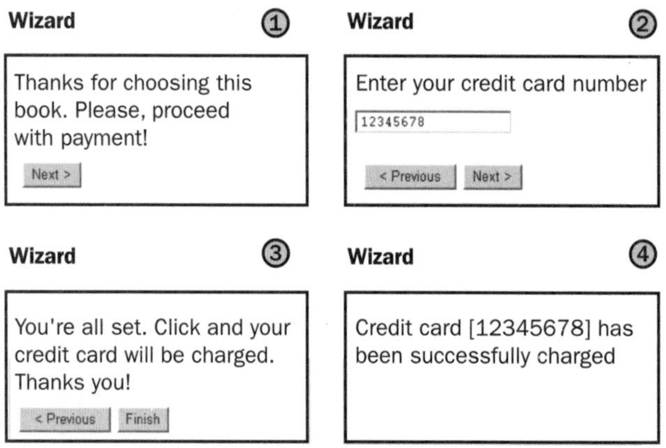

Figure 1-12 The ASP.NET 2.0 *Wizard* control in action

The following code represents the final step of the wizard that finalizes the whole operation.

```
void Finished(object sender, EventArgs e)
{
    // Perform the operation
    ⋮

    // Give feedback
    string msg = "Credit card <b>[{0}]</b> has been successfully charged.";
    FinalMsg.Text = String.Format(msg, CreditCard.Text);
}
```

We'll learn more about this cutting edge control in Chapter 8.

The *BulletedList* Control

I craved a *BulletedList* control in ASP.NET 1.x, so I built one myself. Surprisingly, it wasn't so hard, but I welcome this control in ASP.NET 2.0 with extreme pleasure. The control is a programming interface built around the *<ul>* and *<ol>* HTML tags, with some extra features such as the bullet style, data binding, and support for custom images. The following example uses a custom bullet object:

```
<asp:bulletedlist runat="server" bulletstyle="Square">
     <asp:listitem>One</asp:listitem>
     <asp:listitem>Two</asp:listitem>
     <asp:listitem>Three</asp:listitem>
</asp:bulletedlist>
```

The bullet style lets you choose the style of the element that precedes the item. You can use numbers, squares, circles, and uppercase and lowercase letters. The child items can be rendered as plain text, hyperlinks, or buttons.

The *DynamicImage* Control

The *DynamicImage* class is much more than just a wrapper around the *<img>* tag. It isn't limited to just displaying images. The control has the ability to adapt images based on the capabilities of the requesting browser. You can set a few properties to define the behavior of the *DynamicImage* class when you render images to browsers with limited graphics capabilities. Here's an example of the control:

```
<asp:dynamicimage runat="server"
    ImageFile="image.gif">
</asp:dynamicimage>
```

Interestingly, the source image can be expressed in a variety of ways, including an array of bytes from an external source such as a database, a file, or an image generation service. You can pass the bytes of the image by using the *ImageBytes* property; you use the *ImageFile* property if you're passing a file instead. As you'll see in Chapter 8, ASP.NET 2.0 comes with a special type of HTTP handler that's capable of generating dynamic images using the GDI+ drawing objects. If you intend to display an image obtained in this way, set the *ImageGeneratorUrl* property to the URL of the service. If you need to pass parameters, use the *<asp:parameter>* control. Image generators have the .asix extension.

```
<asp:dynamicimage runat="server"
    ImageType="gif"
    ImageGeneratorUrlImageFile="textimage.asix">
    <parameters>
        <asp:parameter Name="Text" DefaultValue="ASP.NET 2.0" />
    </parameters>
</asp:dynamicimage>
```

We'll discuss the *DynamicImage* control in more depth in Chapter 8.

The *FileUpload* Control

In ASP.NET 1.x, file uploads are possible through the *HtmlInputFile* server control. This control is a simple wrapper built around the *<input type=file>* HTML element. The new *FileUpload* control in ASP.NET 2.0 is nearly identical in functionality but provides a more abstract interface. Both controls display a text field and a browse button that allow users to select a file on the client computer and upload it to the Web server.

The *FileUpload* control does not automatically save a file to the server after the user selects the file. Typically, you provide a button that the user clicks to cause the postback and the subsequent file upload. As the following code shows, using the *FileUpload* control is pretty straightforward.

```
<asp:fileupload runat="server" id="uploader" />
```

The control does its job when the page posts back. The uploaded file can be accessed by name using the *FileName* property or by stream using the *FileContent* property. To access more specific information about the posted file, you can use the object returned by the *PostedFile* property. Finally, *SaveAs* is the method that makes a copy of posted file to a server-side file. Note that the final folder must exist—otherwise, an exception is thrown.

```
void UploadButton_Click(object sender, EventArgs e)
{
    // Specify the path on the server to save the uploaded file to
    string savePath = @"c:\temp\uploads\";
```

```
    if (FileUpload1.HasFile)
    {
       string fileName = FileUpload1.FileName;
       savePath += fileName;

       FileUpload1.SaveAs(savePath);

       UploadStatusLabel.Text = "File saved as: <i>" + savePath + "</i>";
    }
    else
    {
       // Notify the user that a file was not uploaded
       UploadStatusLabel.Text = "You did not specify a file to upload.";
    }
}
```

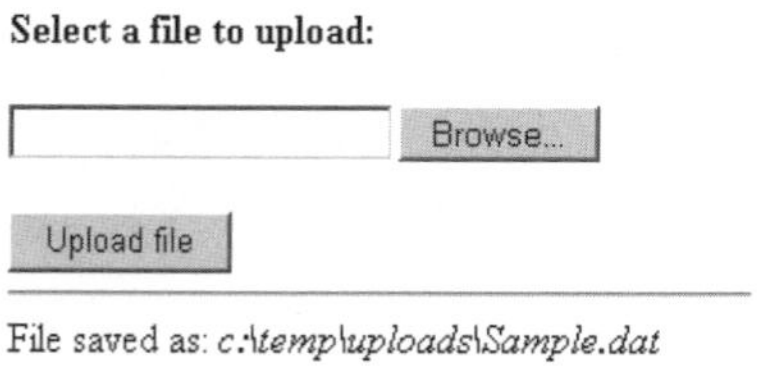

Select a file to upload:

Browse...

Upload file

File saved as: *c:\temp\uploads\Sample.dat*

Figure 1-13 The typical user interface of the upload control

Summary

In this chapter, we covered the three entities that form the foundation of Web applications written with ASP.NET—the development environment, the page object, and the controls. In ASP.NET 2.0, an updated and more powerful designer makes developing Web applications easier than ever, and even pleasant. The ASP.NET designer of Visual Studio 2005 solves all the issues of today's Web development tools and delivers a high-quality IDE that is easier to use and more productive.

The *Page* class is the basis of all the Web forms dynamically created from .aspx resources. The class has been enhanced to support personalization, themes, and a more powerful scripting object model that finds its best expression in cross-page postbacks and script callbacks.

New core controls populate the pages; these include Web wizards, the *MultiView* control, and bulleted lists. Perhaps the most remarkable aspect of ASP.NET 2.0 controls is the unified model that ties together desktop controls and mobile controls. As a result, pagination and control state make their debut in the world of ASP.NET, and a family of more powerful controls can be used to create mobile applications. The adaptive rendering simplifies the design of Web applications, making the optimization for multiple devices a small supplementary application when not simply a form of customization.

In the next chapter, we'll begin exploring the programming world of ASP.NET 2.0. We'll start with the most requested new feature in ASP.NET 2.0: master pages.

2

Working with Master Pages

It took developers little time to realize that something was missing in the ASP.NET approach to creating Web pages and Web sites. Certainly ASP.NET greatly simplified the process. However, after a few months of real-world experience, many developers recognized that they needed more effective and powerful tools to build useful Web applications with the same ease that they could build simple sites.

Almost all Web sites use a similar graphical layout for all their pages. This doesn't happen by chance—it grows out of accepted guidelines for design and usability. A consistent layout is characteristic of all cutting-edge Web sites, no matter how complex. For some Web sites, the layout consists of the header, body, and footer; for others, it is a more sophisticated aggregation of menus, buttons, and panels that contain and render the actual content.

The question is, how can you effectively build such Web sites? I wouldn't be giving you the best advice if I told you to manually duplicate your code and HTML elements. Making your code automatically reusable represents a better approach, but how do you implement it, *in practice*?

Both classic ASP and ASP.NET 1.x provide good workarounds for this type of issue, but neither tackles such a scenario openly and provides a definitive, optimal solution. ASP.NET 2.0 faces up to the task through a new technology—*master pages*—and basically exploits the ASP.NET Framework's ability to merge a "supertemplate" with user-defined content replacements.

The Rationale Behind Master Pages

With ASP.NET 1.x, you can apply a common layout to all the pages of a Web site by wrapping all the common user interface widgets in user controls and reuse them in all the pages. With classic ASP, include files offer the best approach. As you'll see in a moment, though, neither of these approaches (either of which you could also use with ASP.NET 2.0) really hits the target.

A better way to build and reuse pages must fulfill three requirements. First, the pages have to be easy to modify. Second, changes shouldn't require deep recompilation and diffuse retouch of the source code. Third, any change must have minimal impact on the overall performance of the application.

Before we look at how ASP.NET 2.0 master pages address these requirements, let's briefly examine what is good and bad about the ASP.NET 1.x and classic ASP approaches so you'll understand how the final architecture of master pages came to be.

User Controls in ASP.NET 1.x

In ASP.NET 1.x, the best approach to authoring pages with a common layout is to employ *user controls*. User controls are aggregates of ASP.NET server controls, literal text, and procedural code. The ASP.NET runtime exposes user controls to the outside world as programmable components. The idea is that you employ user controls to tailor your own user interface components and share them among the pages of the Web site. For example, all the pages that need a navigational menu can reference and configure the user control that provides that feature.

What's Good About User Controls

User controls are like embeddable pages. Turning an existing ASP.NET page into a user control requires only a few minor changes. User controls can be easily linked to any page that needs their services. Furthermore, changes to a user control's implementation do not affect the referencing page and only require you (or the runtime) to recompile the user control into an assembly.

However, the best feature of user controls turns out to be the main drawback as well.

What's Bad About User Controls

If you change the *internal* implementation of the user control, no referencing page will be affected. However, if you alter any aspect of the control's *public* interface (such as the class name, properties, methods, or events), all the pages that reference the control must be updated. This means you must manually retouch all the pages in the application that use the control. Then you must recompile these pages and deploy the assemblies. In addition, the next time a user views each page, the ASP.NET runtime will take a while to respond because the dynamic assembly for the page must be re-created.

Architecturally speaking, the solution based on user controls works just fine. In practice, though, it is not a very manageable model for large-scale applications—its effectiveness decreases as the complexity of the application (the number of pages involved) increases. If your site contains hundreds of pages, handling common elements through user controls can quickly become inefficient and unmanageable.

This model forces you to introduce duplicate code in content pages. In fact, all pages must reference user controls and all of them must be updated (and recompiled) whenever you change something in the design of the pages or in the programming interface of the user controls. Touching hundreds of files is simply out of the question.

Another, subtler problem arises when you use user controls to build a pagewide user interface. User controls are individual components and as such should be self-contained and designed as embeddable pages. When individual components are used to build a pagewide user interface, you are likely to end up splitting HTML elements between different user controls. For example, a *<table>* element might begin in one user control and end in another one. Although this is not strictly a syntax error, it clearly indicates a less-than-optimal design.

Include Files in Classic ASP

Classic ASP offers a smaller set of tools than ASP.NET 1.x, but the best practice that emerged after years of real-world experience with classic ASP is philosophically closer to ASP.NET 2.0 master pages than user controls. With classic ASP, developers reuse common user interface widgets (such as a header, a footer, or menus) by wrapping them in external include files. When the ASP runtime builds the response for the browser, the content stored in include files is merged with the main template of the ASP page.

What's Good About Include Files

A typical include file contains the HTML markup for the portion of the page it represents. An include file can contain either static or dynamic content. Changes to any include files are reflected in the final page but don't affect how the final page is built. No performance hit stems from changes to included files; this is due to the different runtime architecture of classic ASP compared to ASP.NET.

The page served to the browser is constructed by importing external content into the main template of the page. However, each page of the application remains an independent object and is considered the root of a small tree whose leaves are the include files. In other words, there are no points of contact between the various pages that share a common layout. ASP.NET 2.0 master pages—supertemplates common to all pages sharing a given layout—are simply an enhancement to this approach.

What's Bad About Include Files

Include files are plain containers of relatively static text, and they are merely a cache of HTML markup that is used throughout the application. The markup is integrated with the existing skeleton of the page; it is typically placed in table cells and rows.

This approach has two main drawbacks. First, there's no object orientation, so integrating this approach with the ASP.NET programming model is hard. Second, include files tags opened in one file are frequently closed in another file (either the .asp page or another include file). This situation makes WYSIWYG designer support virtually impossible.

Outline of a Better Approach

The following aspects of master pages make page layout easy to share, simple to maintain, and functional to the application:

- Definition of a supertemplate—the master page—that individual content pages refer to explicitly
- Attachment of a master at various levels in the application scheme—all pages in the Web space, all pages in a directory, and each individual page
- Support for multiple master pages per Web application
- WYSIWYG support for both master pages and content pages

The master page is a single file that defines the template for a set of pages. Similar to an ordinary .aspx page, the master contains replaceable sections that are each marked with a unique ID. Pages in an application that will inherit the structure defined in the master will reference the master page in their *@Page* directive or programmatically. A page based on a master is called a *content page*. One master page can be bound to any number of content pages.

Master pages are completely transparent to end users. When working with an application, a user sees and invokes only the URL of content pages. If a content page is requested, the ASP.NET runtime applies a different compilation algorithm and builds the dynamic class as the merge of the master and the content page. Figure 2-1 illustrates the overall scheme.

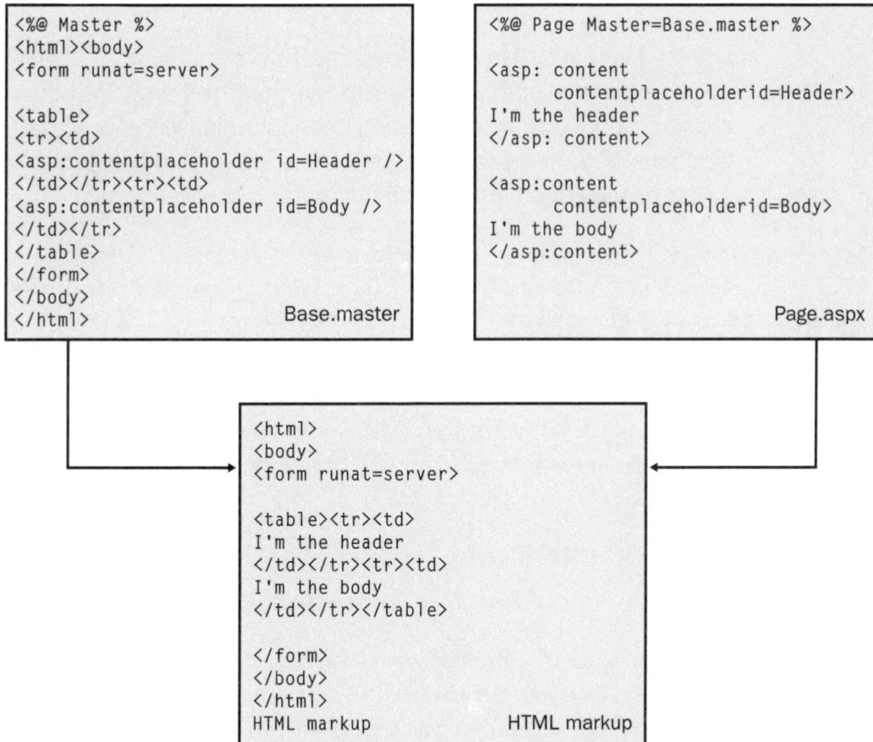
<%@ Master %>
<html><body>
<form runat=server>
<table>
<tr><td>
<asp:contentplaceholder id=Header />
</td></tr><tr><td>
<asp:contentplaceholder id=Body />
</td></tr>
</table>
</form>
</body>
</html>
Base.master
<%@ Page Master=Base.master %>
<asp: content
contentplaceholderid=Header>
I'm the header
</asp: content>
<asp:content
contentplaceholderid=Body>
I'm the body
</asp:content>
Page.aspx
<html>
<body>
<form runat=server>
<table><tr><td>
I'm the header
</td></tr><tr><td>
I'm the body
</td></tr></table>
</form>
</body>
</html>
HTML markup
HTML markup

Figure 2-1 The master page includes one or more content placeholders that define regions where replaceable content will appear.

Master pages are among the hottest new features of ASP.NET 2.0 and address one of the hottest threads in many ASP.NET 1.x newsgroups. By using master pages, a developer can create a Web site in which various physical pages share a common layout. You code the shared user interface and functionality in the master page. The master also contains named placeholders for content that the derived page will provide. The shared information is stored in a single place—the master page—instead of being replicated in each page. Since the master page is a Web page, any pagewide construct begins and ends within the same context. Each content page references the master and fleshes out the placeholders with the actual content. The presence of a master page is not revealed on the client side, and no master file is ever downloaded.

The master page is to some extent similar to ASP.NET templated controls, in which the templates are content pages and the outer markup of the control is the master.

> **Note** Master pages in ASP.NET 2.0 offer one way of building Web pages—not the only way or even the preferred way. You should use master pages only if you're using user controls extensively to duplicate portions of your user interface or if your application lends itself to being (re)designed in terms of master and content pages.

What Are Master Pages?

To build Web pages based on a master, you start by creating the master. A master page is a file with a .master extension. The syntax of a master page is not much different from that of a regular .aspx page. A master page has two key characteristics:

- A new *@Master* directive replacing the *@Page* directive
- One or more *ContentPlaceHolder* child controls

Each embedded *ContentPlaceHolder* control identifies a region of markup text whose real content is provided at run time by content pages. The body of a master page can contain any combination of server controls, literal text, images, HTML elements, and managed code. All this, plus the content bound to placeholders, originates the virtual .aspx source from which the dynamic page class for the user is generated. (See Figure 2-1.)

Master pages work in conjunction with content pages. In fact, neither master pages nor content pages are of any use if used independently. If you attempt to request a .master resource, you'll see an error message because .master represents a forbidden type of resource in ASP.NET. (See Figure 2-2.)

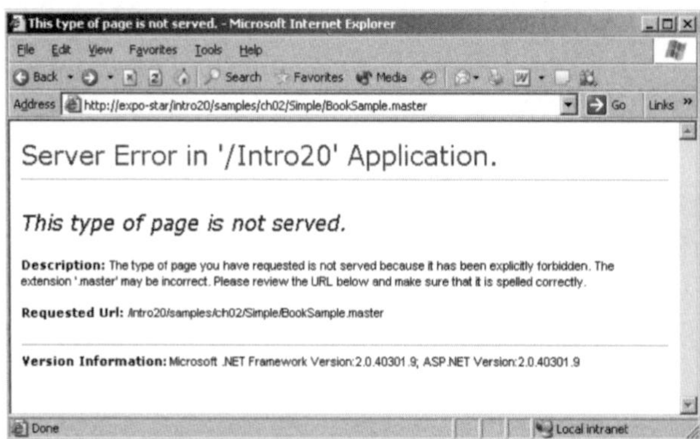

Figure 2-2 Requests for .master resources are received and rejected by the ASP.NET runtime.

Likewise, you see an error message if you request an .aspx resource that's built as a content page but isn't bound to an existing master page. (You'll learn more about content pages in a moment.)

We'll write a sample master/content pair of pages to see how the whole mechanism works and what syntactical elements are involved. Then we'll consider more advanced issues and build a more realistic example of templated pages.

Writing a Master Page

As mentioned, a master page is similar to an ordinary .aspx page except for the top *@Master* directive and the presence of one or more *ContentPlaceHolder* server controls. A master page without content placeholders is technically correct and will be processed correctly by the ASP.NET runtime. However, a placeholderless master fails in its primary goal—to be the supertemplate of multiple pages that look alike. A master page devoid of placeholders works like an ordinary Web page but with the extra burden required to process master pages.

Here's a simple master page named booksample.master:

```
<%@ Master %>
<html>
<head>
    <link rel="Stylesheet" href="styles.css" />
</head>
<form runat="server">

<table border="0" width="100%" bgcolor="beige"
       style="BORDER-BOTTOM:silver 5px solid">
  <tr>
     <td><h2>Introducing ASP.NET 2.0</h2></td>
  </tr>
</table>
<br>
<asp:contentplaceholder runat="server" id="PageBody" />
</form>
</body>
</html>
```

As you can see, the master page looks like a standard ASP.NET page. Aside from the identifying *@Master* directive, the only key difference is the *ContentPlaceHolder* control. A page bound to this master automatically inherits all the contents of the master and has a chance to attach custom markup and server controls to each defined placeholder.

The content placeholder element is fully identified by its *ID* property and normally doesn't require other attributes.

The *@Master* Directive

The *@Master* directive distinguishes master pages from content pages and allows the ASP.NET runtime to properly handle each. The *@Master* directive supports quite a few attributes, including *Language*, *Debug*, *Inherits*, and *ClassName*. These attributes play the same role that they do for ordinary .aspx pages. The *Language* attribute specifies the language used in the master. *Inherits* specifies the base class for the current master, and *ClassName* specifies the name of the actual master class. Finally, *Debug* ensures that debug symbols are added to the compiled page, and it causes the ASP.NET runtime to persist any temporary files (including the source code of the dynamic page class) created during the processing of the page request.

The attributes supported by a *@Master* directive are also the same as those defined on the *@Control* directive for user controls. This is not coincidental. A master page file is compiled to a class that derives from the *MasterPage* class. The *MasterPage* class, in turn, inherits *UserControl*. So, at the end of the day, a master page is treated as a special kind of ASP.NET user control.

> **Note** You can also create master pages programmatically. You build your own class and make it inherit *MasterPage*. Then you create .master files in which the *Inherits* attribute points to the fully qualified name of your class. Rapid application development (RAD) designers such as the one embedded in Visual Studio 2005 use this approach to create master pages.

Table 2-1 details the attributes of the *@Master* directive.

Table 2-1 Attributes of the *@Master* Directive

Attribute	Description
AutoEventWireup	Specifies whether the master page's events are bound to methods with a particular name. The default is *true*.
ClassName	Specifies the name for the class that will be created to render the master page. This value can be any valid class name but should not include a namespace.

Table 2-1 Attributes of the *@Master* Directive

Attribute	Description
CompilerOptions	Specifies a sequence of compiler command-line switches used to compile the master class. The target compiler depends on the language of choice.
Debug	Specifies whether the master page will be compiled with debug symbols. If *true*, the source code of the master will not be deleted and can be retrieved under the Temporary ASP.NET Files folder.
Description	Provides a text description of the master page.
EnableViewState	Specifies whether view state for the controls in the master page is maintained across page requests. The default is *true*.
EnableTheming	Specifies whether themes for the controls in the master page are enabled. The default is *true*.
Explicit	Specifies whether the master page will be compiled using the Visual Basic *Option Explicit* mode. This attribute is ignored by languages other than Visual Basic .NET. It is *false* by default.
Inherits	Specifies a code-behind class for the master page to inherit. This can be any class derived from *MasterPage*.
Language	Specifies the language used throughout the master page.
MasterPageFile	Specifies the name of the master page file that this master refers to. A master can refer to another master through the same mechanisms a page uses to attach to a master. If this attribute is set, you will have nested masters.
Strict	Specifies whether the master page will be compiled using the Visual Basic *Option Strict* mode. This attribute is ignored by languages other than Visual Basic .NET. It is *false* by default.
Src	Specifies the source filename of the code-behind class to dynamically compile when the master page is requested.
WarningLevel	Specifies the compiler warning level at which the compiler will abort compilation of the master page.

Note that the *@Master* directive doesn't override attributes set at the *@Page* directive level. For example, you can have the master set the language to Visual Basic .NET, and one of the content pages can use C#. The language set at the master page level never influences the choice of the language at the content page level.

> **Note** You can use other ASP.NET directives in a master page—for example, *@Import*. However, the scope of these directives is limited to the master file and does not extend to child pages generated from the master. For example, if you import the *System.Data* namespace into a master page, you can call the *DataSet* class within the master. But to call the *DataSet* class from within a content page, you must also import the namespace into the content page.

The *ContentPlaceHolder* Container Control

The *ContentPlaceHolder* control inherits from the *Template* class and is defined in the *System.Web.UI.WebControls* namespace. It acts as a container placed in a master page. It marks places in the master where related pages can insert custom content. A content placeholder is uniquely identified by an ID. Here's an example:

```
<asp:contentplaceholder runat="server" ID="PageBody" />
```

A content page is an .aspx page that contains only *<asp:Content>* server tags. This element corresponds to an instance of the *Content* class that provides the actual content for a particular placeholder in the master. The link between placeholders and content is established through the ID of the placeholder. The content of a particular instance of the *Content* server control is written to the placeholder whose ID matches the value of the *ContentPlaceHolderID* property, as shown here:

```
<asp:Content runat="server" contentplaceholderID="PageBody">
   ⋮
</asp:Content>
```

In a master page, you define as many content placeholders as there are customizable regions in the page. A content page doesn't have to fill all the placeholders defined in the bound master. However, a content page can't do more than just fill placeholders defined in the master.

> **Note** A placeholder can't be bound to more than one content region in a single content page. If you have multiple *<asp:Content>* server tags in a content page, each must point to a distinct placeholder in the master.

Specifying Default Content

A content placeholder can be assigned default content that will show up if the content page fails to provide a replacement. Each *ContentPlaceHolder* control in the master page can contain default content. If a content page does not reference a given placeholder in the master, the default content will be used. The following code snippet shows how to define default content:

```
<asp:contentplaceholder runat="server" ID="PageBody">
   <!-- Use the following markup if no custom
         content is provided by the content page -->
   ⋮
</asp:contentplaceholder>
```

The default content is completely ignored if the content page populates the placeholder. The default content is never merged with the custom markup provided by the content page.

> **Note** A *ContentPlaceHolder* control can be used only in a master page or a (templated) user control. Content placeholders are not valid on .aspx pages. If such a control is found in an ordinary Web page, a parser error occurs.

Writing a Content Page

The master page defines the skeleton of the resulting page. If you need to share layout or a navigational menu among all the pages, placing it in a master page will greatly simplify management of the pages in the application. You create the master and then think of your pages in terms of a delta from the master. The master defines the common parts of a certain group of pages and leaves placeholders for customizable regions. Each content page, in turn, defines what the content of each region has to be for a particular .aspx page.

The *Content* Control

The key part of a content page is the *Content* control. The class is defined in the *System.Web.UI.WebControls* namespace and inherits *Control*. A *Content* control is a container for other controls placed in a content page. The control is used only in conjunction with a corresponding *ContentPlaceHolder* and is not a standalone control.

The master file that we considered earlier defines a single placeholder named *PageBody*. This placeholder represents the body of the page and is placed right below an HTML table that provides the page's header. The following listing shows a sample content page bound to the booksample.master file:

```
<%@ Page Language="C#" masterpagefile="booksample.master" %>

<script runat="server">
    void OnButtonClick(object sender, EventArgs e)
    {
        msg.Text = "Hello, Master Pages";
    }
</script>

<asp:content runat="server" contentplaceholderID="PageBody">
<div>
   <h1>This is the body of the page</h1>
   <asp:button runat="server" text="Click Me" onclick="OnButtonClick" />
   <asp:label runat="server" id="msg" />
</div>
</asp:content>
```

The content page is the resource that users invoke through the browser. Let's call it withmaster.aspx. When the user points her browser to this page, the output in Figure 2-3 is shown.

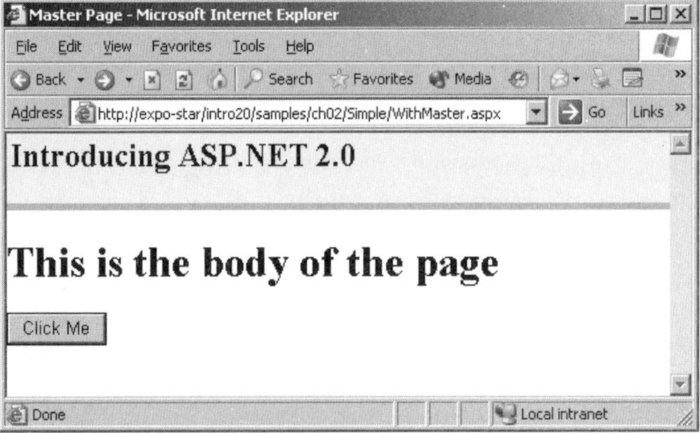

Figure 2-3 The page named withmaster.aspx is obtained by merging the master and the content page.

The replaceable part of the master is filled with the corresponding content section defined in the derived pages. In the previous example, the *<asp:Content>* section for the *PageBody* placeholder contains a button and a label. The server-side code associated to the button is defined in the content page. You should notice that the *Language* attribute points to a different language in the *@Master* directive than it does in the *@Page* directive. In spite of this, the page is created and displayed correctly.

Attaching Pages to a Master

In the previous example, the content page is bound to the master using the new *MasterPageFile* attribute in the *@Page* directive. The attribute points to a string representing the path to the master page. Page-level binding is just one possibility—the most common one.

You can also set the binding between the master and the content at the application or folder level. Application-level binding means that you link all the pages of an application to the same master. You configure this behavior by setting the *Master* attribute in the *<pages>* element of the principal web.config file:

```
<configuration>
   <system.web>
      <pages masterpagefile="WwwContosoCom.master" />
   </system.web>
</configuration>
```

If the same setting is expressed in a child web.config file—a web.config file stored in a site subdirectory—all ASP.NET pages in the folder are bound to a specified master page.

Note that if you use this approach, all the Web pages in the application must have *Content* controls mapped to one or more placeholders in the master page. Application-level binding prevents you from having (or later adding) a page to the site that is not configured as a content page. Any page that contains server controls will throw an exception. A page that is bound to a master is not permitted to host server controls outside of an *<asp:Content>* tag.

Device-Specific Masters

Like all ASP.NET pages and controls, master pages can detect the capabilities of the underlying browser and adapt their output to the specific device in use. The great news about ASP.NET 2.0 is that it makes choosing a device-specific master easier than ever. If you want to control how certain pages of your site appear on a particular browser, you can build them from a common master and design the master to address the specific features of the browser. In other words, you can create multiple versions of the same master, each targeting a different type of browser.

How do you associate a particular version of the master and a particular browser? In the content page, you define multiple bindings using the same *MasterPageFile* attribute, but prefixed with the identifier of the device. For example, suppose you want to provide ad hoc support for Microsoft Internet Explorer and Netscape browsers and use a generic master for any other browsers that users employ to visit the site. You use the following syntax:

```
<%@ Page ie:masterpagefile="ieBase.master"
    netscape:masterpagefile="nsBase.master"
    masterpagefile="Base.master" %>
```

The ieBase.master file will be used for Internet Explorer; the nsBase.master will be used in contrast if the browser belongs to the Netscape family. In any other case, a device-independent master (Base.master) will be used. When the page runs, the ASP.NET runtime automatically determines what browser or device the user is using and selects the corresponding master page.

The prefixes you can use to indicate a particular type of browser are those defined in the *<browserCaps>* section of the machine.config file. It goes without saying that you can distinguish not just between uplevel and downlevel browsers but also between browsers and other devices such as cellular phones and personal digital assistants (PDAs). If you use device-specific masters, you must also indicate a device-independent master.

Underpinnings of Master Pages

The use of master pages slightly changes how pages are processed and compiled. For one thing, a page based on a master has a double dependency—on the .aspx source file (the content page) and on the .master file (the master page). If either of these pages changes, the dynamic page assembly will be re-created. Although the URL that users need is the URL of the content page, the page served to the browser results from the master page fleshed out with any replacement provided by the content page. Let's see in a bit more detail how a content page merges with the master page.

Merging Master and Content Pages

When the user requests an .aspx resource mapped to a content page—that is, a page that references a master—the ASP.NET runtime begins its job by tracking the dependency between the source .aspx file and its master. This information is persisted in a local file created in the ASP.NET temporary files folder. Next, the runtime parses the master page source code and creates a Visual Basic .NET or C# class, depending on the language set in the master page. In the previous example, the booksample.master master page is parsed to a Visual Basic .NET class. (If the *Language* attribute is not specified, Visual Basic .NET is assumed.) The class inherits *MasterPage* and is then compiled to an assembly.

The *MasterPage* Class

The *MasterPage* class is pretty simple—just a small wrapper built around the *UserControl* class:

```
public class MasterPage : UserControl
{
}
```

The dynamic class that the ASP.NET runtime builds from the master page source code extends *MasterPage* by adding any public members defined in line. For example, it adds new properties, methods, and events. In addition, a few protected and private members are added by the framework. In particular, a protected member is added for each *ContentPlaceHolder* server tag found in the .master source. The name of the property matches the ID of the server tag in the source file. Based on the aforementioned simple.master file, the protected property looks like the following snippet:

```
Protected PageBody As System.Web.UI.WebControls.ContentPlaceHolder
```

In addition, a template member is added to represent the content dynamically bound to the placeholder. The property is of type *ITemplate* and is set with actual content provided by the content page for that placeholder.

The overall structure of the source code extracted out of a master page is not much different from that of a classic ASP.NET page. In ASP.NET pages, for each control marked with a *runat* attribute, the runtime generates the code to instantiate and configure the corresponding class. The same occurs with the *ContentPlaceHolder* class; it is instantiated, named, and bound to the matching property on the master page class—the *PageBody* property set above. The final step in this procedure is the instantiation of the template within the placeholder control:

```
// __ctrl is the placeholder control
// Template_PageBody is the internal template member
// representing the dynamically set content of the placeholder
Template_PageBody.InstantiateIn(__ctrl);
```

The templated property is defined but not assigned any value in the master page class. The template is populated while the content page is processed.

Note If multiple .master files are found in the same directory, they are all processed at the same time. Thus a dynamic assembly is generated for any master files found, even if only one of them is used by the ASP.NET page whose request triggered the compilation process. Therefore, don't leave unused master files in your Web space—they will be compiled anyway. Also note that the compilation tax is paid only the first time a content page is accessed within the application. When a user accesses another page that requires the second master, the response is faster because the master is precompiled.

Importing Compiled Templates

Any ASP.NET page bound to a master page must have a certain structure—no server controls or literal text are allowed outside the *<asp:Content>* tag. As a result, the layout of the page looks like a plain collection of content elements, each bound to a particular placeholder in the master. The connection is established through the ID property.

The *<asp:Content>* element works like a control container, much like the *Panel* control of ASP.NET or the HTML *<div>* tag. All the markup text is compiled to a template and associated with the corresponding placeholder property on the master class.

The master page is a special kind of user control. In fact, the ASP.NET Framework calls the *InitializeAsUserControl* method—an internal method on the *UserControl* class—which completes the initialization phase of user controls. The method wires automatic event handlers (such as *Page_Load*, *Page_Unload*) to the control.

The construction of the final page continues with the addition of the filled master page to the control tree of the current instance of the page. No other controls are present in the final page except those brought in by the master. Figure 2-4 shows the skeleton of the final page served to the user.

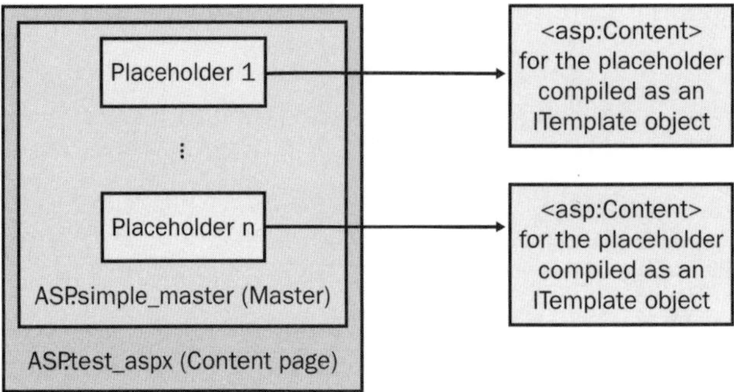

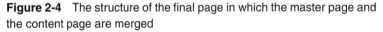

Figure 2-4 The structure of the final page in which the master page and the content page are merged

Nested Masters

So far we've seen a pretty simple relationship between a master and a collection of content pages. However, the topology of the relationship can be made as complex and sophisticated as needed. A master can, in fact, be associated with another master and form a hierarchical, nested structure. Figure 2-5 shows an example.

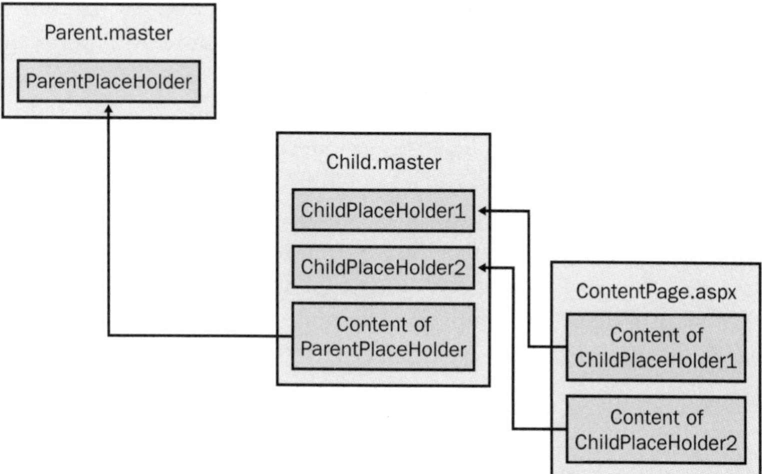

Figure 2-5 Complex sites (such as portals) require the use of interrelated master pages that end up forming a hierarchical structure.

Designing Nested Masters

When nested masters are used, any child master is seen and implemented as a plain content page in which extra *ContentPlaceHolder* controls are defined for an extra level of content pages. Put another way, a child master is a content page that contains a combination of *<asp:Content>* and *<asp:ContentPlaceHolder>* elements. Like any other content page, a child master points to a master page and provides content blocks for its parent's placeholders. At the same time, it makes available new placeholders for its child pages.

There's no architectural limitation in the number of nesting levels you can implement in your Web sites. Performance-wise, the depth of the nesting has a negligible impact on the overall functionality and scalability of the solution. The final page served to the user is always compiled on demand and never modified as long as dependent files are not touched.

Let's extend the previous example so it encompasses a nested structure of master pages.

Building an Example

Many Web sites—most of them portals—have such a complex structure that they can't be rendered using a flat master/content relationship. Suppose you need to have a global menu on top of the page and then a second-level menu whose options vary quite a bit depending on which logical group the page belongs to. In addition, suppose that the second-level menu is not the only visual element to be displayed—a search box or a login text box is also required.

Even from this simple description, it's clear that the portal contains two distinct sets of widgets. Hence, two distinct but interrelated masters are needed to render it in code.

The parent master (BookSample.master) defines the overall layout of the pages—header, body, and footer. The child master (Body.master) expands the body for a certain group of pages, meaning that the Web site will be made of pages belonging to different groups, each with a differently laid out structure. We define a child master in which a toolbar is expected. The content page is responsible for providing the buttons for the toolbar. We'll use a slightly modified version of the BookSample.master page we considered earlier as the parent master in this example. Here's the code:

```
<%@ Master Language="C#" %>
<html>
<head>
    <link rel="Stylesheet" href="/intro20/styles.css" />
    <title>Master Page</title>
</head>
<body style="margin:0;font-family:verdana;">
<form runat="server">
<table width="100%" bgcolor="beige" style="BORDER-BOTTOM:silver 5px solid">
<tr>
    <td><h1>Introducing ASP.NET 2.0</h1></td>
</tr>
</table>
<br>
<table width="100%" style="border:solid 1px black;">
<tr><td>
   <asp:contentplaceholder runat="server" id="Toolbar" /></td></tr>
<tr><td>
   <asp:contentplaceholder runat="server" id="PageBody" /></td></tr>
<tr><td align="center" style="background-color:lightcyan;">
   All rights reserved.</td></tr>
</table>
</form>
</body>
</html>
```

The following code shows the source of the child master—a file named Body.master:

```
<%@ Master Language="VB" MasterPageFile="BookSample.master" %>
<asp:content runat="server" contentplaceholderID="Toolbar">
<table width="100%">
    <tr bgcolor="lightcyan">
       <td width="100%"><h3>Great choice!</h3></td>
```

```
    </tr>
    <tr>
      <td width="100%" style="text-align:center">
        <asp:contentplaceholder runat="server" id="Menu" />
      </td>
    </tr>
</table>
</asp:content>

<asp:content runat="server" contentplaceholderID="PageBody">
<table>
    <tr>
    <td><img src="/Intro20/Images/cover.jpg" align="right"></td>
    <td>
      <h1>Introducing ASP.NET 2.0</h1>
      <h2>Dino Esposito</h2>
      <h2>Microsoft Press, 2004</h2>
      <h2><a href="http://www.microsoft.com/mspress/books/6962.asp">
          Click to learn more</a></h2>
    </td>
    </tr>
</table>
</asp:content>
```

The *@Master* directive contains a new attribute, *MasterPageFile*, that specifies the master page this page is related to. The child master is two things at once. It is a content page with respect to the parent master (and, in fact, it contains a collection of *<asp:Content>* regions). At the same time, it is a master with respect to other content pages in that it features one or more content placeholders—for example, *Menu*.

The following code illustrates a sample content page that originates from the two nested masters. Figure 2-6 shows the final page in the browser.

```
<%@ Page language="C#" masterpagefile="Body.master" %>
<script runat="server">
    void OnBuy(object sender, EventArgs e)
    {…}
    void OnReview(object sender, EventArgs e)
    {…}
    void OnView(object sender, EventArgs e)
    {…}
</script>

<asp:content runat="server" contentplaceholderID="Menu">
<div>
    <asp:button runat="server" text="View TOC"
```

```
            onclick="OnView" width="90px" />
           
        <asp:button runat="server" text="Buy"
            onclick="OnBuy" width="90px" />
        <asp:button runat="server" text="Review"
            onclick="OnReview" width="90px" />
</div>
</asp:content>
```

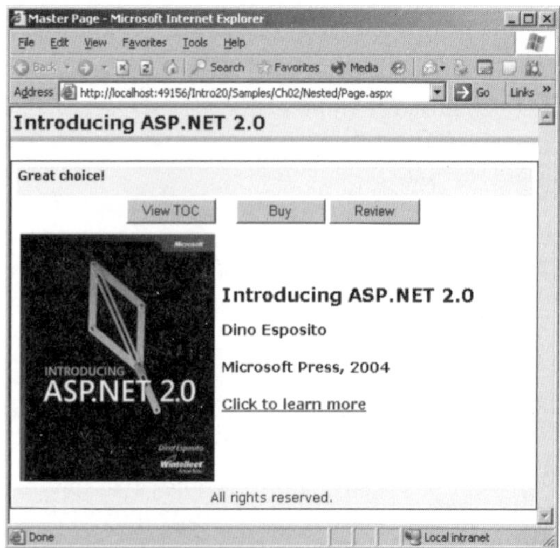

Figure 2-6 The page shown in the browser was created using two interrelated masters—one for the main structure (header, footer, toolbar, and body) and one for the details (subtitle and menu) of the toolbar.

Event Handling

As mentioned earlier, you can configure master pages and content pages to use different languages. In the previous example, in fact, parent and child masters use different languages. But what are languages for? As in ordinary ASP.NET pages, the *Language* attribute specifies the language used to write any procedural code bound to the page. The code can be defined in line or placed in an external file. It typically contains event handlers or public and private methods.

Both master pages and content pages can contain event handlers for embedded controls. Events fired by controls defined in the content page can't be handled at the master-page level. Likewise, controls defined in a master page appear inaccessible to a content page and related events can't be handled.

Page-level events, on the other hand, can be hooked in both the master and the content page. If the same page-level event is handled by both master and content page, handlers are invoked in order, according to the rules set by the page/user control relationship. Once the replaceable regions of a master page are filled, the generated page is hosted within the final page as a user control. (That's why the *MasterPage* class inherits *UserControl*.)

For example, let's consider the order in which the *Page_Init* and *Page_Load* events are captured. Bear in mind that default events are automatically wired up for master pages. If handlers exist in the master and the content page, the order in which they fire will depend on the particular event and will be the same order you'd expect with user controls. As Figure 2-7 shows, the *Init* event reaches the master page before the content page does; for the *Load* event, the order is reversed and the content page is hit first.

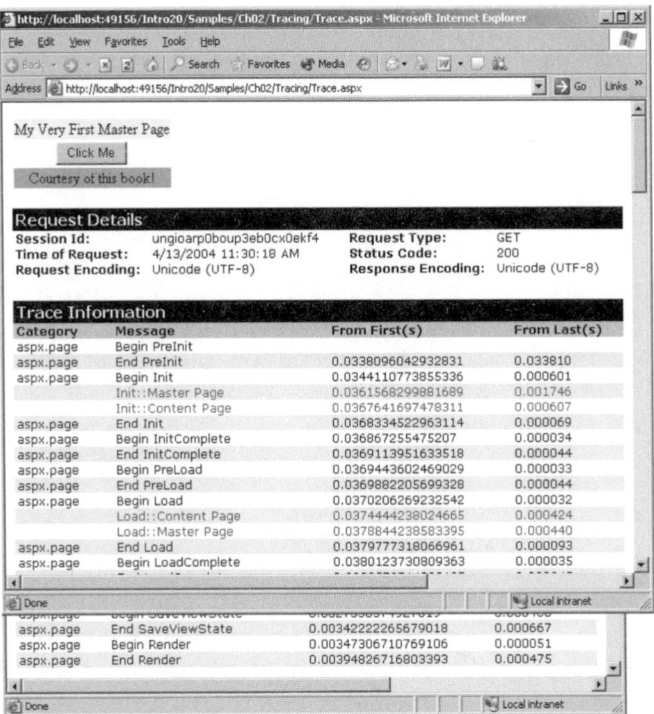

Figure 2-7 Event handlers can be defined in the master page as well as in the content page.

A Realistic Example

Master pages are an incredibly powerful technology that fulfill an important requirement of ASP.NET developers—building similar-looking and similar-working pages quickly and effectively. Former users of the .NET Framework 1.x know about Windows Forms visual inheritance. In brief, it is a Visual Studio .NET feature that allows developers to build new forms from existing ones. There's no magic behind this feature—only pure class inheritance. So why is this feature unavailable to ASP.NET programmers?

I admit that my first guess was laziness or time constraints on the part of the ASP.NET team. The truth is a bit more complex. Master pages are the closest you can get in ASP.NET to visual inheritance *à la* Windows Forms. You'll soon see, though, that they are an equivalent solution.

Master Pages and Visual Inheritance

Let's say it up front. True visual inheritance *à la* Windows Forms is not a goal of ASP.NET 2.0 master pages. Period. The contents of a master page are merged into the content page and dynamically produce a new page class served to the user upon request. The merge process takes place at compile time and only once. In no way do the contents of the master serve as a base class for the content page.

In Windows Forms applications, you can take an existing form—a class derived from *Form*—and use it as the basis for all the new forms you're building. As a result, your new forms inherit any control and any logic built into the base forms. With master and content pages, the final result is pretty much the same, but the underlying mechanism is more complex. In both cases, though, you take a base entity—an existing form or a master page—and build a new entity with the same aspect and capabilities. So why did the ASP.NET team go for master pages instead of true inheritance?

Only a member of the team can provide a definitive answer. However, we can make a few guesses. The team clearly wanted to provide a form of inheritance for Web developers. They also wanted designers (such as the one in Visual Studio 2005) to be able to use such a powerful feature easily. Ideally, a designer would show the master layout when editing a content page and would also restrict users from editing outside the content placeholders. Keeping master and content clearly separate helps to achieve this. Figure 2-8 shows how to edit master pages in Visual Studio.

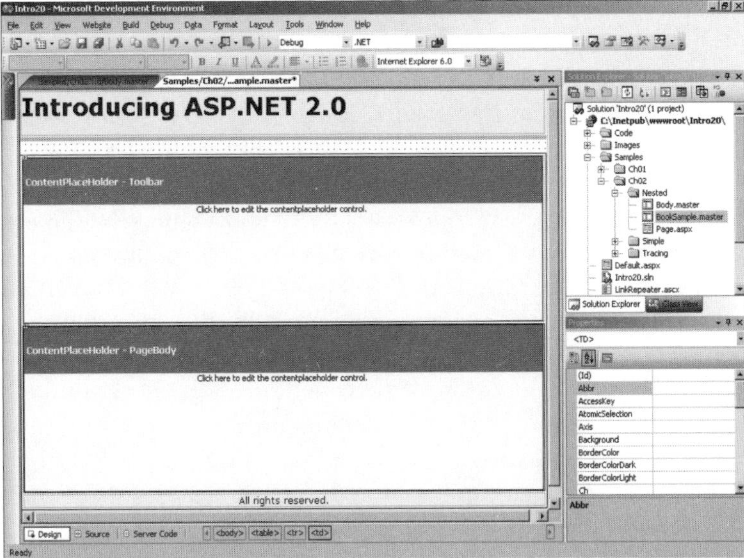

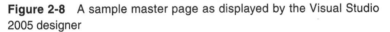

Figure 2-8 A sample master page as displayed by the Visual Studio 2005 designer

Figure 2-9 shows the look and feel of a content page in Visual Studio.

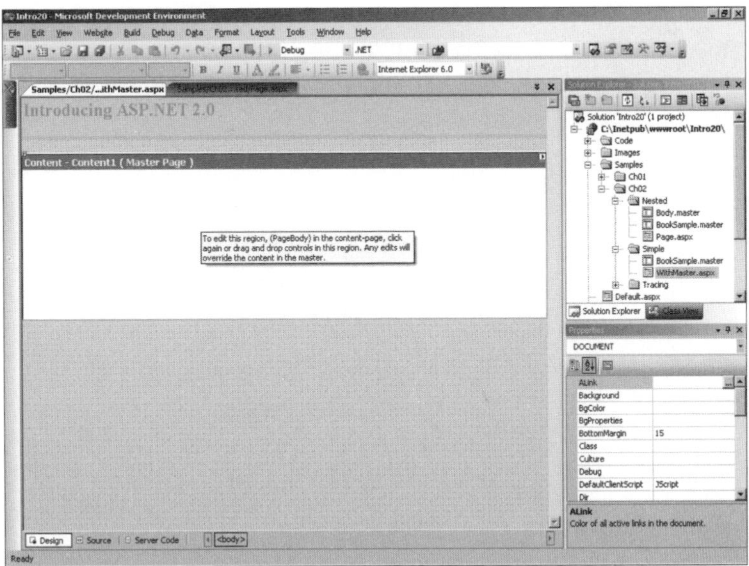

Figure 2-9 A sample content page as displayed by the Visual Studio 2005 designer

The compilation mechanism behind Web pages is too complex to enable a pure inheritance-based approach. A Web form is formed by two indissoluble elements—markup and procedural code. In theory, you could build Web pages using only C# or Visual Basic .NET code. In this case, simply inheriting your Web form from that class instead of *Page* would do the trick—just like in Windows Forms. However, in practice that would force many ASP.NET developers into an unnatural way of working and, more important, would make Web Form editing quite hard. Visual Studio .NET is built to parse markup code; nonempty base pages (those different from *Page*) would either need the ability to convert controls back to markup or a totally different WYSIWYG editor.

In Windows Forms, this works for the simple reason that no markup is involved. A button is a button with a fixed location and attributes. The Visual Studio .NET editor simply renders each control at its own position, using the persisted attributes. New controls are added (or removed) in the same direct way. Simply put, the markup-based nature of server pages (inherited from classic ASP) prevents true visual inheritance in ASP.NET.

Master pages provide the same function—forms inheritance—but by using a totally different set of tools.

> **Note** Visual Studio 2005 doesn't support visual editing of pages with nested masters. If you have two or more nested master pages, neither the child masters nor the content pages can be visually edited. You get an error message that suggests switching to the source view and entering changes codewise.

Layout of the Pages

Figure 2-10 shows a sample Web page based on a master. The master defines five insertion points—that is, content placeholders for developers to add custom code and markup. The figure includes indicators that identify the replaceable regions of the page.

Each content page based on this master would fill one or more regions with custom markup code and any procedural code that is needed to achieve the desired result. The following code shows the master on which the page in Figure 2-10 is based.

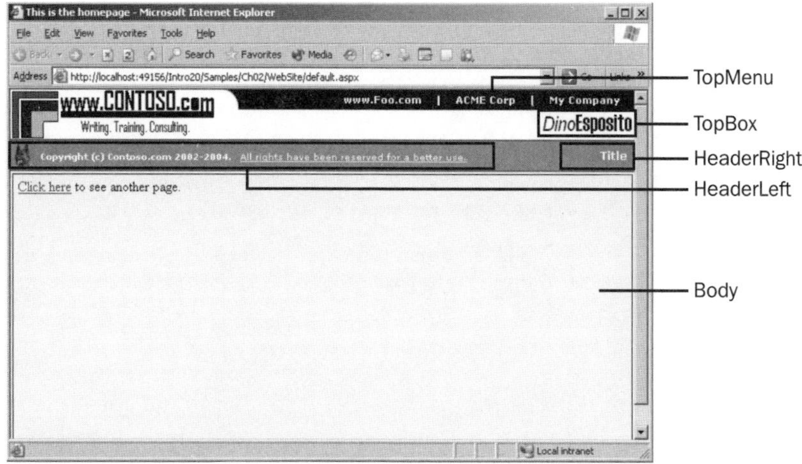

Figure 2-10 A sample Web page based on a master

```
<%@ Master Language="C#" %>
<html>
  <head runat="server">
    <title>Homepage</title>
    <link rel="Stylesheet" href="websitestyles.css" />
  </head>

<body runat="server" style="margin:0">
<form id="Main" runat="server">
  <table cellspacing="0" cellpadding="0" border="0" width="100%">
   <tr>
      <td valign="Top" rowspan="2" style="width:1px;">
        <img src="images/contoso.gif" /></td>
      <td align="Right" valign="Top">
        <img src="images/curve.gif" /></td>
      <td align="Right" class="topMenu">
       <asp:ContentPlaceHolder runat="server" ID="TopMenu" /></td></tr>
   <tr>
      <td align="Right" valign="Top" colspan="3">
       <asp:ContentPlaceHolder runat="server" ID="TopBox" /></td></tr>
  </table>

  <table cellspacing="2" cellpadding="2" border="0" class="headerStrip">
   <tr>
      <td align="Left">
        <asp:ContentPlaceHolder runat="server" ID="HeaderLeft" /></td>
```

```
        <td align="Right">
           <b><span runat="server" id="__titleBar">Title</span> </b>
        </td>
    </tr>
</table>

<div style="margin:2;border:solid 1px black;">
   <asp:ContentPlaceHolder runat="server" ID="Body" />
</div>

</form>
</body>
</html>
```

The master defines the body as well as the single form element of each ASP.NET page. Note that if both the master and the content page define a server-side *<form>* tag, an exception is raised because the final page would end up having multiple forms. The structure of the page is based on a couple of tables—one representing the topmost bar with the menu and one representing the header strip divided in two parts—left (replaceable through a placeholder) and right (modifiable through a property). The topmost table presents two replaceable regions. One is the menu with shortcuts to frequently visited sites; the other is content in the bottom-right corner. This latter area is filled with a bitmap in the sample page shown in Figure 2-10.

Contents of the Pages

The default.aspx page shown earlier in Figure 2-10 replaces the *TopMenu* placeholder with a list of hyperlinks; the *TopBox* placeholder is filled with a bitmap. The header contains two HTML strings with different text alignments. The body of the page can be anything that is appropriate for the application. The following listing shows the source code of the default.aspx content page:

```
<%@ Page Language="C#" MasterPageFile="main.master" %>

<asp:Content runat="server" contentplaceholderID="TopMenu">
   <a href="http://www.foo.com" class="topMenuItem">www.Foo.com</a>
         |   
   <a href="http://www.acme.com" class="topMenuItem">ACME Corp</a>
         |   
   <a href="http://www.mycompany.com" class="topMenuItem">My Company</a>
         
</asp:Content>

<asp:Content runat="server" contentplaceholderID="TopBox">
    <img src="images/dinologo.gif" />
</asp:Content>
```

```
<asp:Content runat="server" contentplaceholderID="HeaderStripLeft">
    <img src="images/jerry.gif"
         alt="Our beloved VP"
         align="absmiddle" width="20" height="25" /> 
    <b>Copyright (c) Contoso.com 2002-2004.  </b>
    <u>All rights have been reserved for a better use.</u>
</asp:Content>

<asp:Content runat="server" contentplaceholderID="Body">
    <asp:panel runat="server" height="300px" backcolor="lightcyan">
        <a href="another.aspx">Click here </a> to see another page.
    </asp:panel>
</asp:Content>
```

Here's the code for a different page designed using the same schema, another.aspx:

```
<%@ Page Language="C#" MasterPageFile="main.master" %>

<asp:Content runat="server" contentplaceholderID="TopMenu">
    <a href="http://mspress.microsoft.com" class="topMenuItem">
    Microsoft Press</a>
          
</asp:Content>

<asp:Content runat="server" contentplaceholderID="TopBox">
    <span class="Normal">Search: </span>
    <asp:textbox runat="server" class="textbox" ID="searchBox" />
    <asp:button runat="server" class="button" Text="Go" />
</asp:Content>

<asp:Content runat="server" contentplaceholderID="HeaderLeft">
    <img src="images/jerry.gif"
         alt="Our beloved VP"
         align="absmiddle" width="20" height="25" /> 
    <b>Copyright (c) Contoso.com 2002-2004.  </b>
    <u>All rights have been reserved for a better use.</u>
</asp:Content>

<asp:Content runat="server" contentplaceholderID="Body">
    <asp:panel runat="server" Height="300px" BackColor="lightcyan">
        <a href="default.aspx">Click here </a> for the home page.
    </asp:panel>
</asp:Content>
```

The new page (shown in Figure 2-11) has a shorter list of hyperlinked Web sites and a different panel below the menu. It also has a search box instead of a bitmap.

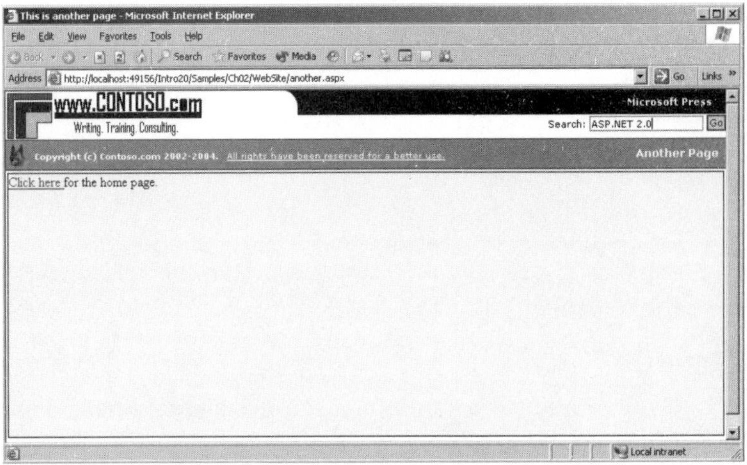

Figure 2-11 Another page based on the same master

Pages built on the same master will differ from each other based on what you add in the content sections. The amount of code (and markup) you need to write is comparable to that needed to set up a derived class in a truly object-oriented application.

Programming the Master

You can use code in content pages to reference properties, methods, and controls in the master page, with some restrictions. The rule for properties and methods is that you can reference them if they are declared as public members of the master page. This includes public page-scope variables, public properties, and public methods. Let's consider a simple scenario—setting the title of the final page.

The *Header* property on the *Page* class exposes the content of the *<head>* tag as programmable entities. To set the title of a content page or to add a stylesheet on a per-page basis, you just add some code to the *Page_Load* event:

```
<script runat="server">
void Page_Load(object sender, EventArgs e)
{
  Header.Title = "This is another page";
}
</script>
```

For this code to run, though, the *<head>* tag must be marked with the *runat* attribute. Note that the *<head>* tag can be defined in either the master or the content page. If you define it in the master, you can modify it programmatically in any content page at the price of adding an additional server control—the *HtmlHead* control.

Exposing Master Properties

To give an identity to a control in the master, you simply set the *runat* attribute and give the control an ID. Can you then access the control from within a content page? Not directly. The only way to access the master page object model is through the *Master* property. If a *TextBox* control named *Search* exists in the master, the following code will throw an exception:

```
Master.Search.Text = "ASP.NET 2.0";
```

As you saw earlier, the *Master* property defined on the *Page* class references the master page object for the content page. This means that only public properties and methods defined on the master page class are accessible.

The page shown in Figure 2-10 has a string of text in the rightmost part of the header set to "Title" by default. In the context of the master and related pages, that string indicates the subtitle of the page. So how can you expose, for example, the subtitle of the final page as a programmable property? Two steps are needed. First you render that string through a server-side control; then you create a public wrapper property to make the control (or one of its properties) accessible from the outside. The following code enhances the main.master file and shows how to define a public *SubTitle* property that wraps the *InnerText* property of the *__titleBar* control:

```
<%@ Master ClassName="MyMaster" Language="C#" %>

<script runat="server">
public string SubTitle
{
    get {return __titleBar.InnerText;}
    set {__titleBar.InnerText = value;}
}
</script>

<html>
⋮
<table cellspacing="2" cellpadding="2" border="0" class="headerStrip">
   <tr>
      <td align="Left">
        <asp:ContentPlaceHolder runat="server" ID="HeaderLeft" /></td>
      <td align="Right">
         <b><span runat="server" id="__titleBar">Title</span></b>
      </td>
   </tr>
</table>
⋮
<html>
```

Just as in ASP.NET 1.x, the *<span>* element marked *runat=server* is mapped to an *HtmlGenericControl* object and its text content is exposed through the *InnerText* property. This property is then wrapped by a new public property—*SubTitle*. Reading and writing the *SubTitle* property gets and sets the value of the *InnerText* property on the *<span>* tag.

Invoking Properties on the Master

When you write a content page, you access any public properties defined on the bound master page through the *Master* property. However, the *Master* property is defined as type *MasterPage* and doesn't contain any property or method definition specific of the master you're creating. The following code won't compile because there's no *SubTitle* property defined on the *MasterPage* class:

```
<script runat="server">
void Page_Load(object sender, EventArgs e)
{
    Master.SubTitle = "Welcome!";
}
</script>
```

What's the real type behind the *Master* property? The *Master* property represents the master page object as compiled by the ASP.NET runtime engine. This class follows the same naming convention as regular pages—*ASP.XXX_master*, where *XXX* is the name of the master file. The *ClassName* attribute on the *@Master* directive lets you assign a user-defined name to the master page class. To be able to call custom properties or methods, you must first cast the object returned by the *Master* property to the actual type:

```
((MyMaster)Master).SubTitle = "Welcome!";
```

Using the above code in the content page does the trick.

Changing the Master Page

The *Page* class defines the *MasterPageFile* property that can be used to get and set the master page associated with the current page. The *MasterPageFile* property is a string that points to the name of the master page file. Note that the *Master* property, which represents the current instance of the master page object, is a read-only property and can't be set programmatically. The *Master* property is set by the runtime after it loads the content of the file referenced by either the *MasterPageFile* attribute or *MasterPageFile* property. If both are set, an exception is thrown.

You can use a dynamically changing master page in ASP.NET 2.0—for example, for applications that can present themselves to users through different skins. You should follow two simple rules when you define a dynamic master page:

- Do not set the *MasterPageFile* attribute in the *@Page* directive.
- Make the page's *MasterPageFile* property point to the URL of the desired master page in the *Page_PreInit* event.

The content of the *@Page* directive is processed before the runtime begins working on the request. The *PreInit* event is fired right before the page handler begins working on the page, and this is your last chance to modify parameters at the page level. If you try to set the *MasterPageFile* property in the *Page_Init* or *Page_Load* events, an exception is raised.

Summary

Many Web sites consist of similar-looking pages that use the same header, footer, and perhaps some navigational menus or search forms. What's the recommended approach for reusing code across pages? One possibility is wrapping these user interface elements in user controls and referencing them in each page. Although the model is extremely powerful and produces highly modular code, when you have hundreds of pages to work with, it soon becomes unmanageable.

ASP.NET 2.0 introduces master pages for this purpose. A master page is a distinct file referenced at the application level as well as the page level that contains the static layout of the page. Regions that each derived page can customize are referenced in the master page with a special placeholder control. A derived page is simply a collection of blocks that the runtime uses to fill the holes in the master.

ASP.NET 2.0 is not the first environment to support template formats. Microsoft FrontPage and Macromedia products support templates, too. However, master pages are different, and compatibility with other template systems is not a goal. Likewise, true visual inheritance similar to that of Windows Forms is not a goal. Master pages promote reusability, but through a totally different mechanism that is not based on class inheritance. Finally, the binding between master and content pages is defined statically and cannot be changed or set programmatically.

ASP.NET 2.0 comes with another mechanism that helps you build a certain type of page quickly and effectively reuse components—Web parts. As you'll see in the next chapter, Web parts provide the infrastructure needed to create Web applications that are modular, content rich, and customizable.

3

Working with Web Parts

Most Web sites, and portals in particular, make a point of showing large amounts of content. This can be a feast for users, but in the long run it can also be a source of confusion. Recent studies on Web usability have concluded that personalization is a key factor in successful Web sites. Giving users the tools to build a personalized view of the content can mean the difference between an average and a superior Web site. You could say that cutting-edge Web sites are rich in content, have a consistent and modular design, and allow users to personalize the content.

How do you build such a Web site? Admittedly, rich content is not a programmatic issue, but being able to handle a wide range of content is a crucial design issue. As a page developer, you are responsible for building a modular site and making it personalizable. Web Parts and the Personalization API are the tools in Microsoft ASP.NET 2.0 that make building modular and customizable Web sites easier, and even pleasant.

In this chapter, we'll take a tour of the ASP.NET 2.0 Web Parts framework and build a small but highly personalizable Web site. We'll cover the Personalization API in Chapter 4.

Building Pages with Web Parts

ASP.NET Web Parts provide an infrastructure for creating Web applications that can handle rich content as well as large amounts of content. You can use Web parts to build sites that enable users to select and receive only the content they want. Web parts are container components that aggregate different types of content. As such, they are particularly useful for creating portal pages.

What Are Web Parts, Anyway?

Figure 3-1 is taken from the My MSN Web site. The page is an aggregation of different blocks, each presenting a particular type of information.

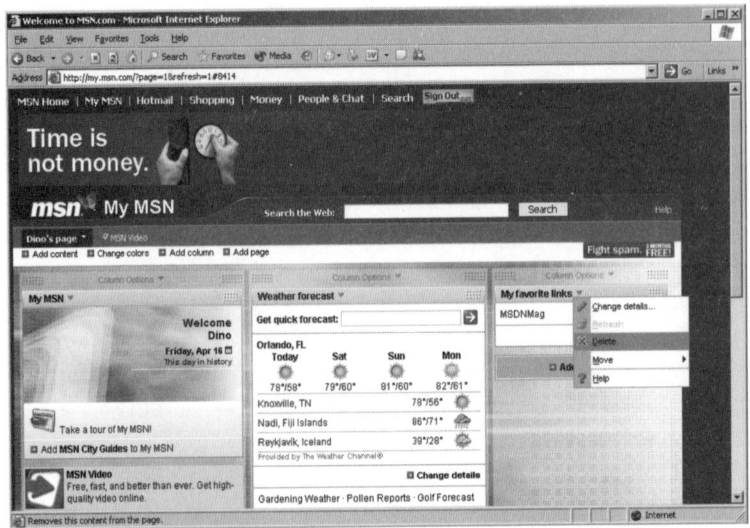

Figure 3-1 The My MSN page of a registered user is composed of all the blocks of information the user selected.

No block displayed in the page is there by chance. By using the Add Content and Change Details links, the user can select which blocks to display and their graphical layout. Each block in the page can be obtained with a Web part in an ASP.NET 2.0 application. Each Web part corresponds to an instance of the *WebPart* control.

Content of a Web Part

You can think of a Web part as a window of information available within the page. Users can close, minimize, or restore that window. The *WebPart* control is essentially a container filled with the usual HTML stuff—static text, link, images, and other controls, including user controls and custom controls. By combining Web Parts and the Personalization API, page developers can easily create pages and controls tailored to the individual user's needs.

The content of a Web part can be any information that is useful to all users, a subset of users, or one user in particular. Most commonly, the content of a Web part is provided by external Web sites—for example, financial, weather, and sports news. The content of a Web part can range from a list of favorite links to a gallery of photos to the results of a search.

Layout of a Web Part

From the developer's perspective, a Web Part component is a sort of smart *Panel* control. Like a panel, a Web part can contain any valid ASP.NET content. The *WebPart* class is actually derived from the *Panel* class.

What makes the Web part more powerful than a simple panel is the support it gets from the Web Part manager (represented by the aptly named *WebPartManager* control) and the extra visual elements it renders. The layout of a Web part mimics that of a desktop window. It has a caption bar with a title, as well as links to common verbs such as minimize, close, and restore.

Although the Web part can act as a container for information from external sites and pages, it is quite different from a frame. A frame points to a URL, and the browser is responsible for filling the area with the content downloaded from the URL. A Web part, on the other hand, is a server-side control that is served to the browser as plain HTML. You can still populate a Web part with the content grabbed from external sites, but you are responsible for retrieving that content, either using HTML scraping or, better yet (when available), Web services.

Introducing the Web Parts Framework

The *WebPart* control is the central element in the Web Parts infrastructure, but it is not the only one. A page employing Web parts uses several components from the Web Parts framework, each performing a particular function. Table 3-1 details these components.

Table 3-1 Components of the Web Parts Framework

Component	Description
WebPartManager	The component that manages all Web parts on a page. It has no user interface and is invisible at run time.
WebPart	Contains the actual content presented to the user. Note that *WebPart* is an abstract class; you have to create your own *WebPart* controls either through inheritance or via user controls.
WebPartZone	Wraps one or more *WebPart* controls and provides the overall layout for the *WebPart* controls it contains. A page can contain one or more zones.
CatalogPart	The base class for catalog *WebPart* controls that present a list of available Web parts to users. Derived classes are *ImportCatalogPart*, *DeclarativeCatalogPart*, and *PageCatalogPart*.
CatalogZone	A container for *CatalogPart* controls.
ConnectionsZone	A container for the connections defined between any pair of Web parts found in the page.

Table 3-1 Components of the Web Parts Framework

Component	Description
EditorPart	The base class for all editing controls that allow modifications to Web parts. An editor part presents its own user interface to let users set properties.
EditorZone	A container for *EditorPart* controls.

Aside from the *WebPartManager* class, the Web Parts infrastructure is made up of three types of components, known as *parts*: Web parts, catalog parts, and editor parts.

A Web part defines the content to show; an editor part lets users edit the structure and the settings of a particular Web part. For example, suppose you have a weather Web part that shows weather information for a few selected cities. An editor part for this Web part would provide a friendly user interface for users to add or remove cities and decide whether to see the temperature in Celsius or Fahrenheit. Based on the weather applet in the My MSN Web site, you enter in edit mode either by clicking the Select Your Cities button of the page or the Edit button in the caption bar. The specific properties you edit differ in each case, but you end up editing the contents of the Web part, as you can see in Figure 3-2.

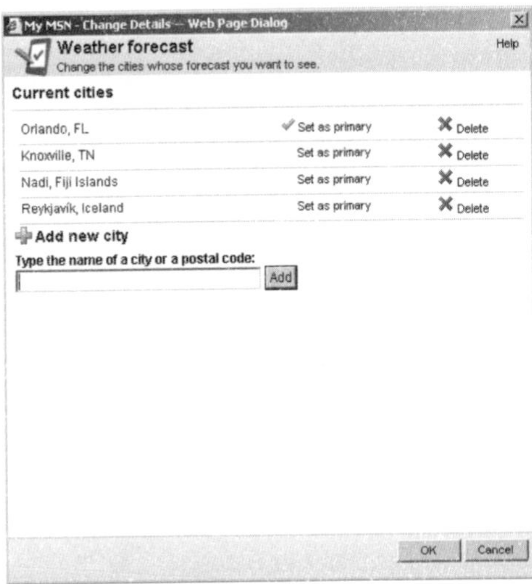

Figure 3-2 Editing the weather content block of the My MSN Web site

The Web Parts infrastructure enables users to choose a personalized set of parts to display on a page and specify their position. The list of available parts is provided by a catalog part control. In this way, users can add parts dynamically. The catalog also acts as a store for the parts that the user has removed from the page by executing the *Close* verb represented by the Delete menu item in Figure 3-1. Removed parts can be restored if a catalog is specified for the page. We'll cover catalog and editor parts in greater depth later in the chapter.

Web Part Zones

The zone object provides a container for parts and provides additional user interface elements and functionality for all part controls it contains. A Web page can contain multiple zones, and a zone can contain one or more parts. Zones are responsible for rendering common user interface elements around the parts it contains, such as titles, borders, and verb buttons, as well as a header and footer for the zone itself.

Each type of part requires its own zone object. The *WebPartZone* is the container for *WebPart* controls. It hosts all the Web part content through a collection property named *WebParts*. In addition, it provides free drag-and-drop functionality when the Web parts are switched to design mode. The design mode is one of the display modes supported by the Web part manager and applies to all Web parts in the page. When you're in design mode, you can modify the layout of the page by moving Web parts around. The drag-and-drop facility is provided by the zone component. The *WebPartZone* control allows you to define a few style properties, such as *PartStyle* (style of the contents), *PartVerbStyle* (style of the action verbs, such as *Minimize* and *Close*), and *PartTitleStyle* (style of the caption bar).

The two other zone types are more specialized. The *EditorZone* is used to contain editor controls to configure existing *WebPart* controls. The *CatalogZone* is used to display the catalog of available *WebPart* controls the user can choose from.

You probably can't wait to see some markup code to illustrate all of this. Here's a quick example:

```
<%@ register tagprefix="x" tagname="News" src="News.ascx" %>
<%@ register tagprefix="x" tagname="Favorites" src="Favorites.ascx" %>

<%@ page language="C#"%>

<html>
<head runat="server">
    <title>WebParts--Headstart</title>
</head>
<body>
    <form runat="server">
    <h1>Demonstrating WebParts zones</h1>
    <div>
      <asp:WebPartManager ID="WebMan" runat="server" />
      <asp:WebPartZone ID="WebPartZone1" runat="server" width="600px"
```

```
                HeaderText="This is Zone #1"
                PartChromeType="TitleAndBorder">
            <PartTitleStyle Font-Size="10pt" Font-Bold="True"
                BackColor="#E0E0E0" Font-Names="verdana" />
            <PartStyle BackColor="#FFFFC0" />
            <PartVerbStyle Font-Size="X-Small" Font-Names="verdana" />
            <CloseVerb Enabled="False" />
            <ZoneTemplate>
                <x:News runat="server" id="News" />
                <x:Favorites runat="server" id="Favs" />
            </ZoneTemplate>
          </asp:WebPartZone>
        </div>
        </form>
</body>
</html>
```

The form contains a *WebPartManager* control that governs the execution and rendering of all child parts. The form also contains one Web zone that contains a couple of parts. The Web part zone is configured to show a title and a border around its content. The *<ZoneTemplate>* tag includes all the Web parts defined in the zone.

The simplest way to incorporate a Web part control is through a user control—an ASCX file. Figure 3-3 shows the page in action.

Demonstrating WebParts zones

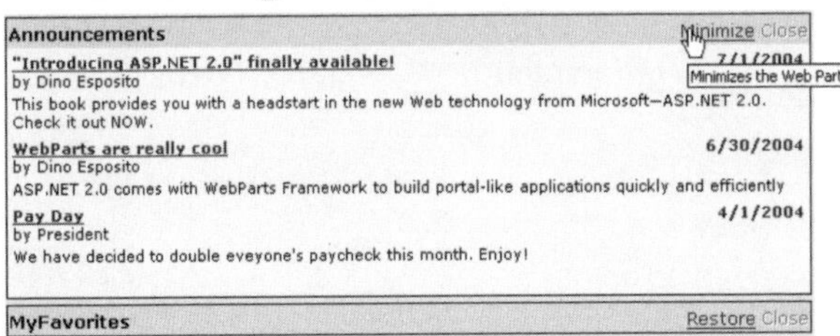

Figure 3-3 A simple WebPart component listing the latest news and useful links

If you click the Minimize button, the page posts back and only the title bar displays on return, as shown in Figure 3-4.

Demonstrating WebParts zones

Announcements Restore Close
MyFavorites Restore Close

Figure 3-4 When a Web part is minimized, a Restore button comes up to let you restore the original panel later.

If you click the Close button (which is programmatically disabled in the previous example), the Web part is hidden from view. It is not destroyed, though. If the page includes a catalog Web part, all closed Web parts are listed in the catalog and users can restore them later.

The *WebPartManager* Class

The *WebPartManager* is a nonvisual control that manages all zones and part controls on a Web page. In particular, the manager maintains a collection of zones and parts and tracks which parts are contained in each zone. Only one *WebPartManager* can be contained in a Web form. In the simplest cases, your interaction with the manager control is limited to adding it to a page:

```
<asp:WebPartManager runat="server" id="MyWebMan" />
```

However, the Web part manager is responsible for more advanced functions that require a bit of coding. For example, it tracks the display mode of the page and notifies zones and parts of any change in the display mode. Depending on the display mode, parts and zones render differently. The default display mode is Normal, which means that catalog and editor zones are hidden and only Web parts are displayed with their own titles and borders. You can access the list of zones via the *Zones* collection.

Finally, the *WebPartManager* is responsible for initiating communication between two part controls. Two part controls within the same page can communicate and exchange information using a special channel represented by a *Connection* object. You can define a *Connection* object for a Web part manager using declarative syntax, as in the following example:

```
<asp:webpartmanager runat="server">
   <StaticConnections>
      <asp:connection runat="server" ID="MyConnection"
           ConsumerID="MyConsumerPart" ProviderID="MyProviderPart" />
   </StaticConnections>
</asp:webpartmanager>
```

Communication between parts is made possible through the use of custom interfaces. A Web part that is intended to provide some information to others would implement the provider's set of interfaces. In this way, a consumer Web part can access properties and methods in a consistent fashion.

We'll look at how connection objects connect to Web parts later in this chapter.

The *WebPart* Class

WebPart is an abstract class that is used only for referencing an existing Web part object. You define the contents of your pages using either a user control or a custom control derived from *WebPart*. Note that if you use a user control, the ASP.NET runtime wraps it into an instance of the *GenericWebPart* control, which provides basic Web Parts capabilities. You can't use the *GenericWebPart* component alone. *GenericWebPart* wraps only one server control. To generate a user interface that aggregates multiple controls, you have two options:

- Create a user control
- Create a new control that inherits *WebPart*

If you use a user control, you can't specify *WebPart*-specific properties such as *Title*. A possible workaround is to implement the *IWebPart* interface in your user control.

Table 3-2 lists the main properties of the *WebPart* class and gives you an idea of the programming power of the Web part controls. The class indirectly inherits *WebControl* and *Panel*, so it also features quite a few extra visual properties, such as *BackColor* and *BackImageUrl* (not listed in the table).

Table 3-2 Properties of the *WebPart* Class

Property	Description
AllowClose	Indicates whether a Web part can be removed from the page.
AllowEdit	Indicates whether a Web part allows you to edit its properties.
AllowHide	Indicates whether a Web part can be hidden on a Web page.
AllowMinimize	Indicates whether a Web part can be minimized.
AllowZoneChange	Indicates whether a Web part can be moved within its zone only or between zones.
Caption	Indicates the caption of the Web part.
ChromeState	Indicates the state of the Web part: normal or minimized.
ChromeType	Indicates the type of the frame for the Web part: border, title, title and border, or none.
Description	The Web part description used in the catalog and as a ToolTip in the title bar.
Direction	Indicates the direction of the text: left-to-right or right-to-left.
HelpMode	Indicates which kind of Help user interface is displayed for a control.
HelpUrl	The URL to a topic in the Web part's help.

Table 3-2 Properties of the *WebPart* Class

Property	Description
Hidden	Indicates whether the Web part is displayed on a Web page.
IsShared	Indicates whether multiple users share the Web part.
ProviderConnectionPoints	Gets the collection of *ConnectionPoint* objects that are associated with the Web part. The *ConnectionPoint* class defines a possible connection in which the Web part is either the provider or the consumer.
Title	Indicates the string used as the first string in the title of a Web part. (See the description of the *Caption* property.)
TitleStyle	A style object used to render the title bar of the Web part.
TitleUrl	Indicates the URL where you can access additional information about the Web part control. If specified, the URL appears in the title bar of the part.
Verbs	The set of verbs associated with the Web part.
Zone	The zone that currently contains the Web part.
ZoneID	ID of the zone that currently contains the Web part.
ZoneIndex	The index of the Web part in the zone it lives in.

The programming interface of the *WebPart* class is all in the properties listed in the table. The class has no methods and events, aside from those inherited from base server controls.

A Sample Web Part Component

Let's build a sample Web part and experiment with its properties. As mentioned, a Web part is a pseudo-window nested in the Web page that contains some sort of information. Like a window, it can be moved around and its content can be configured to some extent. The Web Parts infrastructure provides drag-and-drop facilities for moving the control around and changing the page layout. The programmer is responsible for building any logic and user interface elements for editing and cataloging the content.

The primary goal of a Web part control is delivering information to users. The information can be retrieved in a variety of ways, according to the characteristics of both the Web part and the hosting application. In a portal scenario, the Web part shows through the user's personalized page some content grabbed over the Web and possibly provided by external Web sites.

The BookFinder Web Part

The sample Web part we'll build grabs information about books and authors using a given search engine. You can use the Google or the Amazon API, or you can write your own engine that searches a local or remote database. In this example, I simply want to get information about books written by a certain author. All I need is the author's name. A call to the search engine consists of the following code:

```
private string _dataSource;
_dataSource = SearchEngine.DownloadData(author);
```

The *SearchEngine* class can internally use any search technology you like, as long as it returns an XML string. It goes without saying that the XML schema is totally arbitrary. In the next example, the XML string is transformed in a *DataSet* object and used to populate a *Repeater* control.

The Web Parts component is wrapped into a user control. The body of the user control looks like the following:

```
<div style="overflow:auto;height:280px;margin:3;">
  <asp:TextBox runat="server" id="AuthorName" Text="Dino Esposito" />
  <asp:button runat="server" id="btnGo" Text="Go" onclick="OnSearch" />

  <asp:repeater runat="server" id="Presenter">
    <headertemplate>
        <table style="font-family:Verdana;font-size:8pt;">
    </headertemplate>
    <itemtemplate>
        <tr>
          <td><img src='<%# Eval("ImageUrlSmall") %>' /> </td>
          <td><b><a href='<%# Eval("Url") %>'><%# Eval("ProductName") %>
              </a></b><br />
              <i><%# Eval("Manufacturer") %></i><br />
              <%# Eval("ReleaseDate") %><br /></td>
        </tr>
    </itemtemplate>
    <footertemplate>
        </table>
    </footertemplate>
</asp:repeater>
</div>
```

The data-bound expressions used in the code use the new *Eval* keyword—a more compact replacement for the *DataBinder.Eval* method used in ASP.NET 1.x. We'll cover *Eval* in detail in Chapter 5.

The *Repeater* is bound to a *DataTable* object created from the XML string retrieved by the search engine. The field names used in the previous example are assumed to correspond to columns in the *DataTable* object. The following code snippet shows how to bind data to the *Repeater* control:

```
void BindData() {
   StringReader reader = new StringReader(_dataSource);
   DataSet ds = new DataSet();
   ds.ReadXml(reader);

   // Assume the DataSet contains a table named "Details"
   // (This is the case if you use the Amazon API)
   Presenter.DataSource = ds.Tables["Details"];
   Presenter.DataBind();
}
```

The Web part is inserted in a Web part zone using the following code:

```
<asp:WebPartZone ID="WebPartZone1" runat="server" width="600px"
    HeaderText="This is Zone #1"
    PartChromeType="TitleAndBorder" Height="286px" >
   <zonetemplate>
    <x:bookfinder runat="server" id="Books" />
   </zonetemplate>
</asp:WebPartZone>
```

Figure 3-5 shows the BookFinder Web part in action.

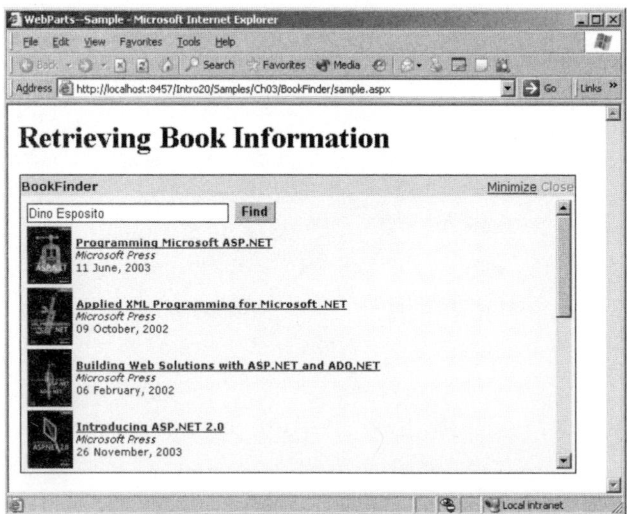

Figure 3-5 The BookFinder Web part retrieves all the books written by Dino Esposito.

> **Note** To implement a real-world book-finder Web part, you must rely on a good search engine. Two of the most popular engines, Amazon and Google, were created with different goals but both expose their services through Web services. If you're interested in the Amazon Web Services API, have a look at the *http://www.amazon.com/gp/aws/landing.html* URL and follow the steps described. Basically, you must download your free developer's kit, get your personal token to issue calls to the methods, and write your application. A similar procedure is required if you want to leverage the services of the Google engine. In this case, you get started at *http://api.google.com*.

Styling the Web Zone

The Web part can embellish its output through styles and visual properties. Note that the actual style of the Web part might depend on the settings of the Web part zone. For example, fonts, colors, and borders are inherited from the zone and apply to all parts in the zone. However, each Web part can override those settings.

The Web zone supports quite a few style properties for customizing the look and feel of the zone and its constituent parts. Table 3-3 lists the supported zone styles.

Table 3-3 Style Properties of the Web Zone

Style	Description
EmptyZoneTextStyle	Defines the style of an empty zone during the change-layout phase.
FooterStyle	Defines the style of the zone's footer.
HeaderStyle	Defines the style of the zone's header.
MenuLabelStyle	Defines the style of the zone's menu.
PartChromeStyle	Defines the style of the Web part's main frame (title, border).
PartStyle	Defines the overall style of the Web part.
PartTitleStyle	Defines the style of the title bar of the Web part.
PartVerbStyle	Defines the style of the verbs in the zone's title bar.

The following code snippet shows the styles that make up the Web part shown earlier in Figure 3-5. You can also use CSS classes defined in a separate stylesheet file.

```
<EmptyZoneTextStyle BackColor="lightyellow" Font-Size="8pt"
      Font-Names="verdana" />
<PartTitleStyle Font-Size="10pt" Font-Bold="True"
      BackColor="#E0E0E0" Font-Names="verdana" />
<PartStyle BackColor="#FFFFC0" />
<PartVerbStyle Font-Size="X-Small" Font-Names="verdana" />
```

You can customize the verbs in the title bar of Web parts. Verbs identify actions users can take on the Web part as a whole—for example, minimizing, restoring, editing, or closing the component. Verbs are enabled using the various *AllowXXX* properties on the Web part. Their style is controlled through *XxxVerb* tags. For example, you can disable the Close button by using the following code:

```
<CloseVerb Enabled="False" />
```

One of the style properties you can set is the text displayed. You can use little bitmaps, too, as shown here:

```
<closeverb imageurl="images/CloseVerb.gif"
    text="Close" description="Closes the WebPart" />
<restoreverb imageurl="images/RestoreVerb.gif"
    text="Restore" description="Restores the WebPart" />
<minimizeverb imageurl="images/MinimizeVerb.gif"
    text="Minimize" description="Minimizes the WebPart" />
```

Note that verb properties belong to the zone, not to the individual Web part. This means that all Web parts in a given zone share the same verb settings. This isn't true of other title attributes, such as the background and colors.

A verb is represented by a *WebPartVerb* object and features a few properties, including *Description* (the tooltip displayed), *Text* (the text or alternative text if an image is used), and *ImageUrl* (the image to render). In addition, you can define click handlers for both the client (*ClientClickHandler*) and the server (*ServerClickHandler*).

Changing the Zones Layout

Let's now consider a sample page that includes more zones and Web parts. We'll define two zones—the Information zone and the Miscellaneous zone. The zones occupy two cells in the same row of a table that spans the whole page.

By default, the Information zone contains the BookFinder Web part, and the Miscellaneous zone contains two other sample Web parts—MyFavorites (mentioned earlier) and MsNbcWeather.

The MyFavorites Web part reads a list of favorite links out of a server-side XML file and displays them through its user interface. The *DataSetDataSource* class (see Chapter 6) is used to load the XML data and bind it to the user interface.

```
<%@ control language="C#" classname="MyFavorites"%>
<asp:datasetdatasource runat="server" id="Source" readonly="False"
    datafile="Favorites.xml" />
<asp:datalist id="DataList1" runat="server" datasourceid="Source">
    <headertemplate>
        <b>My Current Favorite List</b><hr size="1">
    </headertemplate>
    <itemtemplate>
        <table>
          <tr>
             <td valign="top" style="WIDTH: 80%"><b>
               <a runat="server" id="TitleLabel" href='<%# Eval("Url") %>'>
               <%# Eval("Title") %></a></b>
             </td></tr>
          <tr>
             <td colspan="2">
               <asp:label id="DescriptionLabel" runat="server"
                    font-names="verdana" font-size="8pt"
                    text='<%# Eval("Description") %>'></asp:label>
             </td></tr>
        </table>
    </itemtemplate>
</asp:datalist>
```

The MsNbcWeather Web part gets weather information about a U.S. city (identified by a ZIP Code) and displays that in the page. Weather information is provided by the MSNBC Web site. In this case, the information is not retrieved through a Web service call. A ready-to-use page on the *http://www.msnbc.com* site returns a JavaScript object filled with weather information. The Web part invokes this URL and then processes the JavaScript code in the client-side *onload* event of the window.

The sample portal page we're building using these three Web parts is shown in Figure 3-6.

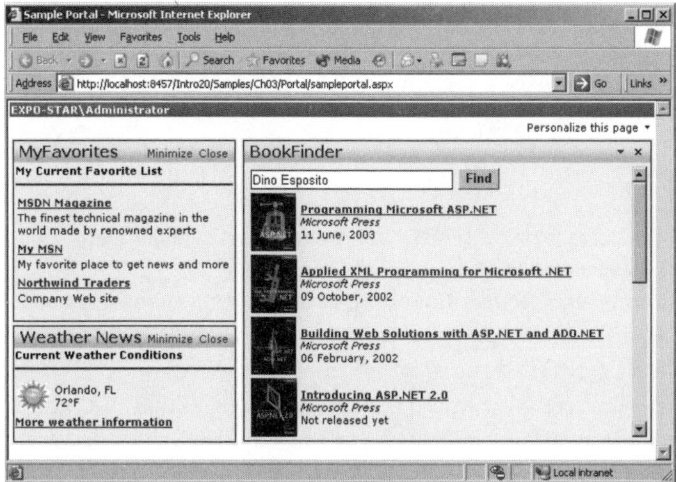

Figure 3-6 The sample portal home page

Note that the two zones have different settings for verbs. In particular, the rightmost zone uses bitmaps for the minimize and close verbs. Two other things in the user interface of the page are worth noting: the login name and the personalization link at the top of the page.

The login name has no meaning other than to serve as a reminder that a portal page is user-specific by design. The sample page uses the new *LoginName* security control to display the name of the current user. (See Chapter 10 for more details about ASP.NET 2.0 security controls.)

When you build portal pages, you should figure out a way to store personalized settings on a per-user basis. The Personalize This Page link button starts a procedure that lets you change the layout of the zones. You attach the personalization link button through the *WebPartPageMenu* control.

```
<asp:WebPartPageMenu ID="WebPartPageMenu1" Runat="server"
    Font-Names="Verdana" Font-Size="8pt"
    Text="Personalize this page">
    <MenuStyle BorderColor="Blue" BorderStyle="Solid"
        Font-Names="Verdana" Font-Size="8pt" BorderWidth="1px" />
</asp:WebPartPageMenu>
```

The control represents a pagewide menu and can be placed anywhere in the page. The page menu does not depend on zones or *WebPart* controls. When clicked, the link button displays a list of options, as shown in Figure 3-7.

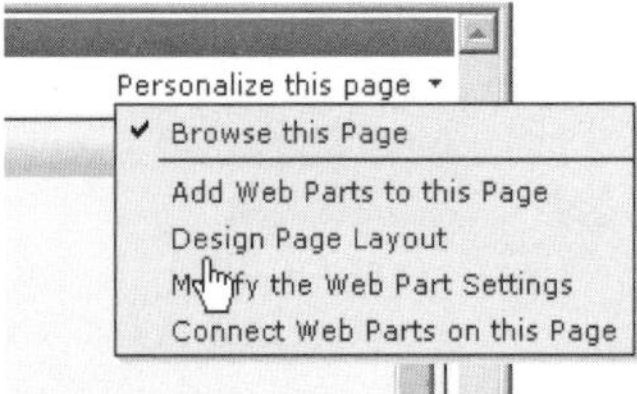

Figure 3-7 The pagewide WebPart menu in its default configuration

The menu items, as well as their state and text, can be modified programmatically. Each menu item represents a verb enabled on the defined Web parts—browse, catalog, design, edit properties, and connect to other Web parts. Each verb is characterized by a property through which you can enable, hide, or label the menu items. The verb properties are *BrowseModeVerb*, *CatalogModeVerb*, *DesignModeVerb*, *EditModeVerb*, and *ConnectModeVerb*. The default mode is Browse.

When you're in design mode (as you can see in Figure 3-8), drag-and-drop facilities let you move Web parts from one zone to another. Once dropped onto a new zone, the Web part inherits the currently active graphical settings, including the title bar and verb settings.

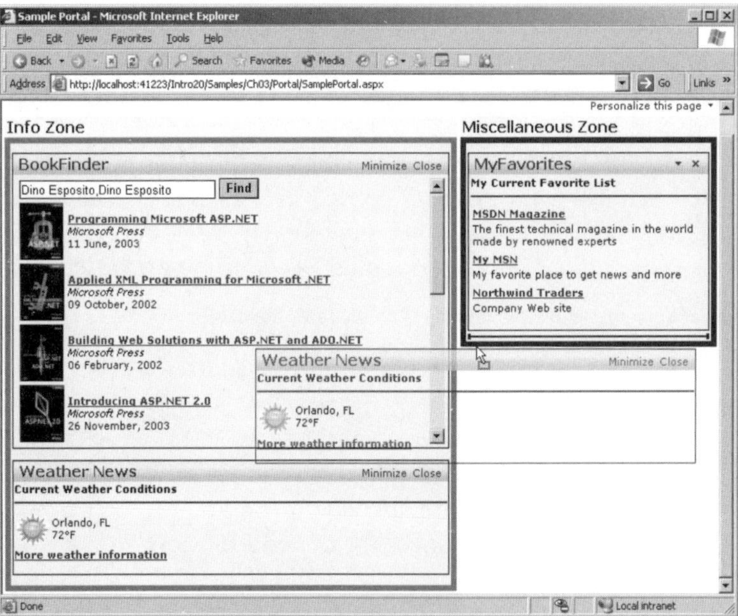

Figure 3-8 In design mode, users can move Web parts around zones using drag-and-drop.

In design mode, each zone sports a border and displays its title text so users can easily spot what Web parts are available for moving. When users finish moving Web parts around, they can click the *Browse* verb to persist the changes.

Persisting Layout Changes

As mentioned, a typical portal page is inherently user-specific. So if the user changes the layout of the zones, the new layout must be stored and used whenever that page is visited. In ASP.NET 2.0, this doesn't require much coding work on your part. All you have to do is configure the application so that it supports personalization. We'll delve into personalization in the next chapter.

In addition to enabling personalization, you must supply (or better yet, declare) a data store. The data store is a Microsoft SQL Server or Microsoft Access database that contains user-specific settings related to personalization. To make the layout changes persistent across application invocations, you run the ASP.NET Configuration applet from the Website menu of Visual Studio 2005. Once in the applet, you click on the Security tab and start the Security Setup Wizard to choose and configure the personalization data store.

When a Web part–driven application finishes the personalization step, modified zone indexes are automatically stored and used to draw the page upon next access, as you can see in Figure 3-9.

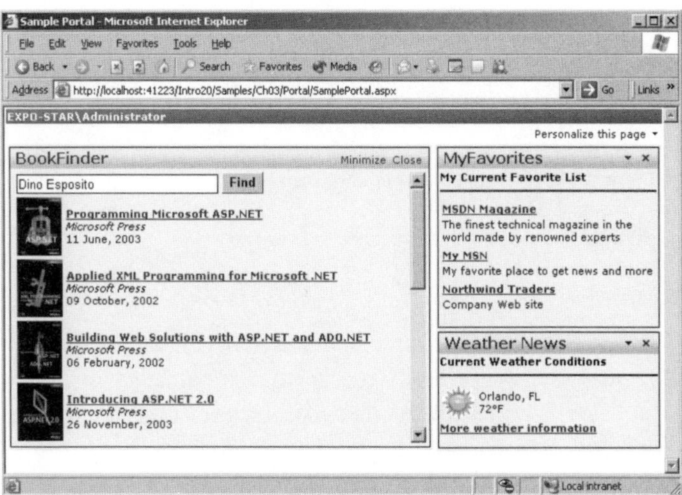

Figure 3-9 The weather Web part has been moved to the Miscellaneous zone and inherits the title and verb local attributes.

Editing and Listing Web Parts

In addition to allowing users to move Web parts from one zone to another, you can allow users to edit various characteristics of the Web parts, including their appearance, layout, and basic behavior. You can also provide users with a list of all available parts and have them choose which ones to activate.

The Web Parts framework provides basic editing and listing functionality for all Web parts. You enable in-place editing by placing one or more editor parts in the page. Listing is enabled by means of a catalog part component. As mentioned, both editing and listing are controlled and activated through the Web part page menu.

Creating an Editor Zone

The first step in enabling dynamic editing on your Web part–driven page is defining an editor zone. The tag to use is *<asp:editorzone>*. You need one editor zone per page. ASP.NET 2.0 supports quite a few types of editors, each designed to edit a particular aspect of Web parts. There are editors to change the values of public and Web browsable properties, the overall behavior of the part, and its layout and appearance.

The Edit Mode

To define an editor zone in a page, you use the following code:

```
<asp:EditorZone runat="server" HeaderText="Enter Your Changes">
    <InstructionTextStyle Font-Names="Verdana" Font-Italic="True" />
    <HeaderStyle BackColor="Blue" ForeColor="White" />
    <ZoneTemplate>
       <asp:AppearanceEditorPart runat="server" />
       <asp:LayoutEditorPart runat="server" />
       <asp:PropertyGridEditorPart runat="server" />
    </ZoneTemplate>
</asp:EditorZone>
```

In addition to specifying some optional style information, you have to create an *<asp:editorzone>* tag and place a *<zonetemplate>* in it. The zone template lists the editors you want to use. The editor zone shows up only in edit mode and appears at the exact position where you defined it in the page. For this reason, you should choose an appropriate placement that doesn't obstruct the editing process.

The Web Parts framework provides a default layout and visual settings for the editor zones. You can change the default settings, though—including the title and the style of the buttons on the footer.

You enter in edit mode, selecting the Modify The Web Parts Settings option on the page menu. When this happens, all Web parts in the page show a little bitmap that represents the edit menu. You click on the menu to make the editors appear, as shown in Figure 3-10.

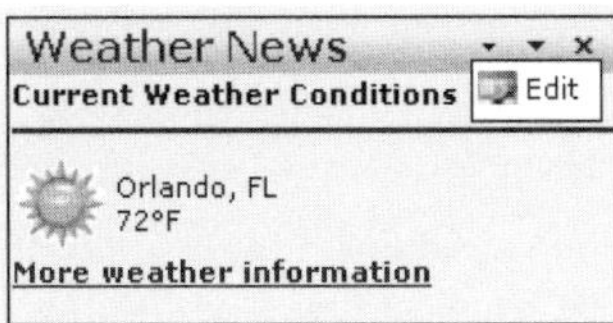

Figure 3-10 Click on the Edit menu to display all referenced Web Parts editors.

Figure 3-11 shows what happens when the Weather Web part is switched to edit mode.

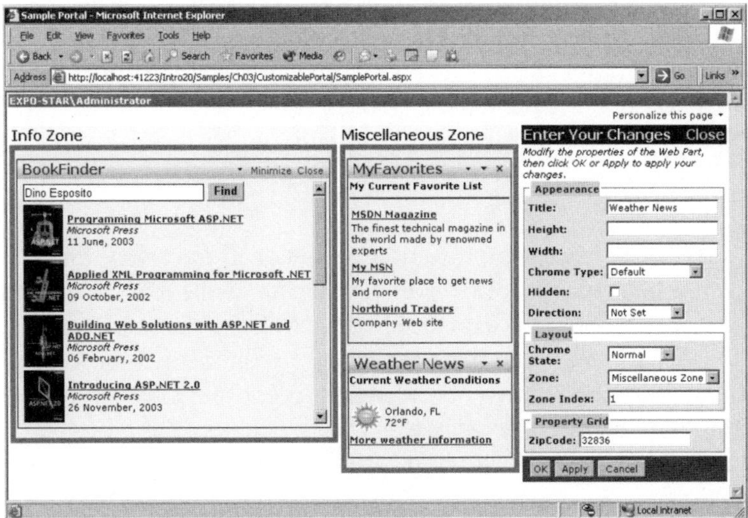

Figure 3-11 When the editors are running, users can change some visual settings for the selected Web part.

The Editor Part Components

Table 3-4 details the editor parts. You can select more than one editor in the same zone. Editors are displayed in the specified order within the editor zone.

Table 3-4 Editor Parts

Editor	Description
AppearanceEditorPart	Lets you edit visual settings such as width, title, direction of the text, and border type.
BehaviorEditorPart	Lets you modify some behavioral settings, such as whether the Web part supports personalization, editing, and minimization. The editor part also lets you edit help and title links.
LayoutEditorPart	Lets you edit the frame style (normal or minimized) and the zone the part belongs to. You can also modify the index of the part within the selected zone.
PropertyGridEditorPart	Lets you edit the custom properties of the Web part component. A custom property is a public property defined on a *WebPart*-derived class marked with the *Personalizable* and *WebBrowsable* attributes.

The footer of the editor zone has a standard toolbar with buttons for saving and exiting (the OK button), saving and continuing (the Apply button), and exiting without saving (the Cancel button). Any change applied during the edit phase is stored in the personalization data store. This feature is provided by the ASP.NET 2.0 framework and requires no additional coding.

> **Important** For the property grid editor to show up, the Web part must have publicly browsable and personalizable properties. The properties must be exposed by the Web part control, not any of its constituent controls. Even though user controls can be employed as Web parts, they have no browsable properties. Adding a browsable property to, say, the .ascx won't work because the property must be exposed by a *WebPart*-derived class. You have to create your own Web part class to be able to edit custom properties through the property grid editor. We'll look at a custom Web part class later in the chapter.

Adding Web Parts Dynamically

A Web part can show a variety of verbs in its title bar, including Close. If you click that button, the Web part is closed and hidden from view, and there's not much you can do to view the Web part again. But is the Web part gone forever? Of course not. Or, more exactly, not if you have designed the Web part page appropriately.

The Catalog Zone

The catalog zone is a Web part component that allows users to add Web parts to the page at run time. A Web parts catalog contains the list of Web parts you want to offer to users. At a minimum, though, the catalog acts as a store for Web parts that the user has removed from the page. The catalog guarantees that no inadvertently closed Web part is lost. You bring up the catalog of a page by choosing the Add Web Parts To This Page menu item.

The following code demonstrates a simple but effective catalog:

```
<asp:CatalogZone runat="server" headertext="Catalog Zone">
    <HeaderVerbStyle Font-Size="8pt" />
    <InstructionTextStyle Font-Italic="True" Font-Size="8pt" />
    <FooterStyle cssclass="EditorZoneFooter" /
>
    <CatalogItemStyle Font-Size="8pt" />
    <PartLinkStyle Font-Names="verdana" Font-Size="8pt" />
    <VerbStyle cssclass="EditorZoneVerb" />
    <HeaderStyle Font-Bold="True" BackColor="Blue" ForeColor="White" />
    <ZoneTemplate>
        <asp:PageCatalogPart runat="server" Title="Available Parts" />
    </ZoneTemplate>
</asp:CatalogZone>
```

Aside from the visual styles that adorn the HTML output of the catalog zone, the only piece of code that really matters is the *<asp:PageCatalogPart>* element. It is the container that will list the available Web parts at run time.

The catalog lists the Web parts that have been closed and gives users a chance to check and add them to one of the existing zones, as you can see in Figure 3-12.

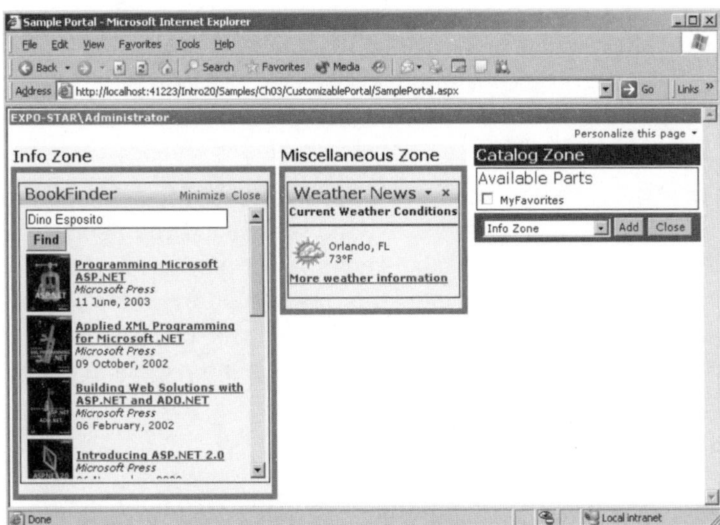

Figure 3-12 The page catalog in action in the sample page

Note The Web Parts framework provides a lot of functionality and a variety of built-in Web dialog boxes. The page catalog and the various editor parts are a few examples. Note that in their native format, these dialog boxes have no visual style set. You are responsible for setting borders, fonts, and colors to give them a professional look.

The Catalog Part Components

The catalog zone can contain two types of catalog parts: a *PageCatalogPart* control and a *DeclarativeCatalogPart* control. As mentioned, the former is a sort of placeholder for the Web parts that the user removes from the page. The *DeclarativeCatalogPart* control contains the list of Web parts that users can add to their page. The Web parts managed by the page catalog are those statically declared in the .aspx source file. The Web parts managed by the *DeclarativeCatalogPart* are not instantiated and managed until they are explicitly added to the page.

The following code defines new externally available Web parts:

```
<ZoneTemplate>
  <asp:declarativecatalogpart runat="server"
       title="Other Parts">
    <webpartstemplate>
       <x:Sample1 Runat="server" id="sample1" />
       <x:Sample2 Runat="server" id="sample2" />
    </webpartstemplate>
  </asp:declarativecatalogpart>
</ZoneTemplate>
```

These Web parts are listed in the catalog side by side with the Web parts declared in the page. You are provided with links to switch between groups of parts. Figure 3-13 shows the appearance of the catalog part.

Important You can also set and control the display mode programmatically. The Web part page menu is helpful if you need to create a fully customizable page, but it forces you to play by its rules and, more importantly, requires advanced browser support. In fact, the menu is displayed through client-side script code based on Dynamic HTML features. You can place simple link buttons in the page and attach some server-side code like the following:

```
MyWebPartManager.DisplayMode = WebPartManager.CatalogDisplayMode;
```

The code sets the display mode of the Web parts to catalog.

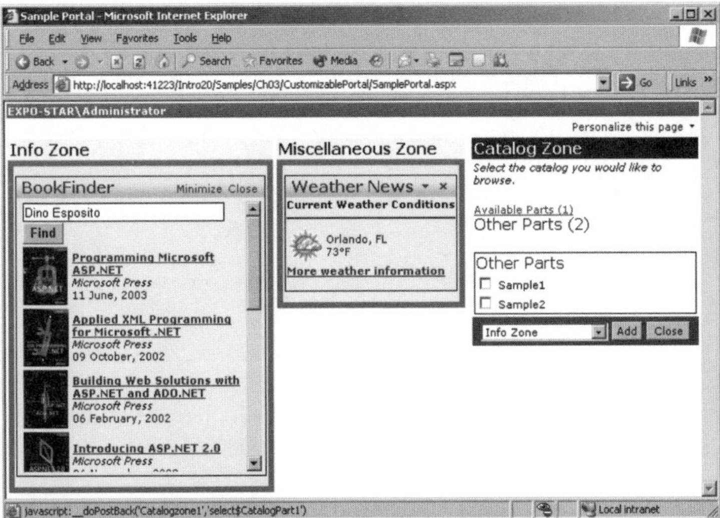

Figure 3-13 The catalog zone lists groups of Web parts that are available to the Web page.

Connecting to Other Web Parts

Web part controls can communicate with other Web parts on the same Web page and exchange data. For this feature to work, each Web part must implement the appropriate interfaces. The communication is one-way and relies on the services of a connection object. The Web part connection object establishes a channel between a Web part control that acts as a provider and a Web part that acts as a consumer.

Two connected Web parts operate in a publisher/subscriber fashion. Any change in the values exposed by the provider are immediately reflected by the consumer. As you can imagine, this model lends itself well to representing master/detail models of data.

The Connection Model

The Web part connection model consists of two interoperating entities—a connection and a connection point. A connection connects two points, one from the provider control and one from the consumer. The connections available in the page are managed by the Web part manager. Web part controls can communicate with more than one other part.

Enabling Web Parts Connectivity

The following code illustrates the key step in a connection-enabled Web page that supports Web parts:

```
<asp:WebPartManager runat="server" id="MyWebPartManager">
    <StaticConnections>
        <asp:connection
             ProviderID="emp"
             ProviderConnectionPointIDname="EmployeeIDProvider"
             ConsumerID="ord"
             ConsumerConnectionPointID="EmployeeIDConsumer" />
    </StaticConnections>
</asp:WebPartManager>
```

All the necessary connection objects are declaratively listed in the body of the Web part manager. A connection is identified by a provider and a consumer object. For both objects, you specify an ID and the name of the corresponding connection point. The *ProviderID* and *ConsumerID* properties must match the ID of existing Web parts. The *ConsumerConnectionPointID* and *ProviderConnectionPointID* properties must match the name of a connection point defined within the Web parts.

> **Note** The Web Parts framework supports static and dynamic connections. Static connections are defined within the body of the *WebPartManager* object and are available to users as soon as they open the page. Dynamic connections enable users to connect and disconnect two Web parts using code.

Connection Points and Interfaces

A connection point defines a possible connection for a *WebPart* control. A connection point doesn't guarantee communication—it simply provides a way for the *WebPartManager* object to establish a communication channel between two parts. A connection point can act as a provider or as a consumer. In the former case, the Web part exposes information through the connection channel that other registered Web parts consume. A consumer connection point, on the other hand, receives incoming data exposed by a provider.

The communication between providers and consumers is defined by a communication contract. The contract set between a provider and a consumer consists of an interface implemented in the provider that the consumer needs to know. This interface can contain properties, events, or methods that the consumer can use once the communication is established. The consumer doesn't need to implement any interface, but it must be aware of the interfaces that its provider supports.

Building a Master/Detail Schema

Let's apply the Web part connection model to a couple of custom Web part controls that inherit from the *WebPart* base class. The provider Web part is named EmployeesWebPart; it exposes the value of employee ID. In addition, the control displays some information about the specified employee.

The consumer component is the *OrdersWebPart* control; it displays all the orders issued by a particular employee. The ID of the employee can be set directly through the programming interface of the component, or it can be automatically detected when the provider Web part signals a change in its state. This link creates a master/detail relationship between the two Web parts.

Provider Web Part Components

When you create a provider Web part, the first thing you define is the communication contract for the connection points. The contract is defined as an interface. The Web part component is a custom ASP.NET control derived from *WebPart* that implements the contract interface.

```
interface IEmployeeInfo
{
   int EmployeeID { get; set; }
}
public class EmployeesWebPart : WebPart, IEmployeeInfo
{
   private int _empID;
   public int EmployeeID
    {
       get { return _empID; }
       set { _empID = value; }
    }
    ⋮
}
```

To make *EmployeeID* show up in the property grid editor, you mark it as browsable and personalizable.

```
[Personalizable(true), WebBrowsable(true)]
public int EmployeeID
{
   get { return _empID; }
   set { _empID = value; }
}
```

To give the Web part a user interface, you can override the *RenderContents* method. Aside from the few features described so far, writing a custom Web part is not much different from writing a custom control.

The next step is creating a provider connection point. You define a function that returns an instance of the current class, and you mark it with the *[ConnectionProvider]* attribute. This function creates the connection point for the data based on the *IEmployeeInfo* interface:

```
[ConnectionProvider("EmployeeIDProvider", "EmployeeIDProvider")]
private IEmployeeInfo ProvideEmployeeInfo()
{
    return this;
}
```

Notice that the name of the connection point must match the *ProviderName* or the *ConsumerName* property of the *<asp:connection>* tag, depending on whether the connection point is for a provider or a consumer.

> **Note** When the *WebPart* provider control implements just one provider interface, as in this case, there's no need to explicitly mention the interface in the connection provider attribute. When multiple interfaces are supported, you must add a third parameter to the *[ConnectionProvider]* attribute to indicate the contract on which the connection is based.
>
> ```
> [ConnectionProvider["Prov", "Prov", typeof(IMyInterface)]
> ```

The sample *EmployeesWebPart* control retrieves and displays some information about the specified employee in SQL Server's Northwind database. Figure 3-14 shows its user interface.

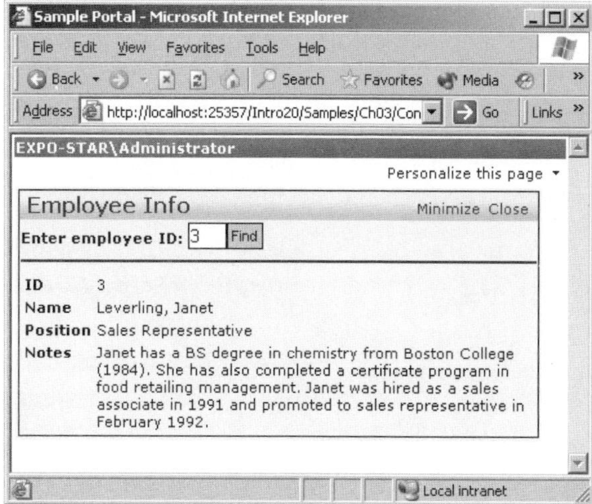

Figure 3-14 The *EmployeesWebPart* control in action

Consumer Web Part Components

A Web part that acts as a consumer is even simpler to write than a provider. Besides generating its own user interface, the Web part has only one duty—creating a consumer connection point for the specified interface.

```
[ConnectionConsumer("EmployeeIDConsumer", "EmployeeIDConsumer")]
private void GetEmployeeInfo(IEmployeeInfo empInfo)
{
   if (empInfo != null)
   {
      _empID = empInfo.EmployeeID;
      FindEmployeeInfo();
   }
   else
      throw new Exception("No connection data found.");
}
```

The ASP.NET runtime creates a consumer connection point that corresponds to a method marked with the *[ConnectionConsumer]* attribute. The method marked with the attribute is taken as the callback to invoke when anything on the specified interface changes.

The user interface is composed using a *DataGrid* control. The grid is filled with the results of a query run against the Orders table in the Northwind database.

Putting It All Together

The two custom Web parts that support connection points must be added to the page using a custom prefix, just like any other custom control. First you compile the two files to an assembly, and then you link it to the page using the *@Register* directive:

```
<%@ Register tagprefix="x" Namespace="Samples" Assembly="MyWebParts" %>
```

If, for some reason, the two classes belong to different namespaces, you use two different prefixes. The code that inserts the Web parts looks like the following:

```
<x:EmployeesWebPart runat="server" id="emp"
     Title="Employee Info" />
<x:OrdersWebPart runat="server" id="ord"
     Scrollbars="Auto" Height="200px"
     Title="Orders 1997" />
```

Let's briefly review the markup code that defines a Web part connection object within the page.

```
<StaticConnections>
    <asp:connection
      ProviderID="emp" ProviderConnectionPointID="EmployeeIDProvider"
      ConsumerID="ord" ConsumerConnectionPointID="EmployeeIDConsumer" />
</StaticConnections>
```

This declaration can be read as a connection set between a Web part with an ID of *emp* and a Web part named *ord*. The former acts as the provider through a connection point name *EmployeeIDProvider*. The latter plays the role of the consumer through a connection point named *EmployeeIDConsumer*.

As a result, any change in any of the properties exposed by the provider results in an internal field-changed event that is resolved, invoking the consumer's callback. The consumer retrieves and displays the orders for the specified employee. The two Web parts work perfectly in sync, as Figure 3-15 shows.

The provider Web part also defines a public and browsable *EmployeeID* property. If you set the *EmployeeID* property on the *EmployeesWebPart* control (the provider), the change is immediately reflected by the consumer, as you can see in Figure 3-16.

Note that, by design, the connection model is a one-way model—to keep the controls completely in sync, you need a second connection in which the provider and consumer roles are swapped. For example, suppose you add a public, browsable *EmployeeID* property to the Orders Web part. To reflect any property changes to the Employees Web part, you must create a second pair of connection points that are completely independent from the first pair.

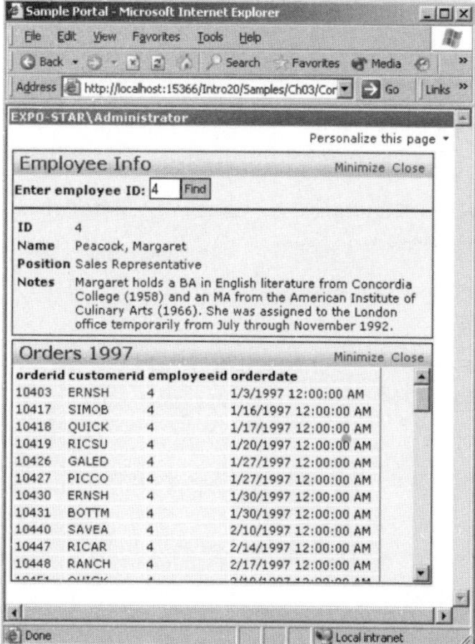

Figure 3-15 A master/detail relationship set using two independent but communicating Web parts

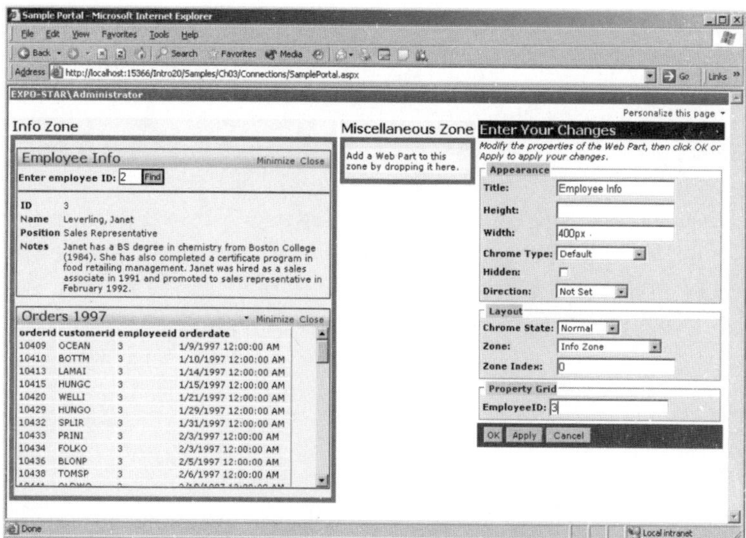

Figure 3-16 Changes to public properties tied to a connection point make the consumer refresh its user interface.

Summary

The Web Parts framework provides a simple and familiar way for ASP.NET developers to create modular Web applications that support end-user personalization. A Web part is a panel-like server control that displays some user interface elements. Like any other server control, it is configurable through properties, methods, and events.

Web parts are integrated into a framework aimed at composing pages with components that are smarter and richer than traditional controls. The surrounding Web Parts framework provides all the magic (or hard infrastructure code, if you will). In particular, you can partition the surface of your Web page into zones and bind one or more parts to each zone. Each Web part is automatically given a frame, a title bar, and some verbs (such as minimize, edit, and close). Overall, a Web part looks like a traditional window of a desktop application.

The Web Parts framework supports a variety of working modes, including design, edit, and catalog. In design mode, users can use drag-and-drop and move parts around, changing the layout of the page. In edit mode, users can also change visual and behavioral properties. The user interface of the editors is provided, free of programming charge, by the Web Parts framework. Finally, in catalog mode the framework lists all available Web parts, including those that the user might have previously closed.

When a user reconfigures the Web parts on a page, the user's settings are automatically persisted. The next time the user visits the page, the last Web parts configuration is restored. Web parts settings are persisted using page personalization. The only requirement is that page personalization be enabled for the page. No code is required to store the user settings, but the page personalization engine must be configured offline. You'll see a lot about page personalization in the next chapter.

4

Personalization: User Profiles and Themes

ASP.NET applications do not necessarily require a rich set of personalization features. However, if you can build an effective personalization layer into your Web application, the application will be friendlier, more functional, and more appealing to use. For some applications (such as portals and shopping centers), though, personalization is crucial. For others, it's mostly a way to improve the visual appearance.

In ASP.NET 2.0, personalization comes in two complementary forms: user profiles and themes. The user profile is designed for persistent storage of structured data using a friendly and type-safe API. The application defines its own model of personalized data, and the ASP.NET runtime does the rest by parsing and compiling that model into a class. Each member of the personalized class data corresponds to a piece of information specific to the current user. Loading and saving personalized data is completely transparent to end users and doesn't even require the page author to know much about the internal plumbing.

The second form of personalization is using themes. Much like Microsoft Windows XP themes, ASP.NET themes assign a set of styles and visual attributes to elements of the site that can be customized. These elements include control properties, page style sheets, images, and templates on the page. A *theme* is the union of all visual styles for all customizable elements in the pages—a sort of super–CSS file. A theme is identified by name and consists of CSS files, images, and control skins. A *control skin* is a text file that contains default control declarations in which visual properties are set for the control. With this feature enabled, if the developer adds a *DataGrid* control to a page, the control is rendered with the default appearance defined in the theme.

With personalization, you can store user-specific information and preferences without the burden of having to write the infrastructural code. With themes, you can easily give the whole site a consistent (and, you hope, appealing) user interface and easily export that look from one application to the next.

Managing User Profiles

At the highest level of abstraction, a user profile is a collection of properties that the ASP.NET 2.0 runtime groups into a dynamically generated class. Any personalization data is persisted on a per-user basis and is permanently stored until someone with administrative privileges deletes it. The layout of the user profile is defined in the configuration file and consists of a list of properties that can take any of the .NET common language runtime (CLR) types.

The data storage is hidden from the user and, to some extent, from the programmers. The user doesn't need to know how and where the data is stored; the programmer simply needs to indicate what type of personalization provider he wants to use. The personalization provider determines the database to use—typically, a Microsoft Access or Microsoft SQL Server database—but custom providers and custom data storage models can also be used.

Creating the User Profile

To use the ASP.NET 2.0 personalization API, you first decide on the structure of the data model you want to use. Then you attach the data model to the page through the configuration file. When the application runs, ASP.NET dynamically creates a profile object that contains, properly typed, the properties you have defined in the data model. The object is then added to the current *HttpContext* object and is available to pages through the *Profile* property. Let's see how to define a data model.

Using Scalar Properties

The simplest way to add properties to the personalization storage medium is through name/value pairs. You define each pair by adding a new property tag to the *<properties>* section of the configuration file. The *<properties>* section is itself part of the larger *<profile>* section, which also includes provider information. The *<profile>* section is located under *<system.web>*. Here's an example of a user profile section:

```
<profile>
   <properties>
      <add name="BackColor" type="string" />
      <add name="ForeColor" type="string" />
      <add name="Height" type="int" />
      <add name="Width" type="int" />
   </properties>
</profile>
```

All the properties defined through an *<add>* tag become members of a dynamically created class that is exposed as part of the HTTP context of each page. The *type* attribute indicates the type of the property. If no type information is set, the type defaults to *System.String*. Any valid CLR type is acceptable. Table 4-1 lists the valid attributes for the *<add>* element. Only *name* is mandatory.

Table 4-1 Attributes of the *<property>* Element

Attribute	Description
allowAnonymous	Allows storing values for anonymous users. False by default.
defaultValue	Indicates the default value of the property.
name	Name of the property.
provider	Name of the provider to use to read and write the property.
readOnly	Specifies whether the property value is read-only. False by default.
serializeAs	Indicates how to serialize the value of the property. Possible values are *Xml*, *Binary*, *String*, and *ProviderSpecific*.
type	The type of property. It is a string object by default.

The User Profile Class Representation

As a programmer, you don't need to know how data is stored or retrieved from the personalization store. However, you must create and configure the store. We skirted this step, but we'll discuss it in detail shortly. The following code snippet gives you an idea of the class being generated to represent the profile's data model:

```
namespace ASP
{
    public class HttpProfile : HttpProfileBase
    {
       public virtual string BackColor
       {
          get {(string) GetPropertyValue("BackColor");}
          set {SetPropertyValue("BackColor", value);}
       }
       public virtual string ForeColor
       {
          get {(string) GetPropertyValue("ForeColor");}
          set {SetPropertyValue("ForeColor", value);}
       }
       public virtual HttpProfile GetProfile(string username)
       {
           object o = HttpProfileBase.Create(username);
           return (HttpProfile) o;
       }
        ⋮
    }
}
```

As you can guess from the code, there's a tight relationship between user accounts and profile information. We'll investigate this in a moment—for now, you need to notice this because anonymous users are supported as well.

Using Collection Types

In the previous example, we worked with single, scalar values. However, the personalization engine fully supports more advanced scenarios such as using collections or custom types. Let's tackle collections first. The following code demonstrates a property *Links* that is an array of strings:

```
<properties>
    <add name="Links"
         type="System.Collections.Specialized.StringCollection"
         serializeAs="Xml" />
</properties>
```

Nonscalar values such as collections and arrays must be serialized to fit in a data storage medium. The *serializeAs* attribute simply specifies how. As mentioned, acceptable values are *String*, *Xml*, *Binary*, and *ProviderSpecific*. If the *serializeAs* attribute is not present on the *<property>* definition, the *String* type is assumed. A collection is normally serialized as XML or in a binary format.

Let's consider the following page-level code that stores values into the *Links* property:

```
Profile.Links.Clear();
Profile.Links.Add("http://www.contoso.com");
Profile.Links.Add("http://www.northwind.com");
```

If you choose the XML format, the previously shown page-level code places an XML string into the storage medium:

```
<?xml version="1.0" encoding="utf-16"?>
<ArrayOfString
      xmlns:xsi="http://www.w3.org/2001/XMLSchema-instance"
      xmlns:xsd="http://www.w3.org/2001/XMLSchema">
  <string>http://www.contoso.com</string>
  <string>http://www.northwind.com</string>
</ArrayOfString>
```

However, as mentioned before, the programmer is not required to know about the storage format and medium. Details of personalization are completely transparent to developers and end users.

> **Important** The XML serialization required by the value of the *serializeAs* attribute shown previously is performed by the *XmlSerializer* class. This means that some of the limitations of the class affect its use with ASP.NET 2.0 personalization. In particular, you can't use hash tables, dictionaries, or classes with circular references. Likewise, before you use a list collection type, you should first make sure it overloads the *Add* method with a single parameter. If you set the *SerializeAs* attribute to *Binary*, the binary .NET formatter is used and all the problems just described disappear instantly.

Using Custom Types

You can use a custom type with the ASP.NET personalization layer as long as you mark it as a serializable type. You simply author a class and compile it down to an assembly. The name of the assembly is added to the type information for the personalization property:

```
<profile>
   <property name="ShoppingCart"
             type="My.Namespace.DataContainer, MyAssem"
             serializeAs="Binary" />
</profile>
```

The assembly that contains the custom type must be available to the ASP.NET application. You obtain this custom type by placing the assembly in the application's Bin directory or by registering it within the global assembly cache (GAC).

Grouping Properties

Like *<property>*, the *<profile>* section can also accept the *<group>* element. The *<group>* element allows you to group a few related properties as if they are properties of an intermediate object. The following code snippet shows an example of grouping:

```
<profile>
  <properties>
     ⋮
     <group name="Font">
        <add name="Name" type="string" defaultValue="verdana" />
        <add name="SizeInPoints" type="int" defaultValue="8" />
     </group>
   </properties>
</profile>
```

The font properties have been declared children of the *Font* group. This means that from now on, any access to *Name* or *SizeInPoints* passes through the *Font* name, as shown here:

```
MyCtl.Style["font-name"] = Profile.Font.Name;
MyCtl.Style["font-size"] = String.Format("{0}pt",
     Profile.Font.SizeInPoints);
```

> **Note** Default values are not saved to the persistence layer. Properties declared with a default value make their debut in the storage medium only when the application assigns them a value different from the default one.

Personalization Providers

In ASP.NET 2.0, the personalization API is composed of two distinct elements—the access layer and the storage layer. The access layer provides a strongly typed model to get and set property values and also manages user identities. As you'll see in the next section, personalization data is associated with identities even though anonymous users can still connect and exploit the feature. The access layer guarantees that the data is retrieved and stored on behalf of the currently logged on user.

> **Note** In general, an ASP.NET 2.0 provider is defined as a pluggable component that extends or replaces system functionality. The personalization provider is just one implementation of the new ASP.NET 2.0 provider model. Other examples of providers are the membership provider and role manager provider, both of which we'll discuss in Chapter 10. At its core, the provider infrastructure allows customers to extend some of the out-of-the-box system functionality and change the underlying implementation while keeping the top-level interface intact. Providers are relatively simple components with as few methods and properties as possible. Only one instance of the provider should exist per application domain.

The second element of the personalization system is the underlying data storage. The system uses ad hoc providers to perform any tasks involved with the storage and retrieval of values. ASP.NET 2.0 comes with two personalization providers, each of which uses a different data engine. The default provider uses an Access database; the other provider is for SQL Server. You can also write custom providers. The provider writes data into the database of choice and is responsible for the final schema of the data. A personalization provider must be able to either serialize the type (by using XML serialization and binary object serialization, for example) or know how to extract significant information from it.

Configuring Personalization Providers

All features, such as personalization, that have providers should have a default provider. Normally, the default provider is indicated via a *defaultProvider* attribute in the section of the configuration file that describes the specific feature. By default, if a preferred provider is not specified, the first item in the collection is considered the default.

As for ASP.NET 2.0 personalization, the default provider is based on an Access database and is named *AspNetAccessProvider*. If you don't mind having your personalization data saved on a per-user basis in an Access database, you don't have to do anything. Otherwise, you can select an alternative provider. ASP.NET 2.0 provides a SQL Server–based provider named *AspNetSqlProvider*. Providers are registered in the *<providers>* section of the configuration file under the main node *<profile>*, as shown here:

```
<profile enabled="true" defaultProvider="AspNetAccessProvider" >
   <providers>
      <add name="AspNetAccessProvider"
           type="System.Web.Profile.AccessProfileProvider"
           connectionStringName="AccessFileName"
           description="Stores and retrieves personalization data from the
                        local Microsoft Access database file" />
      <add name="AspNetSqlProvider"
           type="System.Web.Profile.SqlProfileProvider"
           connectionStringName="LocalSqlServer"
           description="Stores and retrieves personalization data from the
                        local Microsoft SQL Server database" />
   </providers>
   ⋮
</profile>
```

The *<add>* nodes within the *<providers>* section list all the currently registered providers. The previous code is an excerpt from the machine.config file. Attributes such as *name* and *type* are common to all types of providers. Other properties are part of the provider's specific configuration mechanism. Tightly connected with this custom interface is the set of extra properties—in this case, *connectionStringName* and *description*. The *description* attribute is simply text that describes what the provider does. The *connectionStringName* attribute defines the information needed to set up a connection with the underlying database engine of choice. However, instead of being a plain connection string, the attribute contains the name of a previously registered connection string. For example, *LocalSqlServer* is certainly not the connection string to use for a local or remote connection to an instance of SQL Server. Instead, it is the name of an entry in the new <*connectionStrings*> section of the configuration file. That entry contains any concrete information needed to connect to the database.

The Access Personalization Provider

By default, personalization uses a local Access database. The database is created in the Data subdirectory of the application's virtual folder. As you'll see in the section titled "Interacting with the Page," page developers are responsible for creating any personalization databases.

As a developer, you don't need to know about the layout of the table and the logic that governs it; instead, you're responsible for ensuring that any needed infrastructure is created. To do so, you use the Website menu in Visual Studio 2005 to start the ASP.NET administrative tool. (More on this later.)

When you use the Access personalization provider, a database named ASPNetDB.mdb is created in the Data subdirectory. A view of the tables in the database is shown in Figure 4-1.

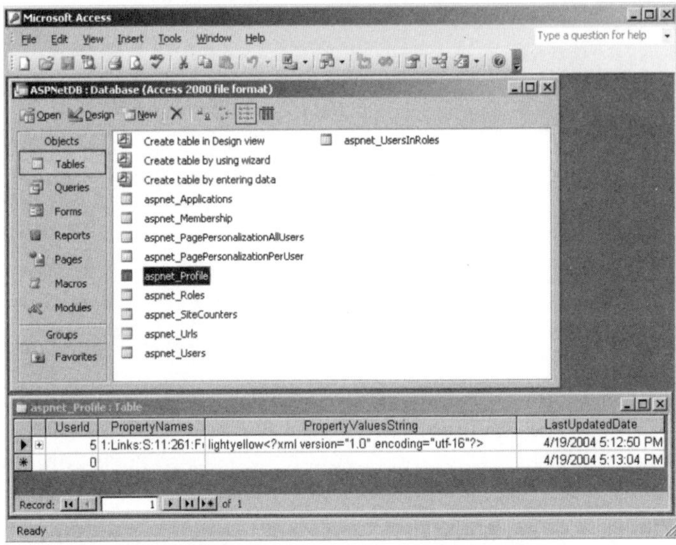

Figure 4-1 The list of tables found in the ASPNetDB Access database and the content of one record in the aspnet_Profile table

Note that the ASPNetDB database isn't specific to the personalization infrastructure. As you can see in the figure, it groups all provider-related tables, including those for membership, site counters, roles, and users. The internal structure of each database is specific to the mission of the underlying provider. The connection string for the Access personalization provider is shown here (located in machine.config):

```
<connectionStrings>
   <add name="AccessFileName" connectionString="~\DATA\ASPNetDB.mdb" />
</connectionStrings>
```

The Access personalization provider is the recommended provider for small applications in Internet scenarios or if you simply want to experiment with the functionality.

The SQL Server Personalization Provider

The Access and SQL Server providers rely on the same schema of data. The data design for default ASP.NET personalization providers shares some tables with the membership and role manager providers. (See Chapter 10.) The tables are aspnet_Users and aspnet_Roles. When the personalization provider is first invoked, any shared table is used if it exists and is created if it doesn't already exist.

The connection string for the SQL server database is shown here:

```
<connectionStrings>
   <add name="LocalSqlServer"
        connectionString="SERVER=127.0.0.1;INTEGRATED SECURITY=SSPI" />
</connectionStrings>
```

The connection string defaults to the local machine and uses integrated security. The structure of the main table that contains personalization data is visible in Figure 4-1. It contains a primary key field named *UserId*, which is the ID of the user because the user is registered in the companion aspnet_Users table. Additional fields are *PropertyNames* and *PropertyValuesString*. The former stores string names for the personalization properties for a specific *UserId*. The latter stores the corresponding values, conveniently serialized. The last field you find in the database is *LastUpdatedDate*, which obviously contains the date of the last update.

Custom Personalization Providers

The Access and SQL Server personalization providers are good at building new applications and are good for personalization data that is inherently tabular. In many cases, though, you won't start an ASP.NET 2.0 application from scratch but will instead migrate an existing ASP or ASP.NET application. You often already have data to integrate with the ASP.NET personalization layer. If this data doesn't get along with the relational model, or if it is already stored in a storage medium other than Access or SQL Server, you can write a custom personalization provider.

Personalization providers push the idea that existing data stores can be integrated with the personalization engine using a thin layer of code. This layer of code abstracts the physical characteristics of the data store and exposes its content through a common set of methods and properties—an interface. A custom personalization provider is a class that inherits *ProfileProvider*.

A custom provider can be bound to one or more personalization properties using the property's *provider* attribute:

```
<properties>
   <add name="BackColor" type="string" provider="MyProviderName" />
   ⋮
</properties>
```

It goes without saying that the provider name must correspond to one of the entries in the *<providers>* section.

Interacting with the Page

To enable or disable personalization support, you set the *enabled* attribute of the *<profile>* element in the web.config file. If the property is *true*, personalization features are enabled for all pages. If personalization is disabled, the *Profile* property isn't available to pages out of the *HttpContext* object.

Creating the Personalization Database

As mentioned earlier, personalization works strictly on a per-user basis and is permanently stored. Enabling the feature simply turns any functionality on, but it doesn't create the needed infrastructure for user membership and data storage.

ASP.NET 2.0 comes with an administrative tool—the ASP.NET Web Application Administration—that is fully integrated in Visual Studio 2005. (See Figure 4-2.) You invoke the tool by choosing ASP.NET Configuration from the Website menu.

The Web Application Administration tool has a wizard-like interface. You select the Security tab and just walk your way through the steps required to set up users, roles, and access permissions for your site. The tool also lets you configure the data store where membership information will be stored. Incidentally, this data storage is partially shared with the personalization engine. Depending on how users will access your site—either from the Internet or a local area network (LAN)—the tool automatically creates an Access or SQL Server database.

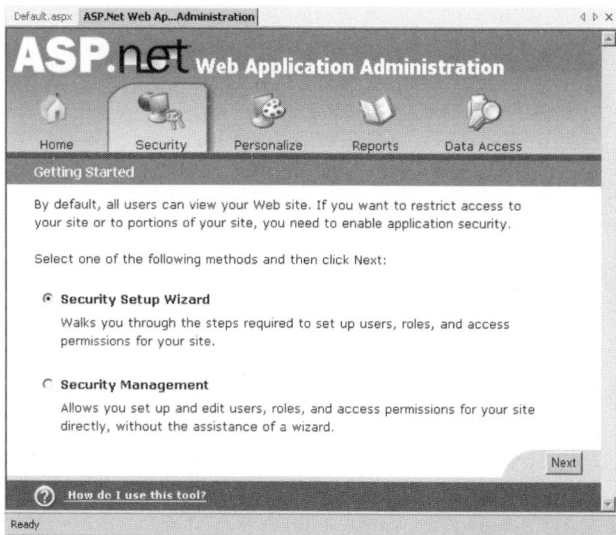

Figure 4-2 The ASP.NET Web Application Administration tool in action

Note that the Web Application Administration tool is just one option—not the only one—for setting up the personalization infrastructure. For example, if you're using a custom provider, the setup of your application is responsible for preparing any required storage infrastructure.

The use of a membership database with users and roles is important because personalization is designed to be user-specific and because a user ID—either a local Windows account or an application-specific logon—is necessary to index data. In our example, which uses the default provider, running a wizard from the Web Application Administration tool creates the Access ASPNetDB database in the Data subdirectory of the virtual root.

Anonymous Personalization

Although personalization is designed primarily for authenticated users, anonymous users can also store personalization data. In this case, though, a few extra requirements must be fulfilled. In particular, you have to turn on the *anonymousIdentification* feature, which is disabled by default.

```
<anonymousIdentification enabled="true" />
```

As you'll see in much greater detail in Chapter 10, anonymous identification is another new feature of ASP.NET 2.0. The purpose of anonymous user identification is to assign a unique identity to users who are not authenticated. This identity, common to all users, can be used to track the user (and handle the user's personalization data) in much the same way that developers do using the session state.

> **Note** Anonymous identification in no way affects the identity of the account that is processing the request. Nor does it affect any other aspects of security and user authentication. Anonymous identification is simply a way to give a "regular" ID to unauthenticated users so they can be tracked as authenticated, "regular" users.

In addition, to support anonymous personalization you must mark properties in the *<profile>* section with the special Boolean attribute *allowAnonymous*. The following code demonstrates how to set up the web.config file to allow for anonymous personalization:

```
<anonymousIdentification enabled="true" />
<profile enabled="true">
   <properties>
      <add name="BackColor"
           type="System.Drawing.Color"
          allowAnonymous="true" />
      <add name="Links"
           type="System.Collections.Specialized.StringCollection"
          allowAnonymous="true"
           serializeAs="Xml" />
   </properties>
</profile>
```

Personalization data has no predefined duration and is permanently stored. It is up to the Web site administrator to delete the information when convenient.

Accessing Personalization Properties

If you want to access personalization data on a page, you can do so through the *Profile* property on the *HttpContext* object. Before the request begins its processing cycle, the *Profile* property is set with an instance of a dynamically created class that was created after the user profile defined in the web.config file.

When the page first loads, the profile properties are set with their default values (if any) or are empty objects. They are never null. When custom or collection types are used to define properties, assigning default values might be hard. In our example, we defined a string collection object—the property *Links*—but giving that a default value expressed as a string is virtually impossible. At run time, though, the *Links* property won't be null—it will equal an empty collection. So how can you manage default values for these properties?

Properties that don't have a default value can be initialized in the *Page_Load* event when the page is not posting back. Here's how you can do that:

```
if (!IsPostBack)
{
   // Store a default value for the Links property
   if (Profile.Links.Count == 0) {
       Profile.Links.Add("http://www.contoso.com");
       Profile.Links.Add("http://www.northwind.com");
   }
}
```

At the end of the request, the contents of the profile object are flushed into the personalization storage medium and are easily retrieved the next time the page is invoked. The following code demonstrates a Web page that loads and saves personalized settings for the anonymous user:

```
<%@Page language="C#" %>
<%@Import namespace="System.Drawing" %>

<script runat="server">
    void Page_Load(object sender, EventArgs e) {
        if (!IsPostBack) {
            // Store a default value for the Links property
            if (Profile.Links.Count == 0) {
                Profile.Links.Add("http://www.contoso.com");
                Profile.Links.Add("http://www.northwind.com");
            }
        }
        ApplyPersonalization();
    }

    void ApplyPersonalization() {
        // Use the BackColor property to paint the body of the page
        theBody.Attributes["bgcolor"] = Profile.BackColor;

        // Use the Links property to create a right-aligned top menu
        Favorites.Controls.Clear();
        foreach (object o in Profile.Links) {
            HyperLink h = new HyperLink();
            h.Text = o.ToString();
            h.NavigateUrl = o.ToString();
            Favorites.Controls.Add(h);
            Favorites.Controls.Add(new LiteralControl("  "));
        }
    }

    void OnSetColor (object sender, EventArgs e) {
        // Change the BackColor property and apply changes to the page
        // The new value is provided by a textbox in the page
```

```
        Profile.BackColor = NewColor.Text;
        ApplyPersonalization();
    }

    void OnAddLink (object sender, EventArgs e) {
        // Add a link to the Links collection and apply changes
        Profile.Links.Add(NewLink.Text);
        ApplyPersonalization();
    }
</script>

<html>
<head runat="server">
    <title>Personalization</title>
</head>
<body runat="server" id="theBody" style="margin:0px">
    <form runat="server">
        <asp:PlaceHolder Runat="server" ID="Favorites" />
        <hr />
        <table><tr>
           <td><asp:textbox runat="server" id="NewColor" /></td>
           <td><asp:button runat="server" text="Save Back Color"
                    onclick="OnSetColor" /></td>
        </tr><tr>
           <td><asp:textbox runat="server" id="NewLink" /></td>
           <td><asp:button runat="server" text="Save Link"
                    onclick="OnAddLink" /></td>
        </tr></table>
     </form>
</body>
</html>
```

The page contains a couple of text boxes you can use to enter the color as a string (yellow, for example) and the URL of a new favorite link, as shown in Figure 4-3. By clicking the buttons next to either text box, you can modify the profile and apply the changes to the current instance of the page.

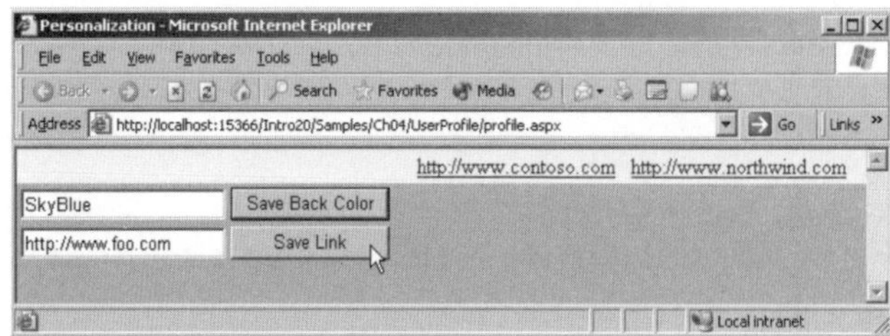

Figure 4-3 If you enter a new URL and click to save it, the menu of the page is permanently modified.

Pages that make intensive use of personalization should also provide a user interface (or a separate editor, much as Web Parts do) to let users modify settings and personalize the visual appearance of the page.

> **Note** The personalization data of a page is all set when the *Page_Init* event fires. ASP.NET 2.0 also defines a *Page_PreInit* event. When this event arrives, no operation has been accomplished yet on the page, not even the loading of personalization data.

Personalization Events

The personalization data is added to the HTTP context of a request before the request begins its processing route. Once bound to the HTTP context object, the personalization data is available through the *Profile* property. But which system component is in charge of loading personalization data? ASP.NET 2.0 employs a new HTTP module for this purpose named *ProfileModule*.

The module attaches itself to a couple of HTTP events and gets involved after a request has been authorized and when the request is about to end. If the personalization feature is off, the module returns immediately. Otherwise, it fires the *Personalize* event to the application and loads personalization data from the current user profile. When the *Personalize* event fires, the personalization data hasn't been loaded yet.

Next the module deals with anonymous users. As mentioned, anonymous users can store and retrieve settings that are persisted using an anonymous unique ID. However, if at a certain point a hitherto anonymous user decides to create an account with the Web site, you might need to migrate to its account all the settings that she made as an anonymous user. This migration doesn't occur automatically. The personalization module fires an event—*MigrateAnonymous*—that, properly handled, allows you to import anonymous settings into the profile of a logged on user. The following pseudocode demonstrates how to handle the migration of an anonymous profile:

```
void Personalization_MigrateAnonymous(object sender,
    AnonymousIdentificationEventArgs e)
{
   // Get the profile of the anonymous user
   HttpProfile anonProfile;
   anonProfile = Profile.GetProfile(e.AnonymousId);

   // Migrate the properties to the new profile
   Profile.BackColor = anonProfile.BackColor;
   ⋮
}
```

You get the profile for the anonymous user and extract the value of any property you want to import. Next you copy the value to the profile of the currently logged on user.

Using Themes

Managing profiles is just one aspect of customizing a Web site. Another important aspect is the visual appearance of individual controls. A golden rule of Web usability is that the look and feel of the pages must be consistent. The use of cascading style sheets (CSS) styles and CSS classes helps a lot in achieving this. You can get the same kind of flexibility that CSS classes provide for visual styles when you work with the properties of ASP.NET controls—by using ASP.NET themes.

ASP.NET themes are closely related to Windows XP themes. Setting a theme is as simple as setting a property, and all the settings the theme contains are applied in a single shot. Themes can be applied to individual controls and also to a page or an entire Web site.

What Are Themes?

ASP.NET offers some predefined themes that you can apply to any ASP.NET Web application. For example, ASP.NET includes a theme called SmokeAndGlass that defines a common style for most server controls. Figure 4-4 shows the new look and feel of our sample page after we apply the SmokeAndGlass theme.

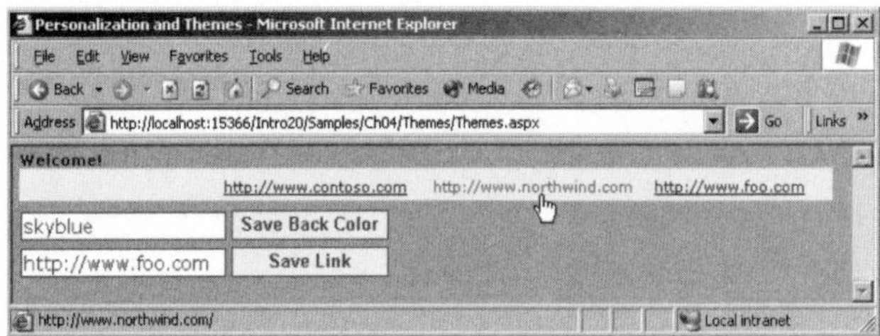

Figure 4-4 The sample page modified using the standard SmokeAndGlass theme

In particular, the theme sets fonts and borders for buttons and text boxes and makes hyperlinks sensitive to the mouse movements. The beauty of ASP.NET themes is that you define how your controls should look and the settings are automatically applied to all the controls you ever create in your page or Web site.

Structure of a Theme

A theme is composed of a collection of CSS files, images, and skin files. Built-in themes are saved in a special location under the installation path of the .NET Framework 2.0:

```
%SystemRoot%\Microsoft.NET\Framework\vX.X.XXXX\ASP.NETClientFiles\Themes\
```

The actual name of the subdirectory labeled *vX.X.XXXX* changes according to the build of ASP.NET 2.0 you're considering. Themes defined in this path are visible to all applications running on the machine. Application-specific themes can be defined, too, but they are stored elsewhere. (More on this in a moment.) Under the folder named Themes, you find child paths, each identifying a distinct theme. The theme's main directory contains .css and .skin files and optionally an Images subdirectory if your theme needs to include images, too. The name of the directory is the name of the theme.

Typically, the CSS file of a theme defines the style of the page body, anchors, headings, input fields. A skin file can be seen as a sort of server-side, ASP.NET-specific style sheet. Basically, by using a skin file you define the style of an ASP.NET control. You don't use CSS style attributes—you assign default values to the visual properties of server controls. For example, you can give default values to fonts, borders, and colors; configure style properties of rich controls such as the *DataGrid*, the *Calendar*, or the *GridView*; and define once and for all the appearance of Web parts.

Once you define a skin, you don't need to set or reference the properties—you just take the default values. The skin just overrides the original default values for skinned properties.

Images are an optional element of a theme. However, since some controls (such as *TreeView*, *DataGrid*, and *Wizard*) might use images to enhance their user interface, skins support images, too. Any images stored in the Images subdirectory of a theme can be used to preconfigure any of the properties of the skinned controls.

Creating Themes

You can create your own themes to apply to your site or individual pages. A page theme is defined in a special Themes folder under the root of a Web application. In the page theme, you define control skins—settings for individual controls such as *Button*, *TextBox*, and *DataGrid* controls. You typically define a control skin for each type of control that you want to use in your application, setting the control's properties so that all the controls have a similar look. The page theme can also include style sheets and graphics.

Note that a theme should configure only visual properties of a control—not properties that influence the runtime behavior of the control.

Working with Themes

A theme includes skins defined for a variety of server controls. When you work with themes, you actually work with control skins. This is also the case when you create custom themes. Skins are a layer of user interface properties placed on top of specified controls. Skins are normally set at design time, but in some cases they can also be modified programmatically.

The SmokeAndGlass Built-In Theme

A skin file is a text file that contains a series of markup declarations, much like the layout part of an .aspx page. The built-in SmokeAndGlass theme contains the following definitions for *Textbox* and *Button* controls:

```
<asp:TextBox runat="server"
     BackColor="#FFFFFF" BorderStyle="Solid"
     Font-Size="0.9em" Font-Names="Verdana"
     ForeColor="#585880" BorderColor="#585880"
     BorderWidth="1pt" CssClass="theme_textbox" />
<asp:Button runat="server"
     BorderColor="#585880" Font-Bold="true"
     BorderWidth="1pt" ForeColor="#585880"
     BackColor="#F8F7F4" />
```

Those settings are the new default values for the controls. Note that if you redefine, say, the *BackColor* property in the markup of the .aspx file, that setting is ignored. The reason is that the theme settings are applied to controls immediately after instantiation. This means, for example, that each *TextBox* control is created with the background color you set in the .aspx markup, but one second later it receives the background color set in the skin.

> **Note** You cannot declaratively override the value of property set in a skin file. If you want to override the skin value of control property, you have to place some code in the *Page_Init* or *Page_Load* event:

```
void Page_Init (object sender, EventArgs e) {
   // Override the default settings of the skin
   NewColor.BackColor = Color.Cyan;
}
```

Theming Your Pages and Controls

Associating a theme with a page is easy. You assign the name of your theme of choice to the *Theme* attribute on the *@Page* directive, and you're all set:

```
<%@Page Language="C#" Theme="SmokeAndGlass" %>
```

Bear in mind that the name of the theme must match the name of a subdirectory under the Themes path, as mentioned earlier. You can automatically give the same theme to all the pages in the site. To do so, you modify the web.config file in the root of the application so that it includes the following block:

```
<configuration>
   <system.web>
      <pages theme="SmokeAndGlass" />
   </system.web>
</configuration>
```

Finally, to ensure that a certain control is rendered according to the look and feel of a particular theme, you set the control's *SkinID* property:

```
<asp:Calendar runat="server" ID="MyCalendar" SkinID="SmokeAndGlass" />
```

The *SkinID* property refers to a particular skin within the page's theme. Using this trick, you can have different controls of the same type using different skins. If the page theme doesn't include a skin that matches the *SkinID* property, the default skin for that control type is used. The following code shows how to create two named skins for a button within the same theme:

```
<!-- Place these two definitions in the same .skin file -->
<asp:button id="skinClassic" BackColor="gray" />
<asp:button id="skinTrendy" BackColor="lightcyan" />
```

A named skin is simply a skin that has an ID. Skins without an ID are said to be the default skins for a control.

By default, any property on any control on a page can be overridden by a skin. You can thus use themes to easily customize a page that has no knowledge of skins, including existing pages written for ASP.NET 1.x. However, the ASP.NET 2.0 theming infrastructure provides the *EnableTheming* property to disable skins for a control and all its children. Note that the *EnableTheming* property can be overridden in a derived class so that theming can be disabled by default. Also, you can block any overriding of the theming capabilities of a control by applying the *EnableTheming* attribute to the control declaration. (This holds true for custom controls only.)

```
[EnableTheming(false)]
public MyControl : Control {...}
```

With the above setting, *MyControl* and any derived controls don't support theming. In ASP.NET 2.0, the *HtmlForm* and the *HtmlHead* controls can't be themed. You can also enable and disable theming on individual properties, by applying the *EnableTheming* attribute to the control's property of choice. By default, all properties can be themed.

> **Note** Themes are similar to CSS style sheets in that both apply a set of common attributes to any page where they are declared. Themes differ from style sheets in several ways, however. Themes can work on a variety of control properties—not just a specific set of style properties. Using themes, you can specify the bitmaps for a *TreeView* control or the template layout of a *GridView* control, thus including auxiliary files. Themes property values always override local property values and do not cascade, as is the case with CSS style sheets. Finally, themes can include style sheet references. The style sheet definitions are applied along with other property values defined in the theme.

Loading Themes Dynamically

You can apply themes dynamically, but this requires a bit of care. The ASP.NET runtime loads theme information immediately after the *PreInit* event fires and immediately after the personalization data has been processed. When the *PreInit* event fires, the name of any theme referenced in the *@Page* directive has already been cached and will be used unless it is overridden during the event. So if you want to enable your users to change theme on the fly, start by creating a *Page_PreInit* event handler:

```
void Page_PreInit (object sender, EventArgs e)
{
      string theme = "";
      if (Page.Request.Form.Count >0)
          theme = Page.Request["ThemeList"].ToString ();
      if (theme == "None")
          theme = "";

      this.Theme = theme;
}
```

The code assumes that the page has a drop-down list named *ThemeList* that contains the names of the available themes. "None" is the name used to indicate that no theme is to be used. What the code does is pretty simple but has a wrinkle. Basically, the event handler retrieves the name of the theme to use and binds it to the *Theme* property of the page object.

Why did we resort to *Page.Request* instead of accessing the drop-down list control directly with a piece of code like the following?

```
string theme = ThemeList.SelectedValue;
```

When the *PreInit* event fires, the drop-down control is initialized, but its view state hasn't been restored yet, nor have posted values been processed. So at this point the *ThemeList* control is not updated with the latest selection. On the other hand, since the page successfully posted back, the posted values are safe and sound in the *Forms* collection of the *Request* object, awaiting processing. Figure 4-5 shows the sample page enhanced to support the dynamic selection of the theme.

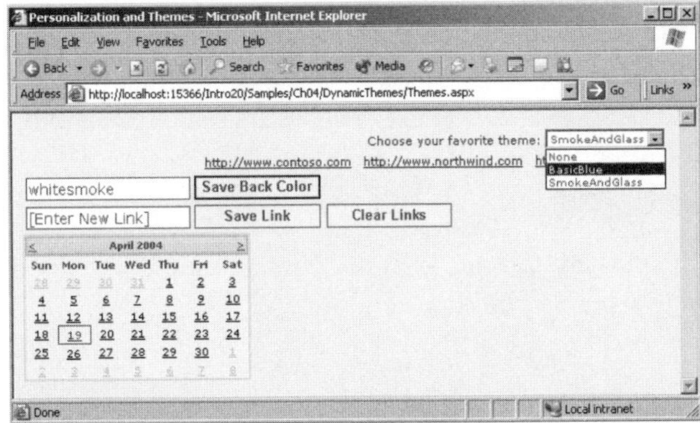

Figure 4-5 The page allows you to select the theme for the user interface.

Summary

In this chapter, we covered two related but significantly different sets of features—site personalization and themes. Both can be, and often are, used to enhance and customize the user interface of a set of pages. However, themes are mostly about visual appearance, whereas personalization encompasses much more than just changes to the appearance of a site.

Personalization is user-specific, but it can also be used for anonymous users. The key to this apparently contradictory behavior is the anonymous ID—another feature specific to ASP.NET 2.0. We'll look at the security aspects in Chapter 10.

Site personalization allows you to write pages that persist user preferences and parametric data off a permanent medium in a totally automated way. As a programmer, you're in charge of setting up the personalization infrastructure, but you need not know anything about the internal details of storage. All you do is call a provider component using the methods of a well-known interface.

Conceptually, ASP.NET 2.0 themes are nearly identical to Windows XP and Windows 2003 Server themes. They provide a skin for a variety of controls. No functionality is altered, and no features are added—only the appearance of the controls changes. For this purpose, you can use any valid element of an ASP.NET theme, including CSS definitions, auxiliary CSS files, templates, and images.

Themes can be registered as global elements of a Web server machine or as application-specific elements. In both cases, the whole application or individual pages can be bound to a theme—you can even control it on a control-by-control level. You could say that themes are the next big thing in styling after CSS files. However, a subtle difference exists between CSS and themes—themes don't cascade their settings, as CSS styles do. Themes can be authored and flexibly applied to a variety of applications. In addition, themes can be manipulated programmatically, making the name of the current theme just another parameter to permanently store as personalization data.

This chapter ends Part I of the book. Part II is devoted to adding data to the application's core engine. We'll start in Chapter 5 with what's new in the ASP.NET data binding model and ADO.NET.

Part II

Data Access

5

What's New in Data Access

To write effective ASP.NET 1.x data-driven applications, you need a deep understanding of ADO.NET objects. You have to be familiar with connections, commands, transactions, and parameters. In Visual Studio 2005, ADO.NET 2.0 is the back-end engine for other, more programmer-friendly objects. Does this mean that ADO.NET objects have become unnecessary? Will ASP.NET 2.0 magically let you write data applications without your having to really know about databases?

ADO.NET objects are still essential pieces of the .NET Framework, but they have been pushed into the back-end infrastructure of most common data-binding operations. In ASP.NET 2.0, you use ADO.NET objects directly much less frequently. And ASP.NET 2.0 does perform a kind of magic—it offers data access code that hides many essential steps from view and buries them in the framework's code. Basically, what many ASP.NET 1.x developers called "that boring ADO.NET boilerplate code" is now packed into a bunch of data source controls (which we'll cover in detail in the next chapter).

All you need to cook up some good data access code is the connection string and the commands to execute. In relatively simple cases, you need very little database know-how to build a data access layer in a Web Forms page.

As mentioned, Chapter 6 is devoted to the new data source model underlying this simplified data binding model. This chapter sets the stage by covering the enhanced data-binding syntax, storage of database connection strings, and enhancements to the ADO.NET object model.

Data-Binding Syntax Enhancements

The biggest change by far in ASP.NET data binding is the introduction of a new data source model. The ASP.NET 2.0 data binding mechanism—the process of connecting a Web control to a data source element—is nearly identical in functionality to the previous version, but the syntax is simpler.

ASP.NET 1.x uses the static method *DataBinder.Eval* for late binding data-store fields to object properties. The method is designed to access information on arbitrary objects, but it is often used in just one scenario. The result is that most pages are filled with similar looking <%# ... %> expressions that are both verbose and redundant. ASP.NET 2.0 comes to the rescue by suggesting an equivalent, but much more compact, syntax for the *DataBinder* class.

The *DataBinder* Class

The *DataBinder* class supports generating and parsing data-binding expressions. Of particular importance is its overloaded static method *Eval*. The method uses reflection to parse and evaluate an expression against a runtime object. Clients of the *Eval* method include RAD tools such as Microsoft Visual Studio designers and Web controls that declaratively place calls to the method to feed properties' dynamically changing values.

The *Eval* Method

The syntax of *DataBinder.Eval* typically looks like this:

```
<%# DataBinder.Eval(Container.DataItem, expression) %>
```

A third, optional parameter is omitted in the preceding snippet. This parameter is a string that contains formatting options for the bound value. The *Container.DataItem* expression references the object on which the expression is evaluated. The expression is typically a string with the name of the field to access on the data item object. It can be an expression that includes indexes and property names. The *DataItem* property represents the object within the current container context. Typically, a container is the current instance of the item object—for example, a *DataGridItem* object—that is about to be rendered.

The code shown earlier is commonly repeated, always in the same form. Only the expression and the format string change from page to page.

A More Compact *Eval*

The original syntax of the *DataBinder.Eval* can be simplified, as the *Eval* method shows here. (The format string argument is optional and is not used in this example.)

```
<script runat="server" language="C#">
void Page_Load (object sender, EventArgs e)
{
   if (!IsPostBack)
   {
      // NOTE:
      // All this code can be replaced with a declarative data
      // control that just takes connection string and command text. The
      // data source is also declaratively bound to controls using an ID.
      // (See Chapter 6)
      SqlDataAdapter adapter;
      adapter = new SqlDataAdapter(
           "SELECT * FROM employees",
           "SERVER=localhost;DATABASE=northwind;UID=sa;");
      DataSet ds = new DataSet();
      adapter.Fill(ds, "Data");
      Repeater1.DataSource = ds;
      Repeater1.DataBind();
   }
}
</script>

<html>
<body>
   <form runat="server">
      <asp:repeater runat="server" id="Repeater1">
         <itemtemplate>
            <p><%# Eval("lastname") %></p>
         </itemtemplate>
      </asp:repeater>
   </form>
</body>
</html>
```

Any piece of code that appears within the <%# … %> delimiters enjoys special treatment from the ASP.NET runtime. Let's briefly look at what happens with this code. When the page is compiled for use, the *Eval* call is inserted in the source code of the page as a standalone call. The following code gives an idea of what happens:

```
object o = Eval("lastname");
string result = Convert.ToString(o);
```

The result of the call is converted to a string and is assigned to a data-bound literal control—an instance of the *DataBoundLiteralControl* class. Then the data-bound literal is inserted in the page's control tree. There's one more point to clarify about the code: What's *Eval*, and where is it defined?

The *Page* class is actually enriched with a new protected (but not virtual) method named *Eval*. The method is defined as follows:

```
protected object Eval(string expression)
{
   return DataBinder.Eval(this.GetDataItem(), expression);
}
```

Eval is a simple wrapper built around the *DataBinder.Eval* method. The base method is invoked using a default container's data item.

Getting the Default Data Item

The pseudocode that illustrates the behavior of the page's *Eval* method shows a rather weird *GetDataItem* method off the *Page* class. What is it? As mentioned, the simplified syntax assumes a default *Container.DataItem* context object. *GetDataItem* is simply the function that returns that object. More precisely, *GetDataItem* is the endpoint of a stack-based mechanism that traces the current binding context for the page. Each control in the control tree is pushed onto this stack at the time the respective *DataBind* method is called. When the *DataBind* method returns, the control is popped from the stack.

Two-Way Data Binding

As you'll see in Chapter 7, ASP.NET 2.0 supports two-way data binding—the ability to bind data to controls and submit changes back to the database. The *Eval* method is representative of a one-way data binding that automates data reading but not data writing. The new *Bind* keyword can be used whenever *Eval* is accepted, and through the same syntax.

```
<asp:TextBox Runat="server" ID="TheNotes"
     Text='<%# Bind("notes") %>' />
```

The big difference is that *Bind* works in both directions—reading and writing. For example, when the *Text* property is set, *Bind* behaves exactly like *Eval*. In addition, when the *Text* property is read, *Bind* stores the value into a collection. Enabled data-bound controls (for example, the new *FormView* control and other templated controls) retrieve these values and use them to compose the parameter list of the insert or edit command to run against the data source. The argument passed to *Bind* must match the name of a parameter in the command. For example, the text box above provides the value for the *@notes* parameter.

The *XPathBinder* Class

Along with the *DataBinder* class, ASP.NET 2.0 provides a class that can bind to the result of XPath expressions that are executed against an object that implements the *IXPathNavigable* interface. This class is *XPathBinder*; it plays the same role as *DataBinder*, except it works on XML data.

The *XPathBinder.Eval* Method

In ASP.NET 2.0, data-bound controls can be associated with raw XML data. You can bind XML data in version 1.x, but you have to first fit XML data into a relational structure such as a *DataSet*. When a templated control such as *DataList* or *Repeater* is bound to an XML data source (such as the new *XmlDataSource* control we'll cover in Chapter 6), individual XML fragments can be bound inside the template using the *XPathBinder* object.

The *XPathBinder.Eval* method accepts an *XmlNode* object along with an XPath expression, and it evaluates and returns the result. The output string can be formatted if a proper format string is specified. *XPathBinder.Eval* casts the container object to *IXPathNavigable*. This is a prerequisite to applying the XPath expression. If the object doesn't implement the interface, an exception is thrown. The *IXPathNavigable* interface is necessary because in the .NET Framework the whole XPath API is built for, and works only with, objects that provide a navigator class. The goal of the interface is creating an XPath navigator object for the query to run.

Like *DataBinder*, the *XPathBinder* class supports a simplified syntax for its *Eval* method. The syntax assumes a default container context that is the same object that is tracked for the data binder. The following example demonstrates using the simplified XPath data binding syntax:

```
<%# XPath("Orders/Order/Customer/LastName") %>
```

The output value is the object returned by *XPathBinder.Eval* converted to a string. Internally, *XPathBinder.Eval* gets a navigator object from the data source and evaluates the expression. The managed XPath API is used.

Enumerating the Node Set

The *XPathBinder* class also features a *Select* method. The method executes an XPath query and retrieves a nodeset—an enumerable collection of XML nodes. This collection can be assigned as a late-bound value to data-bound controls (such as the *Repeater* control). An equivalent simplified syntax exists for this scenario, too:

```
<asp:Repeater runat="server"
    DataSource='<%# XPathSelect("orders/order/summary") %>'>
⋮
</asp:Repeater>
```

XPathSelect is the keyword you use in data-binding expressions to indicate the results of an XPath query run on the container object. If the container object does not implement *IXPathNavigable*, an exception is thrown. Like *Eval* and *XPath*, *XPathSelect* assumes a default data item context object.

.NET Data Provider Enhancements

The .NET data binding model is general enough to accommodate a variety of data and data sources. The most common type of data source is a SQL data source—for example, a SQL-based DBMS such as SQL Server or Oracle. To get SQL data, you use ADO.NET; ADO.NET, in turn, is based on the services of a particular category of objects—the .NET data providers. The common programming model of .NET data providers has been enhanced in Whidbey to support factories and batch operations. The first aspect we'll consider, though, is a core piece of any database operation—the connection string.

Connection String Storage

When we talk about data access objects and strategies, connection strings are perhaps a low-level detail, but they are essential. One of the most frequently asked questions, at least early on in the ASP.NET and Windows Forms adventure, has been "Where should I store my connection strings?" Configuration files (such as the web.config file) support a section named *<appSettings>*, which is used to store name/value pairs. All these values populate the *AppSettings* collection and can be easily retrieved programmatically, as shown here:

```
string connString = ConfigurationSettings.AppSettings["NorthwindConn"];
```

You can use a similar approach to add flexibility to your code because you can keep the connection string out of the compiled code. This way of storing the connection string also makes the information global to the application and easily callable from any modules. You can store any data in the *<appSettings>* section that can be rendered with a flat name/value pair.

However, this approach is far from perfect. Connection strings are a critical parameter for the application and typically contain sensitive data, so at a minimum they need transparent encryption. Although connection parameters can be rendered as semicolon-separated strings, a connection string is more than a plain string and deserves special treatment from the framework.

The *<connectionStrings>* Section

Whidbey configuration files define a new section that was created to contain connection strings (such as SQL connection strings). The section is named *<connectionStrings>*. Its structure is shown here:

```
<connectionStrings>
    <add name="CustomersDB"
         connectionString="SERVER=...;DATABASE=...;UID=...;PWD=...;" />
    <add name="CustAccessDB"
         connectionString="~\DATA\CustDB.mdb" />
</connectionStrings>
```

You can manipulate the contents of the section by using *<add>*, *<remove>*, and *<clear>* nodes. You use an *<add>* node to add a new connection string, *<remove>* to remove a previously defined connection, and *<clear>* to reset all connections and create a new collection. By placing a web.config file in each of the application's directories, you can customize the collection of connection strings that are visible to the pages in the directory.

Note that each stored connection is identified with a name. This name references the actual connection parameters throughout the application. Connection names are also used within the configuration file to link a connection string to other sections, such as the *<providers>* section of *<membership>* and *<personalization>*. The *<connectionStrings>* section is a global and centralized repository of connection information.

Retrieving Connection Strings Programmatically

All the connection strings defined in the web.config file are loaded into the new *ConfigurationSettings.ConnectionStrings* collection. If you are programmatically setting the connection string of an ADO.NET object, this feature makes your code flexible and easy to maintain. For example, consider the following web.config file:

```
<configuration>
  <connectionStrings>
     <add name="NWind"
          connectionString="SERVER=...;DATABASE=northwind;UID=...;PWD=..." />
  </connectionStrings>
</configuration>
```

It registers a connection that points to the Northwind database on a given server, and with certain credentials. To physically open that connection, the following code is acceptable:

```
string cnStr;
cnStr = ConfigurationSettings.ConnectionStrings["NWind"].ConnectionString;
SqlConnection cnObj = new SqlConnection(cnStr);
```

Changes to the connection string parameters do not affect the page or the business object directly.

Declarative Binding of Connection Strings

Can you reference stored connection strings declaratively? At this point in our discussion, this might seem like a nonsense question. How can you manage connections declaratively? As you'll see in the next chapter, ASP.NET 2.0 supports quite a few data source objects. A data source object manages all aspects of data source interaction, including connections and commands. The SQL data source object looks like the following:

```
<asp:SqlDataSource id="MySource" runat="server"
  ProviderName="System.Data.SqlClient"
  ConnectionString='<%#
    ConfigurationSettings.ConnectionStrings["NWind"].ConnectionString %>'
  SelectCommand="SELECT * FROM employees">
```

The object runs the given query against the data source referenced by the connection string. The data provider is specified by the *ProviderName* attribute and is the SQL Server .NET data provider. Later in this chapter, we'll return to this sort of late-bound provider selection, which is a new feature of .NET data providers.

If you use any <%# ... %> data-bound expressions, be aware that they execute only at data-binding time—that is, within the context of a *DataBind* method call. So unless the container to the *SqlDataSource* object has a data-binding operation in progress, the expression isn't evaluated. To work around this, you just place a call to *Page.DataBind* in the *Page_Load* event. However, this short-term trick can cause you trouble if, for some reason, you need to control data binding on individual controls.

Data-bound expressions are not really dynamic expressions because they are evaluated only within the context of a data-binding call. ASP.NET 2.0 provides a made-to-measure infrastructure for dynamic expressions—the expression builder object. Those expressions have a syntax that is similar to that of data binding, *<%$ ... %>*, and they are evaluated when the page compiles. The content of the expression is extracted, transformed into code, and injected into the C# or Visual Basic .NET code created for the page. Let's look at how to rewrite the previous code to declaratively bind connection strings:

```
<asp:sqldatasource id="MySource" runat="server"
     ProviderName="System.Data.SqlClient"
     ConnectionString="<%$ ConnectionStrings:NWind %>"
     SelectCommand="SELECT * FROM employees">
<asp:repeater runat="server" id="Repeater1" DataSourceId="MySource">
     <itemtemplate>
        <p><%# Eval("lastname") %></p>
     </itemtemplate>
</asp:repeater>
```

The expression has two parts, prefix and value, and an underlying object, the expression builder. The expression builder decides on the prefix and how to parse and expand the value. The connection string builder accepts a *ConnectionString* as the prefix and the name of a configuration entry as the value. The expression expands to the following:

```
string conn;
conn = ConfigurationSettings.ConnectionStrings["NWind"].ConnectionString;
MySource.ConnectionString = conn;
```

Protecting Configuration Data

ASP.NET 2.0 introduces a system for protecting sensitive data stored in the configuration system. It uses industry-standard XML encryption to encrypt specific sections of configuration files that might contain sensitive data. XML encryption (see *http://www.w3.org/TR/xmlenc-core*) is a way to encrypt data and represent the result in XML. Prior to version 2.0, only a few specific ASP.NET sections that contain sensitive data support protection of this data using a machine-specific encryption in a registry key. This approach requires developers to come up with a utility to protect their own secrets—typically connection strings, credentials, and encryption keys.

Encryption is optional, and you can enable it for any configuration sections by referencing the name of the section in the *<protectedData>* section of the web.config file, as shown here:

```
<protectedData defaultProvider="RSAProtectedConfigurationProvider">
    <providers>
      <add name="RSAProtectedConfigurationProvider"
           type="..."
           keyName="RSA Key"
           keyContainerName="NetFrameworkConfigurationKey"
           cspProviderName=""
           useMachineContainer="true" />
      <add name="DataProtectionConfigurationProvider"
           type="..."
           keyName="Net Framework DPAPI Key"
           keyEntropy=""
           useMachineProtection="true" />
    </providers>
    <protectedDataSections>
      ⋮
    </protectedDataSections>
  </protectedData>
```

You can specify the type of encryption you want by selecting the appropriate provider from the list of available encryption providers. The list of available protection providers can be found in the *<providers>* section, along with their default configuration.

How can you place encrypted content (say, a connection string) into the web.config file? You can use the newest version of a popular system tool—aspnet_regiis.exe—or write your own tool using the ASP.NET 2.0 configuration API. (We'll take a look at this in Chapter 12.) Here's a simple way to use aspnet_regiis to encrypt connection strings for the Intro20 application:

```
aspnet_regiis.exe -pe connectionStrings -app /Intro20
```

Note that the section names are case sensitive. That connection strings are stored in a protected area is completely transparent to applications, which continue working as before. If you open the web.config file after encryption, you see something like the following:

```
<configuration>
  <protectedData>
    <protectedDataSections>
      <add name="connectionStrings"
           provider="RSAProtectedConfigurationProvider" />
    </protectedDataSections>
  </protectedData>
  <connectionStrings>
    <EncryptedData …>
      ⋮
      <CipherData>
        <CipherValue>cQyofWFQ… =</CipherValue>
      </CipherData>
    </EncryptedData>
  </connectionStrings>
</configuration>
```

To restore the web.config to its original clear state, you use the *–pd* switch in lieu of *–pe* in the aforementioned command line.

Most configuration sections that are processed by the managed configuration system are eligible for protection. However, the *<protectedData>* section itself can't be protected. In this case, clear text is necessary to describe the behavior of the system. Similarly, sections consumed by the CLR from Win32 code or from ad hoc managed XML parsers can't be protected by this system because they don't employ section handlers to consume their configuration. This includes at least the following sections: *<processModel>*, *<runtime>*, *<mscorlib>*, *<startup>*, and *<system.runtime.remoting>*.

The Provider Factory Model

The ADO.NET programming model makes obsolete the universal data access strategy at the root of OLE DB. A universal data access strategy requires programming tools that always perform the same operations, no matter what features are supported by the physical data provider. Consider an SQL data source such as a DBMS. SQL Server, Oracle, and DB2 do the same job, but they work in radically different ways. Normalizing their internal and optimized set of features to the abstract functionality exposed by a suite of universal interfaces results in a loss of performance. It also imposes programming overhead because an extra, more abstract layer of code must be used. ADO provides this common programming interface for a variety of DBMSs.

ADO.NET comes at things from a different angle. It takes into account the particularity of each DBMS and provides a programming model tailor-made for each one. All .NET data providers share a limited set of common features, but each has unique capabilities. The communication between the user code and the DBMS takes place more directly using ADO.NET. This model works better and faster and is probably clearer to the majority of programmers.

But ADO.NET has one snag. Developers must know in advance the data source they're going to access. Generic programming—that is, programming in which the same code targets different data sources at different times—is hard (but not impossible) to do. You can create a generic command object and a generic data reader, but not a generic data adapter and certainly not a generic connection. However, through the *IDbConnection* interface, you can work with a connection object without knowing the underlying data source. But you can never create a connection object in a weakly typed manner—that is, without the help of the *new* operator.

Instantiating Providers Programmatically

ADO.NET 2.0 modifies the provider architecture and introduces the factory class. Each .NET data provider encompasses a factory class derived from the base class *DbProviderFactory*. A factory class represents a common entry point for a variety of services specific to the provider. Table 5-1 lists the main methods of a factory class.

Table 5-1 Principal Methods of a Factory Class

Method	Description
CreateCommand	Returns a provider-specific command object
CreateCommandBuilder	Returns a provider-specific command builder object
CreateConnection	Returns a provider-specific connection object
CreateDataAdapter	Returns a provider a provider-specific data adapter object
CreateParameter	Returns a provider a provider-specific parameter object

How do you get the factory of a particular provider? By using a new class, *DbProviderFactories*, that has a few static methods. The following code demonstrates how to obtain a factory object for the SQL Server provider:

```
DbProviderFactory fact;
fact = DbProviderFactories.GetFactory("System.Data.SqlClient");
```

The *GetFactory* method takes a string that represents the invariant name of the provider. This name is hardcoded for each provider in the configuration file where it is registered. The naming convention suggested is that the provider name equal its unique namespace.

GetFactory enumerates all the registered providers and gets assembly and class name information for the matching invariant name. The factory class is not instantiated directly. Instead, the method uses reflection to retrieve the value of the static *Instance* property on the factory class. The property returns the instance of the factory class to use. Once you hold a factory object, you can call any of the methods listed earlier in Table 5-1.

The following pseudocode gives an idea of the internal implementation of the *CreateConnection* method for the *SqlClientFactory* class—the factory class for the SQL Server .NET data provider:

```
public DbConnection CreateConnection()
{
   return new SqlConnection();
}
```

Enumerating Installed Data Providers

In the .NET Framework 2.0, you can use all .NET data providers registered in the configuration file. The following is an excerpt from the machine.config file:

```
<system.data>
  <DbProviderFactories>
    <add name="Odbc Data Provider"
         invariant="System.Data.Odbc"
         description=".Net Framework Data Provider for Odbc"
         type="System.Data.Odbc.OdbcFactory, System.Data "/>
    <add name="OleDb Data Provider"
         invariant="System.Data.OleDb"
         description=".Net Framework Data Provider for OleDb"
         type="System.Data.OleDb.OleDbFactory, System.Data "/>
    <add name="OracleClient Data Provider"
         invariant="System.Data.OracleClient"
         description=".Net Framework Data Provider for Oracle"
         type="System.Data.OracleClient.OracleFactory,
               System.Data.OracleClient" />
    <add name="SqlClient Data Provider"
         invariant="System.Data.SqlClient"
         description=".Net Framework Data Provider for SqlServer"
```

```
        type="System.Data.SqlClient.SqlClientFactory, System.Data "/>
    ⋮
  </DbProviderFactories>
</system.data>
```

As you can see, each provider is characterized by an invariant name, a description, and a type that contains assembly and class information. The *GetFactoryClasses* method on the *DbProviderFactories* class returns this information packed in an easy-to-use *DataTable* object. The following sample page demonstrates how to get a quick list of the installed providers:

```
<%@ page language="C#" theme="smokeandglass" %>
<%@ import namespace="System.Data" %>
<%@ import namespace="System.Data.Common" %>
<%@ import namespace="System.Data.SqlClient" %>

<script runat="server">
    void Page_Load (object sender, EventArgs e) {
        DataTable providers = DbProviderFactories.GetFactoryClasses();
        provList.DataSource = providers;
        provList.DataBind();
    }
</script>

<html>
<head runat="server"><title>Enum Providers</title></head>
<body>
    <form runat="server">
        <asp:datagrid runat="server" id="provList" />
    </form>
</body>
</html>
```

The final page is shown in Figure 5-1. The page is themed, which allows you to display a rich *DataGrid* control by using just one line of code. Note that a server-side *<head>* tag is necessary for the theme to work.

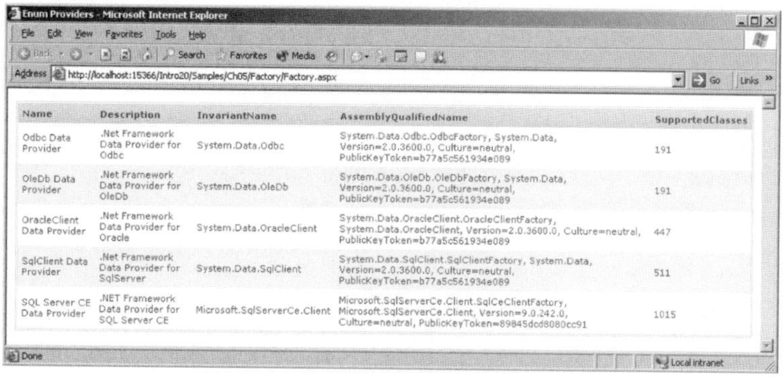

Enum Providers - Microsoft Internet Explorer

Address http://localhost:15366/Intro20/Samples/Ch05/Factory/Factory.aspx

Name	Description	InvariantName	AssemblyQualifiedName	SupportedClasses
Odbc Data Provider	.Net Framework Data Provider for Odbc	System.Data.Odbc	System.Data.Odbc.OdbcFactory, System.Data, Version=2.0.3600.0, Culture=neutral, PublicKeyToken=b77a5c561934e089	191
OleDb Data Provider	.Net Framework Data Provider for OleDb	System.Data.OleDb	System.Data.OleDb.OleDbFactory, System.Data, Version=2.0.3600.0, Culture=neutral, PublicKeyToken=b77a5c561934e089	191
OracleClient Data Provider	.Net Framework Data Provider for Oracle	System.Data.OracleClient	System.Data.OracleClient.OracleClientFactory, System.Data.OracleClient, Version=2.0.3600.0, Culture=neutral, PublicKeyToken=b77a5c561934e089	447
SqlClient Data Provider	.Net Framework Data Provider for SqlServer	System.Data.SqlClient	System.Data.SqlClient.SqlClientFactory, System.Data, Version=2.0.3600.0, Culture=neutral, PublicKeyToken=b77a5c561934e089	511
SQL Server CE Data Provider	.NET Framework Data Provider for SQL Server CE	Microsoft.SqlServerCe.Client	Microsoft.SqlServerCe.Client.SqlCeClientFactory, Microsoft.SqlServerCe.Client, Version=9.0.242.0, Culture=neutral, PublicKeyToken=89845dcd8080cc91	1015

Figure 5-1 The list of the installed .NET data providers

Batch Operations

Using batch processing, you can improve application performance by reducing the number of roundtrips to SQL Server when you apply updates from a *DataSet* object. The batch update feature was introduced with ADO 1.x and enhanced in ADO.NET 2.x. The biggest limitation of the ADO.NET 1.x batch update is that records are always submitted one at a time. For example, if 100 rows have been updated, inserted, or deleted, 100 roundtrips are made to SQL Server to complete the operation.

ADO.NET 2.0 introduces a new property on the data adapter object that lets you control the number of records grouped together and sent to the DBMS in a single shot. The *UpdateBatchSize* property is coded in the *DbDataAdapter* class and, as such, is inherited by all data adapter objects.

The *UpdateBatchSize* Property

The *UpdateBatchSize* property lets you exercise some control over the number of records packed in a single batch statement. The default value of the property is 1, which causes the batch update feature to work as it does in version 1.x. By setting the *UpdateBatchSize* to a value greater than 1, you can force the data adapter to create a statement according to the following pattern:

```
-- size is the value of UpdateBatchSize
exec sp_executesql N'
   BEGIN
      BEGIN statement N        END
      BEGIN statement N+1      END
      ⋮
      BEGIN statement N+size END
   END
', N'list of params'
```

If you give *UpdateBatchSize* a value higher than the number of modified rows, all rows are sent in a single batch. If you set *UpdateBatchSize* to 0, a single roundtrip occurs, regardless of the number of modified rows. However, too large a size can clog the network and result in a loss of performance. You should set a benchmark before you determine what size will work in your production environment.

Profiling Batch Calls

You can use the SQL Server Profiler tool to verify what really happens when changes are submitted in controlled batches. Figure 5-2 shows the profiler in action on a page that uses batch update to submit a couple of changes.

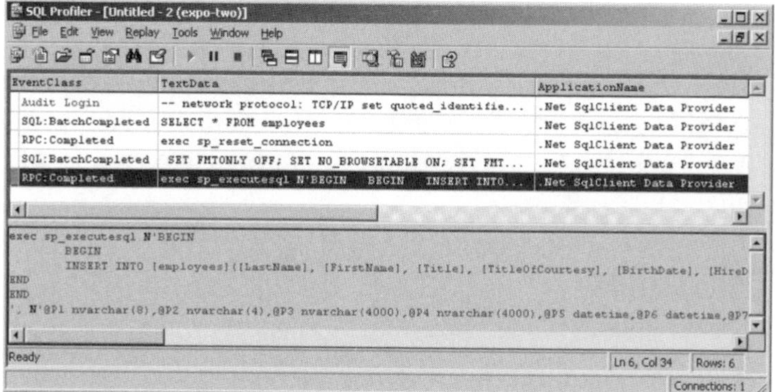

Figure 5-2 The result of a batch update operation with *UpdateBatchSize* set to 0

Batch Update–Related Events and Errors

Data adapter classes have two update-related events: *RowUpdating* and *RowUpdated*. In previous versions of ADO.NET, and in version 2.0 when batch processing is turned off, each of these events is generated once for each row processed. *RowUpdating* is generated before the update occurs; *RowUpdated* is generated after the database update is completed. When batch processing is enabled, the behavior of these events changes.

When batch processing is enabled, several rows are processed before an update is actually performed. Therefore, several *RowUpdating* events are generated before a *RowUpdated* event occurs. Only one *RowUpdated* event is generated for each batch processed. This does not apply to *RowUpdating*, which is still generated once for each row processed.

In ADO.NET 1.x, the row being updated can be accessed using the *Row* property of the corresponding event argument class—*RowUpdatedEventArgs*. However, when a single event is fired for multiple updated rows, the *Row* property is null, and equivalent information is available using the new *CopyToRows* method. The method fills an array of *DataRow* objects. You can determine the right size of the array by looking at the new *RowCount* property on the *RowUpdatedEventArgs* class, which returns the number of rows processed in the batch.

SQL Server Provider Enhancements

Features such as factories and batch operations are not specific to a particular provider—they are changes that apply to the .NET provider model as a whole. Only the SQL Server provider currently implements them, but you can expect to see them fully supported by OLE DB and other .NET providers. Other cool features are available in ADO.NET 2.0 that exploit specific features of SQL Server and, in some cases, the next version of SQL Server (named SQL Server 2005).

New features include asynchronous commands, bulk copy, and (for SQL Server 2005 servers only) notifications, multiple active resultsets, and support for user-defined CLR types.

Asynchronous Commands

A database operation is normally a synchronous operation—the caller regains control of the application only after the interaction with the database is completed. This approach can lead to performance and scalability issues in lengthy operations—a pretty common scenario when you interact with DBMSs. The .NET Framework 1.x supports asynchronous operations, but the model is implemented around user-level code. In other words, you can implement your own procedures asynchronously and connect to databases and run commands as part of the code, but connection management and command execution remain atomic operations that execute synchronously.

ADO.NET 2.0 provides true asynchronous support for executing commands. This offers a clear performance advantage because you perform other actions until the command completes. However, this is not the only benefit. The user interface of the client application isn't blocked while the command runs.

The .NET Asynchronous Pattern

The .NET providers' asynchronous pattern is consistent with the .NET Framework pattern for asynchronous operations. Let's briefly review the basics. The .NET Framework allows you to call any method of any class asynchronously. You first define a delegate with the same signature as the method to call, and the CLR defines a pair of methods—*BeginInvoke* and *EndInvoke*—for this delegate. For example, suppose you have a class method named *ReverseString*, which takes a string and returns a string with characters reordered from right to left. The delegate for this method looks like the following:

```
public delegate string ReverseStringDelegate(string data);
```

You initiate the asynchronous call by creating a new instance of the delegate and calling *BeginInvoke*:

```
MyStringHelper str = new MyStringHelper();
ReverseStringDelegate dlgt;
dlgt = new ReverseStringDelegate(str.ReverseString);
IAsyncResult ar = dlgt.BeginInvoke("Text", null, null);
```

BeginInvoke takes the same parameters as the original method, plus two. The extra two parameters are the delegate to call back when the asynchronous operation is complete and state information is passed to the delegate. *BeginInvoke* returns an *IAsyncResult* needed to obtain the return values from the method call later.

BeginInvoke starts the asynchronous operation and returns. At some point in the code, however, you must synchronize your primary thread and the secondary thread on which the asynchronous request is working. You can do this in a few ways. For example, you can block the primary thread waiting for the other to terminate:

```
// Returns only when the asynchronous call completes
ar.AsyncWaitHandle.WaitOne();
```

Using a *WaitHandle* object is a common thread synchronization technique. It lets you perform additional processing after the asynchronous call completes but before you retrieve the results by calling *EndInvoke*. The signature of *EndInvoke* includes all output parameters plus an object of type *IAsyncResult* as the last parameter. It returns the original return type from the original method signature and throws all exceptions that have happened in the meantime on the delegate:

```
string ret = dlgt.EndInvoke(ar);
```

You can detect the end of the operation by polling or using callback functions.

Executing a Command Asynchronously

The support for asynchronous operations is built into the *SqlCommand* class and is limited to executing nonquery commands and getting a reader or an XML reader. Let's see how it works with the *ExecuteReader* method of *SqlCommand*.

You can use three approaches to build commands that work asynchronously: nonblocking, polling, and callback. Nonblocking is the simplest. Users start the operation and then do something unrelated; then they come back to get the results. Alternatively, the client can check the status of a running asynchronous operation and poll for completion. Finally, they can start the database operation and continue with the application without waiting. Later, when the operation is done, they can receive a callback.

Whatever the model, the first step is calling a *BeginExecuteXXX* function. For example, if you want to execute a reading command, you call *BeginExecuteReader*.

```
// Start a nonblocking execution
IAsyncResult iar = cmd.BeginExecuteReader();

// Do something else in the meantime
⋮

// Block the execution until done
SqlDataReader reader = cmd.EndExecuteReader(iar);

// Process data here ...
Repeater1.DataSource = reader;
Repeater1.DataBind();
```

The *BeginExecuteReader* function returns an *IAsyncResult* object that you use later to complete the call. Note that *EndExecuteReader* is called to finish up the operation; it blocks execution until the ongoing command terminates. Note that to enable asynchronous operations, you must set the new *Async* attribute to *true* in the connection string.

The *EndExecuteReader* function syncs up the command with the rest of the application, blocking the code whenever the results of the command are not ready. You can avoid this blocking schema by periodically polling for completion. The following code illustrates the polling option with a nonquery statement.

```
// Executes a nonquery statement
IAsyncResult ar = cmd.BeginExecuteNonQuery();

// Do some work in the meantime
do {
   ⋮

   // Poll from time to time
   while(!ar.IsCompleted) {
      done = true;
 } while (!done)

  // Sync up
  cmd.EndExecuteNonQuery(ar);
}
```

Note that if *ar.IsCompleted* returns *true*, the *EndExecuteNonQuery* will not block the application.

You can also pass a callback function to a *BeginExecuteXXX* method and any information that constitutes the state of the particular call. The state is any information you want to pass to the callback function. In this case, we just pass a reference to the command object:

```
// Begin executing the command
IAsyncResult ar = cmd.BeginExecuteReader(
   new AsyncCallback(PopulateRepeaterCallback), cmd);
```

After initiating the asynchronous operation, you can forget about it and do any other work. If there's a place in your code that you can't move away from without the results of the query, place a synchronizer there so your code will automatically stop until the other thread terminates and invokes the callback:

```
// Optionally wait to sync
ar.AsyncWaitHandle.WaitOne();
```

The specified callback function is invoked at the end of the operation. The callback must have the following layout:

```
public void PopulateRepeaterCallback(IAsyncResult ar)
{
   // Retrieve the context of the call
   SqlCommand cmd = (SqlCommand) ar.AsyncState;

   // Finalize the async operation
   SqlDataReader reader = cmd.EndExecuteReader(ar);
   ⋮
}
```

The context of the call you specified as the second argument to *BeginExecuteReader* is packed in the *AsyncState* property of the *IAsyncResult* object.

> **Important** The primary thread doesn't execute the callback code. The callback code runs under the control of the secondary thread spawned to accomplish the asynchronous operation. This poses a problem with the user interface of applications, especially Windows Forms applications. It's up to you to ensure that the UI is refreshed in the right thread.

Bulk Copy Operations

Bulk copy functionality provides a much faster way to transfer large amounts of data into a SQL Server table. You typically get much better performance using a specialized operation such as a bulk copy than using an *INSERT* statement. In SQL Server 7.0 and later, the *BULK INSERT* statement copies into a SQL Server table formatted data stored in an ASCII file. You can use this statement from within any .NET Framework 1.1 application that uses an appropriate *SqlCommand* object.

Note that this technique is completely unrelated to the bulk copy functionality provided by the SQL Server .NET data provider in ADO.NET 2.0. In other words, the *SqlBulkCopy* class of ADO.NET 2.0 is not exactly a bare wrapper around the T-SQL *BULK INSERT* statement. As you'll see in a moment, it is even more efficient than a plain call to the *BULK INSERT* statement.

The *SqlBulkCopy* Class

The *SqlBulkCopy* class represents a bulk copy operation to execute against a SQL Server database. Unlike the equivalent T-SQL statement, though, no formatted disk file is managed, either implicitly by the framework or explicitly by the programmer. Interestingly enough, you copy data to SQL Server from an ADO.NET data reader or a *DataTable* object.

The programming interface of the *SqlBulkCopy* class consists of the properties listed in Table 5-2.

Table 5-2 Properties of the *SqlBulkCopy* Class

Property	Description
BatchSize	Specifies the number of rows in each batch of a bulk copy operation. The default is 0, which means that the copy occurs in a single step.
BulkCopyTimeout	Specifies the amount of time, in seconds, before a bulk copy operation times out. The default is 30 seconds.
ColumnMappings	A collection object that defines the mapping between the data source and the destination table.
DestinationTableName	Specifies the name of the destination SQL Server table.
NotifyAfter	Specifies the number of rows to process before the *SqlRowsCopied* notification event is generated. The default is 0, which means that just one event is raised.

The *ColumnMappings* collection is empty by default. You must fill this column only if a mapping between source and target columns is required. In addition, the class features a couple of methods—*Close* and *WriteToServer*. The former releases any held resources, and the latter copies the specified information to the destination table. The *WriteToServer* method comes with the overloads listed in Table 5-3.

Table 5-3 Overloads of the *WriteToServer* Method

Parameter	Description
IDataReader	Copies all of the rows from the specified data reader
DataRow[]	Copies all of the rows from the specified array of *DataRow* objects
DataTable	Copies all of the rows from the specified *DataTable*
DataTable, DataRowState	Copies all of the rows from the specified *DataTable* that are in the specified state (such as deleted or added)

Copying Data from Table to Table

Let's look at how to use the services of the *SqlBulkCopy* class to copy a sample table from one database to another. Suppose you want to make a Test database in one instance of SQL Server a perfect copy of the default Northwind database. The following code shows how to duplicate the [Order Details] table using a data reader:

```
SqlConnection connSrc = new SqlConnection(connStringSrc);
SqlCommand cmd = new SqlCommand(cmdText, connSrc);
connSrc.Open();
SqlDataReader reader = cmd.ExecuteReader();
```

The first step is opening the source data reader. You connect to the source instance of SQL Server, execute a command, and get a *SqlDataReader* object. Next you instantiate the *SqlBulkCopy* class, set the destination table, and optionally set the *BatchSize* and *NotifyAfter* properties:

```
SqlConnection connTgt= new SqlConnection(connStringTgt);
connTgt.Open();
SqlBulkCopy bulk = new SqlBulkCopy(connTgt);
bulk.DestinationTableName = "[Order Details]";
```

At this point, you're ready to initiate the bulk copy. You simply add a call to one of the *WriteToServer* overloads and release the connections.

```
bulk.WriteToServer(reader);
connTgt.Close();
reader.Close();
connSrc.Close();
bulk.Close();
```

If the source table and the target table have slightly different schema (different column names), you can make adjustments by using the *ColumnMappings* collection of mappings:

```
// Map source columns to target columns
bulk.ColumnMappings.Add("orderid", "order_id");
```

If an error occurs during a bulk copy, the operation is aborted and a *SqlException* is generated. It provides details about the server error that occurred. If the *BatchSize* property was set to a value greater than 1, any blocks of rows already committed remain committed. Changes to uncommitted rows are lost.

Note that the destination table and database must exist. Also, the *SqlBulkCopy* class just appends rows to the table, regardless of any primary key constraints you may have. You should be careful not to duplicate rows inadvertently. If a unique constraint is defined, an exception is thrown; otherwise, duplicates are created.

> **Important** The *SqlBulkCopy* class doesn't use the *BULK INSERT* T-SQL statement internally. Instead, it uses an undocumented, low-level SQL Server feature—a variation of the *INSERT* statement—to open a bulk channel. Records flow into this channel and hit the SQL Server engine as the lines of an ASCII file do when the *BULK INSERT* is used. Basically, both the *SqlBulkCopy* class and the *BULK INSERT* statement use the same underlying engine with different input data—ADO.NET objects and the contents of a disk file, respectively.

Bulk Copy and the *bcp* Utility

The *SqlBulkCopy* class works with SQL Server 7.0 and SQL Server 2000. It is also supported in Yukon. The *bcp* command-line utility in SQL Server is a tool that is frequently used to perform bulk operations. The *SqlBulkCopy* class has no relationship to this utility. As mentioned, the class doesn't support input files, nor does it supply the export functionality of the utility (the *out* keyword) that allows you to create text files from the contents of a SQL Server table.

Tracking a Bulk Copy Operation

The *NotifyAfter* property is designed for user interface clients that track the progress of the bulk operation. If you want your Windows Forms application to display a progress bar that tracks the operation, you can set *NotifyAfter* to a value greater than 1—for example, 1/10 of the estimated number of rows to process. The application receives the *SqlRowsCopied* event, which notifies it that a block of rows has been processed.

You should note a couple of points. First, *BatchSize* and *NotifyAfter* are totally unrelated properties. Second, receipt of a *SqlRowsCopied* event doesn't necessarily imply that rows have been committed.

If you close the bulk operation in the event handler using the *Close* method, an exception is thrown. If you want to abort the ongoing operation, set the *Abort* property of the *SqlRowsCopiedEventArgs* instead. You receive an instance of the class as the argument of the *SqlRowsCopied* event. *Abort* is a Boolean property; set it to *true* to abort the bulk copy.

Each step of the bulk copy (the number of steps depends on the *BatchSize* property) runs in its own transaction that is automatically committed or rolled back as the batch terminates. If you choose to abort a bulk copy, nothing happens to the rows that have been processed in earlier batches—they have already been committed. If you're running the bulk copy as a part of your own transaction, you are totally responsible for the commit or rollback of the entire operation. No automatic rollback or commit occurs on your transaction.

SQL Server 2005–Specific Enhancements

The .NET data provider for SQL Server also has new features that are tied to the enhancements in SQL Server 2005 and its MDAC 9.0 libraries. To test the features briefly described in this section, you must have at least the Beta 1 of SQL Server 2005.

SQL Server 2005 introduces significant enhancements in various areas, including data type support, query dependency and notification, and multiple active resultsets.

A Unified Model for Large Data Types

In SQL Server, large values are stored using data types such as *text*, *ntext*, and *image*. SQL Server 2005 also lets you store large values in *varchar*, *nvarchar*, and *varbinary* columns. In fact, these data types can contain up to 2^31-1 bytes. This allows for a unified programming model for regular and large values.

In ADO.NET 1.x and 2.0, you can use the *GetChars* and *GetBytes* methods on the *SqlDataReader* class to improve application performance (but only if you create the reader using the *SequentialAccess* command behavior). When you work sequentially, the data reader doesn't cache the currently selected record, but it lets you freely move the cursor. This lets you optimize your code when you're using large objects. However, you can't, for example, move back to the second field after you access the fourth field. This limitation doesn't exist in the default scenario because the entire record is cached.

Support for CLR Types

The great news in SQL Server 2005 is that it supports any CLR types. In addition to default types, you can store into and retrieve from SQL Server tables any object that is a valid .NET type. This includes both system types—such as a *Point*—and user-defined classes. This extended set of capabilities is reflected in the ADO.NET 2.0 provider for SQL Server.

CLR types appear as objects to the data reader, and parameters to commands can be instances of CLR types. The following code snippet demonstrates how to retrieve a value from the MyCustomers table that corresponds to an instance of user-defined *MyCustomer* class:

```
string cmdText = "SELECT CustomerData FROM MyCustomers";
SqlConnection conn = new SqlConnection(connStr);
SqlCommand cmd = new SqlCommand(cmdText, conn);
cmd.Connection.Open();
SqlDataReader reader = cmd.ExecuteReader();
while(reader.Read())
{
   MyCustomer cust = (MyCustomer) reader[0];
   // Do some work
}
cmd.Connection.Close();
```

A SQL Server 2005 user-defined type is stored as a binary stream of bytes. The *get* accessor of the data reader gets the bytes and deserializes them to a valid instance of the original class. The reverse process (serialization) takes place when a user-defined object is placed in a SQL Server column.

Support for XML as a Native Type

SQL Server 2005 natively supports the XML data type, which means you can store XML data in columns. At first glance, this feature seems to be nothing new because XML data is plain text and to store XML data in a column you only need the column to accept text. However, native XML support in SQL Server 2005 means something different—you can declare the type of a given column as native XML, not plain text adapted to mean markup text.

In ADO.NET 1.x, the *ExecuteXmlReader* method allows you to process the results of a query as an XML stream. The *ExecuteXmlReader* method of *SqlCommand* builds an *XmlTextReader* object on top of the data coming from SQL Server. Therefore, for the method to work, the entire resultset must be XML. Scenarios in which this method is useful include when the *FOR XML* clause is appended or when you query for a scalar value that happens to be XML text.

In ADO.NET 2.0, when SQL Server 2005 is up and running, you can obtain an *XmlTextReader* object for each table cell (row, column) whose type is XML. The following code snippet provides a useful example:

```
string cmdText = " SELECT * FROM MyCustomers";
SqlCommand cmd = new SqlCommand(cmdText, conn);
SqlDataReader reader = cmd.ExecuteReader();
while(reader.Read())
{
   // Assume that field #3 contains XML data

   // Get a XmlTextReader out of the column data
   SqlXmlReader sqlxml = reader.GetSqlXmlReader(3);
   XmlTextReader reader = sqlxml.Value;

   // Process XML data using the XmlTextReader object
}
```

The *SqlXmlReader* class is a wrapper built around the *XmlTextReader* class. The *Value* property of the *SqlXmlReader* class exposes the XML reader to use to process data.

SQL Notifications and Dependencies

Applications that display volatile data or maintain a cache would benefit from friendly server notification whenever their data changes. SQL Server 2005 offers this feature—it notifies client applications about dynamic changes in the resultset generated by a given query. Suppose your application manages the results of a query such as *SELECT * FROM authors*. If you register for a notification, your application is informed if something happens at the SQL Server level that modifies the resultset generated by that query. This means that if a record originally selected by your query is updated or deleted, or if a new record is added that meets the criteria of the query, you're notified.

But where does ADO.NET 2.0 fit in? The SQL Server provider in ADO.NET 2.0 provides two ways to use this notification feature and two related classes—*SqlNotificationRequest* and *SqlDependency*. *SqlNotificationRequest* is a lower-level class that exposes server-side functionality, allowing you to execute a command with a notification request. The following code snippet executes a command with a notification request:

```
SqlCommand cmd = new SqlCommand("SELECT * FROM Authors", conn);
SqlNotificationRequest req = new SqlNotificationRequest();
req.Id = "MyAppRequest";
req.Service = "MyAppQueue";
cmd.Notification = req;
cmd.ExecuteReader();
```

When a T-SQL statement is executed in SQL Server 2005, it keeps track of the query, and if it detects a change that might cause the resultset to change, it sends a message to the queue that you set in the *Service* property. A queue is a new database object that you create and manage with a new set of T-SQL statements. You can place messages only in the specified queue, but how the queue is polled and how the message is interpreted is strictly application-specific. This is where the *SqlDependency* class gets in the game.

The *SqlDependency* class provides a high-level abstraction of the notification mechanism and allows you to set an application-level dependency on the query so changes in the server can be immediately communicated to the client application. The following code binds a command to a SQL dependency:

```
SqlCommand cmd = new SqlCommand("SELECT * FROM Authors", conn);
SqlDependency dep = new SqlDependency(cmd);
dep.OnChanged += new OnChangedEventHandler(OnDependencyChanged);
cmd.ExecuteReader();
```

The *OnChanged* event on the *SqlDependency* class fires whenever the class detects a change that affects the resultset of the command. Here's a typical handler:

```
void OnDependencyChanged(object sender, SqlNotificationsEventArgs e) {
    // Do some work like
    //    - invalidate the cache
    //    - repeat the query
    //    - echo the notification to the user
}
```

The *SqlDependency* class creates an internal notification object and polls the queue. When a change is detected, it fires the event to the application. Easy and effective.

Multiple Active Resultsets

Version 1.x of the SQL Server managed provider, along with the SQL Server ODBC driver, supports only one active resultset per connection. The (unmanaged) OLE DB provider and the outermost ADO library appear to support multiple active resultsets, but this is an illusion. In OLE DB, the effect is obtained by opening additional and nonpooled connections.

In SQL Server 2005, the Multiple Active Result Set (MARS) feature is natively implemented and allows an application to have more than one *SqlDataReader* open on a connection, each started from a separate command. Having more than one data reader open on a single connection offers a potential performance boost because multiple readers are much less expensive than multiple connections. Note that you must create each instance of the data reader from a distinct *SqlCommand* object, as shown in the following code:

```
SqlCommand cmd1 = new SqlCommand(cmdText1, conn);
SqlCommand cmd2 = new SqlCommand(cmdText2, conn);
SqlDataReader reader1 = cmd1.ExecuteReader();
SqlDataReader reader2 = cmd2.ExecuteReader();
// Do some work using both readers on the same connection
```

In ADO.NET 2.0, the MARS feature is enabled by default when SQL Server 2005 is the database server. To disable MARS, you set the *MultipleActiveResultSets* attribute to *false* in the connection string.

> **Note** MARS-like behavior is available in the .NET Framework 2.0 versions of the OLE DB and Oracle managed providers. The Oracle provider doesn't support the MARS attribute on the connection string, but it enables the feature automatically. The OLE DB provider doesn't support the connection string attribute either—it simulates multiple resultsets when you connect to earlier versions of SQL Server or when the MDAC 9.0 library is not available. When you operate through OLE DB on a version of SQL Server 2005 equipped with MDAC 9.0, multiple resultsets are active and are natively implemented.

ADO.NET Class Enhancements

Let's wrap up the chapter by reviewing changes to some of the classes in the *System.Data* namespace—the ADO.NET classes that are not directly involved with managed providers and data storing and retrieval. This group includes central ADO.NET classes such as *DataSet*, *DataView*, and *DataTable*. Compared to the rich set of new features we've examined for managed providers, the list of changes in the ADO.NET data container classes appears minimal. All of the classes have been refined and enhanced, but no extraordinary new features have been added.

The *DataSet* class is nearly identical to its ADO.NET 1.x counterpart, while the *DataTable* is now a first-class citizen in the ADO.NET world and enjoys some of the features reserved for *DataSet*s only in version 1.x. Key enhancements to *DataTable* objects are the support for readers and full XML serialization obtained both through read/write embedded methods and the XML serializer. However, the biggest change for both classes is the introduction of a more compact serialization format when the two objects are sent over a .NET Remoting channel.

DataTable and *DataSet* Readers

In ADO.NET 2.0, the contents of an in-memory table can be read in two ways: by using the classic relational programming interface made up of row and column collections, and by using a new approach based on readers. Just as readers are used to read database rows, XML nodes, and bytes from a file, they are used to return table rows from ADO.NET container objects such as *DataTable* and *DataSet*. The new class that provides this service is *DataTableReader*.

The *DataTableReader* Class

DataTableReader is a reader class that retrieves the contents of a *DataTable* or a *DataSet* object in the form of one or more read-only, forward-only resultsets. It provides a fast, cursor-like way of scrolling and reading the contents of in-memory objects. You obtain an instance of this reader class using the *GetDataReader* method on a *DataTable* or a *DataSet* object.

On the *DataSet* class, the *GetDataReader* method has the following prototype. It takes an array of *DataTable* objects and builds a reader for all of them. The resulting reader object includes the specified tables as multiple resultsets.

```
public DataTableReader GetDataReader(DataTable[] dataTables);
```

The prototype is only slightly different if the method is called on the *DataTable* class:

```
public DataTableReader GetDataReader();
```

In this case, no parameter is necessary, and the returned reader object will work on the current table object. Note that the reader object here has nothing to do with a DBMS-specific data reader. The *DataTableReader* is merely a class that behaves like an in-memory reader.

The *Read* method of the reader moves initially to the first record on the first table. The *NextResult* method moves the internal pointer to the next resultset, if any. When you create a reader from a *DataTable*, the resulting object contains one resultset with the same data as the table from which it was created, except for any rows that have been marked as deleted. The columns appear in the same order as in the original table. When the reader originates from a *DataSet*, the resultsets are in the same order as the tables in the *DataSet*.

> **Note** Which programming interface should you use to access the contents of a *DataSet* or a *DataTable*? Using the *DataTableReader* is the fastest way to scroll through the rows of a table, but it's a read-only interface and doesn't provide for random movements over rows. The *Rows* and *Columns* collections allow full access.

Filling a Table Using a Data Reader

Both the *DataTable* and *DataSet* boast a new *Load* method, which you can use to populate those objects with the contents of a data reader object. The prototype for the *DataSet* class is shown here. The method has two overloads.

```
public void Load(IDataReader, LoadOption, DataTable[])
public void Load(IDataReader, LoadOption, String[])
```

Both overloads take a data reader object and a flag that indicates how to load rows. In the first case, the third argument is the array of the *DataTable* object where resultsets will be stored. In the second case, the array of strings contains the names of the tables to populate with the contents of the reader. The acceptable values for the *LoadOption* enumeration are shown in Table 5-4.

Table 5-4 The *LoadOption* Enumerated Type

Constant	Description
OverwriteRow	Incoming values are written as the current and original values for each column in the row.
PreserveCurrentValues	Incoming values are written as the original values of the row. Current values are not touched.
UpdateCurrentValues	Incoming values are written as the current values of the row. Original values are not touched.

When the *Load* method is called on a *DataTable*, it fills the current object with incoming values. If the *DataTable* already contains rows, the data from the source is merged with the existing rows. The prototypes are shown here:

```
public void Load(IDataReader)
public void Load(IDataReader, LoadOption)
```

Serializing a *DataTable* to XML

In ADO.NET 1.x, the *DataTable* class supports runtime object serialization through the .NET formatter classes, but not any form of XML serialization. The *DataSet* object, for example, has *ReadXml* and *WriteXml* methods that allow you to save to and restore from an XML stream. Serializing the *DataTable* to XML is not hard—you just create a temporary *DataSet*, copy the *DataTable* to it, and serialize the *DataSet*. The same functionality is now natively exposed from the same *DataTable* class.

The *WriteXml* Method

The *WriteXml* method comes with a long list of overloads. You can write the contents of a *DataTable* to a stream, file, XML writer, or text writer. Using the *WriteXml* method, you can write data only or both data and schema to an XML document. You can control the output format by setting the *XmlWriteMode* parameter:

```
public void WriteXml(String)
public void WriteXml(String, XmlWriteMode)
```

Acceptable values for the *XmlWriteMode* parameter are *WriteSchema*, *IgnoreSchema* (the default), and *DiffGram*. The first two options serialize the *DataTable* with or without schema. The last one uses the *DiffGram* XML format. When the default XML format is used, *WriteXml* generates the following markup:

```
<DocumentElement>
   <TableName>
       <Column1>...</Column1>
       <Column2>...</Column2>
       <Column3>...</Column3>
   </TableName>
   <TableName>
       <Column1>...</Column1>
       <Column2>...</Column2>
       <Column3>...</Column3>
   </TableName>
   ⋮
</DocumentElement>
```

The markup is nearly identical to that of a *DataSet* except for the root node, which defaults to *DocumentElement*. If you want to include a schema, you pass *WriteXml* the appropriate write mode parameter. If you want to output only the schema of the table, you're better off using the *WriteXmlSchema* method.

The *ReadXml* Method

The *ReadXml* method reads XML schema and data into a *DataTable* object by using the specified stream, file, or reader. The method always take one parameter and returns a value excerpted from the *XmlReadMode* enumeration. The return value denotes the mode used to read the data. The modes are listed in Table 5-5.

Table 5-5 Modes for Reading a Relational Schema into a *DataTable*

Mode	Description
DiffGram	Creates the table based on the content of a DiffGram file.
Fragment	Reads XML documents, such as those generated by executing FOR XML queries, against SQL Server.
IgnoreSchema	Ignores any inline schema and reads data into the current table schema.
InferSchema	Ignores any inline schema and infers schema from the data.
InferTypedSchema	Ignores any inline schema and infers the schema and data type from the data. If the type cannot be inferred from the data, it is interpreted as string data.
ReadSchema	Reads any inline schema and loads the data.

If the XML document contains an inline schema, the inline schema is used to extend the existing structure. The operation takes place before the data is loaded. If conflicts occur (if, for example, the same column in the same table is defined with different types), an exception is raised. If no inline schema exists, the current structure is extended according to the structure of the XML document. A new schema is inferred from the XML document and applied to the table. If the schema cannot be inferred or applied, an exception is raised.

The XML Serializer

XML serialization is the process of converting an object's public properties and fields to an XML format for storage or transport. Some objects, such as the *DataSet* and in ADO.NET 2.0 the *DataTable*, provide their own methods to save contents to XML. The *XmlSerializer* class is a generic XML serializer that saves a fair number of .NET types to XML. The *XmlSerializer* class works with classes that have no circular references and those that implement the *IXmlSerializable* interface—which is not fully documented, even though used, in the .NET Framework 1.x. In version 1.x, the *DataSet* does implement it; the *DataTable* does not.

Why is support for XML serialization important? The key reason is that ASP.NET uses the *XmlSerializer* class to encode XML Web service messages. Subsequently, classes that have circular references and don't implement *IXmlSerializable* can't be used as parameters of a .NET XML Web service method. This is exactly what happens to *DataTable* objects in the .NET Framework 1.x.

In the .NET Framework 2.0 this situation ceases; the *DataTable* class implements the interface and can be used with the *XmlSerializer* class and with Web service methods. The following code is correct with the .NET Framework 1.x, except that it throws an exception. It works just fine in the .NET Framework 2.0.

```
XmlSerializer ser = new XmlSerializer(typeof(DataTable));
StreamWriter writer = new StreamWriter(@"c:\datatable.xml");
ser.Serialize(writer, dt);
```

The .NET Remoting Format

In the .NET Framework 1.x, the *DataSet* and *DataTable* objects suffer from a serialization problem—they always serialize themselves as XML. This means that when you store an instance of these classes in an out-of-process session or move it through .NET Remoting, a large chunk of data is moved.

To get around this limitation, the .NET Framework 2.0 endows the *DataTable* and the *DataSet* objects with a new property—*RemotingFormat*. The property accepts values from the *SerializationFormat* enumerated type—*Binary* or *Xml* (the default). The property influences how the content of the object is serialized.

```
table.RemotingFormat = SerializationFormat.Binary;
```

Set *RemotingFormat* to *Binary*, and you'll get more compact serialization output to improve the performance of remoted *DataSet* and *DataTable* objects.

Managing Views of Data

The *DataView* class represents a data-bindable, customized view of a *DataTable* and is used for sorting, filtering, and searching rows. Properly configured, the *DataView* also allows for editing. The *DataView* and *DataTable* classes are closely related. More view objects can be associated with the same table at the same time, but no view object holds more than references to the underlying table rows. The *DataTable* also has a *DefaultView* property that returns the default view for the table. By setting the *RowFilter* and *Sort* properties of the *DataView*, you can create filtered and sorted views.

We've looked at the general role of the classes, but not as they relate to ADO.NET 2.0. So what's new in Visual Studio 2005 for the *DataView* class?

Creating a Table from a View

As mentioned, a *DataView* is simply a mask on top of a *DataTable* object. When you set a filter or sort the rows, you actually force the *DataView* to import an array of indexes from the table. Each index points to a particular row in the bound table that meets the criteria of the view. When you enumerate the rows in the view, the internal set of indexes is scrolled and the real *DataTable* row is returned for reading or editing. A filtered view of a table is therefore just a software illusion—it's not a real subtable.

ADO.NET 1.x offers no direct way to create a subtable with only the rows that match a certain filter string or sort expression. If you want to do that, you have to do it on your own. The ADO.NET 2.0 *DataView* class provides the *ToTable* method for creating a new *DataTable* object from the current view:

```
// Get a DataTable object
SqlDataAdapter adapter = new SqlDataAdapter(cmdText, connStr);
DataTable dt = new DataTable("MyTable");
adapter.Fill (dt);

// Create a view of the rows sorted by lastname
DataView sortedView = new DataView(dt);
SortedView.Sort = "lastname";

// Save the view to a new DataTable object
DataTable sortedTable = sortedView.ToTable();
```

The new *DataTable* is a new object with the same schema and duplicated rows. Once you have the content of the view as a distinct *DataTable*, you can proceed with XML serialization by using the *DataTable* object's *WriteXml* method.

Selecting Distinct Rows

The *ToTable* method has four possible prototypes:

```
public DataTable ToTable()
public DataTable ToTable(string name)
public DataTable ToTable(bool distinct, string[] colNames)
public DataTable ToTable(string name, bool distinct, string[] colNames)
```

The first two simply flush the content viewed through the *DataView* object into a newly created, and optionally named, *DataTable* object. The latter two overloads take a Boolean parameter that lets you indicate whether you want distinct rows or all the rows. To get distinct rows, you must set the parameter to *true*; otherwise you get all the rows. (This feature resembles the *DISTINCT* T-SQL keyword.) Two rows are considered equal (that is, not distinct) when all column values are identical.

The array of strings parameter determines which columns in the view should be included in the new table. Each column is identified by name. If the array is empty, all columns are copied.

Summary

ADO.NET 2.0 comes with a full bag of new goodies for developers. Most of these new features revolve around the SQL Server .NET data provider and exploits new functionality in SQL Server 2005, the upcoming new version of SQL Server. SQL notifications and asynchronous commands are the most compelling of these features.

Another bunch of enhancements involve the SQL Server provider but not specifically the SQL Server 2005 database engine or the newest network libraries (MDAC 9.0). They include batch processing and the bulk copy object. These are optimizations of operations that can be performed less comfortably and efficiently in ADO.NET 1.x. In particular, batch update can be configured as a real batch process in which multiple rows are sent to the server for update. The bulk copy operation no longer has to be performed using the classic T-SQL *BULK INSERT* statement and disk files. Instead, you use a new object that exploits a powerful low-level communication channel with the TDS parser. As a result, using the new bulk copy object is even more powerful than the *BULK INSERT* itself.

Finally, we have the classes in *System.Data*—the core of ADO.NET. *DataSet* and *DataTable* objects can be read in a read-only and forward-only way using readers, and they can be filled using a data reader object. The *DataTable* fully supports XML serialization, and the *DataView* can flush the range of selected rows to dynamically created *DataTable* objects.

However, looking at data access from an ASP.NET perspective, the biggest change is the introduction of the data source object, which allows for declarative and virtually codeless data binding. You'll learn more about this in the next chapter.

6

The Data Source Object Model

Most Web applications follow a relatively simple pattern. They fetch data from data sources, manipulate it to fit into a nice-looking HTML layout, and then send the resulting markup to the browser. Consequently, developers commonly use ASP.NET (and other server-side programming environments) to display a data-driven user interface.

ASP.NET 1.x has an extremely flexible and generic data binding architecture that is optimized for performance and can give developers full control of the page life cycle. Developers can link data-bound controls such as the *DataGrid* and the *DropDownList* to any collection of data that implements the *IEnumerable* interface (such as the *DataView*) or any objects that support the members of the *IListSource* interface (such as *DataSet* and *DataTable*). While this approach represents a quantum leap from classic ASP, it still requires page developers to learn a lot of architectural details to create even relatively simple read-only pages. A Web developer who knows only ASP, HTML, JavaScript, and a little ADO and SQL (or equivalent tools) will get into trouble if she is left alone to decide how (or whether) to design a distributed query, a scalable update strategy, or a master/detail view. And experienced developers have to continually reimplement the same pattern to access data sources, get data, and make the data consistent with the programming interface of data controls.

The key issue with ASP.NET data binding is a lack of a higher-level and possibly declarative model for data fetching and manipulation (edit, insert, and delete). As a result, an ASP.NET 1.x data access layer is boring to write and requires hundreds of lines of code even for relatively simple scenarios.

The ASP.NET 2.0 data source model addresses this problem. To simplify the data binding mechanism, the architecture of data-bound controls now supports a new family of data components—the data source components—which in turn support a declarative model of binding. The data source control represents a source of data that returns and accepts data over a well-known stream—such as SQL, XML, *DataSet*, and, why not, custom formats such as the Microsoft Excel worksheets. At least for relatively common, fetch-display-edit scenarios, data source objects offer a very approachable schema for any Web developer and a time-saving resource for more seasoned programmers.

The Rationale of Data Source Components

To understand the importance of data sources before we delve into their plumbing and implementation, let's look at a few data binding scenarios that show the inherent simplicity of a declarative approach. It goes without saying that "declarative" here is not a magic word and that a declarative approach is far from the perfect solution for all software troubles. But it helps—a lot—in a significant number of real-world scenarios.

The data binding model of ASP.NET 2.0 provides two ways of connecting—programmatically (as in ASP.NET 1.x) and declaratively (using data source components). ASP.NET 2.0 also continues to provide hooks so developers can gain full control over the data binding mechanism; at the same time, it makes this need far less frequent.

Codeless Data Binding

Codeless data binding is a feature that a few other server-side programming environments supply, and it has been crucial to the rapid adoption of those environments for developing relatively simple data-driven Web sites. ASP.NET 1.x is great for professional sites because it provides a rich set of events and a detailed object model, but it ends up requiring large blocks of code no matter what you really want to obtain.

In ASP.NET 2.0 developers can set up sophisticated Web sites without knowing a lot of SQL or the page life cycle. Codeless data binding, and the data source model in particular, also lets developers work together, each contributing the best of his skills. For example, one developer can create the skeleton of the page and the other can provide the SQL statements or stored procedures needed to perform the basic I/O operations.

The big difference over ASP.NET 1.x is that less-experienced developers can now do most of the work and rely on others only for SQL statements. All the glue code is automatically provided by the data source control and buried in the

ASP.NET framework. ASP.NET 2.0 data binding enables page developers to implement data binding scenarios, including displaying, editing, paging, and sorting data, with no code. In other common scenarios where some code is still required, the new model makes development as simple and intuitive as possible.

An Inspiring Best Practice

Although codeless data binding is generalized and integrated in the ASP.NET 2.0 data source model, it has many points in common with the *<cfquery>* statement of Macromedia ColdFusion. Have a look at the following code, which represents a query—and the resulting data—with a named markup element:

```
<CFQUERY name="EmployeesList" datasource="Northwind_DSN">
    SELECT * FROM Employees ORDER BY lastname
</CFQUERY>
```

ColdFusion developers don't need to know how to set up the connection to the desired database. Nor do they need to know about the most effective way to execute the specified statement—be it a *SELECT*, as in the example above, or *UPDATE*, *INSERT*, or *DELETE*. All they need to know are the name of the data source and the statement to execute. As you can guess, these pieces of information can be easily provided by a more expert fellow programmer. No deep knowledge of connections, transactions, or OLE DB is required.

The data source is identified by name, but the name has to be more than just a unique string. It must reference a connection string and can be anything that gives the underlying infrastructure enough information to establish a link with the database. In ColdFusion, the data source is by default the name of an ODBC Data Source Name (DSN). If other database drivers are used, the data source name changes accordingly to allow a successful connection.

Even though it was inspired by the ColdFusion approach, the newest ASP.NET data source model differs from it in a number of key ways. For example, the ColdFusion *<cfquery>* statement supports only SQL statements, while the ASP.NET data source model extends the same data binding mechanism to a variety of data sources, including XML and *DataSet* objects. It even allows you to bind to Excel worksheets.

> **Note** The ColdFusion API provides more than just tags for executing queries. Tags for updatable statements are defined, too. They are *<cfupdate>*, *<cfinsert>*, and *<cfdelete>*. The ASP.NET data source model provides the same capabilities, but through a different set of tags and attributes. You'll see more on this later in the chapter.

The Equivalent ASP.NET 1.x Code

The declarative code you just saw as an example of ColdFusion's *<cfquery>* tag hides a lot of code—the code to set up the connection, handle possible parameters, execute the statement, and cache the final resultset. Of course, you can emulate the behavior of the *<cfquery>* tag in ASP.NET 1.x, but it will take some lines of code, as shown here:

```
<script runat="server">
void Page_Load(object sender, EventArgs e)
{
   if (! Page.IsPostBack) {
      // Can use a simple string pointing to the actual
      // connection string in the web.config file
      SqlConnection conn = new SqlConnection(connString);
      SqlCommand cmd = new SqlCommand("SELECT * FROM Employees", conn);

   // Execute the statement
      conn.Open();
      SqlDataReader reader = cmd.ExecuteReader();

   // Display the output and close the connection
      ⋮
      conn.Close();
   }
}
</script>
```

This code gives you an idea of what's needed but is too simple for any realistic application. For a real application, you'd have to figure out the connection string, consider caching fetched data, and arrange for display, paging, sorting, and updates. The code would be significantly more complex and, even worse, its underlying pattern would be reimplemented in any segment of the application that required data access. The data source model incorporates a lot of boilerplate code and provides a declarative and codeless data binding model—which can be valuable, at least in commonplace scenarios.

Integration with the Existing ASP.NET Framework

The ASP.NET 2.0 data source model not only offers much more than the ColdFusion API, but everything is tightly integrated with the existing framework of server controls.

ColdFusion developers use the *<cfoutput>* tag (or one of its variations) to merge the results of a query with the rest of the page. The tag represents a placeholder for the rows fetched. Data is inserted using a custom syntax—*#field_name#*—whose functionality is comparable to that of *Eval*. (See Chapter

5.) Each *<cfoutput>* tag references the bound records through the name of the query tag:

```
<cfoutput query="EmployeesList">
#LastName#, #FirstName# <br>
</cfoutput>
```

In ASP.NET, data-bound server controls are the preferred way to display data coming from queries. In version 1.x, you normally link controls to a data source programmatically. The closest you can get to declarative data binding is the approach in the following code snippet:

```
<asp:datagrid runat="server" ID="grid"
    datasource="<%# GetDataTable() %>" />
```

The *DataGrid* control has its *DataSource* property declaratively set, with the object returned by a page method that the developer must write.

ASP.NET 2.0 adds a new property to all data-bound controls so that any control can be successfully bound to a new data source control. The new property, *DataSourceId*, matches the name of a data source control defined in the same page. The following code snippet shows how to list the employees in the Northwind Employees database. The data-bound control used for the output is the *Repeater*.

```
<asp:SqlDataSource runat="server" ID="MySource"
    ConnectionString="SERVER=…;DATABASE=northwind;UID=…;"
    DataSourceMode="DataSet"
    SelectCommand="SELECT firstname, lastname FROM employees" />

<asp:Repeater runat="server" ID="data" DataSourceId="MySource" >
    <ItemTemplate>
            <%# Eval("ProductName") %>
            <%# Eval("Price") %> <br>
    </ItemTempate>
</asp:Repeater>
```

We'll discuss the programming interface of the *SqlDataSource* control in a moment. In the meantime, note how the code uses a more compact syntax—only *Eval*—for binding data to the *Repeater* control's templates. (We discussed the new form of simple binding in Chapter 5.)

The next listing shows how to use a grid control instead. Note that both the standard *DataGrid* control and the new *GridView* control can be bound to a data source. You can pass data to a data-bound control using either the classic *DataSource* property or the new *DataSourceId* property. Note that the two properties are mutually exclusive; if you set both, an exception will be thrown.

```
<html>
<body>
<form runat="server">
    <asp:GridView runat="server" ID="grid"
         DataSourceId="MySource"
         AutoGenerateColumns="true">
    </asp:GridView>

       <asp:SqlDataSource runat="server" ID="MySource"
         ConnectionString="SERVER=…;DATABASE=northwind;UID=…;"
         DataSourceMode="DataSet"
         SelectCommand="SELECT firstname, lastname FROM employees" />
</form>
</body>
</html>
```

The output of the page is shown in Figure 6-1. Note that no code is needed to set up and populate the grid. As you'll see later on, many other features that require code in ASP.NET 1.x (such as sorting, paging, editing, and master/detail) can be added to data sources without needing a single line of code.

Figure 6-1 A grid of data generated using a SQL data source control bound to an instance of the new *GridView* control

A Consistent Model for Heterogeneous Data Sources

Not only are data source components designed to connect to data providers in a codeless way, but they also support a variety of sources using a single model.

Supported data source types include relational databases, XML documents, and custom business objects. ASP.NET 2.0 data-bound controls work with any of these data sources. Microsoft provides a few built-in data sources, but you can define others.

Defining a Standard Set of Data Operations

A data source component is a data control that can implement some or all of a standard set of data operations. Whether a control implements the entire standard set of operations or only a subset depends on the class. For example, you can have a SQL data source control (a data source control that manages relational data) that supports selection and updates and another data source control that provides only selection capabilities.

The standard set of data operations includes the four basic I/O operations: select, delete, insert, and update. The data source component is also expected to return the fetched data as an object. The type of the returned object depends on the particular implementation. The selection should be smart enough to support optional filtering and sorting.

The data source component exposes these operations to page developers through a number of intuitive method calls on the data source control. The methods are grouped in a new interface that characterizes the data source components.

Binding Data Source Components to Controls

The data source object model is not a new API alternative to ADO.NET or OLE DB. Data source components form a layer of code that works between data-bound controls (and data-driven classes) and the low-level API used to retrieve data. This low-level API can be ADO.NET, System.Xml, or perhaps Microsoft Indexing Service or Excel's COM object model, depending on the data being exposed. A data source component implements a number of tailor-made interfaces to communicate with clients—mostly data-bound controls.

In ASP.NET 2.0, data-bound controls have been extended to support a new set of interfaces so they can take their data out of data source components no matter what the real underlying data source is. The binding model was primarily based on the *IEnumerable* interface in ASP.NET 1.x; it is also based on other, richer interfaces in ASP.NET 2.0 that are representative of data source controls.

One difference between data source components and ASP.NET 1.x bindable classes is that the new data source object model allows you to select, insert, delete, and update data stored in a bound source—be it a relational database, an XML file, or an Excel document.

A Richer Design-Time Experience

Data source components were introduced in ASP.NET 2.0 for two main reasons. The first was to simplify the programming model with a set of advanced controls (sort of programmatic wizards) that could perform I/O operations on generic blocks of data. In this respect, I consider data source components as the evolution of the ADO.NET 1.x data access application block—a set of time-saving classes that can speed up development.

As for the second reason, consider that in ASP.NET 1.x, knowledge of page life cycle events is required for building data access layers. Similarly, familiarity with ADO.NET objects and best practices is highly recommended. In ASP.NET 2.0, all common data access scenarios (i.e., stateless scenarios) can be implemented with zero lines of code. The availability of such powerful controls also makes design-time page composition simpler and more effective. Designers can work with realistic (if not real) data at design time. In addition, the schema of the data is known, so a data-bound control can give its user interface a reasonable appearance. This helps developers to more quickly customize the appearance and layout of the data that will be shown in the control. As a result, the design-time user experience is richer and more pleasant.

Data Source Control Internals

A data source control is a .NET Framework class that facilitates the binding of data between data stores and data-bound controls—both existing controls such as the *DataGrid* and new data-bound controls such as *GridView*, *TreeView*, and *DetailsView*. Let's have a look at the plumbing that makes data source controls work as expected.

A data source control represents one or more named views of data. Each view provides an enumeration of data objects (such as collections, *DataSet*, or business objects). The contents of the data source are managed through SQL-like statements such as *SELECT*, *INSERT*, *DELETE*, and *UPDATE*. Data source controls inherit the base class *Control* and come in two flavors—tabular and hierarchical. The *DataSourceControl* abstract class serves as the base class for all data source controls and defines the interface between data-bound controls and the underlying data. Although the data source control has no visual rendering, it is implemented as a control to allow for "declarative persistence" (automatic instantiation during the request processing) as a native part of the .aspx source code and to gain access to the page view state.

A data source control exposes the contents of its underlying data source through a set of properties and methods. Some of these members are specific to the control; others are common to all source controls and are defined as part of the *IDataSource* interface.

The *IDataSource* Interface

All data source controls implement the *IDataSource* interface. Therefore, this interface is the only prerequisite to creating your own custom ASP.NET data source control. A data source control uses the interface's properties and methods to expose the bound content as a set of named views. The *IDataSource* interface provides the basic set of capabilities to retrieve views of data out of a data source.

Members of the Interface

The *IDataSource* interface is quite simple and features one event and a couple of methods. The event, *DataSourceChanged*, requires delegates with the default prototype—the *EventHandler* class. The event is raised whenever something happens around the control and the underlying data source to alter the currently bound data source. A typical action that causes this event to fire is a change in the connection string. Table 6-1 lists the two methods of the interface.

Table 6-1 Methods of the *IDataSource* Interface

Method	Description
GetView	Takes the name of the data source view to retrieve and returns it as a *DataSourceView* object
GetViewNames	Returns a collection of names representing the list of view objects associated with the current instance of the data source control

The *DataSourceControl* base class doesn't add any extra properties or methods to those automatically inherited from the *Control* class. So any other members available on the programming interface of actual data source controls are defined by the specific type and don't represent items of a contract shared by multiple controls.

Data Source Views

As mentioned, the internal architecture of a data source control looks like a collection of named views. A named view is represented by a data source view object—an instance of the *DataSourceView* class—similar to the *DataView* class in the ADO.NET object model. Like the *DataView* class in ADO.NET, the *DataSourceView* class represents a customized view of data in which special settings for sorting, filtering, and other data operations have been defined. At its core, all that a data source control does is manage views of data loaded from the underlying data source.

The *DataSourceView* class is the base class for all views associated with a data source control. The number of views in a data source control depends on the connection string, the characteristics, and the actual contents of the underlying data source. The data source control uses the *GetViewNames* method to enumerate all the current views and uses the *GetView* method to retrieve a specific view.

Table 6-2 lists the properties of the *DataSourceView* class.

Table 6-2 Properties of the *DataSourceView* Class

Property	Description
CanDelete	Indicates whether deletions are allowed on the underlying data source. The deletion is performed by invoking the *Delete* method.
CanInsert	Indicates whether insertions are allowed on the underlying data source. The insertion is performed by invoking the *Insert* method.
CanPage	Indicates whether the data in the view can be paged.
CanSort	Indicates whether the data in the view can be sorted.
CanRetrieveTotalRowCount	Indicates whether information about the total row count is available.
CanUpdate	Indicates whether updates are allowed on the underlying data source. The update is performed by invoking the *Update* method.
Name	Returns the name of the current view.

In general, the *CanXXX* properties, such as *CanDelete*, indicate not only whether the data source control is capable of performing the specified operation but also whether that operation is appropriate given the current status of the data. The latter is a general guideline that each data source control can take or leave. For example, the view class associated with the *SqlDataSource* control (more on this in a moment) blocks data operations (insert, delete, update) only if no corresponding statement has been specified. The sort operation, on the other hand, is enabled only if the data of the view are cached in a *DataSet*. (This means that SQL Server is never involved with the sort operation.)

Table 6-3 lists all the methods supported by the class.

Table 6-3 Methods of the *DataSourceView* Class

Method	Description
Delete	Performs a delete operation on the data associated with the view
Insert	Performs an insert operation on the data associated with the view
Select	Returns an enumerable object filled with the data contained in the underlying data storage
Update	Performs an update operation on the data associated with the view

All data source view objects support data retrieval through the *Select* method. The method returns an object that implements the *IEnumerable* interface. The real type of the object depends on the data source control and the attributes set on it. As long as the data source control is the *SqlDataSource* class, the *Select* method returns either a data reader or a *DataView* object.

In addition, data source views can optionally perform basic operations such as insert, update, delete, and sort. Data-bound controls discover the capabilities of a data source control by retrieving an associated data source view and querying using the *CanXXX* properties.

Tabular Data Source Controls

Figure 6-2 shows a diagram of the classes that form the data source object model. By the time ASP.NET 2.0 ships, other classes might be added to the tree. Good candidates are data source classes to expose the contents of Excel worksheets, full-text searches conducted by Microsoft Indexing Service, and the Microsoft Outlook Inbox.

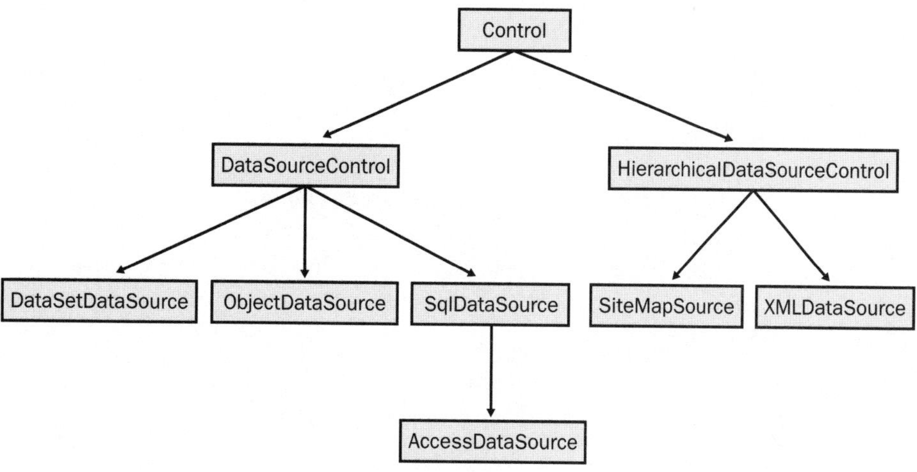

Figure 6-2 The data source controls class hierarchy.

Four data source controls that return tabular data are currently supported. Tabular data is any data that can be expressed as a table of rows and columns. Tabular data source controls are *AccessDataSource*, *DataSetDataSource*, *ObjectDataSource*, and *SqlDataSource*. Each refers to a particular type of data, as described in Table 6-4.

Table 6-4 Tabular Data Source Controls

Class	Description
AccessDataSource	Represents a connection to an Access database. Inherits from the *SqlDataSource* control but throws an exception if you attempt to set the *ConnectionString* and *ProviderName* properties. Use the *DataFile* property to point to the actual MDB file. The control uses the Jet 4.0 OLE DB provider to connect to the database.
DataSetDataSource	Works with the XML representation of a *DataSet* object. The XML data can be specified as a string or through a filename. You can't bind this control to a *DataSet* object—not even programmatically. The class features methods to retrieve the corresponding *DataSet* object and set schema information. Although XML-based, the control supports only the tabular interface and can be bound only to list controls. Mainly used to display XML data in read-only scenarios, the control also supports editing of the underlying XML data.
ObjectDataSource	Allows binding to a custom .NET business object that returns data. The class is specified by name through the *TypeName* property. The control allows developers to structure applications using a three-tier architecture and still take advantage of the ASP.NET 2.0 declarative data binding model. The class is expected to follow a specific design pattern and include, for example, a parameterless constructor and methods with a well-known behavior.
SqlDataSource	Represents a connection to an ADO.NET data provider that returns SQL data, including data sources accessible through OLE DB and ODBC. The name of the provider and the connection string are specified through properties. Do not use this class to connect to an Access database.

Let's have a closer look at the architecture and the implementation of the various tabular data source classes, starting with the one that you'll likely use most often.

The *SqlDataSource* Class

The *SqlDataSource* control is a data source control that represents a connection to a relational data store such as SQL Server or Oracle or any data source accessible through OLE DB and ODBC bridges. As you'll see in a moment, a separate control is available to connect to Access databases, although you can still use the *SqlDataSource* control to work with an .mdb database via OLE DB.

You set up the connection to the data store using two main properties, *ConnectionString* and *ProviderName*. The former represents the connection string and contains enough information to open a session with the underlying engine. The latter specifies the namespace of the ADO.NET managed provider to use for the operation. The *ProviderName* property defaults to *System.Data.SqlClient*, which means that the default data store is SQL Server. To target an OLE DB provider, use the *System.Data.OleDb* string instead.

The *DataSourceMode* property controls how the Select command retrieves data. Data can be fetched using a data adapter or a command object (*SqlCommand*). Depending on your choice, fetched data can be packed in a *DataSet* object or a data reader. The *DataSourceMode* property accepts values defined by the *SqlDataSourceMode* enumeration—*DataSet* and *DataReader*. In the former case, the selection takes place through a data adapter. The results of the query are then cached in a *DataSet* object and stored in memory on the server. When working in *DataSet* mode, the data source control supports advanced scenarios in which sorting and filtering are enabled. When the *DataSourceMode* property is set to *DataReader*, a SQL command is run and a data reader is used to read the rows one at a time in a read-only, forward-only way. The value of the *DataSourceMode* property has no effect on other operations, such as insert, update, or delete.

The following code snippet shows the minimal code necessary to activate a SQL data source control bound to the Northwind database of SQL Server:

```
<asp:SqlDataSource runat="server" ID="MySqlSource"
   ConnectionString="SERVER=…;DATABASE=northwind;UID=…;"
   SelectCommand="SELECT * FROM employees" />
```

The data operations supported by the associated view class are provided by the pairs of properties listed in Table 6-5.

Table 6-5 Properties for Configuring Data Operations

Property Pair	Description
DeleteCommand, DeleteParameters	Gets or sets the SQL statement (and related parameters) used to delete rows in the underlying data store
InsertCommand, InsertParameters	Gets or sets the SQL statement (and related parameters) used to insert new rows in the underlying data store
SelectCommand, SelectParameters	Gets or sets the SQL statement (and related parameters) used to retrieve data from the underlying data store
SelectCountCommand	Gets or sets the SQL statement used to retrieve a row count from the underlying data store
UpdateCommand, UpdateParameters	Gets or sets the SQL statement (and related parameters) used to update rows in the underlying data store

Each *XXXCommand* property is a string that contains the SQL text to be used. The command can optionally contain parameters listed in the associated parameter collection. The way the commands are executed depends on the selected managed provider. The managed provider and its underlying relational engine determine the exact syntax of the SQL to use and the syntax of the embedded parameters. For example, if the data source control points to SQL Server, command parameter names must be prefixed with the @ symbol. If the target data source is an OLE DB provider, parameters are unnamed, identified with a *?* placeholder symbol, and located by position. The following code snippet shows a more complex data source control in which parametric delete and update commands have been enabled:

```
<asp:SqlDataSource runat="server" ID="MySqlSource"
   ConnectionString="SERVER=…;DATABASE=northwind;UID=…;"
   SelectCommand="SELECT * FROM employees"
   UpdateCommand="UPDATE employees SET lastname=@lname"
   DeleteCommand="DELETE FROM employees WHERE employeeid=@TheEmp">
   <!-- parameters go here -->
</asp:SqlDataSource>
```

Another important pair of properties are also supported by the *SqlDataSource* control: *FilterExpression* and *FilterParameters*. A filter expression is a string that creates a filter on top of the data retrieved using the *Select* method. The syntax used for the *FilterExpression* property is the same as the syntax used for the *RowFilter* property of the *DataView* class and is similar to that used with the SQL *WHERE* clause. The *FilterExpression* property can also contain parameters. Filter parameters are prefixed with the @ character and enclosed in single quotation marks. The *FilterParameters* represents the collection of parameters that are evaluated for the placeholders found in the filter expression.

We'll examine all these properties more in detail in a practical scenario later in the chapter, in the "Using the *SqlDataSource* Control" section.

The *AccessDataSource* Class

The *AccessDataSource* control is a data source control that represents a connection to an Access database. It is based on the *SqlDataSource* control and provides a simpler, made-to-measure programming interface. In particular, the *AccessDataSource* control replaces properties such as *ConnectionString* and *ProviderName* with a more direct *DataFile* property. You set this property to the .mdb database file of choice. The data source control resolves the file path at run time and uses the Microsoft Jet 4 OLE DB provider to connect to the database.

The following code shows how to use the *AccessDataSource* control to open an .mdb file and bind its content to a drop-down list control. Note that the control opens Access database files in read-only mode by default.

```
<asp:AccessDataSource runat="server" ID="MyAccessSource"
   DataFile="nwind.mdb"
   SelectCommand="SELECT * FROM Customers" />
Select a Customer:
<asp:DropDownList runat="server" DataSourceId="MyAccessSource" />
```

Several features of the *AccessDataSource* control are inherited from the base class, *SqlDataSource*. In fact, the Access data source control is basically a SQL data source control optimized to work with Access databases. Like its parent control, the *AccessDataSource* control supports two distinct data source modes—*DataSet* and *DataReader*, depending on the ADO.NET classes used to retrieve data. Sorting and filtering can be applied to the selected data only if the fetch operation returns a *DataSet*. In this case, data is cached in memory and can be sorted and filtered.

The *AccessDataSource* can also be used to perform insert, update, or delete operations against the associated database. This is done using ADO.NET commands and parameter collections. Updates are problematic for Access databases when performed from within an ASP.NET application because an Access database is a plain file and the default account of the ASP.NET process (ASPNET or NetworkService, depending on the host operating system) might not have sufficient permission to write to the database file. For the data source updates to work, you should grant write permission to the ASP.NET account on the database file. Alternatively, you can use a different account with adequate permission.

> **Note** Most Internet service providers normally give you one directory in which ASPNET and NetworkService accounts have been granted write permission. In this case, you just place your Access file in this directory, and you can read and write seamlessly. In general, though, Access databases are plain files and as such are subject to the security rules of ASP.NET.

The *ShareMode* property controls how the Access data source opens the database and determines what data operations can be performed. The default value is *Read*, which means that only the *Select* operation can be accomplished. In read mode, the *CanDelete*, *CanInsert*, and *CanUpdate* properties all return *false*, thus blocking the corresponding data operations. To enable read/write operations, set *ShareMode* to *ReadWrite*.

The *DataSetDataSource* Class

The *DataSetDataSource* class takes an XML file or static data (such as an XML string) as input and exposes the *DataSet* representation of this data to data-bound controls. If the XML content is provided through a file, you set the *DataFile* property with the path to the file; otherwise, you set the *Data* property with a string containing the XML data. The XML content provided is parsed to obtain a *DataSet*. The *DataSetDataSource* class instantiates a *DataSet* object and uses the *DataSet* object's *ReadXml* method to parse the XML input. Ideally, the supplied XML data is a DiffGram script or any XML file created by the *DataSet*'s *WriteXml* method.

If the XML data does not also contain schema information, you can specify it as a separate file (by setting the *SchemaFile* property) or as a string (by setting the *Schema* property). The *GetDataSet* method returns the *DataSet* object created based on the supplied XML data. The following listing shows the class in action:

```
<asp:GridView runat="server" ID="grid"
   DataSourceId="MyDataSetSource"
   AutoGenerateColumns="true">
</asp:GridView>

<asp:DataSetDataSource runat="server" ID="MyDataSetSource"
   DataFile="data.xml" />
```

The data source class doesn't have properties to influence select or insert operations. Any data operations take place based on the programming interface of the *DataSet* class. For example, the *Select* method of the corresponding data source view class returns the *DataView* object for the internal *DataTable* whose name matches the name of the data source view. Similarly, the *Insert* method creates a new row on the *DataTable* matching the name of the data source view.

It's also worth mentioning the Boolean *AutoSave* property. When it is set to *true* (the default), the data source control calls its *Save* method to persist changes back to the original file every time a data operation is performed. If *AutoSave* is *false*, the data source does not call *Save* automatically, but changes are temporarily held in memory. This provides a form of batch update to the original file. However, user code can call the *Save* method manually at any time.

The *ObjectDataSource* Class

The *ObjectDataSource* class enables business components to associate their contents to data-bound controls. The class supports declarative parameters that allow developers to pass page-level variables to the object's methods.

The *ObjectDataSource* class makes some assumptions about the objects it wraps. As a consequence, an arbitrary class can't be used with this data source class. In particular, bindable objects are expected to have a default constructor, be stateless, and have methods that easily map to select, update, insert, and delete semantics. Also, the object must perform updates one item at a time; objects that update their state using batch operations are not supported. The bottom line is that managed objects that work well with *ObjectDataSource* were designed with this data source class in mind.

The following listing illustrates a class that can be used with an object data source. The class has a default parameterless constructor and does not maintain any state. The class also features a method—*GetEmployees*—that can be easily mapped to a *Select* statement, with or without filter parameters.

```
using System.Collections;
using System.Data;
using System.Data.SqlClient;
using System.ComponentModel;

namespace Intro20
{
   public class MyBusinessObject
   {
      public MyBusinessObject()
      {}

      public IEnumerable GetEmployees()
      {
```

```
            return GetEmployees(0);
        }
        public IEnumerable GetEmployees(int minID)
        {
            SqlDataAdapter adapter = new SqlDataAdapter(
                "SELECT employeeid, firstname, lastname FROM employees
                                WHERE employeeid >" + minID.ToString(),
                "SERVER=…;DATABASE=northwind;UID=…;");
            DataSet ds = new DataSet("MyData");
            adapter.Fill(ds, "Employees");

            // Return the content of the selected DataTable
            // as an IEnumerable object
            return ((ds.Tables["Employees"]) as IListSource).GetList();
        }
    }
}
```

This class must be accessible from within the .aspx page and can be bound to the *ObjectDataSource* control, as shown here:

```
<asp:ObjectDataSource runat="server" ID="MyObjectSource"
   TypeName="Intro20.MyBusinessObject"
   SelectMethod="GetEmployees" />
```

Similar methods should be defined on the business object to perform update and insert operations using a single call with a few parameters.

The *ObjectDataSource* control is designed to simplify and encourage a common practice among page developers—encapsulating data retrieval and business logic into an additional layer between the presentation page and data provider. This extra layer consists of an object that, designed with the data source model in mind, can provide for free codeless and automatic data binding.

Hierarchical Data Source Controls

Data source controls that represent hierarchical data derive from the abstract *HierarchicalDataSourceControl* class, which is the base implementation of the *IHierarchicalDataSource* interface. The interface defines a single method—*GetHierarchicalView*—that retrieves a hierarchical data source view. The method takes the path of the view to retrieve and returns an object of type *HierarchicalDataSourceView* that represents a single view of the data at the hierarchical level identified by the parameter.

```
HierarchicalDataSourceView GetHierarchicalView(string viewPath);
```

Unlike tabular data source controls, which typically have only one named view, hierarchical data source controls support a view for each level of data that the data source control represents. The *viewPath* parameter indicates the path in the hierarchy to navigate to find the requested data.

Hierarchical and tabular data source controls share the same conceptual specification of a consistent and common programming interface for data-bound controls. The only difference is the nature of the data they work with—hierarchical vs. flat and tabular.

ASP.NET 2.0 comes with a couple of hierarchical data source controls—*SiteMapDataSource* and *XmlDataSource*.

The *SiteMapDataSource* Class

Site maps are a common feature of cutting-edge Web sites. A site map is a graph that represents all the pages and directories found in a Web site. Site map information is used to show users the logical coordinates of the page they are visiting, allow them to access site locations dynamically, and render all the navigation information in a graphical fashion (as shown in Figure 6-3). ASP.NET 2.0 contains a rich navigation infrastructure that allows developers to specify the site structure. We'll cover the site map navigation control in detail in Chapter 8. For now, suffice it to say that the site map is a hierarchical piece of information that can be used as input for a hierarchical data source control. This control is the *SiteMapDataSource* class. The site map information can appear in many ways, the simplest of which is an XML file named web.sitemap located in the root of the application.

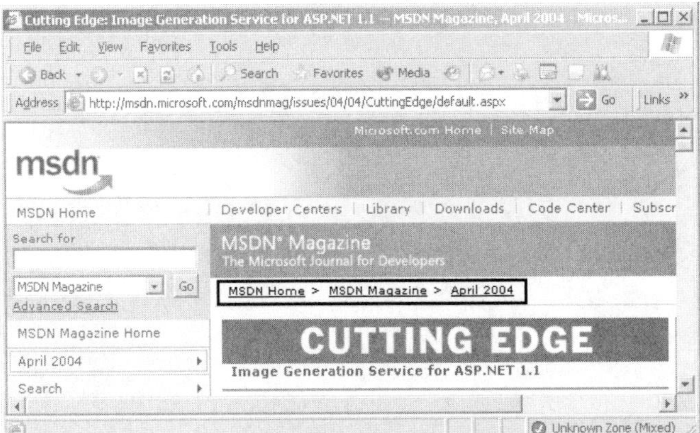

Figure 6-3 The graphical layout that the MSDN Magazine Web site uses to represent the location of a page in the site hierarchy

To give you the essence of site maps and site map data sources, let's briefly review a few usage scenarios. Suppose you're writing a Web site and your client asks for a sequence of hyperlinks that indicate the location of the page in the site map. In ASP.NET 1.x, you have to create your own infrastructure to hold site map information and render the page location. (Typically, you use a configuration file and a user control.) ASP.NET 2.0 provides richer support for site maps. You start by creating a configuration file named app.sitemap in the root of the Web application. The file describes the relationship between pages on the site. Your next step will depend on the expected output.

If the common representation shown in Figure 6-3 (a sequence of hyperlinks with a separator) is what you need, add a *NavigationPath* control to the page. This control (described in more detail in Chapter 8) retrieves the site map and produces the necessary HTML markup. In this simple case, there is no need to resort to a site map data source control. If you need to build a more complex, hierarchical layout—for example, a tree-based representation—you need the *SiteMapDataSource* control.

The *SiteMapDataSource* control pumps site map information to a hierarchical data-bound control (the new *TreeView* control) so it can display the site's structure. Here's an example:

```
<%@ Page Language="C#" %>
<html>
<body>
    <form runat="server">
        <asp:SiteMapDataSource runat="server" ID="MySiteMapSource" />
        <asp:TreeView runat="server" DataSourceId="MySiteMapSource" />
    </form>
</body>
</html>
```

Figure 6-4 shows the final output as it appears to the end user.

Figure 6-4 The site map information rendered through a *TreeView* control

> **Note** As mentioned, ASP.NET 2.0 introduces a new type of data-bound control that was completely unsupported in previous versions—the hierarchical data-bound control. A new base class is defined to provide the minimum set of capabilities: *HierarchicalDataBoundControl*. The *TreeView* and *Menu* controls fall in this category.

The *SiteMapDataSource* class features a couple of properties that relate to the site map provider: *SiteMapProvider* and *SiteMapViewType*. The former specifies the name of the site map provider to use. By default, the XML site map provider is used, which means you have to store site information using a given XML schema. (More on this in Chapter 8.) The *SiteMapViewType* property describes the type of view of the site map data that's generated by the data source control. Feasible view types include a path and a tree-based representation.

Three other properties relate to determining the starting node of the representation: *StartingNodeType*, *StartingNodeUrl*, and *StartingDepth*. They identify the starting node by type, URL, and depth, respectively. If you set more than one property, the order of precedence is *StartingNodeUrl*, *StartingDepth*, and *StartingNodeType*.

The *XmlDataSource* Class

The *XmlDataSource* control is a special type of data source control that supports both tabular and hierarchical views of data. The tabular view of XML data is just a list of nodes at a given level of hierarchy, whereas the hierarchical view shows the complete hierarchy. An XML node is an instance of the *XmlNode* class; the complete hierarchy is an instance of the *XmlDocument* class. The XML data source supports both read-only and read-write scenarios.

The *XmlDataSource* control can accept XML input data as a relative or absolute filename assigned to the *DataFile* property or as a string containing the XML content assigned to the *Data* property. If schema information is not included in the source files, it can be passed in as a separate *SchemaFile* or *Schema* string. (This model is nearly identical to that of *DataSetDataSource*.) Once the input data for the XML data source is supplied, the control exposes that data through the *IDataSource* or the *IHierarchicalDataSource* interface. In general, the *XmlDataSource* control is commonly bound to a hierarchical control, such as the *TreeView*.

To understand how the XML data source works, consider the following small XML file, named data.xml:

```
<warehouse>
   <department name="dairy" deptid="111">
      <category name="yogurt" categoryid="2222">
         <product name="horizon" sku="3333-3333"/>
      </category>
   </department>
</warehouse>
```

Next you bind this file to an instance of the *XmlDataSource* control and the data source to a tree view:

```
<asp:XmlDataSource runat="server" ID="MyXmlSource" DataFile="data.xml" />
<asp:TreeView runat="server" DataSourceId="MyXmlSource">
   <DataBindings>
         <asp:TreeNodeBinding Depth="0" DataMember="Department"
               TextField="Name" ValueField="DeptId" />
         <asp:TreeNodeBinding Depth="1" DataMember="Category"
               TextField="Name" ValueField="CategoryId" />
         <asp:TreeNodeBinding Depth="2" DataMember="Product"
               TextField="Name" ValueField="SKU" />
   </DataBindings>
</asp:TreeView>
```

The final result is shown in Figure 6-5.

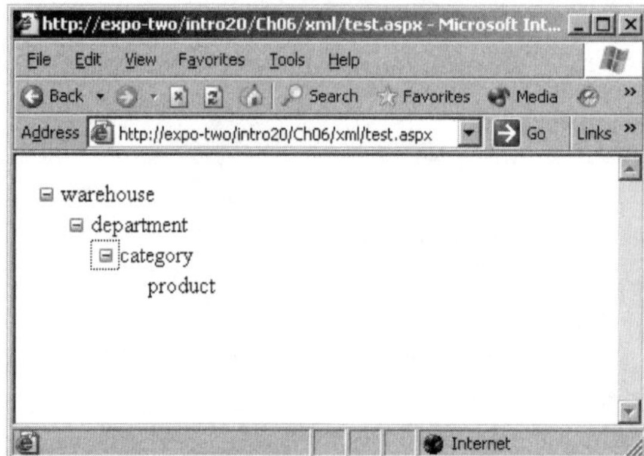

Figure 6-5 The contents of the bound XML file displayed using a *TreeView* control

The *<DataBindings>* section of the *TreeView* control (more on hierarchical controls in Chapter 7) lets you control the layout and the contents of the tree nodes. The *<TreeNodeBinding>* node indicates the depth (attribute *Depth*) of the specified XML node (attribute *DataMember*) as well as which attributes determine the text displayed for the node in the tree view and value associated with the node.

The *XmlDataSource* class can also transform its data using Extensible Stylesheet Language Transformations (XSLT). You set the transform file by using the *TransformFile* property or by assigning the XSLT content to the string property named *Transform*. Using the *TransformArgumentList* property, you can also pass arguments to the style sheet to be used during the XSL transformation. An XSL transformation is often used when the structure of an XML document does not match the structure needed to process the XML data. Note that once the data is transformed, the *XmlDataSource* becomes read-only and the data cannot be modified or saved back to the original source document.

Using the *SqlDataSource* Control

Let's look more closely at the *SqlDataSource* control and how to configure it in real-world situations. As mentioned, the *SqlDataSource* control represents a connection to an ADO.NET managed data provider, such as SQL Server, OLE DB, ODBC, Oracle, or a third-party provider. The control class takes advantage of the ADO.NET common data model, which provides a set of interfaces that all managed data providers implement.

The data source model enables the page author to indicate commands to perform common data operations—query and any sort of update. The text assigned to properties such as *InsertCommand* and *SelectCommand* is parsed to verify that it is a valid SQL command that is compliant with the expected syntax of the corresponding statement (*Insert* and *Select*, in this case). If the syntax doesn't match, the command text is taken as the name of a stored procedure.

Connecting to Data Source Controls

A data source control is the bridge between the physical data provider and the user code. In many cases, the user code is a data-bound server control and the binding takes place declaratively and in a rather codeless way. However, a data source control can also be invoked programmatically, like any other managed class. The following code snippet shows how to accomplish this:

```
<script runat="server">
void Page_Load(object sender, EventArgs e)
{
   SqlDataSource ds = new SqlDataSource();
   ds.ConnectionString = "SERVER=…;DATABASE=northwind;UID=…;";
   ds.DataSourceMode = SqlDataSourceMode.DataSet;
   ds.SelectCommand = "SELECT customerid, companyname FROM customers " +
                      "WHERE country=@TheCountry";
   ds.SelectParameters.Add("TheCountry", "USA");
```

```
    grid.DataSource = ds;
    grid.DataBind();
}
</script>
<asp:GridView runat="server" ID="grid" AutoGenerateColumns="true" />
```

In short, the data source control is a helper class that sets up data access code with a few lines of code—or in a completely codeless manner if a declarative approach is used.

> **Note** The *SqlDataSource* supports events before and after each operation is performed. The *Selecting*, *Inserting*, *Deleting*, and *Updating* events are fired before the associated operation, and the event arguments contain a reference to the provider-specific command object. A developer can set custom properties on the command before an operation's command is executed. The *Selected*, *Inserted*, *Deleted*, and *Updated* events are fired after the associated operation completes.

A data source control tends to incorporate a good number of functions and features. Does this make a data source too rigid and hard to customize? That's definitely not a far-fetched idea. In fact, parameters are an important aspect of data source controls. Both stored procedures and SQL commands can accept parameters.

Data Source Parameters

As mentioned, in the programming interface of the *SqlDataSource* control each command property has its own collection of parameters. A parameter collection is a collection class named *ParameterCollection*. It stores objects whose base class is *Parameter*. The *Parameter* class represents a parameter in a parameterized query, filter expression, or command executed by a data source control. The following code snippet shows how to use parameters to filter the result set generated by a query:

```
<asp:SqlDataSource runat="server" ID="MySource"
    ConnectionString="SERVER=…;DATABASE=northwind;UID=…;"
    DataSourceMode="DataSet"
    SelectCommand="SELECT firstname, lastname FROM employees
                   WHERE employeeid > @MinID">
```

```
    <SelectParameters>
        <asp:ControlParameter Name="MinID" ControlId="EmpID"
            PropertyName="Text" />
    </SelectParameters>
</asp:SqlDataSource>
```

The query contains a placeholder named *@MinID*. The data source control automatically populates the placeholder with the information returned by the *ControlParameter* object—one of the supported parameter types in ASP.NET 2.0. The value of the parameter is determined by the value of a given property on a given control. The name of the property is specified by the *PropertyName* attribute. The ID of the control is in the *ControlId* attribute. For the previous code to work, page developers must guarantee that the page contains a control with a given ID and property. The value of this property is used as the value for the matching parameter.

Parameter Types

The data source control can get the information to set parameters in several ways. How a parameter is bound to a value depends on the type of the parameter. ASP.NET 2.0 supports quite a few parameter types, which are listed in Table 6-6.

Table 6-6 Parameter Types in ASP.NET 2.0

Parameter	Description
ControlParameter	Gets the parameter value from any public property of a server control
CookieParameter	Sets the parameter value based on the content of the specified HTTP cookie
FormParameter	Gets the parameter value from the specified input field in the HTTP request form
ProfileParameter	Gets the parameter value from the specified property name in the profile object created from the application's personalization scheme
QueryStringParameter	Gets the parameter value from the specified variable in the request query string
SessionParameter	Sets the parameter value based on the content of the specified *Session* slot

Each parameter class has a *Name* property and a set of properties specific to its role and implementation. The following code snippet shows the typical way of binding all parameter types:

```
<SelectParameters>
   <asp:ControlParameter Name="TheEmpID"
         ControlId="EmpID" PropertyName="Text" />
   <asp:CookieParameter Name="TheCountry"
         CookieName="Country" />
   <asp:SessionParameter Name="TheOrderID"
         SessionField="OrderID" />
   <asp:QueryStringParameter Name="TheLastName"
         QueryStringField="LastName" />
   <asp:FormParameter Name="TheTitle"
         FormField="Title" />
</SelectParameters>
```

Binding Formal Parameters and Actual Values

The *Evaluate* method of the *Parameter* class updates and returns the value of the parameter object. Different parameter classes override this method and make it return an appropriate value. For example, the *ControlParameter* returns the value of the control that it is bound to, while the *QueryStringParameter* retrieves the current name/value pair from the HTTP request. All parameters support a *DefaultValue* property, for use when the value that the parameter is bound to is unavailable. The following code snippet shows the use of the *DefaultValue* property:

```
<asp:SqlDataSource runat="server" ID="MySource"
   ConnectionString="SERVER=…;DATABASE=northwind;UID=…;"
   SelectCommand="SELECT customerid, companyname FROM customers
                  WHERE @TheCountry='' OR country=@TheCountry">
   <SelectParameters>
     <asp:QueryStringParameter Name="TheCountry"
        QueryStringField="Country" DefaultValue="UK" />
   </SelectParameters>
</asp:SqlDataSource>
```

Figure 6-6 shows a page based on this code in action.

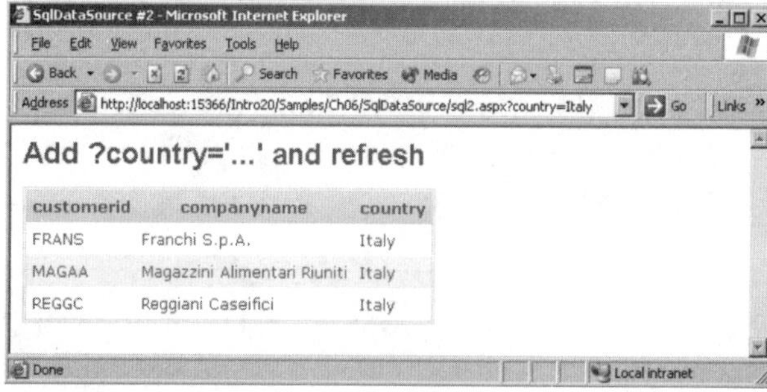

Figure 6-6 The value of the query string *country* parameter is passed to the data source control.

The binding between formal parameters (the placeholders in the command text) and actual values depends on how the underlying managed provider handles and recognizes parameters. If the provider type supports named parameters—as is the case with SQL Server and Oracle—the binding involves matching the names of placeholders with the names of the parameters. Otherwise, the matching is based on the position. Hence, the first placeholder is bound to the first parameter, and so on. This is what happens if OLE DB is used to access the data.

Caching Behavior

Data caching is crucial to any realistic Web application and an important feature to optimize to make the application run faster. Caching is also an important aspect of data source controls. A data source control retrieves data that will be made available to other components within the application. When multiple pages need to access this information, an up-to-date cache provides for a significantly faster response. The *Cache* object of ASP.NET is the preferred place to store in-memory data.

You can instruct the *SqlDataSource* control to cache the results of a query for a certain amount of time—but only if the data source mode is *DataSet*. (You cannot do this if you manage to use a data reader to retrieve the rows.) The *SqlDataSource* control provides automatic caching using a time-based cache expiration policy. It can also support an expiration policy based on the new *SqlCacheDependency* component. (We'll cover state management and the *Cache* object in Chapter 9.)

> **Note** A unique cache key is created for each combination of caching parameters, connection string, and the values of *SelectParameters* and *SelectCommand*. The cache key is hashed to protect the source data used to generate it.

Enabling Automatic Caching

To enable caching on the data source—caching is disabled by default—you set the *EnableCaching* property to *true*. You should also give the *CacheDuration* property a nonzero value. The *CacheDuration* property specifies the number of seconds before the contents of the data source are discarded, to be reloaded on the next request. The following code snippet shows a *SqlDataSource* control that caches ODBC data to expire every hour:

```
<asp:SqlDataSource runat="server"
   ConnectionString="DSN=MyData"
   ProviderName="System.Data.Odbc"
   SelectCommand="SELECT * FROM products"
   EnableCaching="true"
   CacheDuration="3600" />
```

An absolute expiration policy is used by default, but the page developer can configure the policy by using the *CacheExpirationPolicy* property. The property gets and sets the cache expiration behavior that, combined with the duration, fully describes the behavior of the cache that the data source control uses. In the previous example, absolute expiration means that the data source contents expire exactly one hour after their creation. An alternative to absolute expiration is sliding expiration, which means that the duration is reset each time the cache entry is accessed for reading.

> **Note** If the data source gets its data out of a file (such as an Access database or an XML file), an early expiration is forced as soon as the timestamp of the file changes. This occurs no matter what the natural expiration time would be.

SQL Server Cache Dependency

As you'll see in more detail in Chapter 9, in ASP.NET 2.0 the contents of some items in the cache can be bound to the timestamp of a SQL Server table. The class that makes this possible is *SqlCacheDependency*. The *SqlDataSource* control also supports a form of cache expiration based on a dependency between its contents and a table in a SQL Server database.

The dependency is specified as a string property. The syntax has the form "*database:table*". The database part of the string must refer to a database listed under the *<sqlCacheDependency>* section of the web.config file, and the table part must be the name of a table in that database. You can specify multiple table dependencies by separating them with semicolons, as in the following example:

```
<asp:SqlDataSource runat="server"
   ConnectionString="SERVER=…;DATABASE=pubs;UID=…;"
   SelectCommand="sp_getdata"
   EnableCaching="true"
   CacheDuration="3600"
   SqlCacheDependency="pubs:Authors;pubs:TitleAuthor"
/>
```

You can use this feature so that a change in the database can invalidate related values in the cache. This is particularly helpful in Web farm scenarios when an update on a machine can automatically force a refresh on the data of all others.

Summary

The new data binding model defined in ASP.NET 2.0 makes possible a codeless way to incorporate data into a Web application. This is made possible by data source controls that enable declaration and automatic instantiation of data components in a page. Two new interfaces—*IDataSource* and *IHierarchicalDataSource* allow data sources and data-bound controls to work together silently and automatically. These interfaces offer a consistent model of data representation for both run-time and design-time operations.

Does this mean that ASP.NET 2.0 offers a brand-new, exclusive data object model? Not exactly. A key goal of ASP.NET 2.0 architects was to preserve the explicit data binding model of ASP.NET 1.x. This model enables developers to control exactly when and how data access is performed. The new architecture is more automatic in nature, but it works side by side with the old model.

Finally, many ASP.NET 1.x developers complained that only the main ADO.NET objects—*DataSet*, *DataTable*, and *DataView*—could easily be bound to data controls. XML documents and collections of objects needed extra work to be bound to high-end controls such as *DataGrid*.

The introduction of data source controls in ASP.NET 2.0 also enables a consistent model across a variety of data sources. The page developer can use the same data binding model regardless of whether the data source is a SQL table, an XML document, a business object, a site map, or even an Excel worksheet.

In the next chapter, we'll look at the new family of data-bound controls that were designed to take advantage of codeless data binding.

7

Data-Bound Controls

Data binding was one of the most pleasant surprises in ASP.NET 1.x. It was far simpler and more effective than the support for data access in Microsoft Active Server Pages (ASP). But it turned out to have some shortcomings—not in terms of overall functionality but because you had to write a lot of custom code to handle necessary operations such as paging, sorting, editing, and deleting data. As you saw in Chapter 6, the new data source model in ASP.NET 2.0 largely removes these difficulties. The new data source model works with ASP.NET 2.0–specific controls and also enhances the existing data-bound controls with extra features such as codeless data binding.

The *DataGrid* is the principal control of most data-driven ASP.NET 1.x applications. It generates a tabular representation of data and offers advanced functionality such as paging, sorting, and in-place editing. Like all ASP.NET 1.x controls, the *DataGrid* is fully supported in ASP.NET 2.0 but is partnered with a newer control that is meant to replace it in the long run. The new grid control, *GridView*, is complemented by other view controls, such as *DetailsView* and *FormView*.

In this chapter, we'll look at the revised architecture of data-bound controls in ASP.NET 2.0 and examine the most important new data-bound controls—*GridView*, *FormView*, and *DetailsView*.

Hierarchy of Data-Bound Controls

A data-bound control is a control that is bound to a data source and generates its user interface by enumerating the items in the data source. Data-bound controls range from simple list controls (such as *DropDownList* and *ListBox*) that use the data to flesh out the markup, to more complex controls (such as *DataList* and *DataGrid*) that use the bound data to create their own hierarchy of child controls.

In ASP.NET 1.x, the class diagram for data-bound controls is basically made up of three main branches of controls, as shown in Figure 7-1.

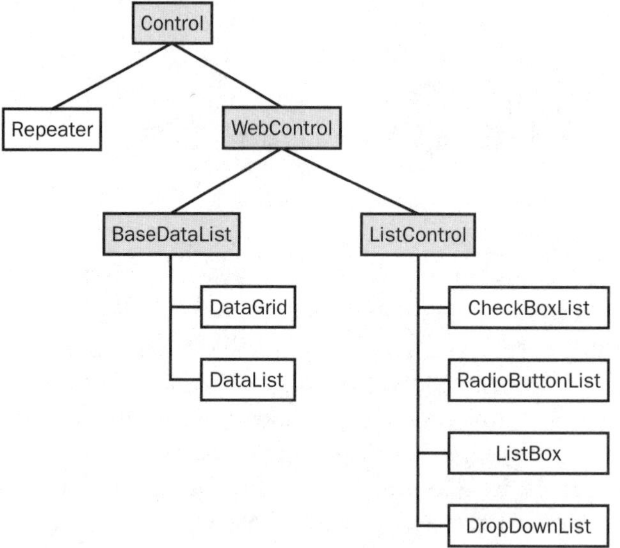

Figure 7-1 The class diagram for data-bound controls in ASP.NET 1.x

The *Repeater* control descends directly from *Control*; *DataGrid* and *DataList* are both specializations of a base data list, which is a templatized class. List controls form yet another group of homogeneous components that are characterized by a list of items.

In ASP.NET 2.0, the class diagram has changed significantly. All controls descend from the same base class—*BaseDataBoundControl*—regardless of the actual implementation or user interface characteristics. *BaseDataBoundControl* branches off into two more specific child classes—*DataBoundControl* and *HierarchicalDataBoundControl*. Figure 7-2 shows the hierarchy of data-bound classes in ASP.NET 2.0.

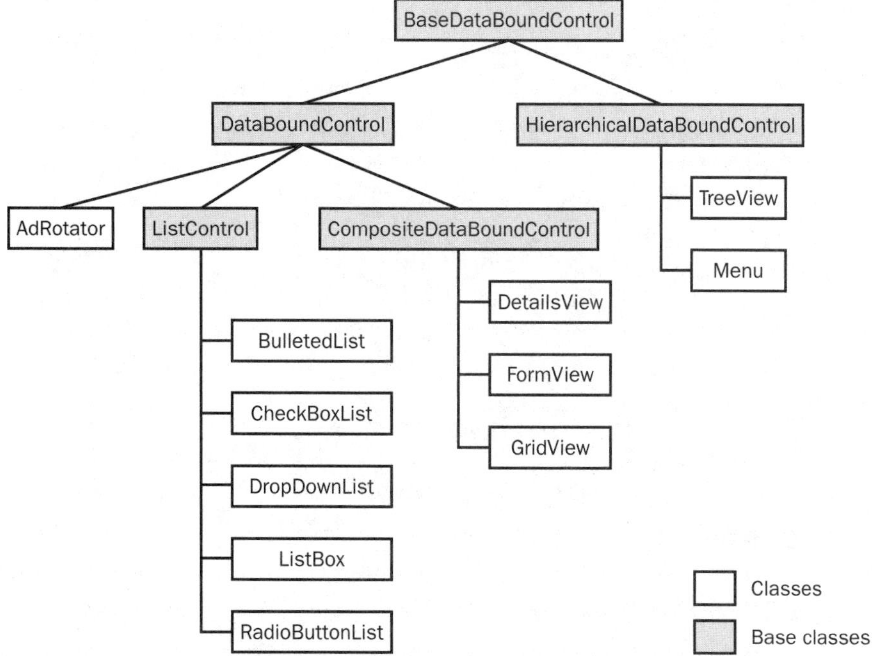

Figure 7-2 The class diagram for data-bound controls in ASP.NET 2.0

> **Note** For completeness, the ASP.NET 2.0 class diagram in Figure 7-2 had to be merged with the diagram shown in Figure 7-1 to include *BaseDataList* classes and the *Repeater* control. These are all fully supported in the newer version of the platform. List controls have been moved one level down in the *System.Web* hierarchy and now inherit from *DataBoundControl* instead of *WebControl*. The same is true of the *AdRotator* control, which inherits *WebControl* in ASP.NET 1.x and *DataBoundControl* in ASP.NET 2.0. (As you'll see in a moment, this doesn't break backward compatibility because *DataBoundControl* in turn inherits *WebControl*.)

The *DataBoundControl* Base Class

DataBoundControl is an abstract base class that defines the common characteristics of flat, nonhierarchical controls that use a data source. The class determines how a data-bound control binds to a collection of data items or to a data source object.

Remarkably, in ASP.NET 2.0 all data-bound controls—with the notable exceptions of *DataList*, *DataGrid*, and *Repeater*—share a common base class. You can group data-bound controls into three categories: simple, composite, and hierarchical controls. Before we look at each of these categories in more detail, let's briefly review the properties and methods that all data-bound controls share.

Properties of the *DataBoundControl* Class

The *DataBoundControl* class inherits from *WebControl* and can thus have all the visual and style properties defined on the base class. Examples of visual properties include *BackColor*, *ForeColor*, *Font*, *BorderStyle*, and the new *SkinID*. The *DataBoundControl* class also features infrastructural properties such as *Context*, *Page*, and *AccessKey*. The class declaration is shown here:

```
public abstract class DataBoundControl : WebControl
```

The *DataBoundControl* class declares only a few data-related properties, which are listed in Table 7-1.

Table 7-1 Data-Related Properties of *DataBoundControl*

Property	Description
DataMember	Selects the list of data that the control should bind to when the data source contains more than one list. For example, it specifies the name of the *DataTable* to pick up when the control is bound to a *DataSet*.
DataSource	Indicates the data source to bind to. The data source must be an object that implements the *IEnumerable* or *IListSource* interface.
DataSourceID	The ID of the data source object to use to retrieve data.

DataMember and *DataSource* are familiar to ASP.NET 1.x developers. In ASP.NET 2.0, they play exactly the same role as before. The *DataSourceID* property is different, however. It refers to the data source object. (Data source objects were discussed in Chapter 6.) The property gets and sets the ID of the bound data source object. Note that *DataSource* and *DataSourceID* cannot be set at the same time. If they are both set, an exception is thrown.

Methods of the *DataBoundControl* Class

The *DataBoundControl* class declares just one data-related public method—the well-known *DataBind* method. Pages and controls call this method when they need to pump data out of the data source:

```
public virtual void DataBind()
```

The method is used in the same way in ASP.NET 2.0, but its internal implementation has been slightly enhanced. In ASP.NET 1.x, the *DataBind* method fires the *DataBinding* event and then recursively invokes *DataBind* on child controls to perform the binding. In ASP.NET 2.0, the behavior of the method is more sophisticated because it has to take into account both old-fashioned, *IEnumerable*-based data sources as well as the new data source controls.

Simple Data-Bound Controls

The term *simple data-bound control* refers to Web controls that have a list-based user interface. The data source provides these controls with data items to populate a list of HTML markup elements. ASP.NET 2.0 has two types of simple data-bound controls—the *AdRotator* control and list controls.

The *AdRotator* Control

Introduced with ASP.NET 1.x, the *AdRotator* control displays an advertising banner on a Web page that changes whenever the page refreshes. The control retrieves ad information from a separate XML file. For each ad, the XML file contains the path to a descriptive image, the URL to go to when the control is clicked, and the frequency of the ad. In ASP.NET 1.x, the control inherits *WebControl* and is not specifically marked as a data-bound control.

The ASP.NET 2.0, the *AdRotator* control is extended to support arbitrary data sources using the default data-binding model. Basically, the ASP.NET 2.0 *AdRotator* control is the same as the one in version 1.x but with full support for data binding. The following code shows how to bind an ad rotator to a Microsoft Access database:

```
<asp:accessdatasource runat="server" id="MyAccessSource"
     DataFile="data/advert.mdb"
     SelectCommand="SELECT * FROM AdTable" />
<asp:adrotator id="Adrotator1" runat="server"
     ImageUrlField="Image"
     NavigateUrlField="Url"
     AlternateTextField="AltText"
     DataSourceID="MyAccessSource" />
```

Note that no matter what the effective data source is, the data passed to the *AdRotator* must match the expected schema format—the same XML schema of version 1.x:

```
<Advertisements>
  <Ad>
     <ImageUrl>images/20245.jpg</ImageUrl>
     <NavigateUrl>books/20245.aspx</NavigateUrl>
     <AlternateText>Get this Book Today!</AlternateText>
     <Keyword>Books</Keyword>
     <Impressions>50</Impressions>
  </Ad>
  ⋮
</Advertisements>
```

The ad records can be loaded from any valid data source as long as they have the correct schema.

> **Note** The *AdRotator* control has a couple of notable new features that aren't strictly related to data binding. In ASP.NET 2.0, the control supports the ability to create pop-up and pop-under ads, in addition to the standard banners. Pop-up and pop-under ads are created in their own window, above or below the browser's window for the page that contains the rotator.

For tracking purposes, the *AdRotator* control supports counters and updates them when an ad is clicked. You can associate each ad with its own counter.

The *BulletedList* Control

In ASP.NET 2.0, list controls are the same as in version 1.x, but with the notable addition of the *BulletedList* control. (Chapter 1 briefly introduced this control.) Typically, you use the *BulletedList* control to create a list of items formatted with bullets. Like all list controls, *BulletedList* allows you to specify individual items by defining a *ListItem* object for each desired entry:

```
<asp:bulletedlist runat="server"
     bulletimageurl="images/bullet.gif"
     bulletstyle="CustomImage">
     <asp:listitem>One</asp:listitem>
     <asp:listitem>Two</asp:listitem>
     <asp:listitem>Three</asp:listitem>
</asp:bulletedlist>
```

However, you usually don't statically generate the list items—you fill the bulleted list via its data binding capabilities. The following code snippet shows how:

```
<asp:SqlDataSource runat="server" id="MySource"
   ConnectionString="SERVER=…;DATABASE=northwind;UID=…;"
   DataSourceMode="DataSet"
   SelectCommand="SELECT customerid, companyname FROM customers
                  WHERE country='Italy' />
<asp:BulletedList runat="server" id="custList"
    BulletImageUrl="images/bullet.gif"
    BulletStyle="CustomImage"
    DisplayMode="LinkButton"
    DataSourceID="MySource"
    DataTextField="companyname" />
```

The bulleted list generated by the code is bound to a Microsoft SQL Server data source and receives the *DataTable* returned by the specified query. The *DataTextField* property selects the column to show, and *DisplayMode* sets the display mode—plain text, link buttons, or hyperlinks. In terms of user interface elements, the link button or hyperlink modes look the same. However, *HyperLink* mode links the page directly to an external URL and the click is handled entirely by the browser. In *LinkButton* mode, the click is handled by the ASP.NET runtime and originates a server-side event. To handle the click event on the server, you define a *OnClick* handler, as follows:

```
void OnClick(object sender, BulletedListEventArgs e)
{
   // Retrieve the item that was clicked
   int itemIndex = e.Index;
   ⋮
}
```

The *Index* property on the *BulletedListEventArgs* class contains the 0-based index of the list item that was clicked. You can customize the style of the bullet by using a personal image or by choosing one of the built-in styles. The *BulletStyle* property controls that.

Other List Controls

The *ListControl* class is an abstract class that provides common basic functionality for the *BulletedList* class and a few other controls. As shown in Figure 7-2, all the ASP.NET 1.x list controls inherit from *ListControl*. They are *DropDownList*, *ListBox*, *RadioButtonList*, and *CheckBoxList*.

All items displayed in the list control are stored in the *Items* collection. You can programmatically specify or determine the index of the selected item in the list control by using the *SelectedIndex* property. You can access the properties of the selected item by using the *SelectedItem* property. If you're interested only in the value of the selected item, use the *SelectedValue* property. The *SelectedIndexChanged* server event is fired whenever the user clicks to change the selection on the control. Note that this event doesn't automatically cause the page to post back unless the *AutoPostback* property is *true*.

ASP.NET 2.0 list controls work the same way as in version 1.x. The only significant difference is that version 2.0 controls also support data source objects through the *DataSourceID* property.

Composite Data-Bound Controls

Composite controls deserve special attention. A composite control manages a tree of child controls, and its output is obtained by merging the markup of the constituent components. In ASP.NET 1.x, the best practice with composite controls was a three-step approach: inherit a base class, build the controls tree, and make the control a naming container.

In ASP.NET 2.0, the architecture of composite controls has been enhanced, and two new base classes have been added—*CompositeControl* and *CompositeDataBoundControl*. As a result, the three steps are generally reduced to two—you derive from the composite base class and build the controls tree.

CompositeControl and *CompositeDataBoundControl* are separate classes with no hierarchical relationship, but they have a similar blueprint. The former addresses the needs of UI-oriented composite controls; the latter defines a common foundation for all composite data-bound controls.

Basic Behavior of Composite Controls

As mentioned, building a composite control in ASP.NET 1.x typically requires three steps. First the control inherits from one of the two control base classes—*WebControl* or *Control*. You choose the class according to your user interface requirements. The key difference between the two base classes is that *WebControl* has the extra visual properties. Typically, you inherit *Control* if you want to be able to control the rendering and assignment of colors, fonts, and border styles. This is a good approach if the layout of the control requires multiple background colors or fonts.

Second, the output of the control shouldn't be generated by overriding the *Render* method. Instead, you should override the *CreateChildControls* protected and virtual method. *CreateChildControls* is invoked just before the control is rendered. All you have to do is build the control tree by instantiating any child control and adding it to the *Controls* collection of the parent. The default implementation of *Render* can then easily iterate through the children and output the markup to the browser.

Last but not least, you should configure the control as a naming container so that any child control is named after its parent. The autogenerated ID for a child control is prefixed with the ID of the parent. This apparently minor change has important repercussions for how the control and its children work. By implementing the *INamingContainer* interface, you guarantee that any event raised by a child control is correctly captured and handled on the server. The *INamingContainer* interface is a marker interface with no methods at all, so to implement it you just add the name of the interface to the class declaration.

The *CompositeDataBoundControl* Class

The *CompositeDataBoundControl* class, which inherits from *DataBoundControl*, is marked as abstract and declares and implements the *Controls* property. The *Controls* property stores references to child controls. The *CompositeDataBoundControl* class also exposes the *CreateChildControls* method:

```
protected virtual int CreateChildControls(
    IEnumerable dataSource,
    bool dataBinding)
```

The behavior of the method depends on the Boolean argument. A value of *true* creates the actual control tree and a value of *false* re-creates the control hierarchy as the control reinitializes from view state. When the *dataBinding* parameter is *false*, the data source parameter is ignored and the child view state and the *Controls* collection are cleared. When the *dataBinding* parameter is *true*, the control creates the tree based on the data source.

In ASP.NET 1.x, *CreateChildControls* is called to accomplish a series of tasks, as shown in the following pseudocode:

```
void CreateChildControls()
{
   Controls.Clear();
   ClearChildViewState();
   TrackViewState();

   // TODO:: Create the controls tree

   ChildControlsCreated = true;
}
```

In ASP.NET 2.0, the programming model is simplified. The code just shown is embedded in a new protected method—*PerformDataBinding*. This method performs all necessary and boilerplate tasks and then calls your implementation of *CreateChildControls*. In other words, when you implement *CreateChildControls* in ASP.NET 2.0 composite controls, you only have to worry about building the control tree; the system does the rest.

Examples of Composite Data-Bound Controls

ASP.NET 2.0 defines a few key composite data-bound controls, such as *GridView*, *FormView*, and *DetailsView*. The *GridView* control can be considered the successor to the *DataGrid*, with the added ability to take advantage of data source controls. As you'll see in more detail in the section titled "The *GridView* Control," the *GridView* control supports several new features, including the built-in ability to sort, edit, page, select, and update data. In short, the *GridView* is what most developers wanted the ASP.NET 1.x *DataGrid* to be.

The *DetailsView* and *FormView* controls have no counterpart in ASP.NET 1.x. Both render a single record at a time from the associated data source, optionally providing paging buttons to navigate between records. The difference between the two is in the use of templates. The *DetailsView* control provides a flexible and customizable user interface but a fixed layout. The *FormView* control is fully templatized. As Figure 7-3 shows, a details view is similar to the Form view of an Access database.

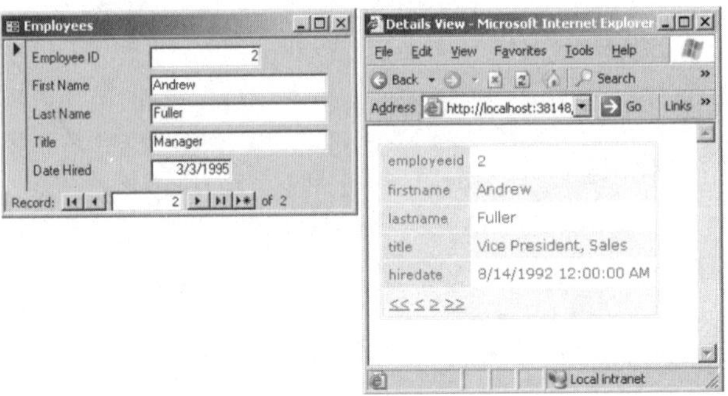

Figure 7-3 Comparing the Access Form view and the ASP.NET details view

The *DetailsView* and *FormView* controls are typically employed to update existing records and insert new ones. They fully benefit from and apply the new two-way binding model that was briefly mentioned in Chapter 5. Both controls lend themselves well to building master/detail views of data when used along with a *GridView* or a *DataGrid*.

Hierarchical Data-Bound Controls

The *HierarchicalDataBoundControl* class is the foundation of hierarchical data-bound controls such as *TreeView* and *Menu*. The class is marked as abstract and, unlike its fellow *CompositeDataBoundControl* class, doesn't provide significant built-in services. The class acts as a logical container for controls that consume hierarchical data. Two of these controls are the *TreeView* and the *Menu*.

Building a Tree-Based Data View

The *TreeView* control can bind to any data source object that supports the *IHierarchicalDataSource* interface. In Chapter 6, you saw examples of such objects, including *XmlDataSource* and *SiteMapDataSource*. The *TreeView* also exposes a *DataSource* property of type *Object*, which can be assigned an *XmlDocument* type. You can bind a *DataSet* with nested relations only if you first transform it into an *XmlDataDocument* or into plain XML. In the latter case, though, you must first set the XML string to the *Data* property of an *XmlDataSource* object and bind using the XML data source control.

By default, the *TreeView* binds XML nodes to its own nodes in a way that reflects the name of the node rather than a particular attribute or the inner text. The result is shown in the left pane of Figure 7-4. As you can see, it doesn't look particularly useful.

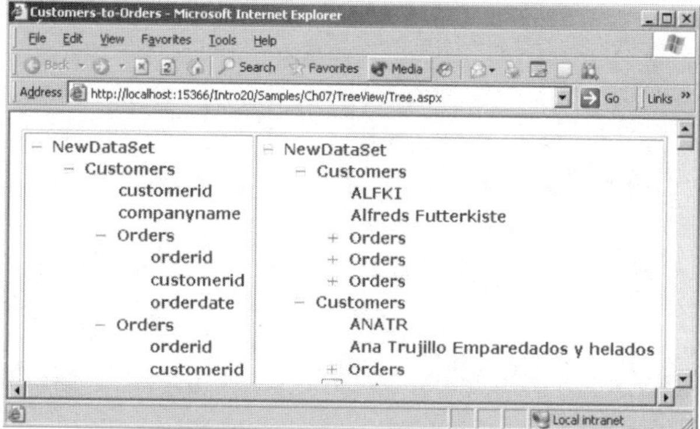

Figure 7-4 A *TreeView* control bound to XML hierarchical data

You can control the node-to-node association by using a bunch of binding parameters. In particular, you can bind the properties of a treeview node to a specific data source field by specifying tree node bindings. A *TreeNodeBinding* object defines the relationship between each data item and the node it is binding to.

```
<asp:treeview id="MyTree" runat="server" DataSourceId="XmlView">
     <DataBindings>
        <asp:TreeNodeBinding Depth="2" DataMember="customerid"
             TextField="#innertext"  />
     </DataBindings>
</asp:treeview>
```

To fully understand this example, consider the XML schema shown earlier in Figure 7-4. The node binding applies at level 2 and involves all the nodes named *customerid*. (The case is important.) By default, the *TreeView* node displays the value returned by the *ToString* method of the data item, which turns out to be just the node name. The *TextField* property of the *TreeNodeBinding* object changes this default to the specified attribute name or the inner text. As a result, the *customerid* node of Figure 7-4 is replaced by the inner text of the node at level 2, or by any other specified attribute. In addition to customizing the node text, you can indicate the ToolTip field, the image URL field, and the URL to navigate to when the node is clicked.

The *TreeView* control can also support graceful expand/collapse functionality, depending on client capabilities, and a customizable look and feel that includes tree node images, plus/minus indicators, selection check boxes, and styles. For performance reasons, individual treeview nodes are not rendered through controls but as plain text.

The *Menu* Control

Menus are pervasive in today's Web sites. ASP.NET 2.0 addresses this reality with a new control—the *Menu* control—to complete the end-to-end site navigation functionality in the ASP.NET control toolbox. The *Menu* control can be bound to any data source and also supports an explicit list of items for the simplest cases. Unlike the *TreeView*, the *Menu* control doesn't support the download-on-demand functionality that brings data down on the browser only when needed. (The *TreeView* does this using the script callback mechanism we discussed in Chapter 1.) This is because the download size of menu controls is typically small and the costs of such a complex feature wouldn't pay off.

An ASP.NET menu object consists of menu items (such as those shown in Figure 7-5) stored in a collection. *MenuItem* is the class that describes a single item, and *MenuItems* is the collection property that returns all the child items of a given menu. The control supports a few static and dynamic styles for constituent elements such as the selected item, submenus, and the item the mouse is currently hovering over. Dynamic styles are applied using the Dynamic HTML object model. An example of a dynamic style is one that is assigned to the menu item currently under the mouse. Static styles are programmatically set and never change after user actions.

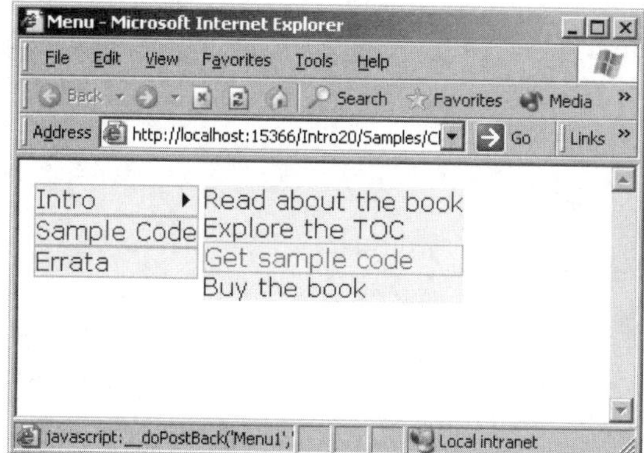

Figure 7-5 A simple *Menu* control in action

Here's a code snippet for the menu shown in the figure:

```
<asp:Menu ID="Menu1" Runat="server">
   <Items>
     <asp:MenuItem Text="Intro">
        <asp:MenuItem Text="Read about the book" />
        <asp:MenuItem Text="Explore the TOC" />
        <asp:MenuItem Text="Get sample code" />
        <asp:MenuItem Text="Buy the book" />
     </asp:MenuItem>
     <asp:MenuItem Text="Sample Code" />
     <asp:MenuItem Text="Errata" />
   </Items>
</asp:Menu>
```

The *GridView* Control

The *GridView* is a major upgrade of the ASP.NET 1.x *DataGrid* control. It provides the same set of capabilities, plus a long list of extensions and improvements. The *DataGrid*—which is still fully supported in ASP.NET 2.0—is an extremely powerful and versatile control, but it has one big drawback: it requires you to write a lot of custom code, even to handle relatively simple (but common) operations such as paging, sorting, editing, or deleting data. The *GridView* control was designed from the ground up to work around this limitation and make two-way data binding happen with as little code as possible. The control is tightly connected to the family of new data source controls and can handle direct data source updates as long as the underlying data source object supports these capabilities.

This virtually codeless two-way data binding is by far the most notable feature of the new *GridView* control, but the enhancements are numerous. The control improves over the *DataGrid* in many ways, including adding the ability to define multiple primary key fields, new column types, and style and templating options. The *GridView* also has an extended eventing model that allows you to handle or cancel events.

The *GridView* Object Model

The *GridView* control provides a tabular, grid-like view of the contents of a data source. Each column represents a data source field, and each row represents a record. The class is declared as follows:

```
public class GridView : CompositeDataBoundControl,
                        IPostBackEventHandler,
                        IPostBackContainer,
                        ICallbackContainer,
                        ICallbackEventHandler,
                        INamingContainer
```

The base class ensures data binding support. The implementation of the *IPostBackEventHandler* and *IPostBackContainer* interfaces allows the control to define a centralized console to handle all the server-side events that constituent controls (such as link buttons) might generate. Any users clicking make the page post back. The postback event is resolved, and control passes to the *RaisePostBackEvent* method on the interface. The method examines the command name carried by the event and decides what to do. Typically, it starts an update, select, or sort operation on the underlying data source. The *ICallbackContainer* and *ICallbackEventHandler* interfaces make possible more effective paging and sorting, supported through client-side, out-of-band calls using the new script callback technology. (See Chapter 1.)

Let's begin our tour of the *GridView* control by looking at the control's programming interface.

Properties of the *GridView*

The *GridView* supports a large set of properties that fall into the following broad categories: behavior, visual settings, style, state, and templates. Table 7-2 details the properties that affect the behavior of the *GridView*.

The *SortDirection* and *SortExpression* properties specify the direction and the sort expression on the column that currently determines the order of the rows. Both properties are set by the control's built-in sorting mechanism when users click a column's header. The whole sorting engine is enabled and disabled through the *AllowSorting* property. The *EnablePagingAndSortingCall-*

backs property toggles on and off the control's ability to use script callbacks to page and sort without doing roundtrips to the server to change the entire page.

Table 7-2 Behavior Properties of the *GridView* Control

Property	Description
AllowPaging	Indicates whether the control supports paging.
AllowSorting	Indicates whether the control supports sorting.
AutoGenerateColumns	Indicates whether columns are automatically created for each field in the data source. The default is *true*.
AutoGenerateDeleteButton	Indicates whether the control includes a button column to let users delete the record that is mapped to the clicked row.
AutoGenerateEditButton	Indicates whether the control includes a button column to let users edit the record that's mapped to the clicked row.
AutoGenerateSelectButton	Indicates whether the control includes a button column to let users select the record that's mapped to the clicked row.
EnablePagingAndSortingCallbacks	Indicates whether paging and sorting should be accomplished using script callback functions. Disabled by default.
SortDirection	A read-only property that gets the direction of the column current sort.
SortExpression	A read-only property that gets the current sort expression.
SummaryViewColumn	Indicates the name of the data column used to provide the summary of the record when the control renders on mobile devices.
UseAccessibleHeader	Specifies whether to render *<TH>* tags for the column headers instead of default *<TD>* tags.

Each row displayed within a *GridView* control corresponds to special type of a grid item. The list of predefined types of items is nearly identical to that of the *DataGrid* and includes items such as the header, rows and alternating rows, footer, and pager. These items are static in the sense that they remain in place for the lifetime of the control in the application. Other types of items are active for a short period of time—the time needed to accomplish a certain operation. Dynamic items are the edit and the selected row templates. New types are the *EmptyData* item, which identifies the body of the grid when bound to an empty data source, and the items introduced for adaptive rendering on mobile devices. The *SummaryTitle*, *DetailLink*, and *DetailTitle* items belong to this group. Each item type has a made-to-measure style property. Table 7-3 details the style properties available on the *GridView* control.

Table 7-3 Style Properties of the *GridView* Control

Style	Description
AlternatingRowStyle	Defines the style properties for every other row displayed in the table
DetailLinkStyle	Defines the style properties for the links in the details view of the control when it's rendered on mobile devices
DetaillTitleStyle	Defines the style properties for the title in the details view of the control when it's rendered on mobile devices
EditRowStyle	Defines the style properties for the row being edited
EmptyDataRowStyle	Defines the style properties for the *EmptyData* row, which is rendered when the *GridView* is bound to empty data sources
FooterStyle	Defines the style properties for the grid's footer
HeaderStyle	Defines the style properties for the grid's header
PagerStyle	Defines the style properties for the grid's pager
RowStyle	Defines the style properties for the rows displayed in the table
SelectedRowStyle	Defines the style properties for the row currently being selected
SummaryTitleStyle	Defines the style properties for the title in the summary view of the control when it's rendered on mobile devices

Table 7-4 lists most of the properties that affect the appearance of the control, and Table 7-5 details the templating properties.

Table 7-4 Appearance Properties of the *GridView* Control

Property	Description
BackImageUrl	Indicates the URL to an image to display in the background
CellPadding	Indicates the amount of space (in pixels) between the contents of a cell and the border
CellSpacing	Indicates the amount of space (in pixels) between cells

Table 7-4 Appearance Properties of the *GridView* Control

Property	Description
DetailNextRowText	Indicates the text for the link to the next row in the details view on mobile devices
DetailPreviousRowText	Indicates the text for the link to the previous row in the details view on mobile devices
DetailSummaryText	Indicates the text for the link to the summary view when the control is rendering on a mobile device
GridLines	Indicates the gridline style for the control
HorizontalAlign	Indicates the horizontal alignment of the control on the page
EmptyDataText	Indicates the text to render in the control when it's bound to an empty data source
PagerSettings	Gets a reference to the *PagerSettings* object that lets you set the properties of the pager buttons
ShowFooter	Indicates whether the footer row is displayed
ShowHeader	Indicates whether the header row is displayed

The *PagerSettings* object groups together all the visual properties you can set on the pager—including the *Mode*, *NextPageText*, *PageButtonCount*, and *PreviousPageText* properties, which will sound familiar to *DataGrid* programmers. The *PagerSettings* class also adds some new properties to accommodate new predefined buttons (first and last pages) and the use of images instead of text in the links.

Table 7-5 Templating Properties of the *GridView* Control

Template	Description
EmptyDataTemplate	Indicates the template content to be rendered when the *GridView* is bound to an empty source. This property takes precedence over *EmptyDataText* if both are set. If neither is set, the grid isn't rendered if it's bound to an empty data source.
PagerTemplate	Indicates the template content to be rendered for the pager. This property overrides any settings you might have made through the *PagerSettings* property.

The final block of properties—the state properties—is shown in Table 7-6. State properties return information about the internal state of the control.

Table 7-6 State Properties

Property	Description
BottomPagerRow	Returns a *GridViewRow* object that represents the bottom pager of the grid.
Column	Gets a collection of objects that represent the columns in the grid. Note that this collection is always empty if columns are autogenerated.
DataKeyNames	Gets and sets an array that contains the names of the primary key fields for the currently displayed items.
DataKeys	Gets a collection of *DataKey* objects that represent the values of the primary key fields set in *DataKeyNames* for the currently displayed records.
EditIndex	Gets and sets the 0-based index that identifies the row currently rendered in edit mode.
FooterRow	Returns a *GridViewRow* object that represents the footer of the grid.
HeaderRow	Returns a *GridViewRow* object that represents the header of the grid.
PageCount	Gets the number of pages required to display the records of the data source.
PageIndex	Gets and sets the 0-based index that identifies the currently displayed page of data.
PageSize	Indicates the number of records to display on a page.
Rows	Gets a collection of *GridViewRow* objects that represent the data rows currently displayed in the control.
SelectedDataKey	Returns the *DataKey* object for the currently selected record.
SelectedIndex	Gets and sets the 0-based index that identifies the row currently selected.
SelectedRow	Returns a *GridViewRow* object that represents the currently selected row.
SelectedValue	Returns the explicit value of the key as stored in the *DataKey* object. Similar to *SelectedDataKey*.
TopPagerRow	Returns a *GridViewRow* object that represents the top pager of the grid.

If you're an experienced *DataGrid* programmer, you'll notice many similarities between *GridView* and *DataGrid*. The *GridView* control is designed to leverage the new data source object model, and it accepts its data through the *DataSourceID* property. The control also supports the *DataSource* property, but if you bind data in that way, some of the features (such as built-in updates and paging) become unavailable. Despite the similarities, 100 percent code compatibility is impossible to achieve. In ASP.NET 2.0 code, you should use the *GridView* control.

Events of the *GridView* Control

The *GridView* control doesn't have methods other than the well-known *DataBind* method. As mentioned, though, in many situations you don't need to call methods on the *GridView* control. The data binding process is started implicitly when you bind a data source control with a data-bound control such as the *GridView*.

In ASP.NET 2.0, many controls, and the *Page* class itself, feature pairs of events of the type doing/done. Key operations in the control life cycle are wrapped by a pair of events—one firing before the operation takes place and one firing immediately after the operation is completed. The *GridView* class is no exception. The list of events is shown in Table 7-7.

Table 7-7 Events Fired by the *GridView* Control

Event	Description
PageIndexChanging, *PageIndexChanged*	Both events occur when one of the pager buttons is clicked. They fire before and after the grid control handles the paging operation, respectively.
RowCancelingEdit	Occurs when the Cancel button of a row in edit mode is clicked, but before the row exits edit mode.
RowCommand	Occurs when a button is clicked.
RowCreated	Occurs when a row is created.
RowDataBound	Occurs when a data row is bound to data.
RowDeleting, *RowDeleted*	Both events occur when a row's Delete button is clicked. They fire before and after the grid control deletes the row, respectively.
RowEditing	Occurs when a row's Edit button is clicked but before the control enters edit mode.
RowUpdating, *RowUpdated*	Both events occur when a row's Update button is clicked. They fire before and after the grid control updates the row, respectively.
SelectedIndexChanging, *SelectedIndexChanged*	Both events occur when a row's Select button is clicked. The two events occur before and after the grid control handles the select operation, respectively.
Sorting, *Sorted*	Both events occur when the hyperlink to sort a column is clicked. They fire before and after the grid control handles the sort operation, respectively.

RowCreated and *RowDataBound* events are the same as the *DataGrid ItemCreated* and *ItemDataBound* events, with new names. They behave exactly as they do in ASP.NET 1.x. The same is true of the *RowCommand* event, which is the same as the *DataGrid ItemCommand* event.

The availability of events that announce a certain operation significantly enhances your programming power. By hooking the *RowUpdating* event, you can cross-check what is being updated and what the new values are. For example, you might want to handle the *RowUpdating* event to HTML-encode the values supplied by the client before they are persisted to the underlying data store. This simple trick helps you to fend off script injections.

The *GridView* Control in Action

The programming interface of the *GridView* control was designed to be as close as possible to that of the *DataGrid*. This doesn't mean that the existing code of the *DataGrid* is 100 percent compatible with a *GridView*, however. Several events and properties have been renamed (for example, *ItemCreated* has been renamed *RowCreated*), and some have been slightly extended (for example, the *DataKeyField* string property is now the *DataKeyNames* array).

In addition, the *GridView* fully supports the data source object model of the new ASP.NET data controls. The *GridView* supports the *DataGrid* programming model but is better suited to working with data source objects.

Simple Data Binding

The following code demonstrates the simplest way to bind data to a *GridView* control. The data source object keeps the page virtually code-free.

```
<asp:TextBox runat="server" ID="Initial" MaxLength="1" />
<asp:SqlDataSource runat="server" ID="MySource"
     ConnectionString="SERVER=…;DATABASE=northwind;UID=…;"
     SelectCommand="SELECT companyname, country FROM customers
                    WHERE companyname LIKE @Initial + '%'">
  <SelectParameters>
     <asp:ControlParameter Name="Initial" ControlId="Initial"
          PropertyName="Text" />
  </SelectParameters>
</asp:SqlDataSource>
<asp:GridView runat="server" id="grid" DataSourceID="MySource"  />
```

Setting the *DataSourceID* property triggers the binding process, which runs the data source query and populates the user interface of the grid. You need not write any code. Note that if you replace the *<asp:gridview>* tag with the corresponding *DataGrid* markup, the final effect—at least in this simple case—is the same. (See Figure 7-6.)

Figure 7-6 The *GridView* in action in a simple scenario

Working with an Empty Data Source

If no data source property is set, the *GridView* control doesn't render. If an empty data source object is bound and an *EmptyDataTemplate* template is specified, the results shown to the user have a more friendly look:

```
<asp:gridview runat="server" datasourceid="MySource">
   <emptydatatemplate>
      <asp:label runat="server">
         There's no data to show in this view.
      </asp:label>
   </emptydatatemplate>
</asp:gridview>
```

The *EmptyDataTemplate* property is ignored if the bound data source is not empty. Figure 7-7 shows the output generated by the empty template.

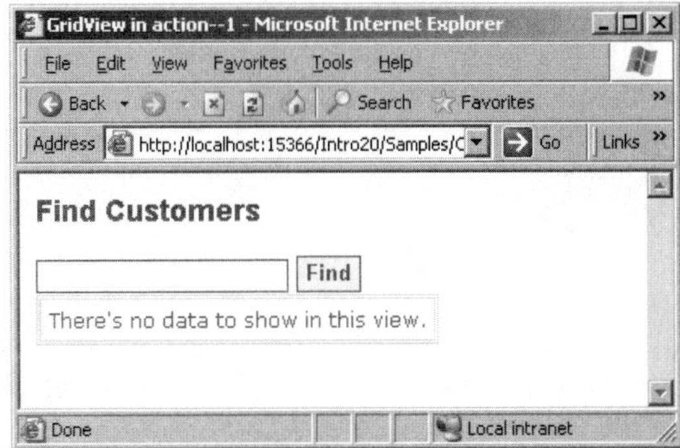

Figure 7-7 The *GridView* in action on an empty data source

Adaptive Rendering

Another important difference between the *DataGrid* and *GridView* controls is that the adaptive rendering engine of Visual Studio 2005 server controls enables the *GridView* to adapt its HTML output to the characteristics of the browser (with special attention paid to mobile devices). Because of their limited screen size, mobile devices often require that the control reorganize the output to make it fit. For devices with small screens, the *GridView* shows only a single record per page and provides additional links to move between records. The initial screen displays only a single column of data defined by the *SummaryViewColumn* property. The *DetailLink* item represents the link to the rest of the current record.

Displaying Data

The most common use of a grid control is to display the results of a database query in a read-only grid for reporting purposes. The *GridView* control makes this easier than ever. You set up a data source object, providing the connection string and the query, and assign the *DataSourceID* property of the *GridView* to the ID of the data source control. At run time, the *GridView* binds to the source and generates appropriate columns of data. By default, however, all the columns in the query are displayed in the grid.

Like the *DataGrid* control, the *GridView* supports custom column fields through the *Columns* collection. If you want to display only a subset of the retrieved data fields or if you simply want to customize their appearance, you can populate the *Columns* collection with objects that represent columns of data. The *GridView* supports a variety of column types, including hyperlink, image, and check box columns.

Configuring Columns

When you use a declared set of columns, the *AutoGenerateColumns* property of the grid is typically set to *false*. However, this is not a strict requirement—a grid can have declared and autogenerated columns. In this case, declared columns appear first. Note also that autogenerated columns are not added to the *Columns* collection. As a result, when column autogeneration is used, the *Columns* collection is empty.

The *Columns* property is a collection of *DataControlField* objects. The *DataControlField* object logically corresponds to the *DataGrid*'s *DataGridColumn* object. It has a more general name because these field objects can be reused in other data-bound controls that do not necessarily render columns (such as the *DetailsView* control). You can define your columns either declaratively or programmatically. In the latter case, you just instantiate any needed data field objects and add them to the *Columns* collection. Columns of data are displayed in the order that the column fields appear in the collection.

```
BoundField field = new BoundField();
field.DataField = "companyname";
field.HeaderText = "Company Name";
grid.ColumnFields.Add(field);
```

To statically declare your columns in the .aspx source file, you use the *<Columns>* tag, as shown here:

```
<columns>
   <asp:boundfield datafield="customerid" headertext="ID" />
   <asp:boundfield datafield="companyname" headertext="Company Name" />
</columns>
```

Table 7-8 lists the column field classes that can be used in a *GridView* control. All the classes inherit *DataControlField*.

Table 7-8 Supported Column Types in *GridView* Controls

Type	Description
BoundField	Default column type. Displays the value of a field as plain text.
ButtonField	Displays the value of a field as a command button. You can choose the link or the push button style. When clicked, the page posts back and fires a *RowCommand* server event.
CheckBoxField	Displays the value of a field as a check box. It is commonly used to render Boolean values.
CommandField	Enhanced version of *ButtonField* that represents special commands such as Edit, Delete, and Select.
HyperLinkField	Displays the value of a field as a hyperlink. When you use this type, you normally bind one data field for the hyperlink's text and one for the hyperlink's URL. When the hyperlink is clicked, the browser navigates to the specified URL. *HyperLinkField* accepts an array of data fields to build multiparameter URLs.
ImageField	Displays the value of a field as an image. The image can come from a database or be specified through a URL.
TemplateField	Displays user-defined content for each item in the column. You use this column type when you want to create a custom column field. The template can contain any number of data fields combined with literals, images, and other controls.

All these classes inherit the base class *DataControlField*. Table 7-9 lists the main properties shared by all column types.

Table 7-9 Common Properties of *GridView* Columns

Property	Description
FooterStyle	Gets the style object for the column's footer.
FooterText	Gets and sets the text for the column's footer.
HeaderImageUrl	Gets and sets the URL of the image to place in the column's header.
HeaderStyle	Gets the style object for the column's header.
HeaderText	Gets and sets the text for the column's header.
ItemStyle	Gets the style object for the various columns' cells.
ShowHeader	Indicates whether the column's header is rendered.
SortExpression	Gets and sets the expression used to sort the grid contents when the column's header is clicked. Typically, this string property is set to the name of the bound data field.

The properties listed in the table represent a subset of the properties that each column type actually provides. In particular, each type of column defines a tailor-made set of properties to define and configure the bound field.

Figure 7-8 shows a few of these columns in action.

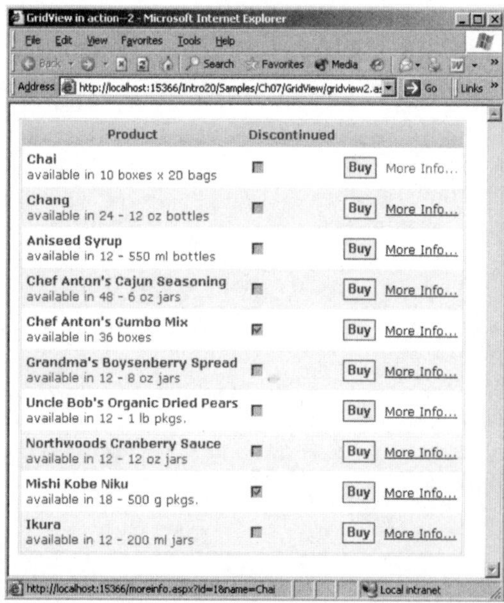

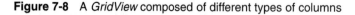

Figure 7-8 A *GridView* composed of different types of columns

The following listing shows the markup code behind the grid in the figure:

```
<columns>
   <asp:boundfield datafield="productname" headertext="Product" />
   <asp:checkboxfield datafield="discontinued"
        headertext="Discontinued" />
   <asp:buttonfield buttontype="Button" text="Buy" />
   <asp:hyperlinkfield text="More Info..."
        datanavigateurlfields="productid,productname"
        datanavigateurlformatstring="/moreinfo.aspx?id={0}&name={1}" />
</columns>
```

The name of the product is displayed using a *BoundField* object. The Discontinued column clearly renders a Boolean value. The sample button column allows you to add the product to the shopping cart; the hyperlink can navigate to a page with more information about the product. In the sample, the button column shows a fixed text for all data items. You get this by setting the *Text* property on the *ButtonField* class. If you want to bind the button text to a particular field on the current data item, you set the *DataTextField* property to the name of that field.

The same pattern applies to the hyperlink column field in regard to the caption of displayed hyperlinks. The URL can be set in either of two ways: through a direct binding to a data source field or by using a hardcoded URL with a customized query string. The second approach is illustrated in the previous sample. You choose the direct binding if the URL is stored in one of the data source fields. In this case, you set the *DataNavigateUrlFields* property to the name of the column. In some situations, though, the URL to access is application-specific and not stored in the data source. In this case, you can set the *DataNavigateUrlFormatString* property with a hardcoded URL and with an array of parameters in the query string. The actual value of the parameters is determined by the comma-separated list of field names passed to the *DataNavigateUrlFields* property. In the example, the product ID and name are used to select the information to show in the helper moreinfo.aspx page. This behavior extends that of the *DataGrid*'s hyperlink column in that it supports multiple parameters.

> **Note** You can format the text displayed in each column by using the *DataTextFormatString* property. The value of the data row is identified by the {0} placeholder.

Templated Fields

A *TemplateField* column gives each row in the grid a personalized user interface that is completely defined by the page developer. You can define templates for various rendering stages, including the default view, in-place editing, header, and footer. The supported templates are listed in Table 7-10.

Table 7-10 Supported Templates

Template	Description
AlternatingItemTemplate	Defines the contents and appearance of alternating rows. If not specified, the *ItemTemplate* is used.
EditItemTemplate	Defines the contents and appearance of the row currently being edited. This template should contain input fields and possibly validators.
FooterTemplate	Defines the contents and appearance of the row's footer.
HeaderTemplate	Defines the contents and appearance of the row's header.
ItemTemplate	Defines the default contents and appearance of the rows.

A templated view can contain anything that makes sense to the application you're building—server controls, literals, and data-bound expressions. Data-bound expressions allow you to insert values contained in the current data row. You can use as many fields as needed in a template. Notice, though, that not all templates support data-bound expressions. The header and the footer template are not data-bound, and any attempt to use expressions will result in an exception.

The following code shows how to define the item template for a product column. The column displays on two lines and includes the name of the product and some information about the packaging. You use data-bound expressions (see Chapter 5) to refer to data fields.

```
<asp:templatefield headertext="Product">
    <itemtemplate>
       <b><%# Eval("productname")%></b> <br />
       available in <%# Eval("quantityperunit")%>
    </itemtemplate>
</asp:templatefield>
```

> **Note** The *TemplateField* class also features an *InsertTemplate* property. However, this type of template is never used by the *GridView* control. The *InsertTemplate* is used by the *FormView* control instead. As mentioned earlier, in ASP.NET 2.0 view controls share some field classes, such as *TemplateField*. As a result, *TemplateField* (and a few more classes) provide a superset of properties that serve the needs of multiple view controls.

Sorting Data

The *GridView* is designed to take advantage of specific capabilities of the underlying data source control. In this way, the grid control can handle common operations on data such as sorting, paging, updating, and deleting. In general, not all data source components support all possible and feasible data operations. Data source components expose Boolean properties (such as the *CanSort* property) to signal whether they can perform a given operation. The *GridView* makes transparent for the page developer the implementation of commonly required features such as sorting and paging.

To enable sorting on a *GridView*, the following code would suffice. As you can see, it is a small fraction of the code required to code the same feature on a *DataGrid*. More important, if you don't need more advanced capabilities (such as a glyph in the header indicating the direction), setting up sorting requires no code at all.

```
<asp:gridview runat="server" id="MyGridView" DataSourceID="MySource"
   AllowSorting="true" AutoGenerateColumns="false">
   <Columns>
      <asp:boundfield datafield="productname" headertext="Product"
           sortexpression="productname" />
      <asp:boundfield datafield="quantityperunit"
           headertext="Packaging" />
   </Columns>
</asp:gridview>
```

When you run this code, each column that has a nonempty *SortExpression* property displays its header text as a hyperlink. When a user clicks there, the page posts back and returns with the grid's contents sorted accordingly. Note that if you click twice on the same column, the order reverts. This is a slick feature that required quite a bit of coding in ASP.NET 1.x. The *GridView*'s *SortExpression* and *SortDirection* read-only properties return at any time the current sort expression and direction.

> **Note** When the *GridView* control fires the *Sorting* event, the *SortExpression* and *SortDirection* properties haven't been updated yet. When *Sorted* fires, the properties are up-to-date. If you click twice on the same column, the *SortDirection* property will contain, say, Ascending in *Sorting* and Descending in *Sorted*.

The *GridView* control doesn't automatically add any visual element to the output that indicates the direction of the sorting. This is one of the few cases in which some coding is needed to complete sorting:

```
<script runat="server">
void MyGridView_RowCreated (object sender, GridViewRowEventArgs e) {
    if (e.Row.RowType == DataControlRowType.Header)
       AddGlyph(MyGridView, e.Row);
}

void AddGlyph(GridView grid, GridViewRow item) {
   Label glyph = new Label();
   glyph.EnableTheming = false;
   glyph.Font.Name = "webdings";
   glyph.Font.Size = FontUnit.XSmall;
   glyph.Text = (grid.SortDirection==SortDirection.Ascending ?" 5" :" 6");

   // Find the column you sorted by
   for(int i=0; i<grid.Columns.Count; i++) {
      string colExpr = grid.ColumnFields[i].SortExpression;
      if (colExpr != "" && colExpr == grid.SortExpression)
         item.Cells[i].Controls.Add (glyph);
   }
}
</script>
```

The idea is that you write a handler for the *RowCreated* event and look for the moment when the header is created. Next you create a new *Label* control that represents the glyph you want to add. Where should the *Label* control be added?

The newly created *Label* control has font and text adequately set to generate a glyph (typically ▲ and ▼) that indicates the direction of the sorting. You must add it alongside the header text of the clicked column. The index of the column can be stored to the view state during the *Sorting* event. Alternatively, it can simply be retrieved, comparing the current sort expression—the grid's *SortExpression* property—to the column's sort expression. Once you know the index of the column, you retrieve the corresponding table cells and add the *Label*:

```
item.Cells[i].Controls.Add (glyph);
```

The results are shown in Figure 7-9. If your page is based on a theme, the font of the *Label* control—essential for rendering the glyph correctly—might be overridden. To avoid that, you should disable theming support for the label control. The *EnableTheming* property does just that.

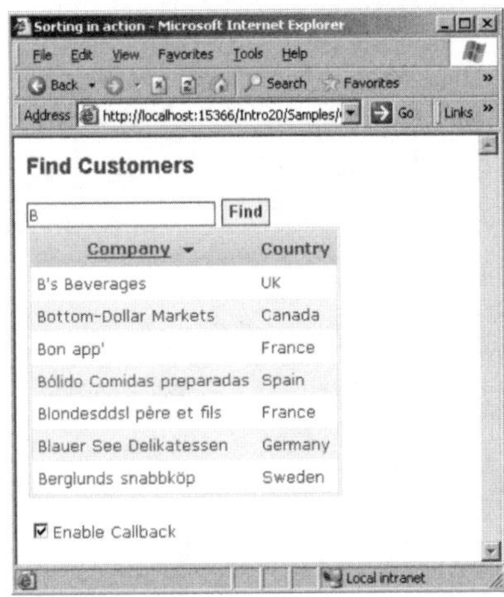

Figure 7-9 Enhancing the sorting capabilities of the *GridView* control

One more item worth mentioning about sorting on a *GridView* control is that you can cancel the sorting operation if need be. You write a handler for the *Sorting* event, get the event argument data (an object of type *GridViewSortEventArgs*), and set its *Cancel* property to *true*. The following code snippet shows how to cancel sorting if the grid is in edit mode:

```
void MyGridView_Sorting(object sender, GridViewSortEventArgs e) {
   if (e.EditIndex > -1) {
       e.Cancel = true;
   }
```

> **Note** As you can see, Figure 7-9 contains a check box to enable callbacks. When that check box is selected, the Boolean *EnablePaging-AndSortingCallbacks* property on the *GridView* is set to *true*. As a result, sorting and paging operations take place without refreshing the whole page. In other words, the page doesn't post back as a whole, but issues an out-of-band call to retrieve the new records to display. When the records are downloaded completely, an internal script call-back function is invoked to update the user interface through Dynamic HTML. This feature requires Internet Explorer 5.5 or later.

Paging Data

The ability to scroll a potentially large set of data is an important but challenging feature for modern, distributed applications. An effective paging mechanism allows customers to interact with a database without holding resources. Like the *DataGrid*, the *GridView* control provides a built-in mechanism for paging over the supplied data source. This form of paging requires that the whole data source be bound to the control. In other words, the *GridView* gets the whole result set from the data source object, caches it internally, and then pages through it.

To enable paging, all you do is enable paging capabilities on the control. The property to use is *AllowPaging*. The following code extends the previous page to support paging:

```
<asp:gridview runat="server" id="MyGridView" datasourceid="MySource"
   autogeneratecolumns="false"
   allowpaging="true" allowsorting="true"
   onrowcreated="MyGridView_RowCreated" >
   <pagersettings firstpagetext="7" lastpagetext="8"
        nextpagetext="4" prevpagetext="3" mode="NextPrevFirstLast" />
   <pagerstyle font-name="webdings" />
   <columnfields>
       <asp:boundfield datafield="productname"
            headertext="Product" sortexpression="productname" />
       <asp:boundfield datafield="quantityperunit"
            headertext="Packaging" />
   </columnfields>
</asp:gridview>
```

When the *AllowPaging* property is set to *true*, the grid displays a pager bar. You can control the characteristics of the pager to a large extent through the *<PagerSettings>* and *<PagerStyle>* tags or their equivalent properties. Unlike the *DataGrid*, the *GridView* pager supports first and last page buttons and lets you assign an image to each button. (This is also possible in version 1.x, but it requires a lot of code.) The pager can work in either of two modes—displaying explicit page numbers or providing a relative navigation system. In the former case, the pager contains numeric links, one representing a page index. In the latter case, buttons are present to navigate to the next or previous page and even to the first or the last. Ad hoc properties—*NextPageText* and *PreviousPageText*—let you set the labels for these buttons as desired. Figure 7-10 shows the page in action.

Figure 7-10 A sortable and pageable *GridView*

Note that the *GridView* control doesn't have an equivalent to the *DataGrid*'s *AllowCustomPaging* property nor limits to exploit the paging capabilities of the underlying data source. Whether page data is queried at every postback or is simply retrieved from some cache doesn't depend on the *GridView* control.

Editing Data

A major strength of the *GridView* control—which makes up for a major shortcoming of the *DataGrid*—is the ability to handle updates to the data source. The *DataGrid* control provides only an infrastructure for data editing. The *DataGrid* provides the necessary user interface elements and fires appropriate events when the user modifies the value of a certain data field, but it does not submit those changes back to the data source. Developers are left with the disappointing realization that they have to write a huge amount of boilerplate code to really persist changes using the *DataGrid* control.

With the *GridView* control, when the bound data source supports updates, the control can automatically perform this operation, thus providing a truly out-of-the-box solution. The data source control signals its capability to update through the *CanUpdate* Boolean property.

Much like the *DataGrid*, the *GridView* can render a column of command buttons for each row in the grid. These special command columns contain buttons to edit or delete the current record. With the *DataGrid*, you must explicitly create an edit command column using a special column type—the *EditCommandColumn* class. The *GridView* simplifies things quite a bit for update and delete operations.

In-Place Editing and Updates

In-place editing refers to the grid's ability to support changes to the currently displayed records. You enable in-place editing on a grid view by turning on the *AutoGenerateEditButton* Boolean property:

```
<asp:gridview runat="server" id="MyGridView" datasourceid="MySource"
    autogeneratecolumns="false" autogenerateeditbutton="true">
:
</asp:gridview>
```

When the *AutoGenerateEditButton* property is set to *true*, the *GridView* displays an additional column, like that shown in Figure 7-11.

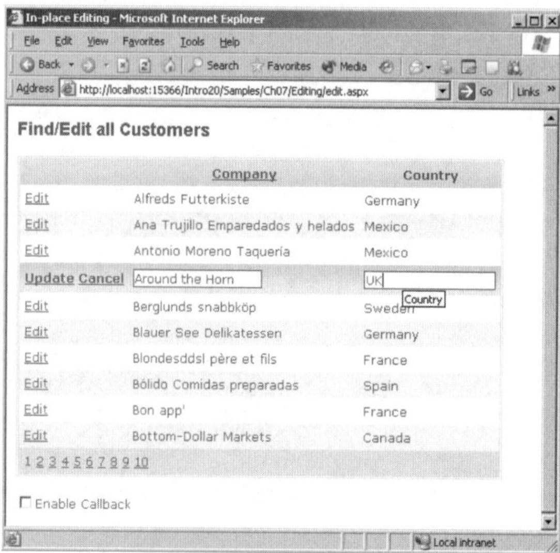

Figure 7-11 A *GridView* that supports editing

When you click to update, the *GridView* searches for an appropriate command object on the underlying data source. As you saw in Chapter 6, a data source object can have a number of command object properties (such as *InsertCommand*, *UpdateCommand*, and *DeleteCommand*), each of which is responsible for the corresponding data operation. When you click to update, the *GridView* fires the *RowUpdating* event and then checks the *CanUpdate* property on the data source. If *CanUpdate* returns *false*, an exception is thrown. Otherwise, the *UpdateCommand* object is invoked to update data. The code is surprisingly compact and simple to write. More important, the exposure to the SQL language is limited to defining the structure of the command; parameters are handled by the *GridView* code! To persist changes when the user clicks Update, you design your code according to the following scheme:

```
<form runat="server">
   <asp:sqldatasource runat="server" id="MySource"
      connectionstring="SERVER=…;DATABASE=northwind;UID=…;"
      datasourcemode="DataSet"
      selectcommand="SELECT employeeid, firstname, lastname
                     FROM employees"
      updatecommand="UPDATE employees SET
                     firstname=@firstname, lastname=@lastname
                     WHERE employeeid=@employeeid">
   </asp:sqldatasource>

   <asp:gridview runat="server" id="MyGridView" datasourceid="MySource"
        AutoGenerateColumns="false"
        DataKeyNames="employeeid" AutoGenerateEditButton="true">
        <columns>
            <asp:boundfield datafield="firstname" headertext="First" />
            <asp:boundfield datafield="lastname" headertext="Last" />
        </columns>
   </asp:gridview>
</form>
```

The *UpdateCommand* attribute is set to the SQL command to use. When you write the command, you declare as many parameters as needed. However, if you stick with a particular naming convention, parameter values are automatically resolved. Parameters that represent fields to update (such as firstname) must match the name of the *DataField* property of a grid column. The parameter used in the WHERE clause to identify the working record must match the *DataKeyNames* property—the key field for the displayed records. Finally, if *UpdateCommand* isn't defined, *CanUpdate* returns *false* and an exception is thrown if you try to submit changes. The successful completion of an update command is signaled using the *RowUpdated* event.

> **Note** The *GridView* collects values from the input fields and populates a dictionary of name/value pairs that indicate the new values for each field of the row. The *GridView* also exposes a *RowUpdating* event that allows the programmer to modify the parameters or values being passed to the data source object. In addition, the *GridView* automatically calls *Page.IsValid* before invoking the *Update* operation on the associated data source. If *Page.IsValid* returns *false*, the operation is canceled, which is especially useful if you're using a custom template with validators.

Deleting Displayed Records

From the *GridView*'s standpoint, deleting records is not much different from updating. In both cases, the *GridView* takes advantage of a data source ability to perform data operations. You enable record deletion by specifying a value of *true* for the *AutoGenerateDeleteButton* property. The *GridView* renders a column of buttons that, if clicked, invokes the *Delete* command for the row on the data source. The data source method is passed a dictionary of key field name/value pairs that are used to uniquely identify the row to delete.

```
<asp:sqldatasource runat="server" id="MySource"
     connectionstring="SERVER=…;DATABASE=northwind;UID=…;"
     datasourcemode="DataSet"
     ⋮
     deletecommand="DELETE employees WHERE
                    employeeid=@employeeid">
</asp:sqldatasource>

<asp:gridview runat="server" id="MyGridView" datasourceid="MySource"
       datakeynames="employeeid"  autogeneratecolumns="false"
       autogenerateeditbutton="true" autogeneratedeletebutton="true">
   <columns>
      <asp:boundfield datafield="firstname" headertext="First" />
      <asp:boundfield datafield="lastname" headertext="Last" />
   </columns>
</asp:gridview>
```

Figure 7-12 shows a grid that supports record deletion.

The *GridView* doesn't provide any feedback about the operation that will take place. Before proceeding, it calls *Page.IsValid*, which is useful if you have a custom template with validators. In addition, the *RowDeleting* event gives you another chance to programmatically control the legitimacy of the operation.

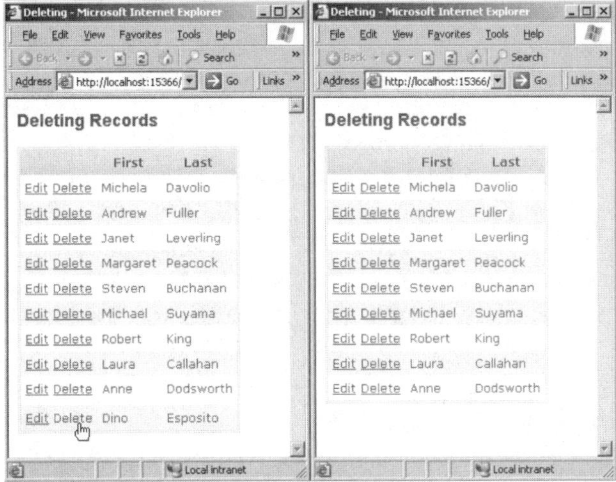

Figure 7-12 When the user clicks the Delete button, the underlying data source is invoked to physically delete the corresponding record.

> **Note** The delete operation fails if the record can't be deleted because of database-specific constraints. For example, the record can't be deleted if child records refer to it through a relationship. In this case, an exception is thrown.

Inserting New Records

In its current form, the *GridView* control doesn't support inserting data against a data source object. This omission is due to the *GridView* implementation and not to the capabilities and characteristics of the underlying data source. In fact, the data source object provides a *CanInsert* property and supports an *InsertCommand* property.

As you'll see in a moment, the insertion of new records is a scenario fully supported by the *DetailsView* and *FormView* controls.

> **Note** In ASP.NET 1.x, it is common practice to make *DataGrid* controls support record insertions by modifying the footer or the pager to make room for empty text boxes and buttons. The *GridView* supports the same model and makes it slightly simpler through the *PagerTemplate* property. This property, in fact, lets you define a custom template for the pager bar where you can subsequently arrange any combination of controls.

The *DetailsView* Control

Many applications need to work on a single record at a time. ASP.NET 1.x has no built-in support for this scenario. Creating a single record view is possible, but it requires some coding. You have to fetch the record, bind its fields to a data-bound form, and optionally provide paging buttons to navigate between records. Displaying the contents of a single record is a common practice when you build master/detail views. Typically, the user selects a master record from a grid, and the application drills down to show all the available fields.

In ASP.NET 2.0, the *DetailsView* fulfills this role. It is the ideal complement to the *GridView* control for building, easily and effectively, hierarchical views of data.

Like the *GridView*, the *DetailsView* control can bind to any data source control and exploit its set of data operations. It can page, update, insert, and delete data items in the underlying data source as long as the data source supports these operations. In most cases, no code is required to set up any of these operations. You can customize the user interface of the *DetailsView* control by choosing the most appropriate combination of data fields and styles, in much the same way that you do with the *GridView*. Finally, the *DetailsView* control fully supports adaptive rendering and renders successfully on mobile devices.

The *DetailsView* control deliberately doesn't support templates. A fully templatized details view control is the *FormView*, which we'll cover shortly.

The *DetailsView* Object Model

The *DetailsView* is to a single record what a *GridView* is to a page of records. Just as the grid lets you choose which columns to display, the *DetailsView* allows you to select a subset of fields to display in read-only or read/write fashion. The rendering of the *DetailsView* is largely customizable using templates and styles. The default rendering consists of a vertical list of rows, one for each field in the bound data item. *DetailsView* is a composite data-bound control. It acts as a naming container and generates postback events through the *IPostBackEventHandler* interface. Much like the *GridView*, the *DetailsView* control also supports out-of-band calls for paging.

```
public class DetailsView : CompositeDataBoundControl,
                           IPostBackContainer,
                           IPostBackEventHandler,
                           ICallbackContainer,
                           ICallbackEventHandler,
                           INamingContainer
```

The typical look and feel of the control was shown earlier in Figure 7-3.

Properties of the *DetailsView*

The *DetailsView* layout supports several properties that fall into the following categories: behavior, appearance, style, state, and templates. Table 7-11 lists them.

Table 7-11 *DetailsView* Behavior Properties

Property	Description
AllowPaging	Indicates whether the control supports navigation.
AutoGenerateDeleteButton	Indicates whether the command bar includes a Delete button. The default is *false*.
AutoGenerateEditButton	Indicates whether the command bar includes an Edit button. The default is *false*.
AutoGenerateInsertButton	Indicates whether the command bar includes an Insert button. The default is *false*.
AutoGenerateRows	Indicates whether the control autogenerates the rows. The default is *true*—all the fields of the record are displayed.
DefaultMode	Indicates the default display mode of the control. It can be any value from the *DetailsViewMode* enumeration (read-only, insert, edit).
EnablePagingCallbacks	Indicates whether client-side callback functions are used for paging operations.
UseAccessibleHeader	Determines whether to render *<TH>* tags for the column headers instead of default *<TD>* tags.

The *DefaultMode* property determines the mode that the control reverts to after an edit or insert operation is performed.

The output generated by the *DetailsView* control is a table in which each row corresponds to a record field. Additional rows represent special items such as the header, footer, pager, and the new command bar. The command bar is a sort of toolbar where all the commands available on the record are collected. Autogenerated buttons go to the command bar.

The user interface of the control is governed by a handful of visual properties, which are listed in Table 7-12.

Table 7-12 *DetailsView* Appearance Properties

Property	Description
BackImageUrl	Indicates the URL to an image to display in the background
CellPadding	Indicates the amount of space (in pixels) between the contents of a cell and the border
CellSpacing	Indicates the amount of space (in pixels) between cells
EmptyDataText	Indicates the text to render in the control when it's bound to an empty data source
FooterText	Indicates the text to render in the control's footer
GridLines	Indicates the gridline style for the control
HeaderText	Indicates the text to render in the control's header
HorizontalAlign	Indicates the horizontal alignment of the control on the page

The properties listed in the table apply to the control as a whole. You can program specific elements of the control's user interface by using styles. The supported styles are listed in Table 7-13.

Table 7-13 *DetailsView* Style Properties

Property	Description
AlternatingRowStyle	Defines the style properties for the fields that are displayed every other row (even positions)
CommandRowStyle	Defines the style properties for the command bar
EditRowStyle	Defines the style properties of individual rows when the control renders in edit mode
FieldHeaderStyle	Defines the style properties for the label of each field value
FooterStyle	Defines the style properties for the control's footer
HeaderColumnStyle	Defines the style properties for the header column item
HeaderStyle	Defines the style properties for the control's header
InsertRowStyle	Defines the style properties of individual rows when the control renders in insert mode
EmptyDataRowStyle	Defines the style properties for the displayed row when no data source is available
PagerStyle	Defines the style properties for the control's pager
RowStyle	Defines the style properties of the individual rows

The *DetailsView* control can be displayed in three modes, depending on the value of the *DetailsViewMode* enumeration—*ReadOnly*, *Insert*, or *Edit*. The read-only mode is the default display mode, in which users see only the contents of the record. To edit or add a new record, users must click the corresponding button (if any) on the command bar. Each mode has an associated style. The current mode is tracked by the *CurrentMode* read-only property. Other state properties are listed in Table 7-14.

Table 7-14 *DetailsView* State Properties

Property	Description
BottomPagerRow	Returns a *DetailsViewRow* object that represents the bottom pager of the control.
CurrentMode	Gets the current mode for the control—any of the values in the *DetailsViewMode* enumeration. The property determines how bound fields and templates are rendered.
DataKey	Returns the *DataKey* object for the currently displayed record. The *DataKey* object contains the key values corresponding to the key fields specified by *DataKeyNames*.
DataKeyNames	An array specifying the primary key fields for the records being displayed. These keys are used to uniquely identify an item for update and delete operations.
FooterRow	Returns a *DetailsViewRow* object that represents the footer of the control.
HeaderRow	Returns a *DetailsViewRow* object that represents the header of the control.
PageCount	Returns the total number of items in the underlying data source bound to the control.
PageIndex	Returns the 0-based index for the currently displayed record in the control. The index is relative to the total number of records in the underlying data source.
Rows	Returns the collection of *DataControlField* objects for the control that was used to generate the *Rows* collection.
Rows	Returns a collection of *DetailsViewRow* objects representing the individual rows within the control. Only data rows are taken into account.
SelectedValue	Returns the value of the key for the current record as stored in the *DataKey* object.
TopPagerRow	Returns a *DetailsViewRow* object that represents the top pager of the control.

If you're not satisfied with the default control rendering, you can use certain templates to better adapt the user interface to your preferences. Table 7-15 details the supported templates.

Table 7-15 *DetailsView* Template Properties

Property	Description
EmptyDataTemplate	The template for rendering the control when it is bound to an empty data source. If set, this property overrides the *EmptyDataText* property.
FooterTemplate	The template for rendering the footer row of the control.
HeaderTemplate	The template for rendering the header of the control.
PagerTemplate	The template for rendering the pager of the control. If set, this property overrides any existing pager settings.

As you can see, the table lists templates related to the layout of the control and doesn't include templates that influence the rendering of the current record. This is by design. For properties such as *InsertTemplate* or *ItemTemplate*, you should resort to the *FormView* control, which is just a fully templatized version of the *DetailsView* control. The *DetailsView* control has only one method, *ChangeMode*. As the name suggests, the *ChangeMode* method is used to switch from one display mode to the next.

```
public void ChangeMode(DetailsViewMode newMode)
```

This method is used internally to change view when a command button is clicked.

Events of the *DetailsView*

The *DetailsView* control exposes several events that enable the developer to execute custom code at various times in the life cycle. The event model is similar to *GridView* in terms of supported events and because of the pre/post pair of events that characterize each significant operation. Table 7-16 details the supported events.

The *ItemCommand* event fires only if the original click event is not handled by a predefined method. This typically occurs if you define custom buttons in one of the templates. You do not need to handle this event to intercept any clicking on the Edit or Insert buttons.

Table 7-16 Events of the *DetailsView* Control

Event	Description
PageIndexChanging, *PageIndexChanged*	Both events occur when the control moves to another record. They fire before and after the display change occurs.
ItemCommand	Occurs when any of the clickable elements in the user interface is clicked. This doesn't include standard buttons (such as Edit, Delete, and Insert), which are handled internally, but it does include custom buttons defined in the templates.
ItemCreated	Occurs after all the rows are created.
ItemDeleting, *ItemDeleted*	Both events occur when the current record is deleted. They fire before and after the record is deleted.
ItemInserting, *ItemInserted*	Both events occur when a new record is inserted. They fire before and after the insertion.
ItemUpdating, *ItemUpdated*	Both events occur when the current record is updated. They fire before and after the row is updated.
ModeChanging, *ModeChanged*	Both events occur when the control switches to a different display mode. They fire before and after the mode changes.

The *PageIndexChanging* event allows you to execute custom code before the *PageIndex* actually changes (before the control moves to a different record). As with the *GridView* events, you can cancel the event by setting the *Cancel* property of the event argument class to *true*.

The *DetailsView* Control in Action

Building a record viewer with the *DetailsView* control is easy and quick. You just drop an instance of the control onto the Web form and add a few settings. The following listing shows the minimum that's needed:

```
<asp:detailsview runat="server" id="det"
    datasourceid="MySource"
    allowpaging="true"
    headertext="Employees">
     <pagersettings firstpageimageurl="images/first.gif"
        lastpageimageurl="images/last.gif"
        nextpageimageurl="images/next.gif"
        prevpageimageurl="images/prev.gif"
        mode="NextPrevFirstLast" />
</asp:detailsview>
```

When the *AllowPaging* property is set to *true*, a pager bar is displayed. You can use text (including rich-formatted text) for each button or just use a bitmap, as in the example. Figure 7-13 shows the results.

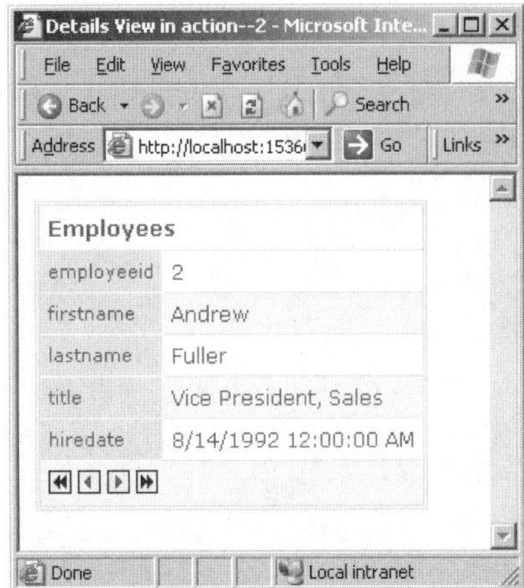

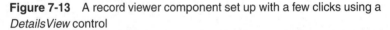

Figure 7-13 A record viewer component set up with a few clicks using a *DetailsView* control

The *DetailsView* paging mechanism is based on the *PageIndex* property, which indicates the index of the current record in the bound data source. Clicking the pager button updates the property; the control does the data binding and refreshes the view.

Editing the Current Record

A detail view like that of the *DetailsView* control is particularly useful if users can perform basic updates on the displayed data. Basic updates include editing and deleting the record. The *DetailsView* command bar gathers all the buttons needed to start data operations. You tell the control to create those buttons by using such properties as *AutoGenerateEditButton* and *AutoGenerateDeleteButton*.

As with the *GridView*, edit and delete operations for the *DetailsView* control are handled by the bound data source control, as long as the proper commands are defined and a key field is indicated through the *DataKeyNames* property:

```
<asp:sqldatasource runat="server" id="MySource"
    connectionstring="server=…;database=northwind;UID=…"
    selectcommand="SELECT employeeid, firstname,
                          lastname, title, hiredate FROM employees"
    updatecommand="UPDATE employees SET
```

```
                           firstname=@firstname, lastname=@lastname,
                           title=@title, hiredate=@hiredate
                      WHERE employeeid=@employeeid"
     deletecommand="DELETE employees WHERE employeeid=@employeeid" />
<asp:detailsview runat="server" id="det"
     datasourceid="MySource"
     allowpaging="true"
     headertext="Employees"
     datakeynames="employeeid"
     autogenerateeditbutton="true"
     autogeneratedeletebutton="true">
     <pagersettings firstpageimageurl="images/first.gif"
          lastpageimageurl="images/last.gif"
          nextpageimageurl="images/next.gif"
          prevpageimageurl="images/prev.gif"
          mode="NextPrevFirstLast" />
</asp:detailsview>
```

Figure 7-14 shows the changed user interface of the *DetailsView* control when it works in edit mode. Note that in edit mode, the default set of buttons in the command is replaced by a pair of update/cancel buttons.

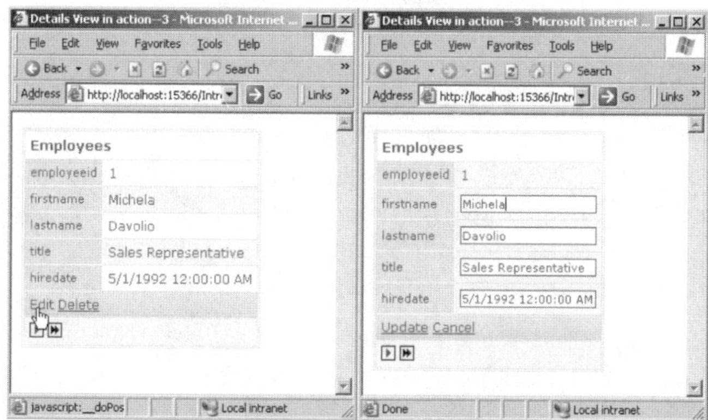

Figure 7-14 A *DetailsView* control working in edit mode

Both the update and the delete operation are handled by a pair of pre- and post-events such as *ItemDeleting/ItemDeleted* or *ItemUpdating/ItemUpdated*.

Inserting a New Record

The process of adding a new record is much like that for editing or deleting. You add an *InsertCommand* string in the bound data source and then tell the *DetailsView* control to create an insert button, and then you are finished. Here is a valid insert command:

```
<asp:sqldatasource runat="server" id="MySource"
     connectionstring="server=…;database=northwind;UID=…"
     :
     insertcommand="INSERT INTO employees
                    (firstname, lastname, title, hiredate) VALUES
                    (@firstname, @lastname, @title, @hiredate)" />
```

Figure 7-15 shows how it works.

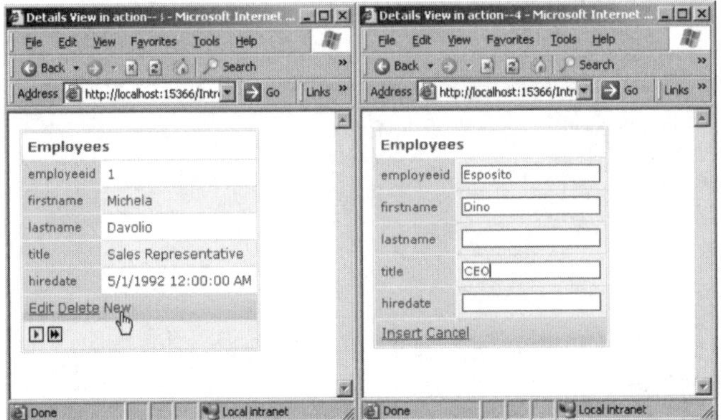

Figure 7-15 A *DetailsView* control working in insert mode

Controlling the Displayed Fields

Just as the *GridView* and the *DataGrid* controls can display only a selected range of columns, the *DetailsView* control can display only a subset of the available fields for the current record. To disable the automatic generation of display fields, you set the *AutoGenerateRows* column to *false*. Then you declare as many fields as needed under the *<Fields>* node, as shown here:

```
<asp:detailsview>
     :
     <fields>
        <asp:boundfield datafield="firstname" headertext="First Name" />
        <asp:boundfield datafield="lastname" headertext="Last Name" />
        <asp:boundfield datafield="title" headertext="Position" />
     </fields>
</asp:detailsview>
```

The *HeaderText* attribute refers to the label displayed alongside the field value. In edit or insert mode, the content of the field is displayed using a text box, which is great for many data types but not all. For example, what if your users need to edit a date? In this case, the *Calendar* control is far more appropriate. As mentioned, you can't use templates to modify the default rendering because the *DetailsView* control doesn't support data-bound templates on rows.

You should use the *FormView* control if template support is an unavoidable necessity.

> **Note** How can you change the layout of the *DetailsView* control, thus simulating the results you would obtain with templates? You can hook up the *ItemCreated* event and modify the layout by adding new controls and/or replacing existing controls.

Creating Master/Detail Views

Combined with another data-bound control such as the *GridView*, the *DetailsView* control greatly simplifies the creation of codeless master/detail views of data. The master control (such as the *GridView*) selects one particular record in its own data source, and that record becomes the data source for a *DetailsView* control in the same form.

Selecting a Record in the *GridView*

In addition to supporting Edit and Delete buttons, the *GridView* control supports another predefined button, the Select button. You enable this button on a per-row basis by setting the *AutoGenerateSelectButton* property to *true*. When the users click this button, the current row enters the selected state and its 0-based index is assigned to the *SelectedIndex* property of the *GridView*. The control also fires the *SelectedIndexChanged* event. Applications can hook up this event and run custom code.

Typically, the *SelectedIndexChanged* event serves to drill down into the contents of the currently selected record; it was often used in ASP.NET 1.x to create master/detail data schemes. Its declaration is shown here:

```
private void Grid_SelectedIndexChanged(object sender, EventArgs e)
{
   ⋮
}
```

You can set the currently selected item manually by clicking or programmatically by setting the *SelectedIndex* property. A value of –1 denotes no selected items.

Drill Down into the Selected Record

With ASP.NET 1.x controls, implementing master/detail views is not particularly hard but certainly not automatic, much less codeless. In ASP.NET 2.0, data source, *GridView*, and *DetailsView* controls (properly configured) support a no-code master/detail scenario. Let's see how.

A master/detail page contains a master control (such as a *GridView*) and a detail control (such as a *DetailsView*), each bound to its own data source. The trick is in binding the detail control to a data source represented by the currently selected record. The following code snippet shows the configuration of the master pair of controls:

```
<asp:sqldatasource runat="server" id="MySource"
     connectionstring="SERVER=…;DATABASE=northwind;UID=…"
     selectcommand="SELECT customerid, companyname, country
                    FROM customers" />
<asp:gridview runat="server" id="Master" datasourceid="MySource"
     pagesize="5"
     allowpaging="true"
     datakeynames="customerid"
     autogenerateselectbutton="true"
     autogeneratecolumns="false">
     <columnfields>
        <asp:boundfield datafield="companyname" headertext="Customer" />
        <asp:boundfield datafield="country" headertext="Country" />
     </columnfields>
 </asp:gridview>
```

The grid shows a Select column, but the page doesn't need to handle the corresponding *SelectedIndexChanged* event. The following code shows the detail pair of controls for completing the codeless implementation of the master/detail scheme:

```
<asp:sqldatasource runat="server" id="MyDetailSource"
     connectionstring="SERVER=…;DATABASE=northwind;UID=…"
     selectcommand="SELECT * FROM customers"
     filterexpression="customerid='@customerid'">
     <filterparameters>
        <asp:ControlParameter Name="customerid" ControlId="Master"
             PropertyName="SelectedValue" />
     </filterparameters>
</asp:sqldatasource>

<asp:detailsview runat="server" id="Detail"
     datasourceid="MyDetailSource">
     <pagersettings firstpageimageurl="images/first.gif"
         lastpageimageurl="images/last.gif"
         nextpageimageurl="images/next.gif"
         prevpageimageurl="images/prev.gif"
         mode="NextPrevFirstLast" />
</asp:detailsview>
```

The *DetailsView* control is bound to the results of a filtered query. The *SqlDataSource* control declares the *FilterExpression* attribute and sets it to an expression used to filter the results of the Select command. The content of the *FilterExpression* property is used to generate the WHERE clause of the query. The *@customerid* parameter is bound to the value of a particular property (*SelectedValue*) on a particular control (the *GridView* control named Master). When a new row is selected on the *GridView*, the *SelectedValue* property is updated to reflect the value of the key fields defined on the grid. (The key field names are in the *DataKeyNames* property.)

The key of the selected record is used to select more information from the containing table and to update the detail view. All of this occurs automatically and with no code from the developer. Figure 7-16 shows the final results.

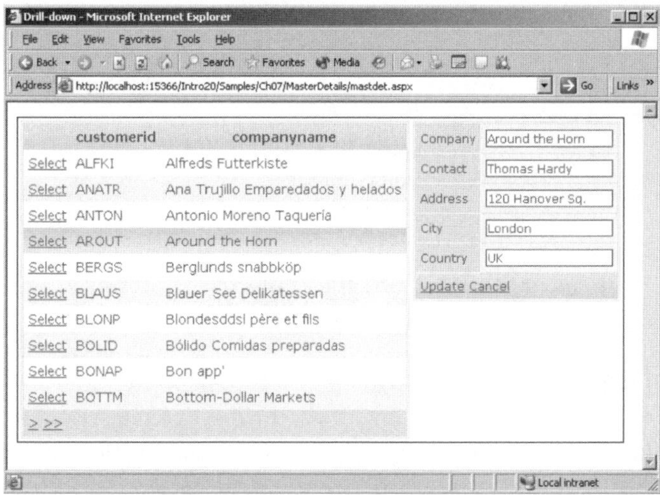

Figure 7-16 A no-code implementation of a master/detail scheme based on a combination of *GridView* and *DetailsView* controls

The *FormView* Control

FormView is a new data-bound control that works like the templated version of the *DetailsView* control. It renders one record at a time picked from the associated data source and optionally provides paging buttons to navigate between records. Unlike the *DetailsView* control, the *FormView* control doesn't use data control fields and requires the user to define the rendering of each item using templates. The *FormView* control can support any basic operation that its data source provides.

The *FormView* Object Model

Designed mostly as a simple update-and-insert interface, the *FormView* control cannot validate against data source schemas and doesn't supply advanced editing features such as foreign key field drop-downs. However, by using templates you can easily provide this functionality.

Two functional aspects mark the difference between *FormView* and *DetailsView*. First, the *FormView* control has *ItemTemplate*, *EditItemTemplate*, and *InsertItemTemplate* properties that—as you've already seen—the *DetailsView* lacks. Second, the *FormView* control lacks the command row, which is a sort of toolbar where available functions are grouped.

Note that the *FormView* control has no default rendering of its own. At the same time, its graphical layout is completely customizable using templates. Therefore, each template includes all command buttons needed by the particular record. The control's definition is shown here:

```
public class FormView : CompositeDataBoundControl,
                        IPostBackContainer,
                        IPostBackEventHandler,
                        ICallbackContainer,
                        ICallbackEventHandler,
                        INamingContainer
```

As you can see, *FormView* has the same root and implements the same interfaces as *DetailsView*.

Members of the *FormView* Control

The *FormView* control exposes many of the properties that you've already seen for the *DetailsView* control. This is no surprise—the two controls are two facets of the same coin—a record viewer control—with and without templates. The difference is only in templates and related styles, as you can see in Table 7-17. See Table 7-11 through Table 7-16 for the complete list of properties and events supported by the *FormView* control.

Supported Templates

The output of the *FormView* control is exclusively based on the templates. This means you must always specify the item template, at a minimum.

It's no coincidence that the *FormView* templates match the three feasible states of the control—ReadOnly, Edit, and Insert. You use the *ItemTemplate* to define the control's layout when in view mode. You use *EditItemTemplate* to edit the contents of the current record, and you use *InsertItemTemplate* to add a new record.

Table 7-17 Data-Bound Templates of the *FormView* Control

Template	Description
EditItemTemplate	Indicates the template to use when an existing record is being updated
InsertItemTemplate	Indicates the template to use when a new record is being created
ItemTemplate	Indicates the template to use when a record is rendered for viewing only

As mentioned, the control doesn't provide any clue or support for building the final user interface. As a developer, you are entirely responsible for providing the user interface from A to Z.

The *FormView* in Action

Let's see how to use templates to configure and run a *FormView* control in a sample ASP.NET Web page. All templates must contain everything needed to accomplish tasks—user interface elements and command buttons. The control itself provides the pager bar and the surrounding table.

Displaying Data

The following code snippet shows the typical code you write to embed a *FormView* in your pages:

```
<asp:FormView ID="EmpDetails" runat="server"
    DataSourceId="MySource" AllowPaging="true">
    <ItemTemplate>
      :
    </ItemTemplate>
    <EditItemTemplate>
      :
    </EditItemTemplate>
    < InsertItemTemplate >
      :
    </InsertItemTemplate>
</asp:FormView>
```

Figure 7-17 illustrates a page that uses a *FormView* control.

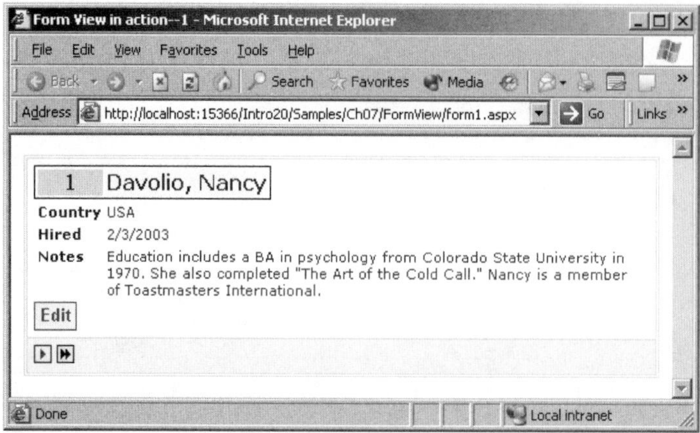

Figure 7-17 The *FormView* control in action

The following code generates the page shown in the figure:

```
<asp:FormView runat="server" id="EmpDetails"
     datakeynames="employeeid"
     datasourceid="MySource" allowpaging="true">
     <ItemTemplate>
        <table style="border:solid 1px black;">
           <tr>
              <td bgcolor="yellow" width="50px" align="center">
                  <b><%# Eval("employeeid") %></b></td>
              <td bgcolor="lightyellow" >
                  <b><%# Eval("lastname") %>,
                  <%# Eval("firstname") %> </b></td>
           </tr>
        </table>
        <table style="font-family:Verdana;font-size:8pt;">
           <tr>
               <td><b>Country</b></td>
               <td><%# Eval("country") %></td>
           </tr>
           <tr>
               <td><b>Hired</b></td>
               <td><%# Eval("hiredate", "{0:d}") %></td>
           </tr>
           <tr>
               <td valign="top"><b>Notes</b></td>
               <td><%# Eval("notes") %></td>
           </tr>
         </table>
         <asp:Button Runat="server" CommandName="Edit" Text="Edit" />
    </ItemTemplate>
</asp:FormView>
```

The Edit button is added using a classic *<asp:Button>* button with the Edit command name. This causes the *FormView* to switch from read-only mode to edit mode and display using the *EditItemTemplate*, if any is defined.

A command name of New forces the control to change to its insert mode and render the contents defined for the *InsertItemTemplate*. Finally, if you add a button with the Delete command name to the item template, the control will invoke the Delete command on the data source when the user clicks.

In view mode, you use the *Eval* function to bind data fields to controls. As you'll see in a moment, *Eval* is useful only in read-only scenarios. For implementing a real two-way data binding, an extension to *Eval* is required—the *Bind* function you saw in Chapter 5.

Editing Data

How do you retrieve values to update or insert a record? To begin with, you design an edit template using interactive input controls such as text boxes, calendars, and drop-down lists. To provide for two-way binding, you fill each control that must edit data using the *Bind* function in lieu of *Eval*. The following code snippet shows a sample multiline text box control bound to the *notes* column of the Employees table:

```
<asp:TextBox Runat="server" ID="TheNotes"
    Text='<%# Bind("notes") %>' />
```

Bind stores the value of the bound control property into a collection of values that the *FormView* control retrieves and uses to compose the parameter list of the insert or edit command. The argument passed to *Bind* must match the name of a parameter in the command. For example, the text box above provides the value for a *@notes* parameter. An exception is raised if such a parameter doesn't exist in the corresponding command of the data source control.

Finally, bear in mind that the edit and insert templates must contain buttons to save changes. These are ordinary buttons with specific command names—Update and Insert to save and Cancel to abort. Buttons trigger update commands whose details are stored in the associated data source object.

The following code snippet shows a sample edit template:

```
<asp:FormView runat="server" id="EmpDetails"
   ⋮
   <EditItemTemplate>
      <table style="border:solid 1px black;">
         <tr>
           <td align="center">
               <b><%# Eval("employeeid") %></b></td>
           <td>
               <b><%# Eval("lastname") %>,
```

```
                <%# Eval("firstname") %> </b></td>
            </tr>
        </table>
        <table style="font-size:8pt;font-family:Verdana;">
            <tr>
                <td><b>Country</b></td>
                <td>
                    <asp:dropdownlist Runat="Server" ID="countries"
                          SelectedValue='<%# Bind("country") %>'>
                        <asp:ListItem>UK</asp:ListItem>
                        <asp:ListItem>USA</asp:ListItem>
                        <asp:ListItem>Italy</asp:ListItem>
                        <asp:ListItem>Australia</asp:ListItem>
                    </asp:DropDownList>
                </td>
            </tr>
            <tr>
                <td valign="top"><b>Hired</b></td>
                <td>
                    <asp:Calendar Runat="Server" ID="Hired"
                          VisibleDate='<%# Eval("hiredate") %>'
                          SelectedDate='<%# Bind("hiredate") %>' />
                </td>
            </tr>
            <tr>
                <td valign="top"><b>Notes</b></td>
                <td>
                    <asp:textbox Runat="Server" TextMoDe="MultiLine"
                          text='<%# Bind("notes") %>' />
                </td>
            </tr>
        </table>

        <asp:Button Runat="server" CommandName="Update" text="Save" />
        <asp:Button Runat="server" CommandName="Cancel" text="Cancel" />
    </EditItemTemplate>
    ⋮
</asp:FormView>
```

Figure 7-18 shows the output of this code.

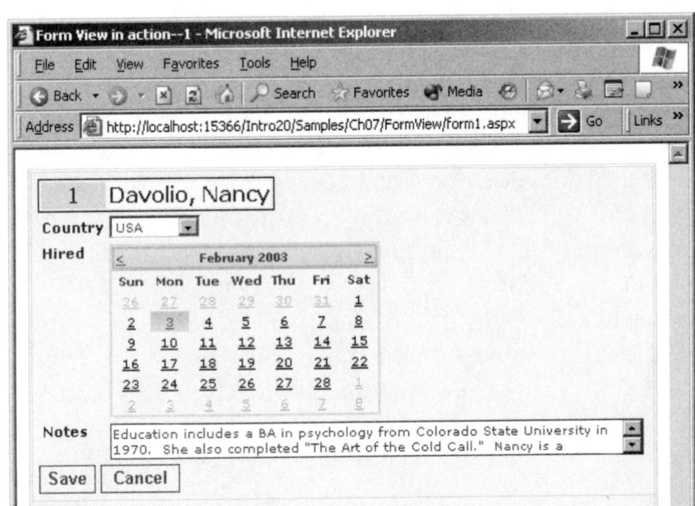

Figure 7-18 A *FormView* control running in edit mode

If you need to do more sophisticated things like pre- or post-processing of data, you write appropriate event handlers for *ItemCommand*, *ItemInserting*, *ModeChanging*, and the like.

Important Be sure to add a proper *WHERE* clause to the *UPDATE* and *DELETE* statements you define—especially when you configure data source components for use with the *DetailsView* and *FormView* controls. The *WHERE* clause must check the primary key field—the field(s) assigned to the *DataKeyNames* property—against a parameter with the same name.

```
UPDATE table SET lastname=@lastname WHERE empID=@empID
```

Summary

Data-bound controls are an essential part of most, if not all, Web applications. To be effective, data-bound controls must be simple and powerful. Ideally, they provide advanced functionalities in a few clicks and use a limited amount of code. Do the ASP.NET 2.0 data-bound controls fulfill these requirements? They do, even though they need a number of changes and improvements.

Data binding in ASP.NET 2.0 can give you a feeling of déjà vu. The *GridView* looks just like the *DataGrid* from ASP.NET 1.x, with just a few of the properties and events renamed. With the exception of the *DetailsView* and *FormView* control, it looks like the same approach to data binding. But a more thoughtful look will reveal that ASP.NET 2.0 data binding is significantly different. The newer object model is simply designed to look like the older one as much as possible.

The key shortcoming of ASP.NET 1.x data binding is that it requires too much code for common, relatively boilerplate operations. This has been addressed with the introduction of data source objects. But data source objects require richer controls that are capable of working with this new model. This explains why ASP.NET 2.0 offers a brand-new control—the *GridView*—rather than just enhancing the existing *DataGrid*. The pair *DetailsView* and *FormView* are the perfect complement to the *GridView*, and they fill another hole in the ASP.NET 1.x data toolbox. The *TreeView* and *Menu* controls are the first attempt in ASP.NET at providing tools to manage hierarchical data. Not that bad for a first try!

Part III

Application Services

8

Rich Controls and Services

Starting with version 1.0, ASP.NET has been characterized by a well-balanced mix of low-level and feature-rich tools. Using low-level tools such as events, HTTP modules, and HTTP handlers, you can plug into the ASP.NET pipeline to influence the processing of requests at every stage. But programming ASP.NET is not only for brave-hearted programmers who can orient themselves in the intricate forest of properties, methods, and cryptic configuration settings. Overall, ASP.NET is a high-level programming tool with a wealth of feature-rich components for those who don't need control over every little step.

The quantity and quality of application services has grown significantly in ASP.NET 2.0, which was designed with the goal of making things happen with the least amount of code. In Chapter 5 through Chapter 7, we examined how the data binding mechanism was extended to make codeless, data-driven applications possible. In Chapter 1, you saw glimpses of rich new controls (such as the *Wizard* control) that provide building blocks for feature-rich Web applications. These off-the-shelf controls bring you application services such as dynamic image generation, site navigation, and counters.

These components are exposed to applications as controls, but they are more than just plain user interface controls. They are feature-rich services that the runtime makes available to Web pages. In this chapter, we'll look in more depth at a few of the components that were introduced in Chapter 1—wizards, image generators, and (last but not least) site navigation functions and counters.

Creating Web Wizards

Wizards are typically used to break up large forms to collect user input. A wizard is a sequence of related steps, each associated with an input form and a user interface. Users move through the wizard sequentially but are normally given a chance to skip a step or jump back to modify some of the entered values. A wizard is conceptually pretty simple, but implementing it over HTTP connections can be tricky. Lots of developers have taken on that challenge and built wizards in their own applications. Everybody involved with serious Web development can now heartily welcome the introduction of a wizard control. In ASP.NET 2.0, a wizard is a composite control named *Wizard* and is located in the *System.Web.UI.WebControls* namespace.

An Overview of the *Wizard* Control

The *Wizard* control supports both linear and nonlinear navigation. It allows you to move backward to change values and to skip steps that are unnecessary due to previous settings or because users don't want to fill those fields. Like many other ASP.NET 2.0 controls, the wizard supports themes, styles, and templates. As mentioned, the *Wizard* is a composite control and automatically generates some constituent controls such as navigation buttons and panels. As you'll see in a moment, the programming interface of the control has multiple templates that provide for in-depth customization of the overall user interface. The control also guarantees that state is maintained no matter where you move—backward, forward, or to a particular page.

All the steps of a wizard must be declared within the boundaries of the same *Wizard* control. In other words, the wizard must be self-contained and not provide page-to-page navigation. As you saw in Chapter 1, though, ASP.NET 2.0 provides a cross-page posting feature to facilitate page-to-page navigation. In addition, the URL of the displayed page doesn't change as the user navigates through the wizard.

Structure of a Wizard

A wizard has four parts: header, view, navigation bar, and sidebar, as shown in Figure 8-1.

The header consists of text you can set through the *HeaderText* property. You can change the default appearance of the header text by using its style property; you can also change the structure of the header by using the corresponding header template property. If *HeaderText* is empty and no custom template is specified, no header is shown for the wizard.

The view displays the contents of the currently active step. The wizard requires you to define each step in an *<asp:wizardstep>* control. All wizard steps must be grouped in a single *<wizardsteps>* tag, as shown here:

```
<asp:wizard runat="server" SideBarEnabled="true">
  <wizardsteps>
    <asp:wizardstep runat="server" steptype="auto" id="step1">
      First step
    </asp:wizardstep>
    <asp:wizardstep runat="server" steptype="auto" id="step2">
      Second step
    </asp:wizardstep>
    <asp:wizardstep runat="server" steptype="auto" id="finish">
      Final step
    </asp:wizardstep>
  </wizardsteps>
</asp:wizard>
```

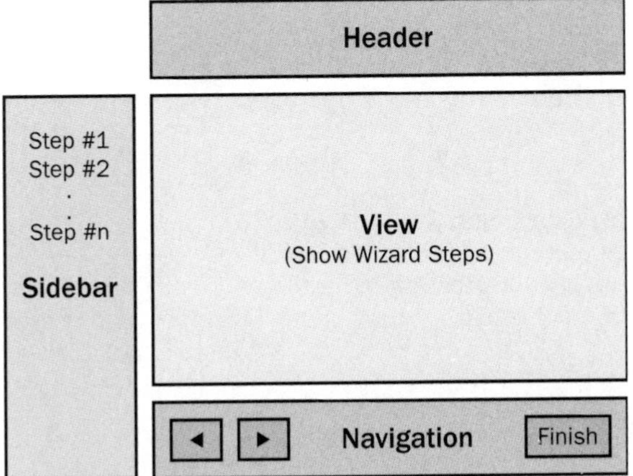

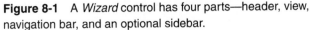

Figure 8-1 A *Wizard* control has four parts—header, view, navigation bar, and an optional sidebar.

The navigation bar consists of autogenerated buttons that provide any needed functionality—typically, going to the next or previous step or finishing. You can modify the look and feel of the navigation bar by using styles and templates.

The optional sidebar is used to display content in the left side of the control. It provides an overall view of the steps needed to accomplish the wizard's task. By default, it displays a description of each step, with the current step displayed in bold. You can customize styles and templates. Figure 8-2 shows the default user interface. Each step is labeled using the ID of the corresponding *<asp:wizardstep>* tag.

Figure 8-2 A wizard with the default sidebar on the left side

Wizard Styles and Templates

You can style all the various parts and buttons of a wizard control by using the properties listed in Table 8-1.

Table 8-1 The *Wizard* Control's Style Properties

Style	Description
CancelButtonStyle	Sets the style properties for the wizard's Cancel button
FinishStepButtonStyle	Sets the style properties for the wizard's Finish button
FinishStepPreviousButtonStyle	Sets the style properties for the wizard's Previous button when at the finish step
HeaderStyle	Sets the style properties for the wizard's header
NavigationButtonStyle	Sets the style properties for navigation buttons
NavigationStyle	Sets the style properties for the navigation area
NextStepButtonStyle	Sets the style properties for the wizard's Next button
PreviousStepButtonStyle	Sets the style properties for the wizard's Previous button
SideBarButtonStyle	Sets the style properties for the buttons on the sidebar
StartStepNextButtonStyle	Sets the style properties for the wizard's Next button when at the start step
StepStyle	Sets the style properties for the area where steps are displayed

The contents of the header, sidebar, and navigation bar can be further customized with templates. Table 8-2 lists the available templates.

Table 8-2 The *Wizard* Control's Template Properties

Style	Description
FinishNavigationTemplate	Specifies the navigation bar shown before the last page of the wizard. By default, the navigation bar contains the Previous and Finish buttons.
HeaderTemplate	Specifies the title bar of the wizard.
SideBarTemplate	Used to display content in the left side of the wizard control.
StartNavigationTemplate	Specifies the navigation bar for the first view in the wizard. By default, it contains only the Next button.
StepNavigationTemplate	Specifies the navigation bar for steps other than first, finish, or complete. By default, it contains Previous and Next buttons.

In addition to using styles and templates, you can control the programming interface of the *Wizard* control through a few properties.

The Wizard's Programming Interface

Table 8-3 lists the properties of the *Wizard* control (excluding style and template properties and properties defined on base classes [such as *WebControl*]).

Table 8-3 Main Properties of the *Wizard* Control

Property	Description
ActiveStep	Returns the current wizard step object. The object is an instance of the *WizardStep* class.
ActiveStepIndex	Gets and sets the 0-based index of the current wizard step.
FinishStepButtonText	Gets and sets the text for the Finish button.
HeaderText	Gets and sets the title of the wizard.
NextStepButtonText	Gets and sets the text for the Next button.
PreviousStepButtonText	Gets and sets the text for the Previous button.
SideBarEnabled	Toggles the visibility of the sidebar. The default value is *False*.
WizardSteps	Returns a collection containing all the *WizardStep* objects defined in the control.

Most of these properties—in particular, the xxx*Text* properties—affect the appearance of the control. *ActiveStep*, *ActiveStepIndex*, and *WizardSteps* indicate the state of the control. A wizard in action is fully represented by its collection of step views and an index that represents the currently selected view.

The wizard's methods allow a couple of actions—getting the history of the wizard and moving through the steps. The first method, *GetHistory*, is defined as follows:

```
public ICollection GetHistory()
```

GetHistory returns a collection of *WizardStep* objects. The order of the items is determined by the order in which the wizard's pages were accessed by the user. The first *WizardStep* object returned—the one with an index of 0—is the currently selected step. The second object represents the view before the current one, and so on.

The second method, *MoveTo*, is used to move to a particular wizard step. The method's prototype is described here:

```
public void MoveTo(WizardStep step)
```

The method requires you to pass a *WizardStep* object, which can be problematic. However, the method is a simple wrapper around the setter of the *ActiveStepIndex* property. If you want to jump to a particular step and not hold an instance of the corresponding *WizardStep* object, setting *ActiveStepIndex* is just as effective.

Table 8-4 lists the key events in the life of a *Wizard* control in an ASP.NET 2.0 page.

Table 8-4 Events of the *Wizard* Control

Event	Description
ActiveViewChanged	Raised when the active step changes
FinishButtonClick	Raised when the Finish button is clicked
NextButtonClick	Raised when the Next button is clicked
PreviousButtonClick	Raised when the Previous button is clicked
SideBarButtonClick	Raised when a button on the sidebar is clicked

The following listing shows a sample wizard. We'll use it to add a new record to the Employees table of the Northwind database.

```
<asp:wizard runat="server" id="MyWizard"
    Font-names="verdana"
    BackColor="lightcyan" forecolor="navy"
    Style="border:outset 1px black"
```

```
    SideBarEnabled="true"
    HeaderText="Add a New Employee">
    <sidebarstyle backcolor="snow" borderwidth="1" font-names="Arial" />
    <headerstyle horizontalalign="Right" font-size="120%" />
    <navigationbuttonstyle width="80px" borderstyle="Solid" />
    <stepstyle backcolor="gainsboro" borderwidth="1" />

    <sidebartemplate>
      <div>
        <img src="images/wizard.jpg" />
        <asp:datalist runat="server" id="SideBarList">
           <ItemTemplate>
             <asp:linkbutton runat="server" id="SideBarButton" />
           </ItemTemplate>
        </asp:datalist>
      </div>
    </sidebartemplate>

  <WizardSteps>
     ⋮
  </WizardSteps>
</asp:wizard>
```

Figure 8-3 shows the wizard in action. The source code lacks a definition for the wizard steps. We'll add those and discuss them in a moment.

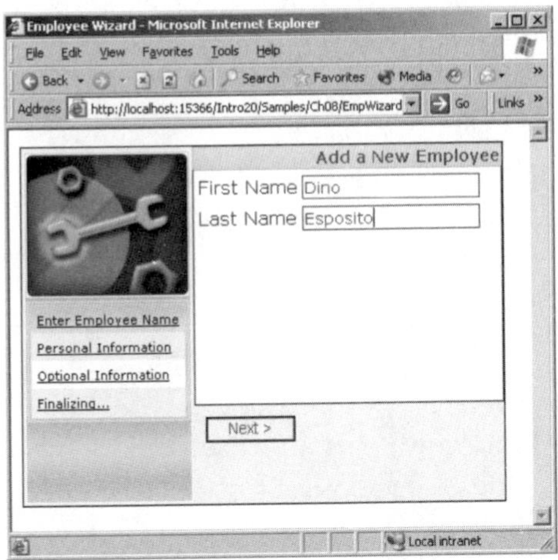

Figure 8-3 The sample wizard control in action

For better graphical results, you might want to use explicit heights for all steps and the sidebar as well. Likewise, the push buttons in the navigation bar might look better if you make them the same size. You do this by setting the *Width* property on the *NavigationButtonStyle* object.

> **Note** The *<SideBarTemplate>* tag should contain a *DataList* with a well-known ID and internal structure. The *DataList* must be named *SideBarList*, and its *ItemTemplate* block must contain a button object named *SideBarButton*. Any other template set on the *DataList* might cause runtime errors.

Adding Steps to a Wizard

A *WizardStep* object represents one of the child views that the wizard can display. The *WizardStep* class derives from *View* and adds just a couple of public properties to it—*StepType* and *Title*. A *View* object represents a control that acts as a container for a group of controls. A view is hosted within a *MultiView* control. (See Chapter 1.) To create its output, the wizard makes internal use of a *MultiView* control. However, the wizard is not derived from the *MultiView* class.

You define the views of a wizard through distinct instances of the *WizardStep* class, all grouped under the *<WizardSteps>* tag. The *<WizardSteps>* tag corresponds to the *WizardSteps* collection property exposed by the wizard control:

```
<WizardSteps>
   <asp:WizardStep>
     ⋮
   </asp:WizardStep>
   <asp:WizardStep>
     ⋮
   </asp:WizardStep>
</WizardSteps>
```

Each wizard step is characterized by a title and a type. The *Title* property provides a brief description of the view. This information is not used unless the sidebar is enabled. If it is, the title of each step is used to create a list of steps, as in Figure 8-3. If the sidebar is enabled but no title is provided for the various steps, the ID of the *WizardStep* objects is used to populate the sidebar.

Types of Wizard Steps

The *StepType* property indicates how a particular step should be handled and rendered within a wizard. Acceptable values for the step type come from the *WizardStepType* enumeration, as listed in Table 8-5.

Table 8-5 Wizard Step Types

Property	Description
Auto	The default setting, which forces the wizard to determine how each contained step should be treated.
Complete	The last page that the wizard displays, usually after the wizard has been completed. The navigation bar and the sidebar aren't displayed.
Finish	The last page used for collecting user data. It lacks the Next button, and it shows the Previous and Finish buttons.
Start	The first screen displayed, with no Previous button.
Step	All other intermediate pages, in which the Previous and Next buttons are displayed.

When the wizard is in automatic mode—the default type *Auto*—it determines the type of each step based on the order in which the steps appear in the source code. For example, the first step is considered type *Start* and the last is marked as *Finish*. No *Complete* step is assumed. If you correctly assign types to steps, the order in which you declare them in the .aspx source is not relevant.

Creating an Input Step

The following code shows a sample wizard step used to collect the first and last name of a new employee. For better graphical results, the content of the step is encapsulated in a fixed-height *<div>* tag. If all the steps are configured in this way, users navigating through the wizard won't experience sudden changes in the overall page layout. Similarly, you might want to define a custom navigation bar where all the buttons are always displayed and those that don't apply to the current step are disabled. This ensures that the buttons remain in the same position as users move through the pages of the wizard.

```
<asp:wizardstep runat="server" steptype="auto"
     title="Enter Employee Name">
     <div style="height:200px">
        <table>
            <tr><td>First Name</td><td>
               <asp:textbox runat="server" id="FirstName" />
               <asp:requiredfieldvalidator runat="server"
                    text="*"
                    errormessage="Must indicate first name"
                    setfocusonerror="true"
                    controltovalidate="FirstName" />
            </td></tr>
            <tr><td>Last Name</td><td>
```

```
                <asp:textbox runat="server" id="LastName" />
                <asp:requiredfieldvalidator runat="server"
                    text="*"
                    errormessage="Must indicate last name"
                    setfocusonerror="true"
                    controltovalidate="LastName" />
            </td></tr>
            <tr><td height="100px"></td></tr>
        </table>
        <asp:validationsummary runat="server" displaymode="List" />
    </div>
</asp:wizardstep>
```

A wizard is usually created for collecting input data, so validation becomes a critical issue. You can validate the input data in two nonexclusive ways—using validators and using transition event handlers.

The first option involves placing validator controls in the wizard step. This guarantees that invalid input—empty fields or incompatible data types—is caught quickly and perhaps on the client. Figure 8-4 shows the error messages you get from the sample wizard of Figure 8-3 if you try to proceed to the next page without entering a first and a last name.

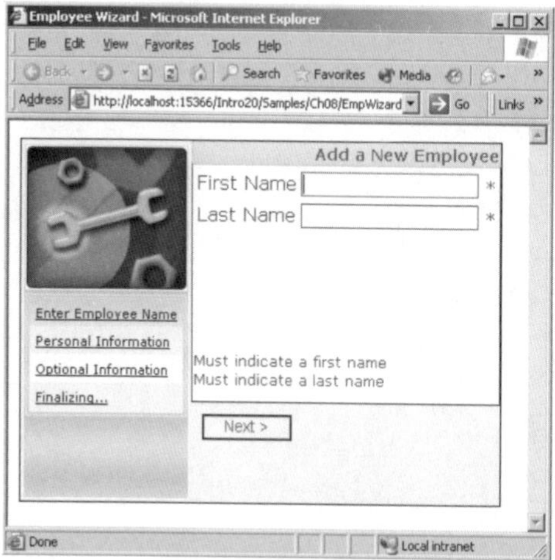

Figure 8-4 The wizard doesn't let you proceed to the next page if the fields don't contain valid entries.

If you need to access server-side resources to validate the input data, you're better off using transition event handlers. A transition event is one of the events the wizard raises when it is about to switch to another view. The events are detailed in Table 8-4.

Navigating Through the Wizard

When a button is clicked to move to another step, an event is fired to the hosting page. It's up to you to decide when and how to perform critical validation. In most cases, you'll want to perform server-side validation only when the user clicks the Finish button to complete the wizard. You can be sure that whatever route the user has taken within the wizard, Finish will complete it. Any code you bind to the *FinishButtonClick* event is executed only once, and only when strictly necessary.

By contrast, any code bound to the Previous or Next button executes when the user moves back or forward. The page posts back on both events; be aware that you don't save any round trips by omitting *PreviousButtonClick* and *NextButtonClick* event handlers.

Filtering Page Navigation with Events

You should perform server-side validation if what the user can do next depends on the data she entered in the previous step. This means that in most cases you just need to write a *NextButtonClick* event handler:

```
<asp:wizard runat="server" id="MyWizard"
    ⋮
    OnNextButtonClick="OnNext">
    ⋮
</asp:wizard>
```

If the user moves back to a previously visited page, you can usually ignore any data entered in the current step. Since she's moving back, you can safely assume she's not going to use any fresh data. Likewise, when a back movement is requested, you can assume that any preconditions needed to visit that previous page are verified. This is by design if your users take a sequential route.

If the wizard sidebar is enabled, users can jump from page to page in any order. If the logic you're implementing through the wizard requires that preconditions be met before a certain step is reached, you should write a *SidebarButtonClick* event handler and ensure that the requirements have been met. A wizard click event requires a *WizardNavigationEventHandler* delegate.

```
public delegate void WizardNavigationEventHandler(
   object sender,
   WizardNavigationEventArgs e);
```

The *WizardNavigationEventArgs* structure contains two useful properties that inform you about the 0-based indexes of the page being left and the page being displayed. The *CurrentStepIndex* property returns the index of the last page visited; the *NextStepIndex* returns the index of the next page. Note that both properties are read-only.

The following code shows a sample handler for the Next button. The handler prepares a summary message to show when the user is going to the Finish page.

```
void OnNext(object sender, WizardNavigationEventArgs e)
{
   // Collect the input data if going to the last page
   // -1 because of 0-based indexing, add -1 if you have a Complete page
   // In case of a Complete step, the Finish step is the next to last one
   if (e.NextStepIndex == MyWizard.WizardSteps.Count - 2)
   {
       // Show a summary message
       StringBuilder sb = new StringBuilder ("");
       sb.Append ("You're about to add: <br><br>");
       sb.AppendFormat ("{0} {1}<hr>", FirstName.Text, LastName.Text);
       sb.Append ("<b><br>Ready to go?</b>");
       ReadyMsg.Text = sb.ToString();
   }
}
```

Each page displayed by the wizard is a kind of panel (actually, a view) defined within a parent control—the wizard. This means that all child controls used in all steps must have a unique ID. It also means that you can access any of these controls just by name. For example, if one of the pages contains a text box named FirstName, you can access it from any event handler by using the FirstName identifier, as in the preceding code snippet.

Canceling Events

The *WizardNavigationEventArgs* structure also contains a read/write Boolean property named *Cancel*. If you set this property to *True*, you just cancel the transition to the page being performed. The following code shows how to prevent the display of the next step if the user is on the start page and types in a last name of Esposito:

```
void OnNext(object sender, WizardNavigationEventArgs e)
{
    if (e.CurrentStepIndex == 0 &&
        LastName.Text == "Esposito")
    {
        e.Cancel = true;
        return;
    }
}
```

You can cancel events from within any event handler and not just from the *NextButtonClick* event handler. This trick is useful to block navigation if the server-side validation of the input data has failed. In this case, though, you're responsible for showing some feedback to the user.

Finalizing the Wizard

All wizards have some code to execute to finalize the task. If you use the ASP.NET 2.0 *Wizard* control, you place this code in the *FinishButtonClick* event handler. Figure 8-5 shows the final two steps of a wizard that completed successfully.

```
void OnFinish(object sender, WizardNavigationEventArgs e)
{
    // Add the employee
    if (!AddEmployee())
    {
       e.Cancel = true;
       return;
    }

    // Show a final message if you don't have a Completed step
    FinalMsg.Text = "The operation completed successfully.";
}
```

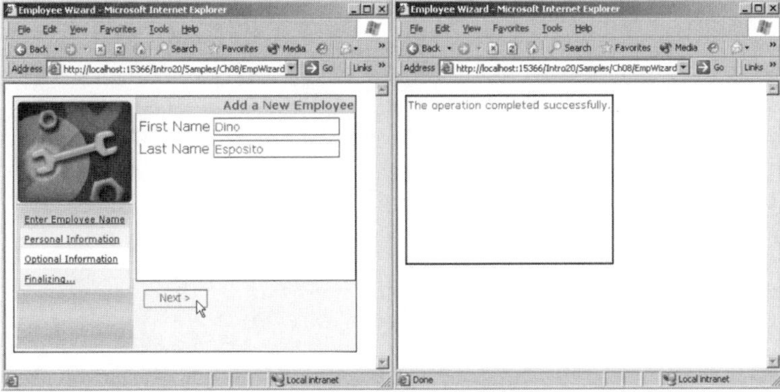

Figure 8-5 The final two steps of a wizard that has completed successfully

If the wizard contains a *Complete* step, that page is displayed after the Finish button is clicked and the final task has completed successfully. If something goes wrong with the update, you should cancel the transition to prevent the *Complete* page from appearing, and give the user another chance.

Generating Dynamic Images

In ASP.NET 1.x, image generation and manipulation are possible, but the implementation costs are shifted to the programmer. By writing some code, you can reference dynamically generated images in your ASP.NET pages and display bytes stored in disk files, database fields, and memory. Whatever the source of the bytes, you can link an image to a page only through a URL-based *<img>* tag. If the image has to be dynamically generated (e.g., fetched from a database), you must reference it through an ad hoc HTTP handler or a page.

The following code snippet shows the typical way of retrieving database images in ASP.NET 1.x:

```
<img src='<%# "photo.aspx?id=" + theID.Text %>'>
```

The image element is bound to the output of a tailor-made ASP.NET page that retrieves and returns the bytes of an image. The image is retrieved based on the input parameters specified on the URL query string. The structure of the photo.aspx page is a sort of boilerplate code:

```
<script runat="server">
void Page_Load(object sender, EventArgs e) {
   // Prepare the SQL command
   // TO DO

   // Execute the command and get the image bytes
   SqlConnection conn = new SqlConnection(conn_string);
   SqlCommand cmd = new SqlCommand(cmdText, conn);
   conn.Open();
   byte[] img = (byte[]) cmd.ExecuteScalar();
   conn.Close();

   // Output the image bytes
   Response.ContentType = "image/jpeg";
   Response.OutputStream.Write(img, 0, img.Length);
}
</script>
```

The code is nearly identical in classic ASP, with the obvious changes related to the use of ADO.NET classes. You end up maintaining multiple image manipulation pages—one per each logical group of images and image data stores. What's missing in classic ASP and ASP.NET 1.x is an ad hoc image generation service and more powerful image controls. ASP.NET 2.0 fills that gap.

> **Note** In ASP.NET 1.x, using a made-to-measure HTTP handler instead of a plain ASPX page results in slightly more efficient code because an HTTP handler with an .ashx extension (or a custom extension) doesn't go through the same long pipeline as a regular Web page. An HTTP handler engages the HTTP runtime less than a regular page does. As you'll see in a moment, the same pattern is maintained in ASP.NET 2.0.

The *DynamicImage* Control

ASP.NET 1.x has the *Image* control, which is little more than a wrapper around the *<img>* HTML tag. The *Image* control provides a thin layer of abstraction over some of the *<img>* properties. In the end, it allows you to reference images only by URL and to set some of the image layout attributes.

In the real world, images can have a variety of origins. An image can be the content of a file, it can be stored in a database field, or it can be dynamically generated in memory using a graphic API such as the GDI+ classes. As you can see, only the first case—when a disk file is used—is well served by the *<img>* tag and the ASP.NET 1.x API. In all other cases, programmers must write their own code.

In spite of the many possible sources for image bytes, the Web page still handles the same logical entity—an image. Ideally, you should always be able to reference images in the same way, irrespective of the storage medium. But the *<img>* tag and the ASP.NET *Image* class are patently inadequate for the job.

ASP.NET 2.0 provides one more image-related control that you met back in Chapter 1: *DynamicImage*. It derives from *DynamicImageBase*, which in turn derives from *Image*.

Architecture of Dynamic Image Controls

The *DynamicImage* control acquires the image bytes from a variety of sources and renders them on all image-capable devices. Each supported source is bound to a property, as shown in Table 8-6.

Table 8-6 Sources for Dynamic Images

Property	Description
Image	The image is stored as an instance of a GDI+ image class. The property is of type *System.Drawing.Image.* This format is ideal for dynamically created images.
ImageBytes	The image is stored as an array of bytes. It is suitable for images stored in databases.
ImageFile	The image is stored in the specified URL.
ImageGeneratorUrl	The image is returned by the specified HTTP handler. ASP.NET defines a new, image-specific HTTP handler. The extension is .asix.

Whatever the source format, the image is internally normalized to a *System.Drawing.Image* object and cached in the ASP.NET *Cache* with a randomly generated key. What kind of markup code is sent to the browser to accommodate images stored in the cache? Have a look at Figure 8-6.

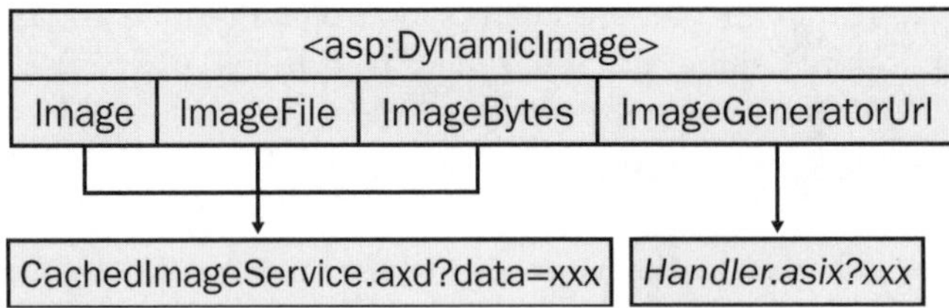

Figure 8-6 The internal architecture of the *DynamicImage* class

If you set the image using the *Image*, *ImageBytes*, or *ImageFile* property, the control generates an *<img>* tag that points to the URL of an internal image-generation service named CachedImageService.axd. Consider the following ASP.NET code:

```
<asp:dynamicimage runat="server" id="MyFileImage"
    ImageFile="images/tools.jpg" />
```

When the page runs, the following markup is generated for an HTML browser:

```
<img id="MyFileImage"
    src="CachedImageService.axd?data={guid}"
    alt=""
    style="border-width:0px;" />
```

The CachedImageService.axd URL is a built-in HTTP handler. It retrieves the image from the ASP.NET *Cache* object and serializes its bytes to the browser using the proper content type. The *data* parameter in the handler's query string is the key used to select the image in the ASP.NET *Cache*. Each cached image is identified with a dynamically generated GUID. If you need to know the exact URL of the image being generated, you can use the *ImageUrl* (read-only) property.

The CachedImageService.axd service converts the size and type (such as JPEG or GIF) of images based on the display capabilities of the browser. If the browser cannot render the type of image, the service converts the image to a type supported on that browser.

The Programming Interface of Dynamic Image Controls

Table 8-7 lists the properties of the *DynamicImage* class. The list includes the properties inherited from the *DynamicImageBase* class, but not those inherited from *WebControl* and *Image*.

Table 8-7 Properties of the *DynamicImage* Class

Property	Description
DesktopScaling	A Boolean property that indicates whether the image should be resized before it's stored in the cache. This allows you to resize images for the desktop (create thumbnails).
Height	Inherited from *DynamicImageBase*, this property gets and sets the height of the image in pixels.
Image	An object of type *System.Drawing.Image*, this property gets and sets the source of the dynamic image.
ImageBytes	Gets and sets a reference to a byte array that contains the dynamic image.
ImageFile	Gets and sets the name of the file that contains the image.
ImageGeneratorUrl	Gets and sets the URL of the HTTP handler image-generation service to use.
ImageType	Inherited from *DynamicImageBase*, this property gets and sets the preferred image type for the dynamic image.
ImageUrl	Inherited from *DynamicImageBase*, this property gets the URL used to generate the dynamic image. More precisely, the property is declared read/write, but if you try to set it, an exception is thrown because the operation is not supported. This behavior is by design.
MobileScaling	Gets information about how the image will be scaled for use on mobile devices.
Parameters	Gets a collection of parameters to pass to the image-generation service. This property is used primarily when an HTTP handler is used to generate the image.
Width	Inherited from *DynamicImageBase*, this property gets and sets the width of the image in pixels.

The *DesktopScaling* and *MobileScaling* properties are totally independent and don't affect each other's rendering. Desktop scaling concerns image resizing and caching. When the *DesktopScaling* property is set to *true*, the image is resized or scaled on the server before being stored in the cache. This is an effective way to resize images and create thumbnails. Note that if only one dimension (height or width) is specified, the scaled image maintains the same aspect ratio; otherwise, it is scaled to the specified dimensions or raises an exception if neither the height nor the width are known. In all cases, you can output the final size of the image to the browser by setting the *width* and *height* attributes of the *<img>* tag.

The *MobileScaling* property is defined as an instance of the *ImageScaling* class and refers to sizing (reducing) images for mobile devices only. The *ImageScaling* class contains two properties—*PercentScreenCover* and *ScaleMode*. The former gets or sets the percentage of the requesting browser's screen that the image should occupy. The latter, of type *ImageScaleMode*, indicates whether and how the image is scaled. Acceptable values include *NoScaling*, *FitBasedOnXxx*, and *ScaleBasedOnXxx*, where *Xxx* can be *Width* or *Height*. The difference between scale and fit mode is that in scale mode you can have one dimension of an image exceed the device's screen. Fit mode always ensures that both dimensions fit the available screen.

> **Important** When you set the width and height for a dynamic image, you must use pixels. If you try to define width or height using percentages, no compile error is returned but an exception is thrown at run time.

The *ImageUrl* property is read-only for dynamic images and is not used to set a URL. You should use it only to read the actual URL for the image that is sent to the browser. Use one of the properties in Table 8-6 to select an image. Note, though, that if more than one of these properties is set, an exception is thrown.

Displaying Images in ASP.NET Pages

ASP.NET 2.0 offers two image server controls—*Image* and *DynamicImage*. You use the former to reference a static image stored to a server-side file. If you can reference an image using a URL, by all means use the *Image* control, which produces the following, quite familiar, markup:

```
<img src="url" />
```

Referencing static images via a URL remains the fastest way to have an image downloaded to a client. No extra code is required, and the browser and the Web server handle it automatically without involving the ASP.NET runtime.

The *DynamicImage* control provides a familiar programming interface in addition to alternative ways to get image bytes. You should use the *DynamicImage* control when the image you want to return cannot be addressed using a static and immutable URL. If the image resides in a database or is created on the fly, using *DynamicImage* results in much better performance—primarily because the image-generation service running behind the control implements caching. Also, the *DynamicImage* control always uses an optimized HTTP handler to return images to the browser. Performance-wise, this is better than writing an ASPX page that returns a content type of JPEG or GIF. Let's look at how to use the *DynamicImage* control.

Images from Files

The *ImageFile* property requires you to indicate a virtual path to a displayable image. If you specify a physical path such as *c:\image.gif*, an exception is thrown. So if image files are involved, where's the difference between *Image* and *DynamicImage*? First let's look at the *Image* control:

```
<asp:image runat="server" ImageUrl="image.jpg" />
```

Image generates a direct reference to the image's URL, and the content of that file is returned to all browsers that make a request. If the *DynamicImage* control is used, no direct link to the image is stored, which results in worse performance compared to *Image*. However, the referenced image can be adapted to the effective capabilities of the requesting browser, is automatically cached on the server, and can have the format changed on the fly.

```
<asp:dynamicimage runat="server" id="MyFileImage"
ImageFile="image.jpg" />
```

The image that the *ImageFile* property references is loaded in memory, cached as a *System.Drawing.Image* object, and manipulated to meet the browser's capabilities if need be. If you use *DynamicImage* with virtual filenames, you pay a price in performance but gain a lot in flexibility with downlevel and mobile browsers.

Images from Databases

The *ImageBytes* property lets you specify the contents of an image using a byte array. For example, images stored within the BLOB field of a database are expressed and returned as an array of bytes. As the following listing shows, the

ImageBytes property is data-bindable and can be declaratively set using a data-bound expression:

```
<asp:dynamicimage runat="server" id="MyDatabaseImage"
     ImageBytes='<%# GetEmployeePhoto(Int32.Parse(EmpID.Text)) %>'
/>
```

The *GetEmployeePhoto* function returns a byte array obtained from a BLOB field. The parameter passed to the function is used to select the right picture. The following code shows a possible implementation of the *GetEmployeePhoto* function:

```
private string ConnString = "SERVER=…;DATABASE=northwind;UID=…;";
public byte[] GetEmployeePhoto(int empID)
{
   SqlConnection conn = new SqlConnection(ConnString);
   SqlCommand cmd = new SqlCommand();
   cmd.Connection = conn;
   cmd.CommandText = "SELECT photo FROM employees WHERE employeeid=" +
                     empID.ToString();
   conn.Open();
   byte[] img = (byte[]) cmd.ExecuteScalar();

   // Must pass through a MemoryStream object because the photo
   // field on the Northwind.Employees table has a 78-byte prefix
   // to skip. Just return img if this is not the case for your database
   MemoryStream ms = new MemoryStream (img, 78, img.Length - 78);
   conn.Close();
   return ms.ToArray();
}
```

Note that when you use <%# … %> data-bound expressions, you must also ensure that a call to *Page.DataBind* is made to fire the data-binding process. Without a pagewide (or control-specific) *DataBind* call, the *ImageBytes* property isn't bound to data. Note, though, that *ImageBytes* can be set programmatically at any time.

Dynamically Generated Images

The *DynamicImage* control also supports images exposed as instances of a class derived from *System.Drawing.Image*—for example, *Bitmap*. In this case, you use the *Image* property. Like *ImageBytes*, *Image* is data-bindable and can be used in data-bound expressions. The following code shows how to display a dynamically generated image that represents a random number:

```
<asp:dynamicimage runat="server" id="MyImage"
     Image='<%# GetRandomNumber(Int32.Parse(MaxNum.Text)) %>' />
```

The function *GetRandomNumber* builds and returns a *System.Drawing.Image* object, as shown here:

```
public System.Drawing.Image GetRandomNumber(int max)
{
   Font f = new Font("Impact", 20);
   Random gen = new Random();

   // Get the number
   int number = gen.Next(max);

   // Generate the image
   Bitmap bmp = new Bitmap(100, 60);
   Graphics g = Graphics.FromImage(bmp);
   g.Clear(Color.LightCyan);
   g.DrawString(number.ToString(), f, Brushes.Blue, 10, 10);

   f.Dispose();
   g.Dispose ();
   return bmp;
}
```

In all these cases, the image is served to the browser through the ASP.NET internal image-generation service, CachedImageService.axd.

Using a Custom Image-Generation Service

ASP.NET 2.0 reserves a new file extension along with the familiar .aspx, .asmx, and .ashx extensions. The new extension. .asix, identifies user-defined HTTP handlers that return images. An .asix file defines a class that inherits *ImageGenerator*—the class that provides base functionality for custom image-generation services. Image-generation handlers are compiled at run time as *ImageGenerator* objects and then cached in server memory.

The following listing illustrates an image generator that takes a string and creates an image that represents it. We'll call this component *textgen.asix*.

```
<%@ Image Class="TextGenerator" Language="C#" %>
using System;
using System.Drawing;
using System.IO;
using System.Web.UI.Imaging;

public class TextGenerator : ImageGenerator
{
   protected override void RenderImage(Graphics g)
   {
      string text = "<No Parameters>";
         int fontSize = 20;
```

```
        if (Request["Text"] != null)
            text = Request["Text"].ToString();
        else
        if (Parameters["Text"] != null)
           text = Parameters["Text"].ToString();
        else
        {
               fontSize = 8;
        }

        Font f = new Font("Arial", fontSize);
        g.FillRectangle(Brushes.LightCyan, g.ClipBounds);
        g.DrawString(text, f, Brushes.Black, g.ClipBounds);
           f.Dispose();
    }
}
```

To write a new image generator, at a minimum you inherit *ImageGenerator* and override the *RenderImage* protected method. The *RenderImage* method receives a *Graphics* object that represents the logical surface where the image will be created. You reference the image using the *ImageGeneratorUrl* property and make it point to the ASIX handler:

```
<asp:dynamicimage runat="server" id="MyAsixImage"
     ImageGeneratorUrl="textgen.asix" />
```

An image generator object can receive input in two ways—through the URL query string and using the *DynamicImage*'s *Parameters* collection. In the former case, the browser ends up referencing the image as follows:

```
textgen.asix?param1=…&param2=…
```

The image generator retrieves query string parameters using the *Request* object and the *QueryString* collection. This approach is viable when you programmatically bind to the image generator, but it doesn't lend itself well to declarative binding. In this case, the *Parameters* collection is more helpful:

```
<asp:dynamicimage runat="server" id="MyAsixImage"
     ImageGeneratorUrl="textgen.asix">
 <parameters>
    <asp:parameter Name="Text" DefaultValue="I love ASP.NET 2.0" />
 </parameters>
</asp:dynamicimage>
```

The code defines a single parameter named *Text*, which is set to a default value. The ASIX generator should look for this parameter in both the *Request* and *Parameters* collections exposed by its base class. As a final note, consider that parameters can also be defined programmatically using the typical interface of name/value collection classes.

Figure 8-7 shows a page formed by four images, each obtained using one of the techniques discussed so far.

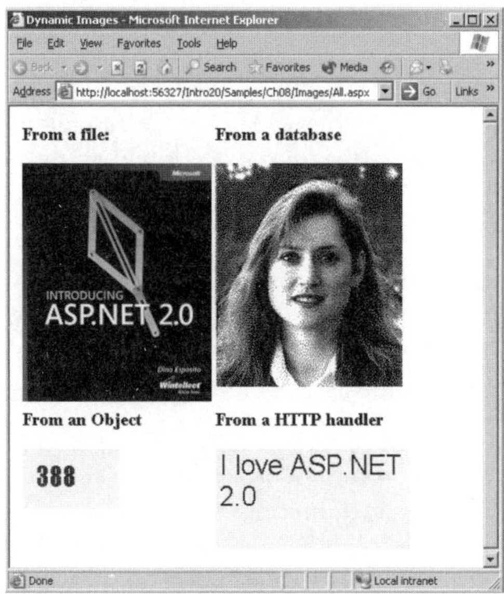

Figure 8-7 Dynamic images created using the techniques supported by ASP.NET 2.0

Advanced Site Functionality

The more a Web site grows in complexity and functionality, the more the administrator will appreciate statistics about user activity. The more a Web site grows in size, incorporating new pages and directories, the more users need help to orient themselves in the forest of links, URLs, and references. ASP.NET 2.0 addresses both points with a site navigation API and a site counter service.

Site Structure and Navigation

The idea of content navigation is tightly connected to the idea of the Web. In the beginning, though, the URL of a page, and perhaps its directory information, were enough to easily identify the desired resource. The URL itself was the key to accessing a resource, and the short descriptive text displayed by the hyperlink was more than helpful. But what was true for the Web of 8 or 10 years ago is completely inadequate for the Web of today, in which the complexity of many sites makes it virtually impossible to retrieve a resource by URL.

We can safely assume that all sites now require some form of content navigation. ASP.NET 2.0 comes with a built-in navigation infrastructure for configuring, storing, and rendering site navigation. This infrastructure has three key components:

- **Site structure** A common programming interface lists the inherently hierarchical structure of a Web site. This programming interface is exposed via a site map object that site map provider components fill with information read from a given data store. The default data store is a root-level XML file tentatively named app.sitemap.
- **Site navigation** Each node defined in the site map is associated with a URL so that page developers can easily retrieve and use at run time the root URL of a site section. In other words, any element defined in the site structure must be bound to a URL for run-time access.
- **Site structure display** This component renders the site navigation user interface in an intelligent fashion and maps user-friendly URLs to appropriate ASPX file paths.

To understand the importance of built-in tools for site navigation, consider the following common scenario. In a large Web site that contains thousands of files, how do you organize a consistent site navigation mechanism? Large Web sites (such as portals) are usually changing constantly, and many different groups of developers and designers work on the site. ASP.NET 2.0 makes it possible to use several files and different data stores to specify a site's structure. Each team can freely manage the pages they own, but they are bound to a common programming interface, which greatly simplifies access to the site navigation structure from any page.

Defining the Site Map

A site map is the logical container for a hierarchical collection of nodes, each representing a page in the application. Within a site map, individual pages are grouped together in folders that might or might not correspond to a physical folder. In ASP.NET 2.0 the default representation of a site map is usually an XML file named web.sitemap, like the one shown here:

```
<siteMap>
  <siteMapNode title="Home" url="default.aspx">
    <siteMapNode title="Articles" url="articles/articles.aspx">
      <siteMapNode title="Article 1" url="articles/demoart1.aspx" />
```

```
      <siteMapNode title="Article 2" url="articles/demoart2.aspx" />
    </siteMapNode>
    <siteMapNode title="Picture Gallery" url="Photo/Albums.aspx">
      <siteMapNode title="Meetings" url="Photo/Album.aspx?id=1" />
      <siteMapNode title="Activities" url="Photo/Album.aspx?id=2" />
      <siteMapNode title="Training" url="Photo/Album.aspx?id=3" />
    </siteMapNode>
  </siteMapNode>
</siteMap>
```

The site map file, if any, is parsed and transformed into a *SiteMap* object. The *SiteMap* object is globally accessible through a bunch of static methods.

The XML file shown above is made up of a hierarchy of *<siteMapNode>* elements, each containing a *title* and a *url* attribute, and an optional *description* attribute. The former returns a friendly name for the element; the latter indicates the URL to jump to when that portion of the site is selected. You can also specify the contents of a site map node by referencing an external file, as the following code snippet demonstrates:

```
<siteMap>
  <siteMapNode title="Home" url="default.aspx" />
  <siteMapNode title="About Us" url="about.aspx" />
</siteMap>
```

To reference an external site map file, you use the *siteMapFile* attribute on the *<siteMapNode>* element.

```
<siteMap>
  <siteMapNode title="Home" url="default.aspx" />
  <siteMapNode siteMapFile="picturegallery.sitemap" />
  ⋮
</siteMap>
```

The child site map file has the same structure as the parent and begins with a root *<siteMap>* node.

Accessing Site Map Information

The *SiteMap* object acts as an interface to site navigation information. This information is expressed in the form of *SiteMapNode* objects. The site map information exposed through the *SiteMap* object is loaded by a registered site map provider. The default site map provider is the *XmlSiteMapProvider* class, which works with the aforementioned XML configuration file named web.sitemap. A site map provider is a class that implements the *ISiteMapProvider* interface. A provider can store its site map information in any way, including in databases.

The *SiteMap* object doesn't maintain the relationships between the nodes; it delegates this responsibility to the site provider. The *SiteMap* object exposes the static properties listed in Table 8-8.

Table 8-8 Static Properties of the *SiteMap* Object

Property	Description
CurrentNode	Gets a *SiteMapNode* that represents the currently requested page
Provider	Returns the site provider object for the current site map
Providers	Returns a collection of named site provider objects that are available to the *SiteMap* object
RootNode	Gets a *SiteMapNode* that represents the top-level page of the site's navigation structure

The following code shows how to programmatically access any site map information and build the user interface of the home page. The following page contains a horizontal bar showing a brief description of the home page and a vertical menu:

```
<html>
<head runat="server">
    <title>My Site</title>
</head>
<body>
  <form runat="server">
      <asp:panel runat="Server" backcolor="cyan" width="100%">
         <h1><asp:label runat="server" id="Caption" /></h1>
      </asp:panel>
      <table width="100%"><tr>
         <td style="width:200;" bgcolor="lightcyan" valign="top">
           <asp:bulletedlist runat="server" id="MyLinks"
                displaymode="HyperLink" />
         </td>
         <td style="width:10;" bgcolor="lightcyan"></td>
         <td valign="top">Content of the page</td>
      </tr></table>
  </form>
</body>
</html>
```

This structure is populated at run time using the following code, which uses site map information:

```
<script runat="server">
    void Page_Load (object sender, EventArgs e) {
        InitSiteMap();
    }
```

```
    void InitSiteMap () {
        Caption.Text = SiteMap.RootNode.Title;
        foreach(SiteMapNode node in SiteMap.RootNode.ChildNodes) {
            ListItem li = new ListItem();
            li.Text = node.Title;
            li.Value = node.Url;
            MyLinks.Items.Add (li);
        }
    }
</script>
```

Based on the web.sitemap file shown earlier, the root node has two child nodes—About Us and Products. For each of these nodes, an entry into a bulleted list control is created. Figure 8-8 shows the final results.

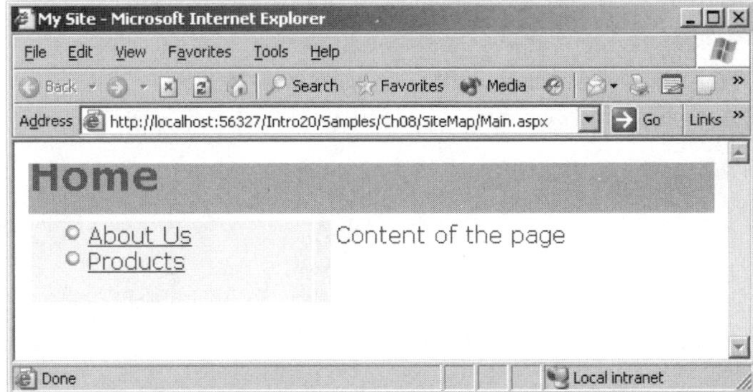

Figure 8-8 Building the home page of a Web site using site map information

Binding Site Map Information to Controls

Site map information is hierarchical data and as such can be automatically handled by hierarchical data-bound controls such as *TreeView*. As you saw in Chapter 6, ASP.NET 2.0 provides a site map–specific data source control that was designed to work with *TreeView* and *Menu* hierarchical controls. The following code shows how to declare a site map data source object and bind it to a tree view and a menu control:

```
<asp:sitemapdatasource runat="server" id="MySiteMap" />
<asp:treeview runat="server" datasourceid="MySiteMap">
   <rootnodestyle font-bold="true" />
   <parentnodestyle font-bold="true" />
   <nodestyle font-size="0.8em" />
   <databindings>
      <asp:treenodebinding navigateurlfield="url" textfield="title" />
   </databindings>
</asp:treeview>
<asp:Menu runat="server" DataSourceID="MySiteMap" />
```

The tree view is bound to the site map data source object through the *DataSourceId* property and is instructed to show nodes based on the *title* and *url* attributes in the site map. Figure 8-9 shows the final results.

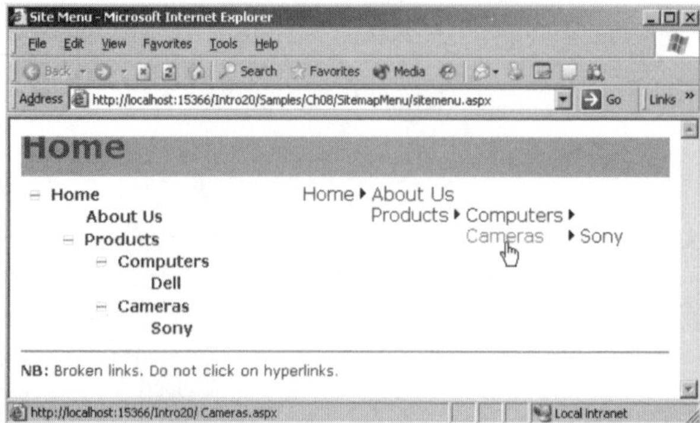

Figure 8-9 Site map information bound and displayed using *TreeView* and *Menu* controls

The *SiteMapPath* Control

Along with bindable site map information, ASP.NET 2.0 also provides a ready-to-use control that shows where a given page lives in the site hierarchy. Once you have configured a site map provider and defined the actual site map, this is as easy as dropping a *SiteMapPath* control on the page:

```
<asp:sitemappath runat="server" />
```

The *SiteMap* object is found, and any needed information is extracted and displayed. There is no need to add a *SiteMapDataSource* object if all you want is to display the site path to the current page. Figure 8-10 shows the default output of the site map path control.

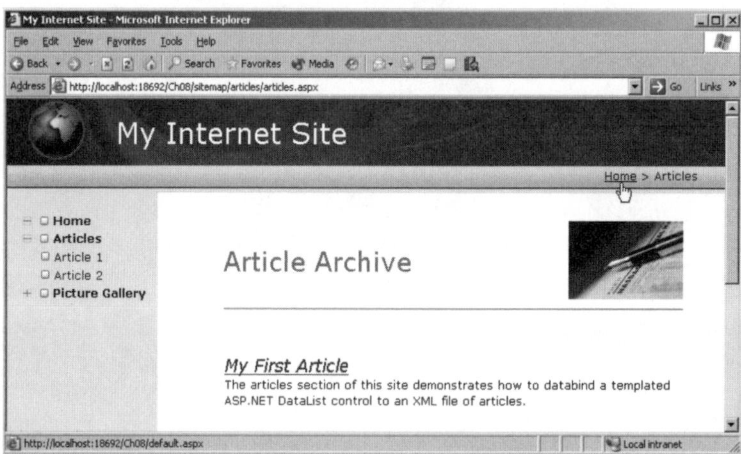

Figure 8-10 Site map information bound and displayed by a treeview control

By default, a site map path control returns a string in which all the site map nodes found along the way to the physical path are concatenated using a > separator. Each element is rendered as a hyperlink that points to the corresponding page. The appearance of the control can be customized to some extent using style properties such as *CurrentNodeStyle*, *HoverNodeStyle*, *RootNodeStyle*, and *NodeStyle*. You can customize the path separator, too, using your preferred colors, font, and style.

Site Counters

Monitoring visitor activity is an important administrative task for improving the quality and contents of the site. Impressions and click-throughs are two metrics commonly used to evaluate activity on a Web site. An *impression* is a viewing of some specific content, such as a page or an advertisement. A *click-through* is a user's click to see specific content. To measure the effectiveness of an advertisement, both impressions and click-throughs are usually tracked. The ratio of clicks to impressions—the click-through rate—gives an idea of how site visitors receive the advertising.

ASP.NET 2.0 provides a few built-in counters to track user activity, particularly impressions and click-throughs. The site counter API collects counts and write-related and read-related data to a database via an ad hoc provider. The underlying API on which these counters are based can also be used by server control developers to create their own counters.

Applications can collect counter data in two nonexclusive ways: by enabling built-in counters and by directly using the site counter API to write counts. Built-in counters include page view counters and counters for clicks on server controls such as *HyperLink* and *AdRotator*. The information collected is sent to the provider, which stores it to a persistent medium—typically, a SQL Server or Access database. Site counter information can be collected later both programmatically and through Web Administration tool reports.

Counting Clicks on Server Controls

Some server controls provide a built-in implementation of the site counter service. This results in a handful of new properties added to some ASP.NET button-like controls. The controls with built-in support for counters are *AdRotator*, *HyperLink*, *Button*, *ImageButton*, *LinkButton*, *PhoneLink*, and *ImageMap*. The site counter service is disabled by default, but it is turned on when the programmer sets the *CountClicks* Boolean property to *true*. This can be done both programmatically and declaratively.

To support the site counter service, the preceding controls expose additional properties, listed in Table 8-9. All the properties are read/write.

Table 8-9 Site Counter Properties

Property	Description
CountClicks	Gets or sets whether click-through events should be counted each time the control is clicked. It is set to *false* by default.
CounterGroup	Gets or sets the (optional) group name of the click-through counter to use. By default, it is set to the class name of the control.
CounterName	Gets or sets the name of the click-through counter to use. By default, the target URL of the control is used.
CountViews	Gets or sets whether displaying a control is an event that should be counted. It's set to *false* by default. (More later.)
RowsPerDay	Gets or sets the number of rows of data that should be collected for a given day. For example, if the number is 24, one row is collected every hour.
SiteCountersProvider	Gets or sets the name of the provider to be used by the control. If this is set to an invalid provider, an exception is thrown. It is the empty string by default, which means that the default provider will be used.
TrackApplicationName	Indicates whether the application name will be tracked by the SiteCounters service and stored in the database. It's set to *true* by default.
TrackNavigateUrl	Indicates whether the destination URL of the click-through event is tracked. It's set to *true* by default.
TrackPageUrl	Indicates whether the URL for the page that contains the control will be tracked. It's set to *true* by default.

Note that not all controls that support site counters expose all the properties listed in the table. In particular, *CountViews* appears only on *AdRotator*, whereas *TrackNavigateUrl* is specific to *HyperLink* and *AdRotator*.

For the properties to work, the site counter service must be enabled in the configuration file. You control the state of the service through the *enabled* attribute on the *<siteCounters>* section. The service is enabled by default. An ASP.NET application that wants to use site counters must have the site counter database set up before it starts. You set up the provider and the related database using the Web Site Administration tool. The default provider, AspNetAccessProvider, uses the same Access aspnetdb.mdb database in which personalization data is stored. (See Chapter 4.)

> **Note** *TrackApplicationName*, *TrackNavigateUrl*, and *TrackPageUrl* are Boolean properties, so you can specify only whether the application name, the target, and the page URL are tracked. You cannot indicate the name or the URL to track.

The following code shows a hyperlink control configured to track clicks:

```
<asp:hyperlink id="Hyperlink1" runat="server"
    navigateurl="http://www.contoso.com"
    text="Visit us at Contoso.com"
    countclicks="true" countername="Contoso.com" />
```

As Figure 8-11 shows, the hyperlink doesn't point directly to the specified URL. This is reasonable; how could the click be tracked otherwise? The destination URL is counters.axd—a new HTTP handler that registers the event and then redirects to the original URL. The handler receives information about counters and the URL in encoded form. Site counter–enabled controls use the machine key code to scramble the query string. Finally, notice that multiple clickable controls in the application can be linked to the same counter.

Figure 8-11 A hyperlink control with counting enabled doesn't point to the original URL. (See the status bar.)

Tracking Page Views

You can designate a page for counting by tweaking one of the application's web.config files. In particular, you must turn on the *enabled* attribute in the *<pageCounters>* section. The page counter is disabled by default. Depending on the scope of the tweaked web.config file, all pages or a group of pages can be designated for counting.

```
<system.web>
   <siteCounters>
      <pageCounters enabled="true" />
   </siteCounters>
</system.web>
```

Enabling the page view tracking doesn't significantly affect overall page performance. The site counter service is implemented as an HTTP module. This module intercepts the *Application_EndRequest* event and writes data out to the site provider. As a result, counter data is written only when the request has completed and doesn't affect generation of the markup. The time taken to log counters is negligible compared to the time needed to render page content to the client, even for very simple pages.

Accessing Counters Programmatically

In addition to using counters declaratively from pages and server controls, you can also update counters programmatically. You use the static members of the *SiteCounters* class, which represents the public API for reading and writing counter data. The following code shows how you can write data when a few controls are clicked on a page:

```
void OnRate(object sender, BulletedListEventArgs e) {
    Rate(e.Index);
}
void Rate (int index) {
   string displayRate = Feedback.Items[index].Text;
   string rate = Feedback.Items[index].Value;

   string baseText = "You rated this book as <b>{0}</b>.<br>";
   Thanks.Text = String.Format (baseText, displayRate);

   SiteCounters.Write("Book Feedback", "IntroAspNet20", rate,
       null, true, true);
}
```

The *OnRate* event handler is bound to the *Click* event of a *BulletedList* control:

```
<h2>How would you rate this book?</h2>
<asp:bulletedlist runat="server" id="Feedback"
     displaymode="LinkButton"
     onclick="OnRate" >
   <asp:listitem value="5">Outstanding</asp:listitem>
   <asp:listitem value="4">Excellent</asp:listitem>
   <asp:listitem value="3">Great</asp:listitem>
   <asp:listitem value="99">More than I can say...</asp:listitem>
</asp:bulletedlist>
```

The value associated with each list item is written to the counter database when the corresponding item is clicked.

The *Write* method of the *SiteCounters* class has several overloads. The one we use here requires you to specify the counter group, the counter name, some text that describes the event, the target URL (if any), and whether you want the application name and page URL be tracked. In this case, we write some optional information associated with the event—the feedback. This information, known as the *counter event data*, is coded as a string and can be useful for grouping data, as you'll see in moment.

The *SiteCounters* class has a few methods for extracting data from the provider's database. For example, the *GetRows* methods returns a *DataSet* object filled with the whole site counter table. Figure 8-12 shows the actual content of the *DataSet* in the sample application (rendered in a *GridView*).

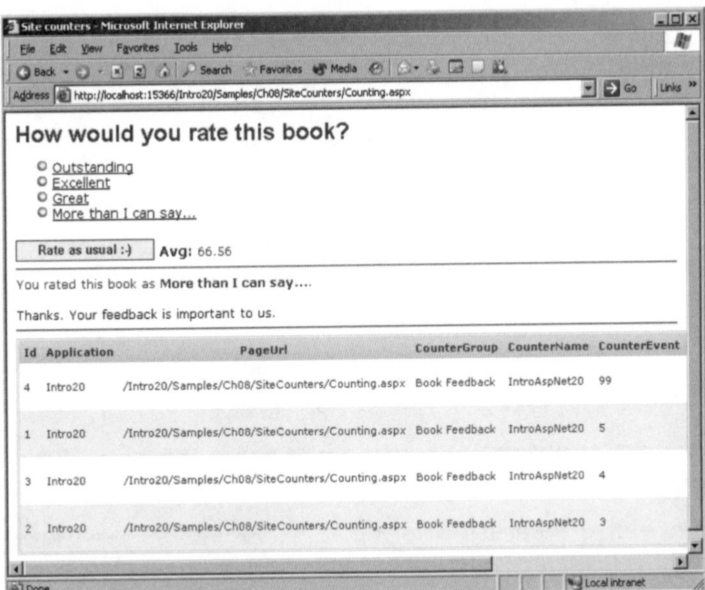

Figure 8-12 The *DataSet* object that contains the current snapshot of the site counter database

You get the data and bind it to a *GridView* control using the following code:

```
DataSet data = SiteCounters.GetRows(DateTime.MinValue,
    DateTime.MaxValue, "Book Feedback", "IntroAspNet20");
Results.DataSource = data;
Results.DataBind();
```

The *GetRows* method requires a time interval—all records are selected in the preceding snippet—plus the counter group and counter name. Once you hold counter data as a *DataSet*, you can easily implement custom functions over the data. For example, you can calculate the average rate by summing the counter event data and dividing it by the total number of clicks:

```
int total = 0;
int clicks = 0;
foreach(DataRow row in data.Tables[0].Rows)
{
   int eventClicks = (int) row["Total"];
   int eventTotal = Int32.Parse((string)row["CounterEvent"]) * eventClicks;
   total += eventTotal;
   clicks += eventClicks;
}
Avg.Text = String.Format ("{0:f}", ((float)total / (float)clicks));
```

Site Counter Providers

The site counter service relies on the services of a site provider object to implement persistent data storage. ASP.NET 2.0 comes with two built-in providers—one using an Access database and one using a SQL Server table. Script are provided to create and configure the databases off line. You can accomplish the same task through the visual interface of the Web Administration Tool integrated into Microsoft Visual Studio.

ADO.NET classes are used to manage writing and reading on these tables. You can explore the structure of the default site counter table by looking at the aspnetdb.mdb file in the Data subdirectory of the application. The site counter table is named *aspnet_SiteCounters*.

Summary

Several times in this book, you've seen the word *codeless* used in a discussion of programming to describe features that allow you to create relatively simple pages with no code at all. Will the day come when programmers become useless? Of course not—or at least not because of incredibly powerful software tools. Codeless programming will probably remain an unreachable ideal, even though the ASP.NET 2.0 literature liberally uses the words *codeless* and *programming* together. Codeless programming is possible in ASP.NET 2.0, but it is worthwhile in only a small number of real-world situations—specifically, in the case of application services.

Application services help programmers build more advanced functions with less code. An application service can be provided by controls as well as low-level ASP.NET pipeline components such as HTTP modules and handlers. This chapter discussed a few of the new application services in ASP.NET 2.0. In particular, we focused on the cutting-edge *Wizard* control and a couple of services that run alongside your code—dynamic image generation and site counters. As part of the ASP.NET infrastructure, all these features come at a cost. However, site counters and dynamic images add value to your overall application and the extra cost is negligible.

9

State Management

For applications to work on top of a stateless protocol such as HTTP, state maintenance is essential. Web pages are destroyed and re-created during each round trip to the server, so page information cannot exist beyond the life cycle of a single page request. State management is the process by which you maintain state and page information over multiple requests. ASP.NET provides multiple ways to maintain state between server round trips, which fall into two general categories: client-side and server-side approaches. The right approach depends on the application; you must consider the amount and sensitivity of the information, where you want to store it, your performance goals, and other factors.

In ASP.NET, the client-side options are the view state, hidden fields, and cookies. Server-side storage media include some intrinsic objects such as *Application*, *Session*, and *Cache*. Storing page information on the client means you don't use any server resources, but you risk the confidentiality and security of the information unless you encrypt the data. There is also a practical limit on how much information you can send to the client for storage. Server-side options for storing page information are generally preferable because of the higher security standards. On the downside, valuable Web server resources are consumed, which can lead to scalability issues if the size of the information store is large.

To balance data security and performance, ASP.NET 1.x introduced the *Cache* object in addition to supporting the familiar ASP *Application* and *Session* objects. The *Session* object was also redesigned from the ground up. ASP.NET 2.0 introduces even more enhancements:

- Control state for custom ASP.NET controls
- Custom session-state management options
- Mechanism for handling custom cache dependencies, including SQL Server database dependencies

From a custom control's perspective, the new client-side storage medium, control state, is more reliable than view state. It is not only independent of view state, but it is also completely customizable in terms of programming interface and data format. The session state can be persisted in any data storage medium for which you can get or write a session state provider object. Any information placed in the ASP.NET cache can be invalidated by user-defined events. An insightful example of this technique comes as a separate feature, too. In ASP.NET 2.0, you can cache the results of a SQL Server query and have it invalidated when one of the displayed records is updated.

The Control State

An ASP.NET server control can participate in state management by using the view state object. All controls inherit the *ViewState* property from the base class *Control* and can use it to store state information as name/value pairs. The *ViewState* property returns an instance of the *StateBag* class—a sort of specialized dictionary object. What's the control state, then, and how does it differ from the ASP.NET 1.x view state?

At a high level of abstraction, the control state and the view state are similar. The key difference is that the control state is completely handled by the control. No page or application-level setting can affect the structure, storage, or even availability of the control state. In a certain way, the control state is the control's private view state.

Control State vs. View State

It is not uncommon for a server control to persist information across postbacks. For example, consider what happens to a *DataGrid* control that supports auto-reverse sorting. When the user clicks to sort by a column, the control compares the current sort expression and the new sort expression. If the two coincide, the sort direction is reversed. How does the *DataGrid* track the current sort expression? There's the rub. It doesn't.

Drawbacks of the View State

Because you want your pages to show a fully sortable grid, you must find a workaround. As a smart ASP.NET developer, you decide to derive a new control from the *DataGrid* class and add a new property to it—say, *SortExpression*. You set the *SortExpression* property when the grid fires the *SortCommand* event, after the user clicks on the header of a sortable column. Unfortunately, if you don't place the *SortExpression* property in the control's view state, the sort expression will be lost as soon as the control renders to the browser.

To work around the issue, you implement a *get* and *set* accessor for the property that reads from and writes to the view state. This is a solution you can be proud of. But what happens if the control is used in a page that has the view state disabled? In ASP.NET 1.x, the control feature just stops working. You might see unexpected behaviors (that cause will you headaches) when you use rich custom controls—especially if these controls are not well documented.

When to Use Control State

Few built-in server controls make "private" use of the view state, and most often this is limited to particular features. Private use of the view state occurs when a control stores the content of nonpublic properties in the view state. In fact, the application can't access these properties due to the protection level, and not even default values can be restored. By storing internal properties to the view state, the control uses the view state privately. This action is perfectly legal, but it becomes dangerous when the view state is disabled. The necessity of using the view state for private or protected members grows with the complexity of the control. As mentioned, few ASP.NET controls make private use of the view state. The *TextBox* control persists its text between posts to the server for the *TextChanged* event to work correctly.

In ASP.NET 2.0, the control state replaces the private use of the view state. It is safer to use the control state than the view state because application and page-level settings cannot affect it. If your custom control has private or protected properties stored in the view state, you should move all of them to the control state in ASP.NET 2.0. Anything you store in the control state remains there until it is explicitly removed. The more data you pack into it, the more data is moved back and forth between the browser and the Web server. Unlike with the view state, though, there's no way to control the size of the control state. You should use control state in ASP.NET 2.0, but you should do so carefully.

Programming the Control State

The implementation of the control state is left to the programmer, which is both good and bad. It's bad because you have to implement serialization and deserialization for your control's state. It's good because you can control exactly how the control works and tweak its code to achieve optimal performance in the context in which you're using it.

The page infrastructure takes care of the actual data encoding and serialization. The control state is processed along with the view state information and undergoes the same treatment as for binary serialization and Base64 encoding. The control state is also persisted within the view state's hidden field.

Maintaining State for a Control

You store custom data to the control's view state by adding items to a dictionary object exposed through the *ViewState* property. This property is defined on the *Control* class and is inherited by all server controls. The *ViewState* property returns an object of type *StateBag*—a dictionary-like type.

There's no ready-made dictionary object to hold the items that form the control state. You no longer have to park your objects into a fixed container such as the *ViewState* state bag—you can maintain data in plain private or protected members. Among other things, this means that access to data is faster because it is more direct and is not mediated by a dictionary object. For example, if you need to track the sort direction of a grid, you can do so using the following variable:

```
private int _sortDirection;
```

In ASP.NET 1.x, you have to resort to the following:

```
private int _sortDirection
{
   get {return Int32.Parse(ViewState["SortDirection"]);}
   set {ViewState["SortDirection"] = value;}
}
```

In ASP.NET 2.0, you are responsible for the initialization of any private state property upon loading. The ASP.NET runtime takes care of restoring the view state when the page posts back and serializing it back to the browser when the page renders. You must do the same for the control state. Let's see how.

Persisting the Control State

When a page loads, the ASP.NET 2.0 runtime first restores the view state and then recursively calls into a new overridable method for all child controls, *LoadControlState*. The following pseudocode shows the control's typical behavior:

```
private override void LoadControlState(object savedState)
{
   // Make a copy of the saved state.
   // You know what type of object this is because
   // you saved it in the SaveControlState method.
   object[] currentState = (object[]) savedState;
   if (currentState == null)
      return;
```

```
    // Initialize any private/protected member you stored
    // in the control state. The values are packed in the same
    // order and format you stored them in the SaveControlState method.
    _myProperty1 = (int) currentState[0];
    _myProperty2 = (string) currentState[1];
  ⋮
}
```

The *LoadControlState* method receives an object identical to the one you created in *SaveControlState*. As a control developer, you know that type very well and can use this knowledge to extract any information that's useful for restoring the control state. For example, you might want to use an array of objects in which every slot corresponds to a particular property.

The following pseudocode gives an idea of the structure of the *SaveControlState* method:

```
protected override object SaveControlState()
{
   // Declare a properly sized array of objects
   object[] stateToSave = new Object[…];

   // Fill the array with local property values
   stateToSave[0] = _myProperty1;
   stateToSave[1] = _myProperty2;
   ⋮

   // Return the array
   return stateToSave;
}
```

You allocate a new data structure (such as an array of objects, a hashtable, or a custom type) and fill it with the private properties to persist across postbacks. The method terminates, returning this object to the ASP.NET runtime. The object is then binary-serialized and encoded to a Base64 stream. The class that you use to collect the control state properties must be serializable.

Extending the Session State Mechanism

Session state consists of a dictionary-based API that developers use to store user-specific data for the duration of a session. In ASP.NET 1.x, the session state mechanism uses an HTTP module to hook a few state-related application events. When the state is being acquired to serve the incoming request, the module retrieves the ID of the current session or generates a new session ID if a new session is being started. A new session ID is also generated if the user didn't store any data in the session state in previous requests.

The session ID is retrieved from an HTTP cookie (the default) or extracted from the URL (for cookieless sessions). In the case of cookieless sessions, the module redirects the browser to a fake URL, which has just been modified to embed the session ID. Once the module knows the ID of the current session, it attempts to load the state associated with it. Session state is a collection of name/value pairs that is retrieved from a storage medium and copied into the *HttpSessionState* object. This is the object you access through the familiar *Session* property.

In ASP.NET 1.x, the session HTTP module supports three storage modes for session data: *InProc*, *StateServer*, and *SqlServer*. When the session is configured to work in *InProc* mode, the data is stored in the ASP.NET *Cache* object—that is, in the ASP.NET worker process memory. *StateServer* mode stores data in the memory of a process separate from the ASP.NET worker process. This process is a Windows NT service called aspnet_state.exe that must be started manually. Finally, in *SqlServer* mode, session data is maintained in a SQL Server table.

In ASP.NET 2.0, developers can define custom data stores for session state. For example, if you need the robustness that a database-oriented solution can guarantee but you work with Oracle databases, you need not install SQL Server as well. You can support an Oracle session data store while using the same *Session* semantics and classes.

The extensibility model for session state offers two options: customizing bits and pieces of the existing ASP.NET session state mechanism (for example, creating an Oracle session provider or controlling the generation of the ID) and replacing the standard session state HTTP module with a new one. The former option is easier to implement but provides a limited set of features you can customize. The latter option is more complicated to code but provides the greatest flexibility. Let's review the conceptual specification of both these new features.

The Default Session State Module

Before going any further with customization and replacement, let's briefly review the behavior of the default session state module so you can fully understand the changes you can implement. The whole session mechanism is controlled by the HTTP session module. This module hooks up three application events—*AcquireRequestState*, *ReleaseRequestState*, and *EndRequest*. The tasks accomplished by each event handler are described in Figure 9-1.

If you're content with the preceding logic, you probably don't need to replace the session module altogether. Otherwise, you should use the steps outlined next as a basis for building your own module.

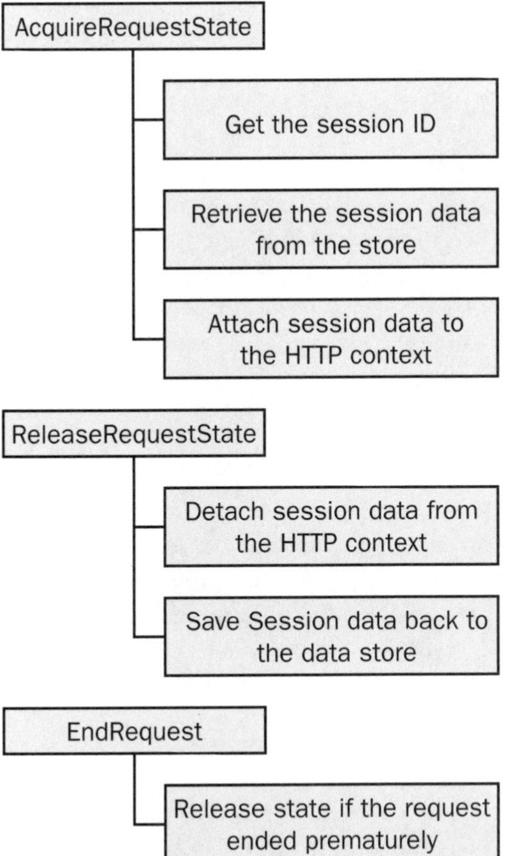

Figure 9-1 The overall behavior of the default session state module

Acquiring the State for the Request

When the *AcquireRequestState* event fires, the session module gets the ID of the current session. The ID can be read from a cookie or excerpted from the URL. If a new ID must be generated, the session module calls into another HTTP module. This module is a class that implements the *ISessionIDModule* interface. The name of the session ID generator is stored in the web.config file. By writing a custom class that behaves like a session ID module, you can completely customize the process that generates the ID of the session.

Next, the default session module uses this ID as a selector to load the session data from the data store. The data store is identified based on the information found in the web.config file. In ASP.NET 1.x, the data store can be the ASP.NET cache, SQL Server, or a Windows NT service. Using the session data obtained in the last step, the module populates a dictionary and adds it to the current HTTP context object. A valid dictionary for the session state is an object that implements the *IHttpSessionState* interface. Finally, if this is a new session, the module fires the *Session_OnStart* event.

Releasing the State for the Request

When the ASP.NET runtime is about to release the state for the current request, the session module detaches the session state dictionary from the HTTP context. If the session has been abandoned, it raises the *Session_OnEnd* event and removes the session data from the data store. If the session continues, the session module saves data back to the data store.

Note that the default session handler doesn't create an entry in the data store if the session state is empty. This causes a new session ID to be generated on the next request within the session.

Terminating the Request

The default session HTTP module also handles the *EndRequest* event—the last event in the life cycle of a HTTP request. This handler is only for clearing possible errors. Basically, if a request terminates prematurely due to an error, no *ReleaseStateRequest* event is raised. So the *EndRequest* is a sort of sentinel that ensures that any request state is correctly released anyway.

Customizing the Session State Module

If the logic and the data structures employed by the default session module don't completely satisfy you, the first option you have as a developer is to replace portions of ASP.NET session state functionality without reinventing all of it. The default session module probably does what you need about 99 percent of the time. If you want to support functionality not covered by the standard module, you should consider replacing the session state module.

You can customize and adapt four aspects of the session state module: the data store, the session state item, the data dictionary, and the session ID. For this purpose, ASP.NET 2.0 introduces a few new attributes and elements to the *<sessionState>* section of the web.config file.

Replacing the Session Data Store

The session data store is the layer of code in charge of reading and writing the session data to a particular storage medium. ASP.NET 1.x supports three media—the ASP.NET *Cache*, a well-known separate process, and a well-known SQL Server table. ASP.NET 2.0 lets you specify a custom data store.

In its most general form, a session data store is a class that inherits the *SessionStateStoreProviderBase* class. The main methods of the interface are listed in Table 9-1.

Table 9-1 Methods of the *SessionStateStoreProviderBase* Class

Method	Description
BeginRequest	Called by the default session state module when it begins to handle the *AcquireRequestState* event.
CreateNewStoreData	Creates a new object to contain all the state information specific to a session. Returns an object of type *SessionStateStoreData*.
Dispose	Releases all resources (other than memory) used by the session data store object.
EndRequest	Called by the default session state module when it begins to handle the *EndRequest* event.
GetItem	Gets the session data from the data store. The method serves requests from applications that use the read-only session state. (The *EnableSessionState* attribute is set to *ReadOnly*.)
GetItemExclusive	Gets the session data from the data store and locks it. Used for requests originated by applications in which the *EnableSessionState* attribute is set to *ReadWrite*.
Init	Receives an object packed with configuration settings for a custom session state and initializes the provider class.
ReleaseItemExclusive	Unlocks a session state item that was previously locked by a call to the *GetExclusive* method.
RemoveItem	Removes a session data store item from the session data store. Called when a session ends or is abandoned.
ResetItemTimeout	Resets the expiration time of a session state item based on the session's *Timeout* value. Invoked when the application has session support disabled.
SetAndReleaseItemExclusive	Writes a session data item to the data store.
SetItemExpireCallback	The module calls this method to notify the data store class that the caller has registered a *Session_OnEnd* handler.

Classes that inherit the *SessionStateStoreProviderBase* class work with the default ASP.NET session state module and replace only the part of it that handles session state data storage and retrieval. Nothing else in the session functionality changes. The *Get* and *Set* methods are responsible for reading and writing the data object that contains all session data. When the session starts, the *CreateNewStoreData* method is called to create a new object to store the contents of the session data. For example, in the default session module, the session data store is placed in the ASP.NET *Cache* or is serialized in a row within the SQL Server session table.

Note that the data store doesn't handle individual data items such as those you read or write in your pages through the *Session* property. At the data store level, the session data is managed as a single, all-encompassing object named the *session data store*. This object is administered using *Get*, *Set*, *Remove*, and the like.

To take advantage of custom session data providers, you must modify the *<sessionState>* configuration section as follows:

```
<sessionState mode="Custom"
    customType="Samples.MyDataStore, MyDataStoreLib">
    ⋮
</sessionState>
```

Based on this configuration script, ASP.NET uses the *Samples.MyDataStore* class to access the session data. The class is loaded from the *MyDataStoreLib* assembly. Of course, the *Samples.MyDataStore* class inherits the *SessionStateStoreProviderBase* class.

Replacing the Session State Item

The session data store is the class that combines a dictionary of user-defined data—the actual slots of data managed through the familiar *Session* property—and the static objects available for the current context. Session static objects are objects that are declared in the global.asax file and scoped to session. Figure 9-2 provides a graphical overview of the session state architecture.

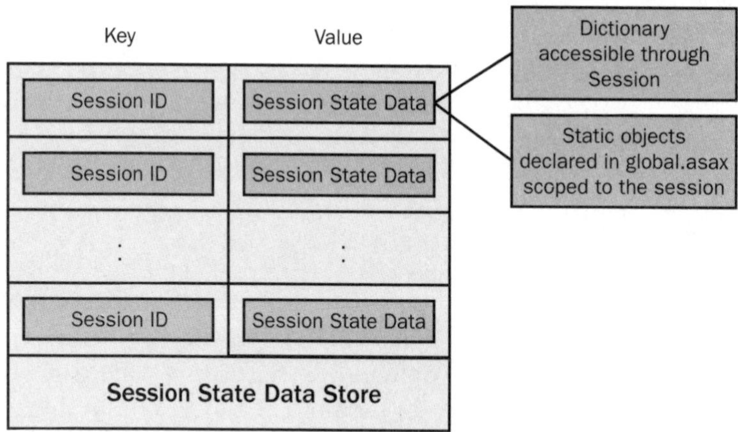

Figure 9-2 How the pieces of the session puzzle fit together

In ASP.NET 2.0, the default session state item class is named *SessionStateStoreData*. You can inherit from this class to create your own session data store class.

Replacing the Session Data Dictionary

As shown earlier in Figure 9-2, the *SessionStateStoreData* class has two main components—the dictionary of user-defined items and the collection of static objects. Only the *Items* and *StaticObjects* are properties on the *SessionStateStoreData* class. A third property is defined on the class—*Timeout*. As the name suggests, *Timeout* indicates how long, in minutes, the session state item is valid. The default value is 20 minutes.

The *Items* collection is actually exposed to the page through the *Session* property. By default, it is an instance of the *HttpSessionState* class. You can replace the default dictionary class with your own. All you have to do is create a class that implements the *ISessionSessionItemCollection* interface. The following code snippet shows a possible implementation of the *CreateNewStoreData* method on the data store. The method returns an instance of the default *SessionStateStoreData* class in which the timeout and the internal dictionary have been modified.

```
SessionStateStoreData CreateNewStoreData()
{
   SessionStateStoreData mySessionData = new SessionStateStoreData();

    // Provide an empty session dictionary object
    mySessionData.Dictionary = new Samples.MyDictionaryClass();

    // Set the timeout to 10 minutes
    mySessionItem.Timeout = 10;

    // Set the StaticObjects property to the static objects for
    // the current context.
    mySessionItem.StaticObjects =
        SessionStateUtility.GetSessionStaticObjects(
        HttpContext.Current);

   return mySessionData;
}
```

Notice the use of the *SessionStateUtility* helper class. The class contains optional helper methods that custom session state data storage providers can use. In particular, the *GetSessionStaticObjects* used above returns the default collection of static objects.

Generating a Custom Session ID

ASP.NET 2.0 uses an HTTP module named *SessionIDModule* to generate the session ID. The class implements the *ISessionIDModule* interface. You can replace this component with a custom module if your HTTP module implements the same *ISessionIDModule* interface. To help you decide whether you really need a custom session ID generator, let's review the facts about the default module.

The *SessionIDModule* class generates a session ID as a 120-bit random number. The session is represented as a string of 20 alphanumeric characters. The session ID can be stored in either an HTTP cookie or a mangled URL, based on the value of the *cookieless* attribute in the *<sessionState>* configuration section. By default, cookies are used. The default cookie name is *ASP.NET_SessionId*, but you can override it by setting the *cookieName* attribute in the configuration file.

When cookieless sessions are used, the session ID module is responsible for adding the ID to the URL and redirecting the browser. In this case, the browser is redirected to a fake URL like the following:

```
http://www.contoso.com/test/(session_id)/page.aspx
```

How can a request for this fake URL be served correctly? In the case of a cookieless session, the Session ID module depends on a small and simple ISAPI filter (aspnet_filter.dll, which is also available to ASP.NET 1.x) to dynamically remove the session ID from the request URL. In this case, the request is served correctly, but the path on the address bar doesn't change. The removed session ID is placed in a request header named *AspFilterSessionId*.

If the filter is disabled on the Web server machine, a custom Session ID module is called to replace it. You can do this by using a handler that subscribes to the *HttpApplication.BeginRequest* event. Table 9-2 details the methods available on the *ISessionIDModule* interface. You should implement all of them if you want to install your own ID generator.

Table 9-2 Methods of the *ISessionIDModule* Interface

Method	Description
CreateSessionID	Creates a unique session identifier for the session
GetSessionID	Gets the session ID from the context of the current request
RemoveSessionID	Deletes the session ID from the cookie or from the URL
SaveSessionID	Saves a newly created session ID to the HTTP response
Validate	Confirms that the session ID is valid

Once you have created a custom session ID module, you register it in the configuration file. Here's how to do it:

```
<httpModules>
   <remove name="SessionID" />
   <add name="MySessionID" type="Samples.MyIDModule, MyLib" />
</httpModules>
```

You first remove the default session ID HTTP module and then add your own.

Writing a Custom Session State Module

A custom session state module is an HTTP module class that intercepts three key application events—*AcquireRequestState*, *ReleaseRequestState*, and *EndRequest*. Capturing these events is mandatory not so much because you would otherwise get error messages or runtime exceptions, but because without them you couldn't implement a serious session state module.

Initialization of the Module

An HTTP module implements the *IHttpModule* interface, which consists of two methods, *Init* and *Dispose*. In the *Init* method, you start by reading any configuration information from the web.config file. Based on that, you configure the state of the module and prepare it for handling the current configuration.

In the *Init* method, the module also subscribes to the aforementioned application events and gets a reference to the session ID module to use. A reference to the currently loaded module that implements the *ISessionIDModule* interface can be obtained through the following code:

```
ISessionIDModule idModule;
HttpApplication app = HttpContext.Current.ApplicationInstance;
idModule = SessionStateUtility.GetSessionIDModule(app);
```

The *GetSessionIDModule* method on the *SessionStateUtility* helper class just returns the current session ID module, which is then stored in an internal variable for further use. Next the module instantiates and initializes the session provider object by calling the *Init* method on the *SessionStateStoreProviderBase* object, which any session provider must inherit.

Acquiring Session State

When the *AcquireRequestState* event fires, the module retrieves the session ID for the request by calling the *GetSessionID* method (listed earlier in Table 9-2). In implementing this method, you should take into account cookies or implement alternative schemes for client storage of the session ID. If no session ID is found, the module creates a new ID and saves it to the *Response* object. You save the newly created session ID to the *Response* object by calling *SaveSessionID* on the *ISessionIDModule* interface. The following pseudocode shows how to store the session ID using a cookie:

```
string cookieText = UrlEncode(id);
HttpCookie cookie = new HttpCookie(cookieName, cookieText);
cookie.Path = "/";
context.Response.Cookies.Add(cookie);
```

After retrieving the session ID, the module connects to the data store and retrieves the data associated with the given ID. This data is stored in a class such as the *SessionStateStoreData* class you saw earlier. Using the session data obtained in the previous step, you create a session state object—a dictionary that will be bound to the context of the current request and will be made available to applications through the *Session* property. Finally, if this is a new session, the *Start* event should be raised.

Releasing Session State

The *ReleaseRequestState* event fires when the request is about to terminate. The module should detach the session state object from the HTTP context and then save it back to the data store. A new session is created if the session state is empty; if this is the case, the session module doesn't write anything to the data store. If you write a custom session state module, you can customize this aspect, too.

If you want to support *Session_OnStart* and *Session_OnEnd* in your session state module, you should use the name *Session* when you register the custom module. Use the following script to replace the session module:

```
<httpModules>
   <remove name="Session" />
   <add name="Session" type="Samples.MySession, MyLib" />
</httpModules>
```

When the session state module is replaced, all the settings in *<sessionState>* are irrelevant unless the custom module uses them.

The ASP.NET *Cache* Object

ASP.NET 1.x introduced a container object named *Cache*, which joined the other two popular containers in classic ASP, *Application* and *Session*. *Cache* is a hashtable used to store frequently accessed data. As with *Application* (but not *Session*), any data stored in *Cache* is global to the application and is visible from within each currently active session. The structure and API of the three objects is similar, and all provide access using a familiar name/value notation.

Session and *Cache* differ in that *Session* is a block of memory set aside for each user and *Cache* manages globally accessible data. The key difference between *Application* and *Cache* is the *Cache* object's support of item dependencies. *Cache* can remove cached items when certain events occur. First and foremost, it drops the least-used items if the Web server runs low on memory. You can also define item dependencies so cached items are removed after a specific duration of time, at a certain time, or when one or more files or cached items change. This characteristic makes the *Cache* object an important tool for building highly scalable, fast Web applications. One instance of the *Cache* class is created per application domain, and it shares the lifetime of the domain.

The *Cache* Dependency Functionality

The cache dependency mechanism is encapsulated in the *CacheDependency* class. This class can represent a single file or directory, an array of files or directories, or an array of cached items logically related to a particular item added to the cache. To establish a dependency between a cached item and an external component, you add the item using a specific overload of the *Insert* method, as shown here:

```
CacheDependency dep = new CacheDependency(fileName);
Cache.Insert(key, value, dep);
```

The added item is removed from the cache when the specified file changes. Let's review in more detail the mechanism that the *Cache* uses to implement dependencies. You'll see the limitations in the version 1.x functionality and get an introduction to the new features in ASP.NET 2.0.

Tracking Changes in Files and Directories

You can tie the lifetime of a cached item to the timestamp of a file or a directory. When the file or directory changes (by being modified, deleted, or moved), the file system change is detected and the cached item is marked as obsolete and removed from the memory. A file dependency is based on a file monitor object—an instance of the *FileSystemWatcher* class. This class is a managed wrapper around a Windows operating system feature—the file notification change functionality—which is extensively used by various modules within ASP.NET.

Note that a file dependency can also be established with an array of files and directories. Also note that you can create dependencies only by using the *Insert* method or the *Add* method.

```
// Various approaches to cache items
Cache[key] = value;      // set accessor of the Item property
Cache.Insert(key, value, dep);
```

If you use the *set* accessor of the *Item* property to add a new item, the item will be correctly inserted but no dependency will ever be created.

Tracking Changes in Cached Items

Cached items can also be bound to other cached items. Interestingly, this can happen in addition to file dependencies, as the following code demonstrates:

```
// Use string arrays for file(s) and key(s)
CacheDependency dep = new CacheDependency(fileNames, otherKeys);
Cache.Insert(key, value, dep);
```

The cached item is subordinate to the specified files or folders and the array of keys. When either of the two changes, the item is invalidated and removed. To make an item dependent only on a cache item, you set the filename parameter to *null* in the constructor shown above.

The *CacheDependency* class also supports a few more combinations that let you create effective dependencies between cached items and other elements of the application. For example, a cached item can expire at a certain time (absolute expiration) or after a certain duration of time (sliding expiration). In addition, you can add a time to each cache dependency to make it start tracking changes only at a certain moment. Finally, a cache dependency can be subordinate to another cache dependency. This feature is useful in implementing cascading changes to stored items.

What Cache Dependencies Cannot Do in ASP.NET 1.x

In ASP.NET 1.x, a cached item can be subject to four types of dependencies: time, files, other items, and other dependencies. The ASP.NET 1.x *Cache* object addresses many developers' needs and made building in-memory webs of frequently accessed data much easier and more effective. However, this mechanism is not perfect, nor is it extensible.

Like many other aspects of ASP.NET, the *Cache* object merely whetted developers' appetites. Let's briefly consider a real-world scenario. What type of data do you think a distributed data-driven application would place in the ASP.NET *Cache*? In many cases, it would simply be the results of a database query. But unless you code it yourself—which can really be tricky—the object doesn't support database dependency. A database dependency would invalidate a cached result set when a certain database table changes. Furthermore, in ASP.NET 1.x the *CacheDependency* class is a sealed class—it is closed to any form of customization that gives developers a chance to invalidate cached items based on user-defined conditions.

As far as the *Cache* object is concerned, the biggest difference between ASP.NET 1.x and ASP.NET 2.0 is that version 2.0 supports custom dependencies. This was achieved by making the *CacheDependency* class inheritable (instead of a sealed class) and providing a made-to-measure *SqlCacheDependency* cache that provides built-in database dependency limited to SQL Server 7.0 and later.

Designing a Custom Dependency

Let's say it up front: writing a custom cache dependency object is no picnic. You should have a very good reason to do so, and you should carefully design the new functionality before proceeding. As mentioned, in ASP.NET 2.0 the *CacheDependency* class is inheritable—you can easily derive your own class from it. However, the memory footprint of your class will be bigger than it needs to be because the cache dependency class picks up all of the base class functionality (including aspects you don't need, such as constructors that accept arrays of files or create dependencies on other cached items).

On the other hand, a public constructor on the *CacheDependency* class saves you from having to do a lot of work. First, there's no risk of breaking existing code and no risk that your class will misbehave with the *Cache* object. The base class handles all the wiring of the dependency object to the ASP.NET cache and all the issues surrounding synchronization and disposal. It also saves you from implementing a start-time feature from scratch—you inherit that capability from the base class constructors. (The start-time feature allows you to start tracking dependencies at a particular time.)

Let's review the extensions made to the *CacheDependency* class to allow for custom dependencies.

Extensions to the *CacheDependency* Base Class

In ASP.NET 1.x, the *CacheDependency* class is sealed (not inheritable) and therefore not meant to be extensible. To fully support derived classes and to facilitate their integration into the ASP.NET cache, a bunch of new methods have been added. They are summarized in Table 9-3.

Table 9-3 New Members of the *CacheDependency* Class

Member	Description
DependencyDispose	Protected method that releases the resources used by the class.
GetUniqueId	Public method that retrieves a unique string identifier for the object.
NotifyDependencyChanged	Protected method that notifies the base class that the dependency represented by this object has changed.
SetUtcLastModified	Protected method that marks the time when a dependency last changed.
HasChanged	Public Boolean read-only property that indicates whether the dependency has changed. This property also exists in version 1.x.
UtcLastModified	Public read-only property that gets the time when the dependency was last changed. This property exists also in version 1.x, but it is not publicly accessible.

As mentioned, a custom dependency class relies on its parent for any interaction with the *Cache* object. The *NotifyDependencyChanged* method is called by classes that inherit *CacheDependency* to tell the base class that the dependent item has changed. In response, the base class updates the values of the *HasChanged* and *UtcLastModified* properties. Any cleanup code needed when the custom cache dependency object is dismissed should go into the *DependencyDispose* method.

Getting Change Notifications

As you might have noticed, nothing in the public interface of the base *CacheDependency* class allows you to insert code to check whether a given condition—the heart of the dependency—is met. Why is this? The *CacheDependency* class was designed to support only a limited set of well-known dependencies—against file or other item changes.

To detect file changes, the *CacheDependency* object internally sets up a file monitor object and receives a call from it whenever the monitored file changes. The *CacheDependency* class creates a *FileSystemWatcher* object and passes it an event handler. A similar approach is used to establish a programmatic link between the *CacheDependency* object and the *Cache* object and its items. The *Cache* object fires a *CacheDependency* event when one of the monitored items changes. What does this all mean to the developer?

A custom dependency object must be able to receive notifications from the data source it is monitoring. In most cases, this is really complicated if you can't bind to an existing notification mechanism (such as file system monitor or SQL Server 2005 notifications). We'll consider a practical example in a moment.

The *AggregateCacheDependency* Class

In addition to creating a single dependency on an entry in the ASP.NET *Cache*, you can also aggregate dependencies. For example, you can make a cache entry dependent on both a file and a SQL Server table. The following code snippet shows how to create a cache entry, named *MyData*, that is dependent on two different files:

```
// Creates an array of CacheDependency objects
CacheDependency dep1 = new CacheDependency(fileName1);
CacheDependency dep2 = new CacheDependency(fileName2);
CacheDependency deps[] = {dep1, dep2};

// Creates an aggregate object
AggregateCacheDependency aggDep = new AggregateCacheDependency();
aggDep.Add(deps);
Cache.Insert("MyData", data, aggDep)
```

Any custom cache dependency object, including *SqlCacheDependency*, inherits *CacheDependency*, so the array of dependencies can contain virtually any type of dependency.

In ASP.NET 2.0, the *AggregateCacheDependency* class is built as a custom cache dependency object and inherits the base *CacheDependency* class.

A Web Service–Based Cache Dependency

Suppose your application gets some data from a Web service. The Web service method returns a *DataSet* that is stored to the *Cache*. Since you want the cached data to be invalidated when the source data changes, you create a made-to-measure cache dependency class. The initialization code of your new class should configure and start up a hooking mechanism that promptly detects changes on the monitored resource and communicates any detected changes to the custom dependency object.

Generally speaking, if the target data source provides you with a built-in and totally asynchronous notification mechanism (such as the command notification mechanism of SQL Server 2005), you just use it. Otherwise, to detect changes in the monitored data source, you can only poll the resource at a reasonable rate.

Designing the *WeatherCacheDependency* Class

To better understand the concept of custom dependencies, think of the following example. You need to cache the return value of a Web service method—say, the currently reported temperature in a particular city. You can define a custom dependency class that caches the current value upon instantiation and polls the Web service to detect changes. When a change is detected, the cached key is invalidated.

A good way to poll a local or remote resource is through a timer callback. Let's break the procedure into a few steps:

1. The custom *WeatherCacheDependency* class gets ready for the overall functionality. It initializes some internal properties and caches at least the polling rate and the current temperature.
2. After initialization, the dependency object sets up a timer callback to poll the Web service for up-to-date information. Polling the Web service means calling a particular Web method at regular intervals.
3. In the callback, the result of the Web method—the current temperature in the city—is compared to the previously stored temperature. If the two temperatures differ, the linked cache key is promptly emptied.

There's no need for the developer to specify details on how the cache dependency is broken or set up. The *CacheDependency* class in ASP.NET 2.0 takes care of it entirely.

Implementing the Dependency

The following source code shows the core implementation of the custom *WeatherCacheDependency* class:

```
namespace Intro20
{
    public class WeatherCacheDependency : CacheDependency
    {
        // Internal members
        static Timer _timer;
        int _pollSecs = 10;
        string _zipCode;
        int _temperature;

        // Ctor
        public WeatherCacheDependency(string zipCode, int pollTime)
        {
            // Set internal members
            _zipCode = zipCode;
            _pollSecs = pollTime;
```

```
            // Get the current temperature
            _temperature = GetTemperature();

            // Set up the timer
            if (_timer == null) {
                int ms = _pollSecs * 1000;
                TimerCallback cb = new TimerCallback(WeatherCallback);
                _timer = new Timer(cb, this, ms, ms);
            }
        }

        // Current temperature
        public int Temperature
        {
            get { return _temperature; }
        }

        // Event raised every N seconds
        public void WeatherCallback(object sender)
        {
            // Get a reference to THIS dependency object
            WeatherCacheDependency dep = (WeatherCacheDependency) sender;

            // Check for changes and notify the base class if any is found
            int currentTemp = GetTemperature();
            if (_temperature != currentTemp)
                dep.NotifyDependencyChanged(dep, EventArgs.Empty);
        }

        // Returns the current temperature accessing the Web service
        int GetTemperature()
        {
            // Uses a custom Web service to get the info
            MsNbcWeather service = new MsNbcWeather();
            return service.GetTemperature(_zipCode);
        }

        // Clean up internal resources
        protected override void DependencyDispose()
        {
            // Kill the timer and then as usual
            _timer = null;
            base.DependencyDispose();
        }
    }
}
```

When the cache dependency is created, the Web service method is invoked and the value is stored in an internal member. At the same time, a timer is started to call the same Web service method at regular intervals. The return value is compared against the value stored in the constructor code. If the two are different, the *NotifyDependencyChanged* method is invoked on the base *CacheDependency* class to invalidate the linked content in the ASP.NET *Cache*.

Testing the Web Service Dependency

How can you use this dependency class in a Web application? You simply use it in any scenario where a *CacheDependency* object is acceptable. For example, you create an instance of the class in the *Page_Load* event and pass it to the *Cache.Insert* method:

```
void Page_Load(object sender, EventArgs e)
{
   if (!IsPostBack)
   {
      WeatherCacheDependency dep;
      dep = new WeatherCacheDependency(Zip.Text, 5);
      Cache.Insert("Weather-" + Zip.Text, dep.Temperature, dep);
   }

   // Consume the data
   ShowTemperature();
}
```

You write the rest of the page as usual, paying attention to accessing the specified *Cache* key—because of the dependency, the key could be null. Here's an example:

```
// Read the temperature from the cache
string msg = "[No data available at this time.]";
object o = Cache["Weather-" + Zip.Text];
if (o != null)
    msg = o.ToString();

// Display the temperature
TempLabel.Text = msg;
```

The weather Web service has a *GetTemperature* method that takes a Zip code and returns an integer. The Web service, the cache dependency object, and the preceding sample page work out the following output, shown in Figure 9-3.

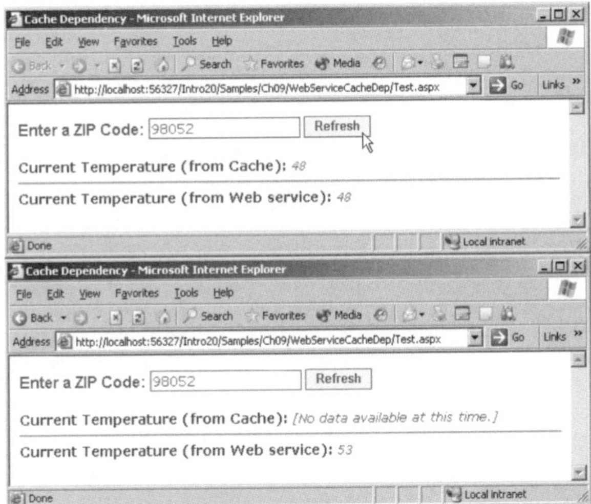

Figure 9-3 The custom dependency object in action on a sample page

The page on the top is generated when the content of the ASP.NET *Cache* and the Web service return value coincide. The page at the bottom is what you get when the cached value is invalidated because of a change in the return value of the monitored Web service method.

SQL Server Cache Dependency

One common scenario that is not addressed by the ASP.NET 1.x *Cache* is database dependencies. A database dependency is a special case of custom dependency and results in the cached item removal when the contents of a certain database table change. ASP.NET 2.0 provides an ad hoc class—*SqlCacheDependency*—that inherits *CacheDependency* and supports dependencies on SQL Server tables. More precisely, the class implements a feature compatible with MSDE, SQL Server 7.0, and subsequent SQL Server versions, including SQL Server 2005, in which even more features are supported.

Enabling Databases to Support Notifications

For the *SqlCacheDependency* class to work correctly, any tables on which you want to make dependencies must have notifications enabled. This means creating ad hoc triggers and stored procedures that will handle any incoming UPDATE, INSERT, or DELETE statements. This task must be accomplished before the application is published. You can use either the command-line tool *aspnet_regsqlcache* or the methods of *SqlCacheDependencyAdmin*. The following code enables the Northwind database for notifications:

```
SqlCacheDependencyAdmin.EnableNotifications("Northwind");
```

(Note: The Northwind string in the command is not the actual name of the database—it's simply the name of an entry in the application's web.config file.)

```
<configuration>
<connectionStrings>
   <add name="Local_Northwind"
        connectionString="SERVER=…;DATABASE=…;UID=…;" />
</connectionString>
<system.web>
  <caching>
    <sqlCacheDependency enabled="true" pollTime="60000" >
      <databases>
        <add name="Northwind" connectionName="Local_Northwind" />
      </databases>
    </sqlCacheDependency>
  </caching>
</system.web>
</configuration>
```

The database entry is bound to a connection string entry. The preceding configuration script enables polling on the Northwind database every 60 seconds. The poll component accesses a newly created table in the Northwind database to see whether one of the other tables has changed. Figure 9-4 shows how the database table looks in design mode.

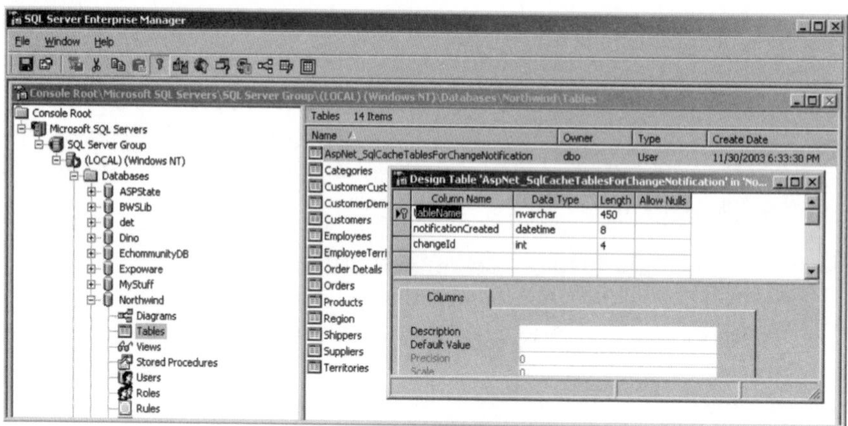

Figure 9-4 The *SqlCacheDependencyAdmin* class adds a new table to the Northwind database to enable notifications for all tables.

So far, no table in the Northwind database has actually been added to the list of monitored tables. You can do that programmatically using the following code:

```
SqlCacheDependencyAdmin.EnableTableForNotifications(
    "Northwind", "Employees");
```

This code defines a trigger on the Employees table that is sensitive to insertions, updates, and deletions. Whenever any of these operations takes place, the trigger increments the value of the *changeId* column in the row that corresponds to the Employees table. (See Figure 9-4.) Figure 9-5 shows the trigger.

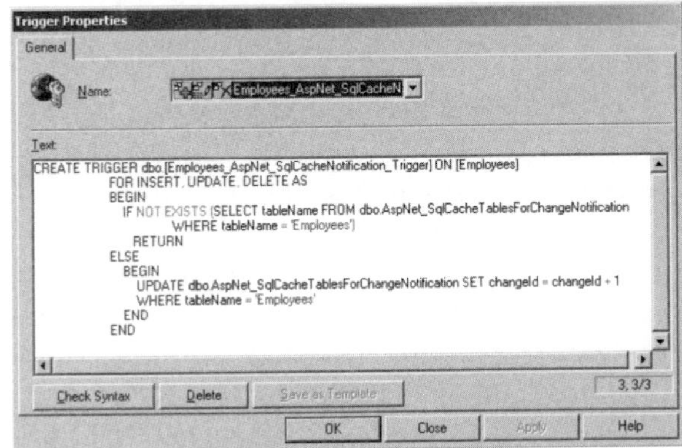

Figure 9-5 The trigger defined to track changes on the Employees table

So much for the offline configuration. Let's see now how to create and use a *SqlCacheDependency* object.

Creating SQL Server Dependencies

The *SqlCacheDependency* class has two constructors. The first takes a *SqlCommand* object (more on this later), and the second accepts two strings—the database name and the table name. The following code creates a SQL Server dependency and binds it to a cache key.

```
SqlCacheDependency dep = new SqlCacheDependency(database, table);
Cache.Insert("SqlSource", data, dep);
```

The data stored in the cache probably comes from the monitored table, but you get notification based on changes in the table as a whole. For example, suppose you're displaying a data set that results from the following:

```
SELECT * FROM customers WHERE country='USA'
```

If a new record is added to the Customers table, you get a notification no matter what the value in the *country* column is. SQL Server 2005 offers a finer level of control over the monitored output and involves the other constructor of the *SqlCacheDependency* class. We'll look at this in a moment.

Overview of the Implementation

It should be clear by now how the SQL Server dependency mechanism really works. The trigger detects changes to the table and writes data to a helper table. This table contains at most one row per table. A new row is added only when a table is enabled for notifications. The tableName column (as shown earlier in Figure 9-4) is set to the name of the table. The ASP.NET trigger works just like any other SQL Server trigger and is completely unaware of which module created it and why.

This situation means that the SQL Server cache dependency feature offers no guarantee that a change in the database will be immediately reflected in the ASP.NET *Cache*. The change is reflected in the ASP.NET environment only when an ASP.NET component polls the table.

A key architectural component is the cache dependency manager object, which periodically accesses the table, reads the *changeId* field, and informs the corresponding cache object if a change has occurred to the table. The cache dependency object is informed about the change in an indirect way. When created, each SQL cache dependency object is made dependent on a helper cache key, whose name depends on the table and the database. Guessed what happens? The dependency manager object just removes the helper cache entry so that the original *SqlCacheDependency* object is invalidated.

Cache Dependencies in SQL Server 2005

As mentioned, the *SqlCacheDependency* class has two constructors, one of which takes a *SqlCommand* object as its sole argument:

```
// data is a DataTable filled using this same command
SqlCommand cmd = new SqlCommand(
   "SELECT * FROM Customers WHERE country='USA'",
   conn);
SqlCacheDependency dep = new SqlCacheDependency(cmd);
Cache.Insert("SqlSource", data, dep);
```

When called in this way, the *SqlCacheDependency* class sets up a dependency relationship with SQL Server 2005 known as *command notification*. (See Chapter 5.) As a result, whenever something happens to the involved tables that modifies the output of the command, the notification is sent to the caller. Nicely enough, the caller this time is just the *SqlCacheDependency* class. Internally, the *SqlCacheDependency* class handles the event and lets the parent know through *NotifyDependencyChanged*.

Summary

In ASP.NET 2.0, state management is much the same as in ASP.NET 1.x. Sure, you get a few cool new features, but the underlying architecture is nearly identical. In most cases, the changes are ones that would have fit into version 1.x if the team had had more time. Overall, the new state management features are in response to user requirements or are necessary enhancements. For example, control state was introduced to avoid common errors and pitfalls in control development.

The new session and cache features clearly resulted from repeated user requests, particularly the database cache dependency (which is available only for SQL Server 7.0 and later). You cannot use the *SqlCacheDependency* class to control changes to an Oracle or a Microsoft Access database. However, the cache dependency mechanism has been abstracted enough that smart developers can write custom invalidation mechanisms.

10

ASP.NET Security

To restrict access to a Web site to registered users, an ASP.NET developer can choose between three authentication types—Windows (the default), Passport, and Forms authentication. The type of authentication is declared in the application's configuration file and can't be changed dynamically. When you use Windows authentication, information about users and groups is often stored in the Security Accounts Manager (SAM) database, but you can also place that information in the care of the Active Directory services. With Passport authentication, user information is stored in the internal Passport database. And with Forms authentication, you can specify where to store user and role data. Typically, it goes in a custom database.

Windows authentication is commonly used in intranet scenarios. Like Passport authentication, it provides the user interface and back-end code needed to collect and verify user credentials. The developer doesn't have to know about the structure of the data storage or how users and roles are checked. The identity of the application's logged-in user is any authenticated identity passed in from Microsoft Internet Information Services (IIS). For Internet applications, this model is often inadequate; Passport and Forms authentication are better choices.

The Passport authentication mechanism is a Microsoft centralized authentication service. Passport provides a way to authenticate users coming across all the sites that participate in the initiative. Users do a single login, and if they are successfully authenticated they can move freely through all the member sites. In addition to the single login service, Passport also offers core profile services for member sites. The Passport authentication service is used throughout the industry.

Neither Windows authentication nor Passport authentication is practical for real-world Web sites. In ASP, you typically place some relatively boilerplate code on top of each nonpublic page and redirect the user to a login page. On the login page, the user is prompted for credentials, and the credentials are verified against a list of authorized users. If all goes fine, the user is redirected to the originally requested page. None of this code is rocket science, but you have to write it yourself and use it over and over.

ASP.NET 1.x introduced Forms-based authentication, a built-in infrastructure with an easy-to-use API that greatly simplifies the setting up of this login pattern. Forms-based authentication is probably the only viable approach to restricting access to real-world Web sites. In ASP.NET 2.0, the custom Forms authentication engine is even easier and quicker to use.

Using Forms Authentication

You set up an ASP.NET application for Forms authentication by tweaking its root web.config file. You enter the following script:

```
<configuration>
  <system.web>
      <authentication mode="Forms">
         <forms loginUrl="login.aspx" />
      </authentication>
  </system.web>
</configuration>
```

Note that this code doesn't make your application ask users to log in. The login form is displayed only to users who have explicitly been denied access. The following code snippet uses the *<authorization>* section in the web.config file to block the anonymous user (identified with the ? symbol):

```
<authorization>
  <deny users="?" />
</authorization>
```

All blocked users are redirected to the login page, where they are asked to enter their credentials.

> **Note** The Forms authentication mechanism protects any ASP.NET resource located in a folder for which Forms authentication and authorization is specified. Note that only resource types explicitly handled by ASP.NET are protected. The list includes .aspx, .asmx, and .ashx files, but not plain HTML pages or ASP pages.

Forms Authentication Control Flow

Accessing a protected page involves a four-step process. The first step is the request for the protected page—say, default.aspx. An HTTP module implementing the Forms authentication service intercepts the request and looks for an authentication ticket. If it finds no such a ticket, the browser is redirected to the specified login page. Information about the originating page is placed in the query string by using the *ReturnUrl* key. For security reasons, you might want to use a Secure Sockets Layer (SSL) channel to keep the user's credentials from being sent in clear text.

The login page is then displayed. The programmer creates this page, which, at a minimum, contains text boxes for the username and the password and a button for submitting credentials. The handler for the button click event validates the credentials using an application-specific algorithm and data storage media. If the credentials are authenticated, the user code redirects the browser to the original URL (which is in the request's query string). Authenticating a user means that an authentication ticket is issued as a cookie. The cookie is attached to the request and is retrieved by the HTTP module when the request for the original page is processed.

Cookie-Based Forms Authentication in ASP.NET 1.x

In ASP.NET 1.x, Forms authentication is based on cookies. The cookie is named after the value of the *name* attribute in the *<forms>* section of the web.config file. The cookie contains any information that helps to identify the user making the request. This information is known as the *authentication ticket*.

In the *<forms>* section of the configuration file, you can declaratively set some properties of the cookie, including the duration and the protection level. By default, an authentication cookie lasts 30 minutes and is protected using both data validation and encryption. Data validation ensures that the contents of the cookie has not been tampered with along the way. Encryption uses the Triple-DES (3DES) algorithm to scramble the content.

> **Note** If you are running multiple Web applications on a single server machine and each application requires a unique authentication cookie (that is, each application requires a different authentication back end), you must configure the cookie name in each application's web.config file.

A Cookieless Approach in ASP.NET 2.0

Using cookies requires some support from the client browser. In ASP.NET 1.x, cookies are mandatory if you want to take advantage of the built-in authentication framework. In ASP.NET 2.0, the core API also supports cookieless semantics. More precisely, the whole API has been reworked to make it expose a nearly identical programming interface but also support dual semantics—cookied and cookieless.

You can implement cookieless authentication in several ways. For example, you can append the ticket to the query string or store it as extra path information and retrieve it from the *PATH_INFO* server variable. But ASP.NET 2.0 takes a different approach, which is consistent with the implementation of cookieless sessions. The authentication ticket is packed into the URL, as shown here:

```
/SampleApp/(XYZ1234)/default.aspx
```

This solution requires an ISAPI filter to intercept a request, extract the ticket, and rewrite the correct path to the application. The filter also exposes the authentication ticket as another request header. You'll see how to set up cookie semantics and review the changes in the next section.

Configuring Forms Authentication

Forms authentication is driven by the contents of the *<forms>* section within the *<authentication>* section. The overall syntax of the section is shown here:

```
<forms name="cookie"
    loginUrl="url"
    protection="All|None|Encryption|Validation"
    timeout="30"
    requireSSL="true|false"
    slidingExpiration="true|false">
    path="/"
    cookieless="UseCookies|UseUri|AutoDetect|UseDeviceProfile"
    defaultUrl="url"
    domain="string">
   <credentials passwordFormat="Clear|SHA1|MD5]">
      <user name="…" password="…" />
   </credentials>
</forms>
```

The attributes shown in italic are new in ASP.NET 2.0. The rest of the declaration is identical to ASP.NET 1.x.

Table 10-1 describes the role of each attribute defined in ASP.NET 1.x. Note how slight the difference is between ASP.NET 1.0 and ASP.NET 1.1.

Table 10-1 Attributes for Forms Authentication in ASP.NET 1.x

Attribute	Description
loginUrl	Specifies the URL to which the request is redirected for login if no valid authentication cookie is found.
name	Specifies the name of the HTTP cookie to use for authentication. The default name is .ASPXAUTH.
path	Specifies the path for the authentication cookies issued by the application. The default value is a slash (/).
protection	Indicates how the application intends to protect the authentication cookie.
requireSSL	Indicates whether a secure (SSL) connection is required to transmit the authentication cookie. The value is *false* by default. *This attribute is not supported in ASP.NET 1.0.*
slidingExpiration	Indicates whether sliding expiration is enabled. *This attribute is not supported in ASP.NET 1.0.*
timeout	Specifies the amount of time, in minutes, after which the cookie will expire. The default value is 30.

The *Cookieless* Attribute

The new *cookieless* attribute specifies whether cookies are used to store the authentication ticket and their overall behavior. It can take any of the values listed in Table 10-2.

Table 10-2 Values for the *cookieless* Attribute

Value	Description
AutoDetect	Uses cookies if the browser has cookie support currently enabled. It uses the cookieless mechanism otherwise.
UseCookie	Always uses cookies, regardless of the browser capabilities.
UseDeviceProfile	Uses cookies if the browser supports them and uses the cookieless mechanism otherwise. When this option is used, no attempt is made to check whether cookie support is really enabled for the requesting device.
UseUri	Never uses cookies, regardless of the browser capabilities.

The default value for the *cookieless* attribute is *UseDeviceProfile*, which ensures compatibility with ASP.NET 1.1 and guarantees support for mobile scenarios.

Setting the Default Return URL

The new *defaultUrl* attribute lets you set the default name of the page to return after a request has been successfully authenticated. This URL is hardcoded to default.aspx in ASP.NET 1.x but is configurable in ASP.NET 2.0. For backward compatibility, the default value is just default.aspx.

The value of the *defaultUrl* attribute is used only if no *ReturnUrl* variable is found in the URL to the login page. If a user is redirected to the login page by the authentication module, the *ReturnUrl* variable is always correctly set. However, if your page contains a link to the login page or if it needs to transfer programmatically to the login page (for example, after the current user has logged off), you must specify the *ReturnUrl* variable, and the *defaultUrl* attribute can help.

Setting the Cookie's Domain

The *domain* attribute specifies an optional domain that is assigned to the *domain* property of the *HttpCookie* class for outgoing authentication cookies. This attribute has no default value and is ignored if it isn't explicitly set. It is useful because it allows you to share authentication cookies between two machines located in the same domain.

For example, suppose you run two Web sites named www.contoso.com and weblogs.contoso.com. If you choose contoso.com as the authentication domain, the two applications will recognize each other's cookies. Setting the *domain* attribute doesn't cause anything to be emitted into the ticket; it simply forces all form authentication methods to properly set the *domain* property on each issued or renewed ticket. The attribute is ignored if cookieless authentication is used.

Note that this setting takes precedence over the domain field used in the *<httpCookies>* section.

The *FormsAuthentication* Class

The helper methods exposed by the *FormsAuthentication* class are quite useful for quickly adding authentication to an ASP.NET application. The class supplies some static methods that you can use to manipulate authentication tickets. You typically use the *RedirectFromLoginPage* method to redirect an authenticated user back to the originally requested URL; likewise, you call *SignOut* to remove the authentication ticket for the current user. Other methods and properties are for manipulating and renewing the ticket and the associated cookie.

Properties of the *FormsAuthentication* Class

Table 10-3 lists the properties of the *FormsAuthentication* class. As you can see, many of them deal with cookie naming and usage and expose the content of configuration attributes.

Table 10-3 Properties of the *FormAuthentication* Class

Property	Description
CookieDomain	Returns the domain set for the authentication ticket. This property equals the value of the *domain* attribute in the *<forms>* section.
CookieMode	Returns one of the four *FormsCookieMode* enumeration values (listed earlier in Table 10-2).
CookiesSupported	Returns *true* if the current request supports cookies. If the *AutoDetect* mode is configured, it also checks for the browser's cookie capability and verifies that cookies haven't been disabled on the client.
DefaultUrl	Returns the configured or default URL for the page to return after a request has been successfully authenticated. Matches the *defaultUrl* configuration attribute.
EnableCrossAppRedirects	Indicates whether redirects can span over different Web applications.
FormsCookieName	Returns the configured cookie name used for the current application. The default name is .ASPXAUTH.
FormsCookiePath	Returns the configured cookie path used for the current application. The default is the root path /.
LoginUrl	Returns the configured or default URL for the login page. Matches the *loginUrl* configuration attribute.
RequireSSL	Gets a value indicating whether a cookie must be transmitted using only HTTPS.
SlidingExpiration	Gets a value indicating whether sliding expiration is enabled.

The properties are initialized with the values read from the application's configuration file when the application starts up.

Methods of the *FormsAuthentication* Class

Table 10-4 details the methods supported by the *FormsAuthentication* class.

Table 10-4 Methods of the *FormsAuthentication* Class

Method	Description
Authenticate	Attempts to validate the supplied credentials against those contained in the configured <*credentials*> section.
Decrypt	Returns a decrypted authentication ticket, given a valid encrypted authentication ticket obtained from an HTTP cookie.
Encrypt	Produces a string containing an encrypted authentication ticket suitable for use in an HTTP cookie.
GetAuthCookie	Creates an authentication cookie for a given username.
GetRedirectUrl	Returns the URL for the original request.
HashPasswordForStoringInConfigFile	Given a password and a string identifying the hash type, this method hashes the password for storage in the web.config.
Initialize	Initializes the *FormsAuthentication* class.
RedirectFromLoginPage	Redirects an authenticated user back to the originally requested URL.
RedirectToLoginPage	Performs a redirect to the configured or default login page.
RenewTicketIfOld	Conditionally updates the sliding expiration on an authentication ticket.
SetAuthCookie	Creates an authentication ticket and attaches it to the cookies collection of the outgoing response. It doesn't redirect to the originally requested URL.
SignOut	Removes the authentication ticket.

The *Initialize* method is called only once in the application's lifetime and initializes the properties in Table 10-3 by reading the configuration file. The method also gets the cookie values and encryption keys to be used for the application.

RedirectToLoginPage is a new entry in the list of class methods and fills a hole in the programming interface of the *FormsAuthentication* class in ASP.NET 1.x. The method is useful when a user signs out, and you want to redirect her to the login page afterwards. When this happens, the method figures out what the login page is and calls *Response.Redirect*.

Setting Up a Forms Authentication Layer

Let's review the steps for setting up a forms authentication layer on top of a Web application. These steps are not much different from what you do in ASP.NET 1.x. However, some of the methods in the *FormsAuthentication* class and some of the new security-specific server controls in ASP.NET 2.0 (more on this in a moment) make programming easier and faster.

The typical web.config file of a secure application looks like the following code snippet:

```
<configuration>
    <system.web>
            <authentication mode="Forms">
                    <forms name=".ASPXAUTH"
                            loginUrl="login.aspx"
                            protection="All" />
            </authentication>
            <authorization>
               <deny users="?" />
            </authorization>
    </system.web>
</configuration>
```

The anonymous user is denied access in the *<authorization>* section, and all users are redirected to a particular login page to enter their credentials. The login page is responsible for authenticating the user and emitting a ticket. According to the code just shown, the authentication ticket is encrypted in the default way and packed into a cookie with the default name. Figure 10-1 shows a reasonable login page.

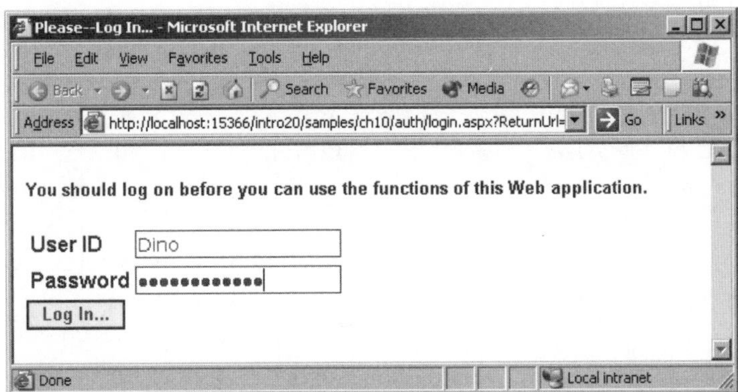

Figure 10-1 The login page of the sample application, in which the user enters credentials and clicks to log in

Note the URL displayed in the address bar. The query string embeds in the *ReturnUrl* variable the originally requested page. Let's review the source code associated with the click event of the form button:

```
void Logon_Click(object sender, EventArgs e)
{
   bool bAuthenticated = false;
   string user = userName.Text;
   string pswd = passWord.Text;

   // Custom authentication
   bAuthenticated = ValidateUser(user, pswd);
   if (bAuthenticated)
      FormsAuthentication.RedirectFromLoginPage(user, false);
   else
      errorMsg.Text = "Sorry, yours seems not to be a valid account.";
}

bool ValidateUser(string user, string pswd)
{
   // TODO:: something useful here
   return true;
}
```

A custom function takes the credentials and validates them against a user-defined data store—typically a SQL Server database. The *AuthenticateUser* function returns a Boolean value, which tells the code whether to display an error message or just redirect to the originally requested page.

In ASP.NET 2.0, *RedirectFromLoginPage* has three overloads:

```
public void RedirectFromLoginPage(String, Boolean)
public void RedirectFromLoginPage(String, Boolean, String)
public void RedirectFromLoginPage(String, Boolean, String, String)
```

The first argument is the name of the user. The Boolean argument indicates whether a persistent cookie must be created. Note, though, that persistent cookies aren't a good idea when the user logs on from a shared computer—you should at least give her a choice between create a temporary or persistent cookie. The third argument, when requested, indicates the cookie path; the fourth specifies the authentication type—cookied or cookieless.

Figure 10-2 shows the main application's page when a registered and authenticated user is being served. The name of the user is displayed in the topmost bar along with a button for logging off.

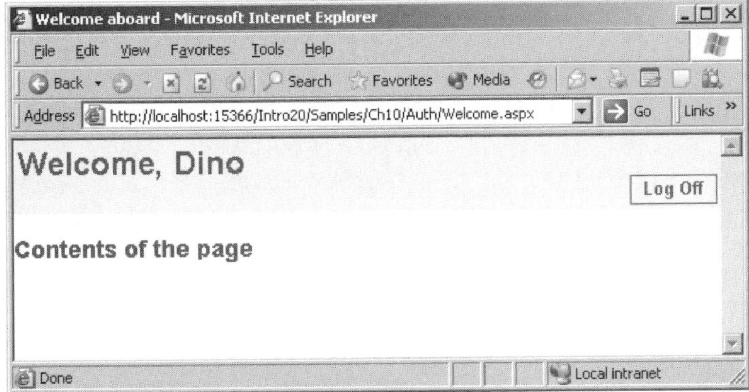

Figure 10-2 The page of the application when a registered user is connected

Anonymous Identification

Anonymous identification is an optional new ASP.NET 2.0 feature that assigns an identity to users who are not authenticated. This feature does not affect the identity of the account that processes the request, nor does it affect any other aspects of user identification and authorization. When enabled, anonymous user identification merely assigns a unique identity to a nonauthenticated user so she looks like a regularly authenticated user. This feature allows you to track the user or assign personalization properties. Functionally, anonymous identification relates to personalization only and doesn't modify any other aspect of the membership subsystem. The unique ID is not customizable by programmers.

The anonymous user's ID is stored in a cookie, much like a Forms authentication ticket is stored. But the membership system doesn't consider an anonymous user to be logged in. If the user's browser doesn't accept cookies, the anonymous identification can be embedded in the URL of requested pages.

If an anonymous user logs in, the anonymous identification information is discarded and the user is treated as an authenticated user. As you saw in Chapter 4, when this happens the user's personalization values can be migrated to the new identity and retained as part of the user identity. The anonymous ID is generated by an HTTP module and stored in a cookie. The behavior of the module and the properties of the cookie are determined by the following configuration setting:

```
<anonymousIdentification enabled="true|false" />
```

The module fires a couple of events—*Remove* and *Create*—when the anonymous ID is removed and created, respectively.

The name of the connected user can be retrieved using the *User* object from the HTTP context. The following expression returns the username:

```
string name = HttpContext.Current.User.Identity.Name;
```

Here the logoff button is a plain submit button. However, you can create both the name of the user and the logoff button by using some new facility controls in ASP.NET 2.0. We'll cover them in detail later in the chapter.

Managing Membership and Roles

In ASP.NET 1.x, you must write the code that validates the user credentials against a data store—typically a database. In many cases, this is boilerplate code that you must write repeatedly. The new *Membership* class in ASP.NET 2.0 saves you from this repetitive task. Not only does it reduce the amount of code needed to authenticate a user, but it also supplies a built-in infrastructure for managing roles.

Using the features of the membership subsystem, you can rewrite the code that authenticates a user as follows:

```
void Logon_Click(Object sender, EventArgs e)
{
   string user = userName.Text;
   string pswd = passWord.Text;
   if (Membership.ValidateUser(user, pswd))
      FormsAuthentication.RedirectFromLoginPage(user, false);
   else
      errorMsg.Text = "Sorry, that's not it.";
}
```

This code doesn't look much different from what you would write for an ASP.NET 1.x application, but there's one big difference: the use of the *ValidateUser* built-in function. As long as you hold, or can obtain, the right data provider, that function call does the authenticating. Earlier in the chapter, you saw a sample function named *ValidateUser* written and used for the same purpose; I left it codeless for simplicity. The *Membership* class's *ValidateUser* function does the same thing, but for real this time as long as you configure the users' data store.

The *Membership* Class

The membership feature consists of a neat and elegant API that doesn't require you to have a deep understanding of the data storage tools and mechanisms (such as SQL Server, stored procedures, and encryption). It shields you from the details of how the credentials are retrieved and compared, and how to encrypt and decrypt. The *Membership* class contains a few static methods that you use to obtain a unique identity for each connected user. This information can also be used with other ASP.NET services, including role-based function enabling and personalization.

Among the members of the class are methods for creating, updating, and deleting users, but not methods for managing roles and programmatically setting what a user can and cannot do. Like the personalization API (discussed in Chapter 4), the *Membership* class works on top of a data provider. If you want to use a custom data store (such as an Active Directory or a personal database), you can create your own provider and just plug it in. You can use multiple providers at the same time, which allows the application to select the right one at run time.

The Programming Interface of the *Membership* Class

The membership subsystem is made up of a set of classes and interfaces that encapsulate the logic for creating and managing users and for authenticating users based on the supplied credentials. Table 10-5 lists the properties exposed by the *Membership* class.

Table 10-5 Properties of the *Membership* Class

Property	Description
ApplicationName	Gets and sets an optional string to identity the application. Defaults to the application's metabase path.
EnablePasswordReset	Returns *true* if the provider supports password reset.
EnablePasswordRetrieval	Returns *true* if the provider supports password retrieval. (Password retrieval is accomplished via the *PasswordRecovery* control—more on this later.)
Provider	Returns an instance of the currently configured provider.
Providers	Returns the collection of all registered providers.
RequiresQuestionAndAnswer	Returns *true* if the provider requires a password question/answer when retrieving or resetting the password.
UserIsOnlineTimeWindow	Specifies the time window, in minutes, during which the user is considered to be online.

The *Provider* property returns a reference to the membership provider currently in use. As you'll see in a moment, the provider is selected in the configuration file. ASP.NET 2.0 comes with a couple of predefined providers that target Access and SQL Server databases. However, many more membership providers are in the works. You can obtain the list of available providers through the *Providers* collection. Some of the properties are provider-specific and are not implemented if the underlying provider doesn't support them.

Table 10-6 details the methods supported by the *Membership* class. This list gives a clearer idea of the tasks the class accomplishes.

Table 10-6 Methods of the *Membership* Class

Method	Description
CreateUser	Creates a new user and fails if the user already exists. The method returns a *MembershipUser* object representing any available information about the user.
DeleteUser	Deletes the user corresponding to the specified name.
FindUsersByEmail	Returns a collection of membership users whose e-mail address corresponds to the specified e-mail.
FindUsersByName	Returns a collection of membership users whose username matches the specified username.
GeneratePassword	Generates a random password of the specified length.
GetAllUsers	Returns a collection of all users.
GetNumberOfUsersOnline	Returns the total number of users currently online.
GetUser	Retrieves the *MembershipUser* object associated with the current or specified user.
GetUserNameByEmail	Obtains the username that corresponds to the specified e-mail. *This method assumes that the e-mail is a unique identifier in the user database.*
UpdateUser	Takes a *MembershipUser* object and updates the information stored for user.
ValidateUser	Authenticates a user using supplied credentials.

The class supports fairly advanced functionality, such as estimating the number of users currently using the application. It uses the value assigned to the *UserIsOnlineTimeWindow* property to determine this number. A user is considered online if he has done something with the application during the previous time window. The default value for the *UserIsOnlineTimeWindow* property is 15 minutes. After 15 minutes of inactivity, a user is considered offline.

Setting Up Membership Support

Let's look at how to use the membership API in ASP.NET 2.0 applications. The membership API relies on a particular data store. The membership model supports a variety of storage media as long as special component—the membership data provider—exists to wrap it. ASP.NET 2.0 comes with a couple of built-in providers; one targets an Access database, and the other works with a SQL Server. Before you deploy the application, you should create and fully set up the membership data store.

The Web Application Administration Tool in Visual Studio 2005 provides a user interface for creating and administering the registered users of your application. Figure 10-3 provides a glimpse of the user interface.

Figure 10-3 The Web Application Administration Tool lets you configure the membership data model

The security wizard you can run from the tool creates the membership database (which is an Access database by default) to which the site administrator can add users and roles. (See Figure 10-4.)

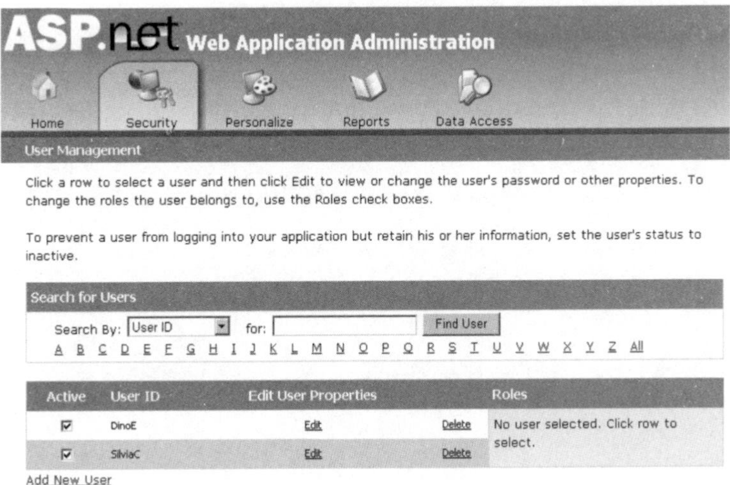

Figure 10-4 Managing users and roles with the Web Application Administration Tool

The Access database is the same .mdb file we worked with in Chapter 4 for personalization. This database contains a table with usernames and related passwords. Once the application is fully configured for membership, you need to enter only a few changes to the code you saw earlier.

```
if (Membership.ValidateUser(user, pswd))
    FormsAuthentication.RedirectFromLoginPage(user, false);
```

You call the *ValidateUser* static method on the *Membership* class to check the username and password against the list of users stored in the database.

Managing Users and Passwords

The *Membership* class provides easy-to-use methods for creating and managing user data. For example, to create a new user programmatically, all you do is place a call to the *CreateUser* method. Let's assume you have a login page with two mutually exclusive panels—one for registered users and one for new users, as shown in Figure 10-5.

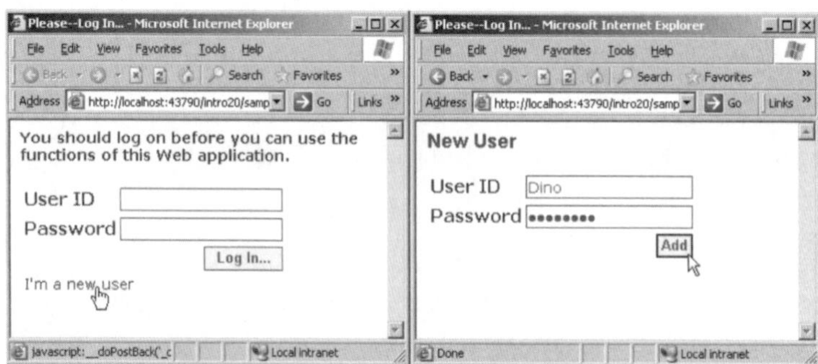

Figure 10-5 A login page that allows new users to register

If you click the button that allows new users to register, the page switches the panels and displays the input form for collecting the name and password of the new user. The click handler for the Add button runs the following code:

```
void AddNewUser_Click (object sender, EventArgs e)
{
    Membership.CreateUser(NewUserName.Text, NewUserPswd.Text);
    NewUserPanel.Visible = false;
    LogUserPanel.Visible = true;

      // Preset the username text box in the log-in panel
    userName.Text = NewUserName.Text;
}
```

To delete a user, you call the *DeleteUser* method:

```
Membership.DeleteUser(userName);
```

You can just as easily get information about a particular user by using the *GetUser* method. The method takes the username and returns a *MembershipUser* object:

```
MembershipUser user = Membership.GetUser("DinoE");
```

Once you've got a *MembershipUser* object, you know all you need to know about a particular user, and you can, for example, programmatically change the password. An application commonly needs to execute several operations on passwords, including changing the password, sending a user her password, or resetting the password, possibly with a question/answer challenge protocol. These functions are all supported by the membership API, but not necessarily by the underlying provider. Note that if the provider does not support a given feature, an exception is thrown if the method is invoked. Here's the code that changes a password:

```
MembershipUser user = Membership.GetUser("DinoE");
user.ChangePassword(user.GetPassword(), newPswd);
```

To use the *ChangePassword* method, you must pass in the old password. In some cases, you might want to allow users to simply reset their password instead of changing it. You do this by using the *ResetPassword* method:

```
MembershipUser user = Membership.GetUser("DinoE");
string newPswd = user.ResetPassword();
```

In this case, the subsystem of your application that calls *ResetPassword* is also in charge of sending the new password to the user—for example, via e-mail. Both the *GetPassword* and *ResetPassword* methods have a second overload that takes a string parameter. If specified, this string represents the answer to the user's "forgot password" question. The Membership API matches the provided answer against the stored answers; if a user is identified, the password is reset or returned.

It goes without saying that the ability to reset the password, as well as support for a password challenge, is specific to the provider and is configured in the web.config file. The password question and the related answer are exposed as read/write members of the *MembershipUser* class. They must be set when the user is created and are stored in the membership database.

The Membership Provider

The beauty of the membership model lies not merely in the extremely compact code you need to write to validate or manage users but also in the fact that the model is abstract and extensible. If you have an existing data store filled with user information, you can integrate it with the Membership API without much effort. All you have to do is write a custom data provider—a class that inherits the *MembershipProvider* class which, in turn, inherits the *ProviderBase* class:

```
public class OracleMembershipProvider : MembershipProvider
{
   // Implements all abstract members of the class and, if
   // needed, defines custom functionality
   ⋮
}
```

The code shows the signature of a custom provider that uses an Oracle database to store its membership information. Once you have written your own made-to-measure provider, the only thing left to do is tell the membership subsystem to use the custom provider. This requires a little change in the application's web.config file, as shown here:

```
<configuration>
<system.web>
  <membership defaultProvider = "Mainframe">
    <providers>
       <add name="OracleMembershipProvider"
            type="Samples.OracleMembershipProvider, samples" />
    </providers>
  </membership>
</system.web>
</configuration>
```

In front of this declaration, the membership API instantiates the specified provider class and uses it through the implemented interfaces. No other action is required on your part.

The *ProviderBase* Class

All the providers used in ASP.NET 2.0 implement a common set of members—those defined by the *ProviderBase* class. The class comes with one method, *Initialize*, and one property, *Name*. The *Name* property returns the official name of the provider class. The *Initialize* method takes the name of the provider and a name/value collection object packed with the content of the provider's configuration section. The method is supposed to initialize its internal state with the values just read out of the web.config file.

The *MembershipProvider* Class

Many of the methods and properties used with the *Membership* class are actually implemented by calling a corresponding method or properties in the underlying provider. Table 10-7 lists the methods defined by the *MembershipProvider* base class.

Table 10-7 Methods of the *MembershipProvider* Class

Method	Description
ChangePassword	Takes a username in addition to the old and new password and changes the user's password.
ChangePasswordQuestionAndAnswer	Takes a username and password and changes the pair of question/answer that allows reading and changing the password.
CreateUser	Creates a new user account and returns a *MembershipUser*-derived class. The method takes the username, password, and e-mail address.
DeleteUser	Deletes the record that corresponds to the specified username.
FindUsersByEmail	Returns a collection of membership users whose e-mail address corresponds to the specified e-mail.
FindUsersByName	Returns a collection of membership users whose username matches the specified username.
GetAllUsers	Returns the collection of all users managed by the provider.
GetNumberOfUsersOnline	Returns the number of users that are currently considered to be online.
GetPassword	Takes the username and the password's answer and returns the current password for the user.
GetUser	Returns the information available about the specified username.
GetUserNameByEmail	Takes an e-mail address and returns the corresponding username.
ResetPassword	Takes the username and the password's answer and resets the user password to an autogenerated password.
UpdateUser	Updates the information available about the specified user.
ValidateUser	Validates the specified credentials against the stored list of users.

All these methods are marked as abstract virtual (must-inherit, overridable according to the Visual Basic .NET jargon) in the class. The *MembershipProvider* class also features a few properties. They are listed in Table 10-8.

Table 10-8 Properties of the *MembershipProvider* Class

Property	Description
ApplicationName	Gets and sets an optional string to identify the application
EnablePasswordReset	Indicates whether the provider supports password reset
EnablePasswordRetrieval	Indicates whether the provider supports password retrieval
RequiresQuestionAndAnswer	Indicates whether the provider requires a question/answer challenge to enable password changes

The provider can also store additional information with each user. You can derive a custom class from *MembershipUser*, add any extra members, and return an instance of that class via the standard *GetUser* method of the membership API. To use the new class, you must cast the object returned by *GetUser* to the proper type, as shown here:

```
MyCompanyUser user = (MyCompanyUser) Membership.GetUser(name);
```

In addition to the members listed in Table 10-7 and Table 10-8, a custom membership provider can add new and custom members. These are defined outside the official schema of the interface and are therefore available only to the users of the custom provider.

For simplicity, the membership API tends to hide the underlying provider from the developer's view. In many cases, the API just routes the calls to the selected provider. However, this works well only if the invoked methods are part of the *MembershipProvider* base class. In the case of custom members, you must explicitly invoke the methods on the provider object. The following code illustrates how to retrieve the instance of a particular membership provider:

```
MyCompanyProvider prov;
prov = (MyCompanyProvider) Membership.Providers["MyCompanyProvider"];
```

Note that the *Providers* collection is also the key property for authenticating users using a dynamically selected provider:

```
MembershipProvider prov;
prov = (MembershipProvider) Membership.Providers["MyCompanyProvider"];
prov.ValidateUser(user, pswd);
```

This feature allows you to support multiple providers and authenticate users via a specific provider. For example, you can design your application to support a legacy database of users through a custom provider while storing new users in a standard SQL Server table. In this case, you use different membership providers for different users.

Built-In Providers

As mentioned, ASP.NET 2.0 comes with two built-in membership providers: *AccessMembershipProvider* (the default) and *SqlMembershipProvider*. The former stores user data in an Access database; the latter uses a SQL Server database. The Access provider is for the situation in which no access to SQL Server (or MSDE) is available. For a real-world enterprise scenario, the choice is a no-brainer—use the SQL Server provider.

The *SqlMembershipProvider* performs all access to SQL Server using stored procedures but doesn't require an extensive knowledge of the syntax and semantics of SQL Server. You decide whether multiple applications will use the same database or whether each application should manage its own database. The ASP.NET 2.0 Framework comes with a T-SQL script that installs (and uninstalls) the membership database and necessary tools.

Configuring a Membership Provider

Any configuration information about membership providers is stored in the *<membership>* section. The section contains a child *<providers>* element under which individual providers are configured. The following is an excerpt from the machine.config file that ships with the PDC build:

```
<membership defaultProvider="AspNetAccessProvider"
            userIsOnlineTimeWindow="15" >
   <providers>
      ⋮
   <providers>
</membership>
```

The *<membership>* section supports a couple of attributes: *defaultProvider*, which indicates the default provider, and *userIsOnlineTimeWindow*, which indicates the maximum number of minutes of idleness before a user is declared offline. The following code snippet shows the typical configuration block for a membership provider:

```
<add name="..."
     type="..."
     connectionStringName="..."
     enablePasswordRetrieval="true|false"
     enablePasswordReset="true|false"
     requiresQuestionAndAnswer="true|false"
     applicationName="/"
     requiresUniqueEmail="true|false"
     passwordFormat="Hashed"
     description="..."
/>
```

No matter the type of the data store—SQL Server, Access, Oracle, or Active Directory—a connection string is always needed. The *connectionStringName* attribute points to another section in the web.config file in which all needed connection strings are held. To add a new provider, you just add an extra, properly configured *<add>* block.

Managing Roles

Roles in ASP.NET simplify the implementation of applications that require authorization. A role is just a logical attribute assigned to a user. An ASP.NET role is a plain string that refers to the logical role the user plays in the context of the application. In terms of configuration, each user can be assigned one or more roles. This information is attached to the identity object, and the application code can check it before the execution of critical operations.

For example, an application might define two roles—Admin and Guest, each granting its users a set of permissions. Users belonging to the Admin role can perform tasks that other users are prohibited from performing.

> **Note** Assigning roles to a user account doesn't add any security restrictions by itself. It is the responsibility of the application to ensure that authorized users perform critical operations only if they are members of a certain role.

In ASP.NET, the role manager feature simply maintains the relationship between users and roles. ASP.NET 1.1 has no built-in support for managing roles. You can attach some role information to an identity, but this involves writing some custom code. Checking roles is easier, but ASP.NET 2.0 makes the whole thing significantly simpler.

The Role Management API

The role management API lets you define roles as well as specify programmatically which users are in which roles. The easiest way to configure role management, define roles, add users to roles, and create access rules is to use the Web Application Administration Tool. (See Figure 10-6.)

You enable role management by adding the following script to your application's web.config file:

```
<roleManager enabled="true" />
```

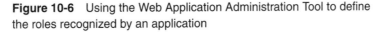

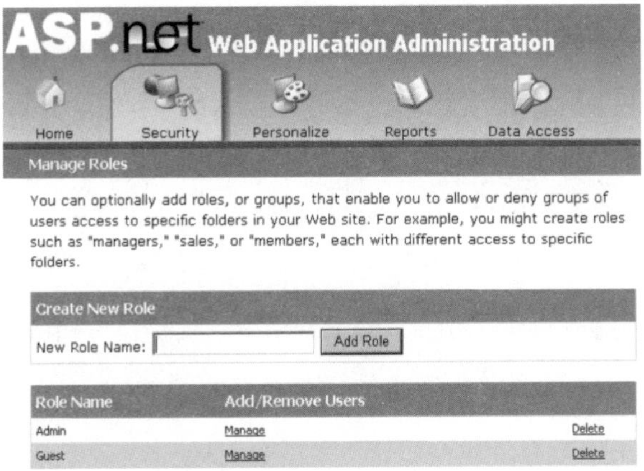

Figure 10-6 Using the Web Application Administration Tool to define the roles recognized by an application

You can use roles to establish access rules for pages and folders. The following *<authorization>* block states that only *Admin* members can access the pages controlled by the web.config file:

```
<configuration>
<system.web>
    <authorization>
       <allow roles="Admin" />
       <deny users="*" />
    </authorization>
</system.web>
<configuration>
```

The Web Administration Tool provides a visual interface for creating associations between users and roles. If necessary, you can instead perform this task programmatically by calling various role manager methods. The following code demonstrates how to create the *Admin* and *Guest* roles and populate them with usernames:

```
Roles.CreateRole("Admin");
Roles.AddUsersToRole("DinoE", "Admin");
Roles.CreateRole("Guest");
string[] guests = new string[2];
guests[0] = "JoeUsers";
guests[1] = "Godzilla";
Roles.AddUsersToRole(guests, "Guest")
```

At run time, information about the logged-in user is available through the *User* object. The following code demonstrates how to determine whether the current user is in a certain role and subsequently enable specific functions:

```
if (User.IsInRole("Admin"))
{
      // Enable functions specific of the role
   :
}
```

When role management is enabled, ASP.NET 2.0 looks up the roles for the current user and binds that information to the *User* object. This same feature had to be manually coded in ASP.NET 1.x.

The *Roles* Class

When role management is enabled, ASP.NET creates an instance of the *Roles* class and adds it to the current request context—the HttpContext object. The *Roles* class features the methods listed in Table 10-9.

Table 10-9 Methods of the *Roles* Class

Method	Description
AddUsersToRole	Adds an array of users to a role
AddUsersToRoles	Adds an array of users to multiple roles
AddUserToRole	Adds a user to a role
AddUserToRoles	Adds a user to multiple roles
CreateRole	Creates a new role
DeleteCookie	Deletes the cookie that the role manager used to cache all the role data
DeleteRole	Deletes an existing role
FindUsersInRole	Returns a string array filled with the names of users in a role where the username contains a match for the specified name. For example, if the name to match is 'user', the users 'user1', 'user2', 'user3' are returned in alphabetical order.
GetAllRoles	Returns all the available roles
GetRolesForUser	Returns a string array listing the roles that a particular member belongs to
GetUsersInRole	Returns a string array listing the users that belong to a particular role
IsUserInRole	Determines whether the specified user is in a particular role
RemoveUserFromRole	Removes a user from a role

Table 10-9 Methods of the *Roles* Class

Method	Description
RemoveUserFromRoles	Removes a user from multiple roles
RemoveUsersFromRole	Removes multiple users from a role
RemoveUsersFromRoles	Removes multiple users from multiple roles
RoleExists	Returns true if the specified role exists

Table 10-10 lists the properties available on the *Roles* class.

Table 10-10 Properties of the *Roles* Class

Property	Description
ApplicationName	Gets and sets an optional string to identify the application.
CacheRolesInCookie	Returns *true* if cookie storage for role data is enabled.
CookieName	Specifies the name of the cookie used by the role manager to store the roles.
CookieProtectionValue	Specifies an option for securing the roles cookie. Possible values are All, Clear, Hashed, and Encrypted.
CookieRequireSSL	Indicates whether the cookie requires SSL.
CookieSlidingExpiration	Indicates whether the cookie has a fixed expiration time or a sliding expiration.
CookieTimeout	Returns the time, in minutes, after which the cookie will expire.
Enabled	Indicates whether role management is enabled.
Provider	Returns the current role provider.
Providers	Returns a list of all supported role providers.

Some of the methods on the *Roles* class need to query continuously for the roles associated with a given user, so when possible, the roles for a given user are stored in an encrypted cookie. On each request, ASP.NET checks to see whether the cookie is present; if so, it decrypts the role ticket and attaches any role information to the *User* object. Note that the cookie is valid only if the request is for the current user. When you request role information for other users, the information is read from the data store using the configured role provider. To enable cookie support, you must ensure that the *cacheRolesInCookie* attribute is set to *true* in the *<roleManager>* configuration section.

The Role Provider

The role management API is completed by two components that work in the background—the role manager HTTP module and the role provider. The role manager is responsible for adding the appropriate roles to the current identity object (such as the *User* object). The module listens for the *AuthenticateRequest* event and does its job.

For its I/O activity, the module uses a provider component. The role provider is a class that inherits the *RoleProvider* class. The schema of a role provider is not much different from that of a membership provider. Table 10-11 details the members of the *RoleProvider* class.

Table 10-11 Methods of the *RoleProvider* Class

Method	Description
AddUsersToRoles	Adds an array of users to multiple roles
CreateRole	Creates a new role
DeleteRole	Deletes the specified role
FindUsersInRole	Returns the name of users in a role matching a given username pattern.
GetAllRoles	Returns the list of all available roles
GetRolesForUser	Gets all the roles a user belongs to
GetUsersInRole	Gets all the users who participate in the given role
IsUserInRole	Indicates whether the user belongs to the role
RemoveUsersFromRoles	Removes an array of users from multiple roles
RoleExists	Indicates whether a given role exists

You can see the similarity between some of these methods and the programming interface of the *Roles* class. This is not coincidental—it's the intention of using patterns in the new ASP.NET 2.0 provider data model. You can select any provider and still have your high-level code work. You can manipulate any data store without being an expert in that syntax.

ASP.NET ships with two built-in role providers—*AccessRoleProvider* (default) and *SqlRoleProvider*. The former stores role information in a new table in the familiar AspNetDb.mdb file; the latter uses a SQL Server table. You can register a custom role provider by using the child *<providers>* section in the *<roleManager>* section:

```
<roleManager
    enabled="false"
    cacheRolesInCookie="true|false"
```

```
    cookieName=".ASPXROLES"
    cookieTimeout="30"
    cookiePath="/"
    cookieRequireSSL="true|false"
    cookieSlidingExpiration="true|false"
    cookieProtection="All"
    defaultProvider="AccessRoleProvider">
    <providers>
       <add  name="..."
             type="..."
             connectionStringName="..."
             applicationName="/"
             description="..." />
    </providers>
    ⋮
</roleManager>
```

Security-Related Controls

In addition to the membership and role management APIs, ASP.NET 2.0 offers several server controls that make programming security-related aspects of a Web application easier than ever: *Login*, *LoginName*, *LoginStatus*, *LoginView*, *PasswordRecovery*, *ChangePassword*, and *CreateUserWizard*. These are composite controls, and they provide a rich, customizable user interface. They encapsulate a large part of the boilerplate code and markup you would otherwise have to write repeatedly.

The *Login* Control

An application based on the Forms authentication model always needs a login page. Aside from the quality of the graphics, all login pages look alike. They contain a couple of text boxes (for username and password), a button to validate credentials, plus perhaps a Remember Me check box—links to click if the user has forgotten his password or needs to create an account. The *Login* control provides all this for free, including the ability to validate the user against the default membership provider.

Setting Up the *Login* Control

The *Login* control is a composite control that provides all the common user interface elements of a login form. Figure 10-7 shows the default user interface of the control. To get it, you simply drop the control from the toolbox onto the Web form, or you just type the following code:

```
<asp:login runat="server" id="MyLoginForm" />
```

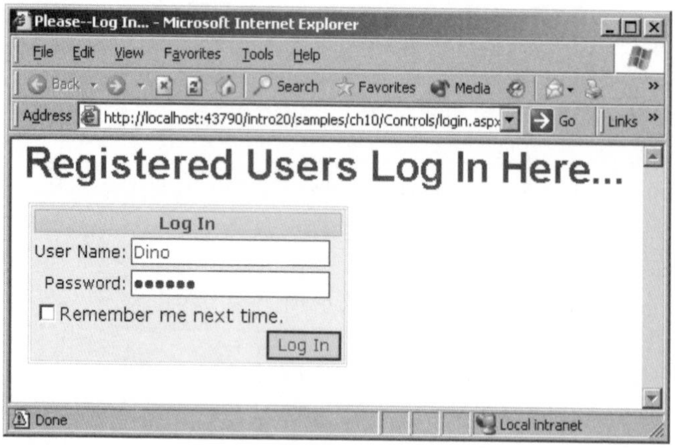

Figure 10-7 The *Login* control in action

The *Login* control also has optional user interface elements for functions such as password reminder, new user registration, help link, error messages, and a custom action in case of a successful login. When you drop the control onto a Visual Studio 2005 form, the AutoFormat verb lets you choose among a few predefined styles, as in Figure 10-8.

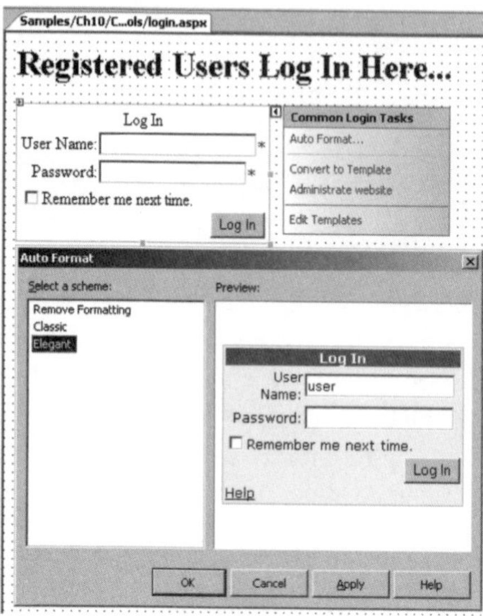

Figure 10-8 The predefined styles of the *Login* control

The appearance of the control is fully customizable through templates and style settings. All user interface text messages are also customizable through properties of the class.

The Programming Interface of the Control

Table 10-12 lists all the properties of the *Login* control. You can see that the control is modularized, and each constituent part can be individually customized.

Table 10-12 Properties of the *Login* Control

Property	Description
CheckBoxStyle	Defines the style of the *Remember Me* check box.
CreateUserText	Gets or sets the text of a link to a registration page for new users.
CreateUserUrl	Gets or sets the URL to the new-user registration page.
DestinationPageUrl	Gets or sets the URL of the page displayed to the user when a login attempt is successful.
DisplayRememberMe	Indicates whether to enable the user to choose to store an authentication cookie on the user's computer.
EnableValidation	Indicates whether to validate the text-entry fields of the control.
FailureAction	Gets or sets the action that occurs when a login attempt fails. Options are *Refresh* (the page is refreshed to display an error message) or *RedirectToLoginPage* (redisplays the login page).
FailureText	Gets or sets the text displayed when a login attempt fails.
FailureTextStyle	Defines the style of the error text.
HelpPageText	Gets or sets the text of a link to the help page.
HelpPageUrl	Gets or sets the URL to the help page.
HyperLinkStyle	Defines the style of the hyperlink controls displayed in the control.
InstructionText	Gets or sets login instruction text for the user.
InstructionTextStyle	Defines the style for instruction text.
LabelStyle	Defines the style of the control labels.
LayoutTemplate	Gets or sets the template used to display the contents of the control.
MembershipProvider	Gets or sets the name of the membership data provider used by the control.

Table 10-12 Properties of the *Login* Control

Property	Description
Orientation	Indicates whether constituent controls should be displayed horizontally or vertically (default).
Password	Gets the password entered by the user.
PasswordLabelText	Gets or sets the text of the label for the Password text box.
PasswordRecoveryText	Gets or sets text of a link to the password recovery page.
PasswordRecoveryUrl	Gets or sets the URL to the password recovery page.
PasswordRequiredErrorMessage	Gets or sets the error message to display when the password field is left blank.
RememberMeSet	Indicates whether the Remember Me check box is set.
RememberMeText	Gets or sets the text of the label for the Remember Me check box.
SubmitButtonImageUrl	Gets or sets the URL of an image to use for the submit button.
SubmitButtonStyle	Defines the style of the submit button.
SubmitButtonText	Gets or sets the text for the submit button.
SubmitButtonType	Gets or sets the type of button to use when rendering the control (push or link button).
TextBoxStyle	Defines the style of text boxes.
TitleText	Gets or sets the title of the control.
TitleTextStyle	Defines the style of the title text.
UserName	Gets the username entered by the user.
UserNameLabelText	Gets or sets the text of the label for the UserName text box.
UserNameRequiredErrorMessage	Gets or sets the error message to display when the username field is left blank.
VisibleWhenLoggedIn	Indicates whether to show the Login form once the user is authenticated.

If you don't like the standard user interface of the control, you can define your own template:

```
<asp:login runat="server" id="MyLoginForm">
    <layouttemplate>
       ⋮
    </layouttemplate>
</asp:login>
```

Your template can include new elements, and you can recycle default components. To do the latter, you should use the same ID for the controls as in the default template. To simplify this operation, right-click on the control in the Visual Studio designer, choose Convert To Template, and switch to Source view. The markup you see is the default template of the control expressed as ASP.NET code. Use it as a starting point for creating your own template.

Events of the Control

The *Login* control fires the events listed in Table 10-13.

Table 10-13 Events of the *Login* Control

Event	Description
Authenticate	Fires when a user is authenticated.
LoggedIn	Fires when the user logs in to the site after a successful authentication.
LoggingIn	Fires when a user submits login information but before the authentication takes place. The operation can still be canceled.
LoginError	Fires when a login error is detected.

In most common cases, though, you don't handle any of these events. The most common use for the *Login* control is to set up the user interface of the login page for use with Forms authentication. The form itself performs membership authentication, displays error messages, and redirects to the originally requested page when the login is successful.

The *LoginName* Control

The *LoginName* control is an extremely simple and useful server control. It works like a sort of label control and displays the user's name on a Web page:

```
<asp:loginname runat="server" />
```

The control captures the name of the currently logged-in user from the *User* intrinsic object and outputs it using the current style. Internally, the control builds a dynamic instance of a *Label* control, sets fonts and color accordingly, and displays the text returned by the following expression:

```
string name = HttpContext.Current.User.Identity.Name;
```

The *LoginName* control has a pretty slim programming interface that consists of only one property—*FormatString*. *FormatString* defines the format of the text to display. It can contain only one placeholder, as shown here:

```
myLogin.FormatString = "Welcome, {0}";
```

If Dino is the name of the current user, the code generates a "Welcome, Dino" message.

The *LoginStatus* Control

The *LoginStatus* control indicates the state of the authentication for the current user. Its user interface consists of a link button to log in or log out, depending on the current user login state. If the user is acting as an anonymous user—that is, he never logged in—the control displays a link button to invite the user to log in. Otherwise, if the user successfully passed through the authentication layer, the control displays the logout button.

Setting Up the *LoginStatus* Control

The *LoginStatus* control is often used in conjunction with the *LoginName* control to display the name of the current user (if any), plus a button to let her log in or out. The style, text, and action associated with the button changes are conveniently based on the authentication state of the user.

The following code creates a table showing the name of the current user and a button to log in or log out:

```
<table width="100%" border="0">
  <tr>
    <td>
      <asp:loginname runat="server" FormatString="Welcome, {0}" />
    </td>
    <td align="right">
      <asp:loginstatus runat="server" LogoutText="Log off" />
    </td>
  </tr>
</table>
```

Figure 10-9 shows the results. The first screenshot demonstrates a page that invites a user to log in; the second shows the *LoginName* and *LoginStatus* controls working together in the case of a logged-in user. To detect whether the current user is authenticated and adapt the user interface, you can use the *IsAuthenticated* property of the *Identity* object.

```
void Page_Load(object sender, EventArgs e)
{
   if (User.Identity.IsAuthenticated)
       Msg.Text = "Enjoy more features";
   else
       Msg.Text = "Login to enjoy more features.";
}
```

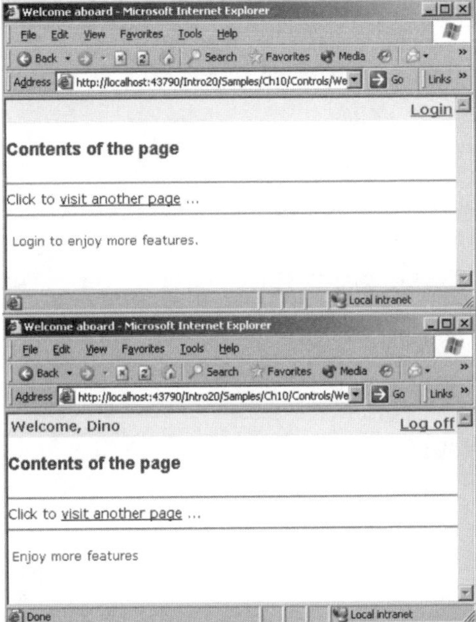

Figure 10-9 The *LoginStatus* control invites a user who is not currently logged in to log in; next, it displays more features reserved to registered users.

The Programming Interface of the Control

Although the *LoginStatus* control is quite useful in its default form, it provides a bunch of properties and events that you can use to configure it. The properties are listed in Table 10-14.

Table 10-14 Properties of the *LoginStatus* Control

Property	Description
LoginImageUrl	Gets or sets the URL of the image used for the login link.
LoginText	Gets or sets the text used for the login link.
LogoutAction	Determines the action taken when a user logs out of a Web site. Possible values are *Refresh*, *Redirect*, and *RedirectToLoginPage*.
LogoutImageUrl	Gets or sets the URL of the image used for the logout button.
LogoutPageUrl	Gets or sets the URL of the logout page.
LogoutText	Gets or sets the text used for the logout link.

The control also features a couple events—*LoggingOut* and *LoggedOut*. The former fires before the user clicks to log off. The latter is raised immediately after the logout process has completed.

The *LoginView* Control

The *LoginView* control allows you to aggregate the *LoginStatus* and *LoginName* controls to display a custom user interface that takes into account the authentication state of the user as well as the role. The control, which is based on templates, simplifies creation of a user interface specific to the anonymous or connected state and particular roles. In other words, you can create as many templates as you need, one per state or per role.

The Programming Interface of the Control

Table 10-15 lists the properties of the user interface of the *LoginView* control.

Table 10-15 Properties of the *LoginView* Class

Property	Description
AnonymousTemplate	Gets or sets the template to display to users who are not logged in to the application
Controls	Returns the collection of controls defined within the body of the login control
LoggedInTemplate	Gets or sets the template to display to users who are logged in to the application
RoleGroups	Returns the collection of templates defined for the supported roles
RoleProvider	Gets or sets the name of the role data provider in use

Note that the *LoggedInTemplate* template is displayed only to logged-in users who are not members of one of the role groups specified in the *RoleGroups* property. The template (if any) specified in the *<rolegroups>* tag always takes precedence.

The *LoginView* control also fires the *ViewChanging* and *ViewChanged* events. The former reaches the application when the control is going to change the view (such as when a user logs in). The latter event fires when the view has changed.

Creating a Login Template

The *LoginView* control lets you define two distinct templates to show to anonymous and logged users. You can use the following markup to give your pages a common layout and manage the template to show when the user is logged in:

```
<asp:loginview runat="server">
   <anonymoustemplate>
     <table width="100%" border="0"><tr><td>
        To enjoy more features,
        <asp:loginstatus runat="server">
     </td></tr></table>
   </anonymoustemplate>
   <loggedintemplate>
     <table width="100%" border="0"><tr>
       <td><asp:loginname runat="server" /></td>
       <td align="right"><asp:loginstatus runat="server" /></td>
     </tr></table>
   </loggedintemplate>
</asp:loginview>
```

Basically, the LoginView control provides a more flexible, template-based programming interface to distinguish between logged-in and anonymous scenarios. It makes the use of the *IsAuthenticated* property seen above unnecessary.

Creating Role-Based Templates

The *LoginView* control also allows you to define blocks of user interface to display to all logged-in users who belong to a particular role. As mentioned, these templates take precedence over the *<loggedintemplate>* template if both apply.

```
<asp:loginview runat="server">
  <rolegroups>
     <asp:rolegroup roles="Admin">
       <contenttemplate>
          :
       </contenttemplate>
     </asp:rolegroup>
     <asp:rolegroup roles="Guest">
       <contenttemplate>
          :
       </contenttemplate>
     </asp:rolegroup>
  </rolegroups>
</asp:loginview>
```

The content of each *<contenttemplate>* block is displayed only to users whose role matches the value of the *roles* attribute. You can use this feature to create a role-specific menu. For the *LoginView* control to work well, role management must be enabled, of course. The default role provider is used, but you can change it through the *RoleProvider* property.

The *PasswordRecovery* Control

The *PasswordRecovery* control is another server control that wraps a common piece of Web user interface into an out-of-the-box component. The control represents the form that enables a user to recover or reset a lost password and receive it back through an e-mail message.

Configuring the Environment

After you drop the *PasswordRecovery* control onto a Web form, you must make some changes to the membership environment before it will work. First you must ensure that the *ensurePasswordRetrieval* attribute in the web.config file is turned on. (It is *false* by default.)

The following configuration script shows how to proceed. You first remove the current definition of the provider of choice (the Access provider in this case) and then add a brand new definition where a few attributes are overridden.

```
<membership>
   <providers>
     <remove name="AspNetAccessProvider" />
     <add name="AspNetAccessProvider" type="..."
          connectionStringName="AccessFileName"
            enablePasswordRetrieval="true"
          enablePasswordReset="true"
          requiresQuestionAndAnswer="false"
            passwordFormat="Clear"
          requiresUniqueEmail="false"
          applicationName="/" />
   </providers>
</membership>
```

Another required change involves how the password is stored in the membership data store. By default, passwords are not stored as clear text; their text is hashed using some system parameters as the key. Unfortunately, hash algorithms are not two-way algorithms. In other words, the hash mechanism is great at encrypting and comparing passwords, but it doesn't retrieve the clear text. If you plan to use the *PasswordRecovery* control, you must set the *pass-*

wordFormat attribute in the *<provider>* section to *Clear* or *Encrypted*. In this way, a clear text string will be returned to users.

Retrieving a Password

Unlike many of the other security-related controls, the *PasswordRecovery* control cannot work without a child element, *MailDefinition*.

```
<asp:passwordrecovery runat="server">
   <maildefinition from="admin@contoso.com" />
</asp:passwordrecovery>
```

The *<maildefinition>* element indicates the sender of the e-mail message that returns the password to the user. For sending e-mails, the control relies on the settings in the *<smtpMail>* section of the web.config file. The following script shows the default content of the section in machine.config:

```
<smtpMail serverName="localhost" serverPort="25" />
```

If the user has a question/answer pair defined and the *requiresQuestionAndAnswer* attribute is turned on (see Figure 10-10), the *PasswordRecovery* control can change its own user interface to display the question and ask for the answer before the password is retrieved and sent back.

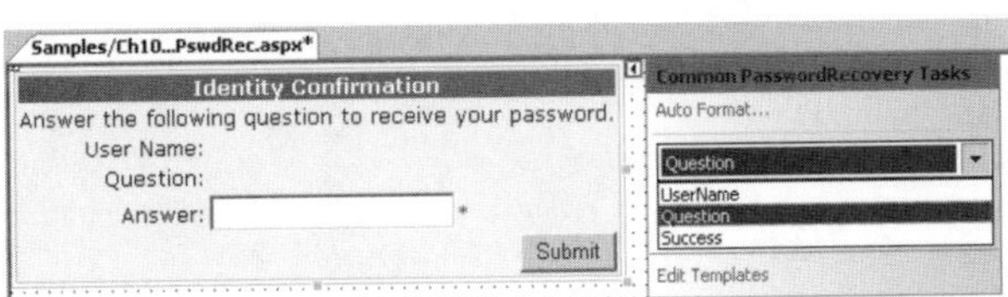

Figure 10-10 Configuring the *PasswordRecovery* control in Visual Studio 2005

The *ChangePassword* Control

The *ChangePassword* control provides an out-of-the-box virtually codeless solution that enables end users to change their password to the site. The control supplies a modifiable and customizable user interface and built-in behaviors to retrieve the old password and save a new one. The underlying API for password management is the same Membership API we discussed earlier in this chapter.

```
<asp:ChangePassword ID="ChangePassword1" Runat="server" />
```

The *ChangePassword* control will work in scenarios where a user may or may not be already authenticated. The control detects if a user is authenticated and automatically populates a username text box with the name. Even though the user is authenticated he or she will still be required to reenter the current password. Once the password has been successfully changed, the control may send—if properly configured—a confirmation e-mail to the user, as you see in Figure 10-11.

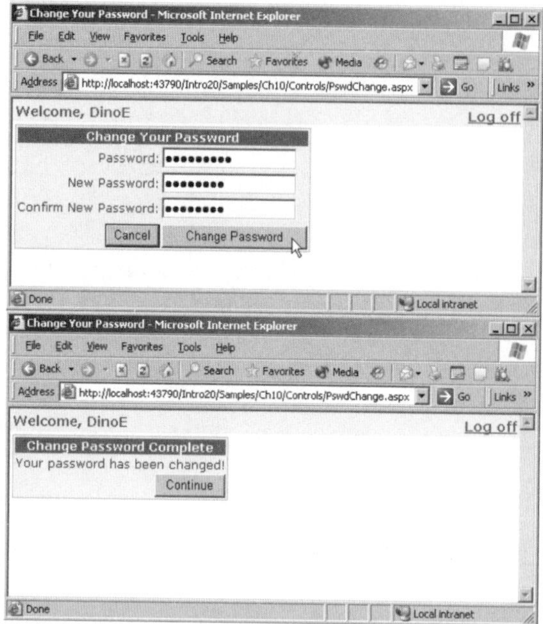

Figure 10-11 The *ChangePassword* control in action

As mentioned, the *ChangePassword* control is extensively based on the Membership API and makes use the *ValidateUser* and *ChangePassword* methods on the *Membership* class.

The *CreateUserWizard* Control337

The *CreateUserWizard* is designed to provide a native functionality for creating a new user using the Membership API. The control offers a basic behavior that the developer can extend to send a confirmation e-mail to the new user and add steps to the wizard to collect additional information like address, phone number, or maybe roles.

Customization is supported in two ways: customizing one of the default steps and by adding more user-defined steps. Figure 10-12 shows the control in action in a sample page.

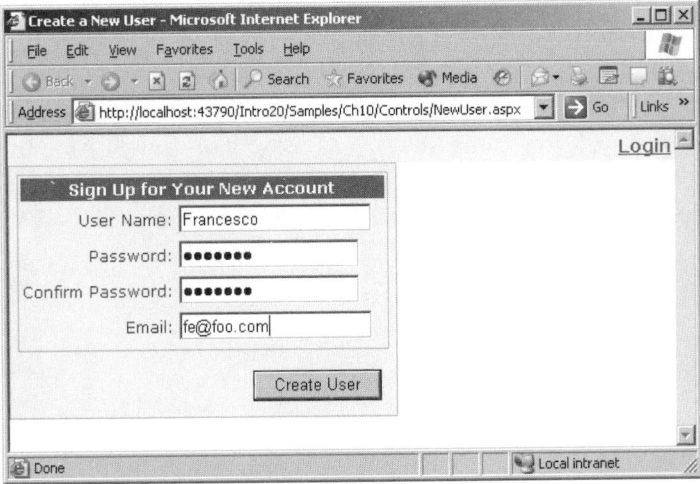

Figure 10-12 The *CreateUserWizard* control in action

Summary

Web applications typically use forms-based authentication for their security layer. The user sees a login form and is asked to specify her credentials. If the credentials are validated, the user is redirected to the originally requested page. Unlike other forms of Web authentication (such as Passport), forms-based authentication requires the developer to provide both the custom logic for validating and authorizing the user and any necessary user interface. Forms authentication in ASP.NET 1.x represents a quantum leap from what was previously available, but you have to write a lot of code even though the entire infrastructure is provided by the system.

In ASP.NET 2.0, the new membership and role management API has greatly improved the machinery of Forms authentication. This API is built around the concept of a provider, which is a component that exposes a suite of data-driven methods that are not tied to the physical data store. This model, which we analyzed in Chapter 4 in terms of personalization, is particularly well-suited to the membership system. The membership and role providers are components that manage users and roles from a particular data store. They make the type of data store irrelevant because the API just talks to a pluggable component with a well-known interface.

A further big improvement in the ASP.NET 2.0 security infrastructure is the security-related server controls, including *Login* and *LoginView*. These controls integrate well with the membership and role management API, and they make building a security layer around ASP.NET 2.0 applications much less complex and tedious than in previous versions of ASP.NET and in classic ASP.

Part IV

Advanced Topics

11

The ASP.NET Runtime Environment

ASP.NET 2.0 is a highly evolved product with new features, new tools, and more abstraction but essentially the same underlying environment as in previous versions. HTTP requests are processed in a nearly identical way, but the HTTP pipeline has been enriched with new handlers, new system events, and more powerful objects. The eventing model—a fundamental piece of the ASP.NET jigsaw puzzle—is also still there, but revised and enhanced.

All in all, the new ASP.NET release builds on top of ASP.NET 1.0 and ASP.NET 1.1, offers some redesigned features, and adds new features to address specific user requests. ASP.NET 2.0 has no breaking changes and is 100 percent compatible with previous versions through the side-by-side execution model.

In this chapter, we'll briefly examine the overall environment that surrounds ASP.NET applications and makes them work. The underlying infrastructure has not radically changed. HTTP handlers and modules are still there and work as expected, but with a few more events and methods. The page served to the browser is still made up of HTML markup and script code, but it is organized differently. The view state works as before. While running, a page is still an instance of a class that is dynamically created out of the .aspx source code. The *runat* attribute plays the same key role, and procedural code can be written both in line and behind classes.

We'll look first at side-by-side compatibility—a neat feature that allows you to install ASP.NET 2.0 without breaking any of your current applications.

Installing ASP.NET 2.0

So you've just gotten your hands on ASP.NET 2.0. What's the next step? Before you install the new framework, you should make sure it won't kill any of the running applications and won't mess up your system.

The great news about ASP.NET is that you can run several versions of the runtime engine at the same time. Many developers faced this issue when they upgraded to ASP.NET 1.1—how to ensure that the new runtime didn't break any existing (and working) applications.

The Microsoft .NET Framework provides support for side-by-side execution, which allows multiple versions of an assembly to be installed on the same computer at the same time. Individual managed applications, including ASP.NET applications, can then select which version of the .NET Framework to use. The choice doesn't affect other applications that require a different version.

Side-by-Side Backward Compatibility

Any version of the .NET Framework, including version 2.0, comes with a redistributable package that includes the ASP.NET engine. The redistributable program is named dotnetfx.exe. When you install it, by default all existing ASP.NET applications are reconfigured to use the version being installed. But this happens only if a few conditions are met.

The version of the .NET Framework you are installing must be newer than the version that is currently mapped to each application. It must also be compatible with the version mapped to the application. Two version numbers that differ only by a minor revision and build number are said to be compatible. Versions whose major revision numbers do not match are considered incompatible. ASP.NET 2.0 is perfectly compatible with previous versions because it has a version number of 2.0.xxxx, where *xxxx* represents the build number.

To prevent the remapping of all existing applications to the installing version of the .NET Framework, you should use the */noaspupgrade* command-line option with the dotnetfx.exe setup program, as shown here:

```
dotnetfx.exe /C:"install /noaspupgrade"
```

The */C* switch overrides the internal command (in this case, *install*) as defined by the programmer. As a result, the above program installs ASP.NET 2.0 but doesn't upgrade existing applications to version 2.0. Note that when you install Whidbey, dotnetfx.exe is the first executable that runs.

Remapping Applications to ASP.NET 1.1

Sadly, you generally get advice about the command-line switches of dotnetfx.exe after it's too late—that is, when you've just finished with the setup of

ASP.NET 2.0. By then, all applications will have been upgraded. How do you recover and make an existing application support ASP.NET 1.1 once it has been upgraded to version 2.0? Do you recall the aspnet_regiis.exe tool in ASP.NET 1.1? It's still the recommended tool for this task.

To make sure that a given ASP.NET application uses the correct runtime files, you must guarantee that all the ASP.NET-related extensions are managed by the correct executable. For example, to make sure that the Foo Web site is bound to ASP.NET 1.1 even after you have upgraded to ASP.NET 2.0, you run the following command-line program:

```
aspnet_regiis.exe -s W3SVC/1/ROOT/Foo
```

Of course, you must use the copy of aspnet_regiis.exe to run from the install directory of the target version of ASP.NET. For example, to remap Foo to ASP.NET 1.1, you run aspnet_regiis from the following folder (the folder of the ASP.NET 1.1 framework):

```
C:\Windows\Microsoft.NET\Framework\v1.1.4322
```

You take a similar approach to uninstall a version of ASP.NET without uninstalling the associated .NET Framework. You use the aspnet_regiis.exe utility of the target version and run it with the *–u* option.

> **Note** By default, when you install ASP.NET 2.0 all applications are updated to use the installing version of ASP.NET as long as no serious compatibility issues exist. However, this procedure does not move any custom configuration settings in the current machine.config file. If your application needs customized configuration settings to work, you must manually update the new machine.config file.

The ASP.NET Underpinnings

The process by which a Web request becomes plain HTML text for the browser is not much different in ASP.NET 1.1 and ASP.NET 2.0. The request is picked up by Microsoft Internet Information Services (IIS), given an identity token, and passed to the ASP.NET ISAPI extension (aspnet_isapi.dll)—the entry point for any ASP.NET-related processing. This is the general process, but a number of key details depend on the underlying version of IIS and the process model in use.

In ASP.NET 2.0, the architecture of the runtime environment has been abstracted and enhanced to support alternative scenarios. The steps and the managed objects that bring an .aspx request to generate plain HTML are nearly the same as in previous versions, but what happens before the HTTP pipeline is activated is remarkably different.

Let's start by reviewing the ASP.NET process model, and then we'll look at the changes in the IIS/ASP.NET infrastructure.

The IIS 5.x Process Model

The *process model* is the sequence of operations needed to process a request. When the ASP.NET runtime runs on top of IIS 5.x, the process model is based on a separate worker process named aspnet_wp.exe. This Win32 process receives control directly from IIS through the hosted ASP.NET ISAPI extension. The extension is passed any request for ASP.NET resources, and it hands them over to the worker process. The worker process loads the common language runtime (CLR) and starts the pipeline of managed objects that make the original request evolve from a HTTP payload to a full-featured page for the browser.

The aspnet_isapi module and the worker process implement advanced features such as process recycling, page output caching, memory monitoring, and thread pooling. The worker process and the ISAPI module communicate through named pipes, and a single instance of the worker process serves all Web applications, except a Web garden is implemented. Each Web application runs in a distinct AppDomain within the worker process. By default, the worker process runs under a restricted, poorly privileged account named ASPNET.

When ASP.NET runs under IIS 6.0, the default process model is different and the aspnet_wp.exe process is not used. Although it is not recommended practice, you can configure ASP.NET to work under IIS 6.0 using the IIS 5.0 process model and isolation mode. In this case, the worker process isolation architecture of IIS 6.0 is disabled and the native process model of ASP.NET is used for all ASP.NET applications on the server machine.

> **Caution** When you set the IIS 6.0 Web application service to work in IIS 5.0 isolation mode, the process model of IIS 6.0 is disabled and IIS dispatches calls as IIS 5.0 would. This feature affects not only ASP.NET applications but all installed applications—as a result, you lose all the features of the IIS 6.0 isolation mode that are based on application pools.

The IIS 6.0 Process Model

When the underlying Web server is IIS 6.0, things change quite a bit. Unless you opt to run the IIS Web service in IIS 5.x isolation mode, ASP.NET applications are hosted by the IIS standard worker process named w3wp.exe, into which the ASP.NET ISAPI extension is loaded to service the request.

IIS 6.0 implements its HTTP listener as a kernel-level module. As a result, all incoming requests, including requests for ASP.NET pages, are first managed by that listener, which is implemented as a driver named http.sys running in kernel mode. The http.sys driver listens for requests and posts them to the request queue of the appropriate application pool. An *application pool* is a worker process and a virtual directory. A module called the Web Administration Service (WAS) reads from the IIS metabase and instructs the http.sys driver to create as many request queues as there are application pools registered in the metabase.

Each application pool is managed by a distinct instance of the same worker process (w3wp.exe). As a result, you can have ASP and ASPX applications managed by the same worker process. Sound weird? Well, it's really not.

The worker process looks up the URL of the request and loads a specific ISAPI extension. For example, it loads aspnet_isapi.dll for ASP.NET-related requests. Under the IIS 6.0 process model, the aspnet_isapi extension is responsible for loading the CLR and starting the HTTP pipeline. All the settings in the *<processModel>* section of the machine.config file are ignored, and similar information is read from the IIS metabase instead. ASP.NET settings that do not relate to the process model continue to be read from the configuration file. The w3wp.exe worker process runs under a restricted account that is functionally similar to ASPNET but is named NetworkService. (It's a built-in service account of Windows Server 2003.)

This description isn't specific to a particular version of ASP.NET. But in ASP.NET 2.0, the interaction between the Web server environment and the ASP.NET runtime environment has been refined by adding a couple of extra layers that abstract the overall design and make it general enough to also support non-HTTP protocols such as SOAP and SMTP. In particular, the SOAP protocol makes room for a parallel runtime aimed at handling the next generation of Web services—code-named Indigo. In ASP.NET 1.1, Web services are treated as a special kind of Web request. The next generation of Web services will have its own set of runtime services hosted by the Web server at the same level of the ASP.NET engine.

The WebHost Application Management System

ASP.NET 2.0 is part of a new process and AppDomain management system whose code name is WebHost. In brief, WebHost is an extensible model for application activation and hosting. It's a common layer of code that hosts and manages applications that can be activated and controlled through messages. Examples of such message-based managed applications are currently limited to ASP.NET 2.0 and Indigo applications. Bits and pieces of WebHost appear in the IIS 6.0 architecture and made their debut in the aspnet_isapi module on IIS 5.0 and Windows 2000.

Starting with the .NET Framework 2.0, the WebHost platform has been finalized as managed components supplied by various providers, including ASP.NET, Indigo, and IIS itself. WebHost manages the lifetime of worker processes, AppDomains, and application components. In doing so, it also provides services such as configuration management, dynamic compilation, and output caching. Applications managed by WebHost must define the high-level components listed in Table 11-1.

Table 11-1 ASP.NET 2.0 Components in the WebHost Platform

Component	Description
Application Manager	Manages the lifetime of AppDomains and application components within the worker process. Already implemented as an internal component of aspnet_isapi 1.x, it is now generalized to handle messages arriving on all protocols (including HTTP) and route them to AppDomains.
Hosting Environment	A library loaded inside the worker process that handles communication with the WebHost host platform (IIS). For example, it answers ping requests. The component also interfaces with the Process Host, a managed object that controls the execution of .NET applications.
Process Host	Provides the ability to host the CLR within the worker process and hosts the application manager and the protocol handlers.
Protocol Handlers	Components that retrieve protocol-specific requests from a queue and service them.

WebHost is expected to provide a number of benefits, such as a single activation and hosting model for all message-activated applications and support for activation over multiple protocols (not just HTTP). WebHost provides a common set of services for all message-activated applications, regardless of the protocol recognized by the particular application. Services include process and AppDomain recycling, health monitoring, and deadlock detection.

If you're a former ASP.NET 1.x programmer and know the basics of IIS 6.0, you think of the WebHost environment as a common layer of code that exposes and personalizes some Web server services to message-activated managed applications. To support these goals, in fact, WebHost clients must implement the process host and application manager components.

> **Important** The WebHost environment is involved with request processing only if the IIS 6.0 process model is used. If ASP.NET 2.0 is hosted on IIS 5.0 or if the IIS 5.0 process model is used, ASP.NET uses its own worker process—aspnet_wp.exe. In this case, the ASP.NET ISAPI extension receives the request and creates the application manager, which in turn creates an instance of the AppDomain's protocol handler to service the request.

The WebHost Process Manager

The WebHost process manager is a Windows service provided by IIS. It starts up and shuts down worker processes and initiates all process management actions, such as recycling and idle detection. The WebHost process manager receives messages from message receivers, which are components that listen to special incoming packets. Message receivers include a component for HTTP messages based on the IIS 6.0 http.sys kernel-mode driver and the SOAP-TCP listener adapter provided with Indigo.

The WebHost process manager passes control to the IIS 6.0 worker process together with information about the WebHost application to start (such as an ASP.NET 2.0 application). The information includes a unique application ID, the root URL and the physical location of the application, the ID of the corresponding IIS 6.0 application pool, the logon account, and a set of protocols that can be used to activate the application. Figure 11-1 shows the overall WebHost architecture.

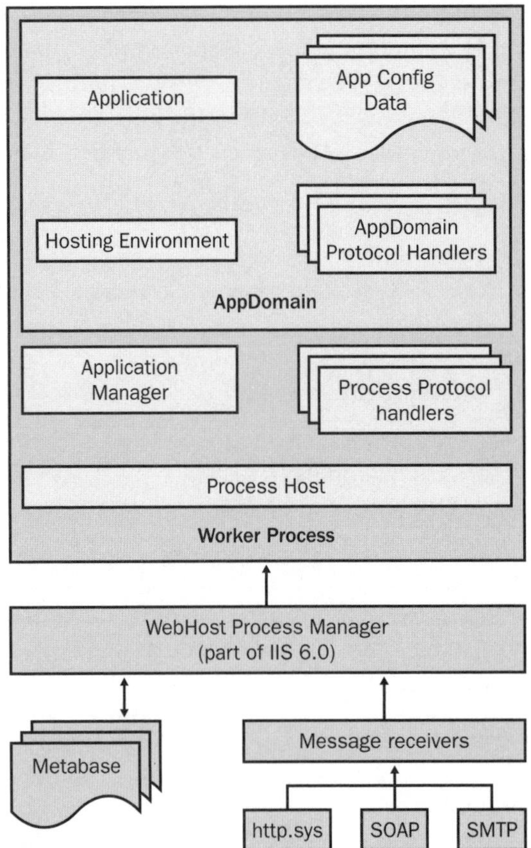

Figure 11-1 The WebHost architecture, which permits the flow of messages from IIS up to the ASP.NET 2.0 runtime environment

Protocol Handlers

In the context of WebHost, protocol handlers play a double role: receiving as well as dispatching messages from the queue. They connect applications with message receivers through a message queue. Each receiver captures messages of a particular type (such as HTTP, TCP, or SOAP) and places them in a protocol-specific queue. As Figure 11-1 shows, there are two kinds of protocol handlers—process handlers and AppDomain handlers.

A process protocol handler is a global component shared by all applications in the pool managed by the worker process. The protocol handler manages all the messages for any pooled application. An AppDomain protocol handler is a component local to each application domain that has visibility only on the messages destined for the AppDomain it lives in.

Walking Through an ASP.NET Request

Once in the worker process, the request is first routed through the IIS core engine that handles requests for static resources (such as HTML or JPG) and dynamic resources (such as ASP or ASPX). Requests for .aspx resources are then dispatched to the ASP.NET ISAPI extension (aspnet_isapi.dll). Thus the ASP.NET ISAPI gets information about the request and creates the process host object.

The process host is responsible for hosting the CLR in the IIS 6.0 worker process and for keeping track of process protocol handlers. The ASP.NET 2.0 process host is an object living inside aspnet_isapi that implements the *IProcessHost* interface. Note that this interface is COM-compatible, so unmanaged hosts can implement it. (In fact, aspnet_isapi.dll is a Win32 library.) The ASP.NET process host creates the application manager—the component responsible for starting, stopping, and managing all AppDomains within the worker process.

The application manager acts as a common tool for pumping requests up to the AppDomains that will actually service them. The application manager also allows enumeration of currently running applications by returning an array of objects representing the state of the individual application. The programming interface of the application manager lets members manage the lifetime of objects in applications and participate in process management actions such as recycling.

In ASP.NET, a request is actually executed within an AppDomain. When the application manager creates an AppDomain, its hosting environment is also created. The hosting environment is represented by an ASP.NET framework class and provides services to the application itself. Each AppDomain contains a single instance of the hosting environment class. This class provides a number of static methods that allow you to register new objects, obtain configuration information, and control the AppDomain lifetime through a reference counting mechanism.

In the AppDomain, the protocol handler continuously pings the corresponding queue, and when a message representing a request for the application is found, it is picked up and processed. The processing happens in much the same way as in ASP.NET 1.x. The protocol handler obtains the request, packs it into a *HttpWorkerRequest* structure, and processes it, passing the object to an AppDomain-specific instance of the *HttpRuntime* class. Just as in ASP.NET 1.x, *HttpRuntime* is the entry point in the HTTP pipeline that processes an ASP.NET request.

After control has passed to the HTTP pipeline, what happens is also much the same as in previous versions. The request is managed by an HTTP handler and filtered by a collection of HTTP modules. A new HTTP handler (one of a handful of new internal handlers) serves images to users more effectively. Quite a few new modules are available as well.

Before we go further, let's get a quick refresher on the ASP.NET runtime components.

> **Note** The WebHost architecture underlies the hosting capabilities of ASP.NET. The application manager, process host, host environment, and protocol handlers are abstractions for common functionality required for hosting ASP.NET outside IIS. In ASP.NET 1.1, the hosting model wasn't rigorously defined. WebHost makes up for that. If you still can't see the big picture, you can take a look at the source code of Cassini—the Microsoft's mini–Web server that hosts the ASP.NET engine. You can get the source code from *http://www.asp.net*. The classes that form the Cassini application map almost 1:1 to the components of the WebHost framework.

ASP.NET Runtime Components

ASP.NET maps each incoming HTTP request to a particular HTTP handler. An HTTP handler is the component that actually serves the request. It is an instance of a class that implements the *IHttpHandler* interface. The *ProcessRequest* method of the interface is the central console that governs the processing of the request. A special breed of component called the *HTTP handler factory* provides the infrastructure for creating the physical instance of the handler to service the request. For example, the *PageHandlerFactory* class parses the source code of the requested .aspx resource and returns a compiled instance of the class that represents the page.

An HTTP handler is designed to process one or more URL extensions. Handlers can be given an application or a machine scope—that is, they can process the assigned extensions within the context of the current application or all applications installed on the machine. HTTP handlers were introduced in ASP.NET 1.0, and their role and base implementation has not changed in ASP.NET 2.0.

HTTP modules are classes that implement the *IHttpModule* interface and handle runtime events. A module can deal with two types of public events: events raised by *HttpApplication* (including asynchronous events) and events raised by other HTTP modules. For example, the *SessionStateModule* in ASP.NET supplies session state services to an application. It fires the *End* and

Start events that other modules can handle through the familiar *Session_End* and *Session_Start* signatures.

Overall, HTTP handlers and modules have the same functionality as Internet Server Application Programming Interface (ISAPI) extensions and filters, respectively, but with a much simpler programming model. All ASP.NET versions allow you create custom handlers and custom modules.

Tools and Executables

Although the ASP.NET ISAPI and the worker process are the key components of the ASP.NET runtime infrastructure, other executables are involved. Table 11-2 lists the main components.

Table 11-2 Main Executables in ASP.NET 2.0

Name	Type	Account
aspnet_isapi.dll	Win32 DLL (ISAPI extension)	LOCAL SYSTEM
aspnet_wp.exe	Win32 EXE	ASPNET
aspnet_filter.dll	Win32 DLL (ISAPI filter)	LOCAL SYSTEM
aspnet_state.exe	Win32 NT Service	ASPNET
aspnet_regiis.exe	Win32 EXE	LOCAL SYSTEM
aspnet_regsql.exe	Win32 EXE	LOCAL SYSTEM
aspnet_compiler.exe	Win32 EXE	LOCAL SYSTEM

As mentioned, if ASP.NET runs under IIS 6.0 using the IIS 6.0 process model, the worker process is not aspnet_wp but the w3wp.exe executable, which is an integral part of the IIS 6.0 platform. In this case, the default account is not ASPNET but NETWORKSERVICE, which has the same limited set of privileges.

The aspnet_filter.dll component is a small Win32 ISAPI filter used to back up cookieless session states for ASP.NET applications. In Windows Server 2003, when the IIS 6.0 process model is enabled, it also prohibits requests for nonexecutable resources located in critical directories under the application root folder. Examples of protected directories include Bin, Code, Resources, and Data.

The optional aspnet_state.exe service is more vital to Web applications because it has to do with session state management. It can be used to store session state data outside of the Web application memory space. The executable is a Windows NT service that can be run locally or remotely. When the service is active, an ASP.NET application can be configured to store any session information into the memory of this process. This means more reliable storage of session data because the data is not subject to process recycling and ASP.NET applications failure. The service runs under the ASPNET local account but can be configured using the Service Control Manager interface.

The aspnet_regiis.exe utility configures the environment for side-by-side execution of different ASP.NET versions on a single computer. It is also helpful for repairing IIS and ASP.NET broken configurations. The utility works by updating the script maps stored in the IIS metabase root and below. (A *script map* is an association set between resource types and ASP.NET modules.) Finally, the tool can be used to display the status of all installed versions of ASP.NET and perform other configuration operations such as granting NTFS permissions to specific folders and create client-script directories.

A couple of new tools in ASP.NET 2.0, aspnet_regsql and aspnet_compiler, address important features of the environment. The aspnet_regsql tool lets you configure all the SQL Server tables needed to implement a few tasks. (Figure 11-2 shows the tool's user interface.)

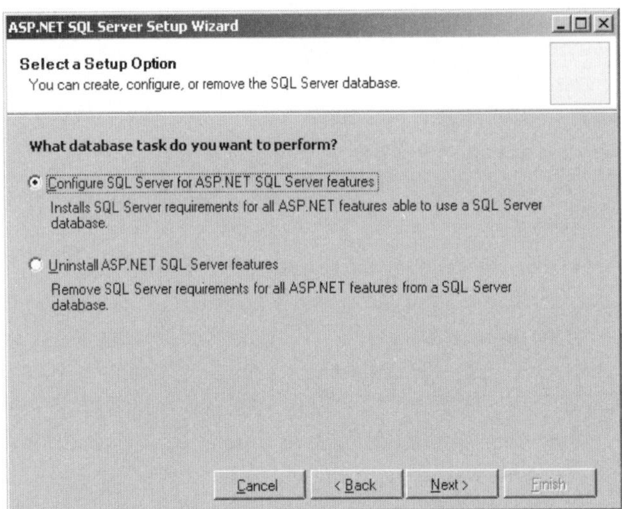

Figure 11-2 The user interface of the aspnet_regsql tool

In ASP.NET 1.x, the use of a SQL Server database was limited to only one situation—storing the session state to a persistent table. To create the necessary database infrastructure, Microsoft provided a couple of T-SQL scripts. ASP.NET 2.0 has three new features that might rely on a SQL Server database: Membership, Personalization, and Role Management. You can use the aspnet_regsql tool's wizardlike command-line utility to help you configure SQL Server as needed.

> **Note** The new database-related features of ASP.NET 2.0 support a provider design pattern that allows for the data store to be interchanged. You can choose data providers other than SQL Server; in such cases, you don't need to run aspnet_regsql utility to set them up.

Finally, the aspnet_compiler tool provides a mechanism for precompiling the pages of a Web application so that all the needed assemblies are generated for all the pages in the application. Based on the command line of the utility, you can precompile the content of a virtual directory to a new physical directory or locally. Here's an example:

```
aspnet_compiler -v /TestApp c:\inetpub\wwwroot\test
```

Built-In HTTP Handlers

ASP.NET 1.x defines a main type of HTTP handler for each of three types of resources: .aspx, .asmx, and .ashx. For completeness, you should add the handlers needed to serve .soap and .rem resources that are invoked when a .NET Remoting object is hosted within IIS. ASP.NET 2.0 has a new handler extension (.asix) for dynamically generated images requested directly over the Web.

The class that handles .asix requests is *ImageGeneratorFactory*. It is a factory class that returns the actual HTTP handler object—an instance of the *ImageGenerator* class. You write ASIX components in a way that closely resembles simple HTTP handlers (ASHX resources) in ASP.NET 1.x. The ASIX resource is a class written in a file that begins with an *@Image* directive. (We discussed a sample ASIX resource in Chapter 8.)

One of the nicest features of HTTP handlers is that you can configure them so the class is invoked whenever a particular URL (or family of URLs) is requested. Note that in this case the HTTP handler is invoked whether or not the specified URL exists. In other words, if you bind a given handler to a fake URL such as *foo.axd*, the handler is invoked whenever a request for the URL is made. You need not have a server-side file with that name. In ASP.NET 1.x, this feature was used to implement the ASP.NET trace viewer.

The trace viewer continues to work in the same way in ASP.NET 2.0. It is an HTTP handler that gets into the game whenever the trace.axd resource is invoked. You won't find a file with that name on your machine, but the ASP.NET infrastructure will detect its invocation and promptly react, as Figure 11-3 shows.

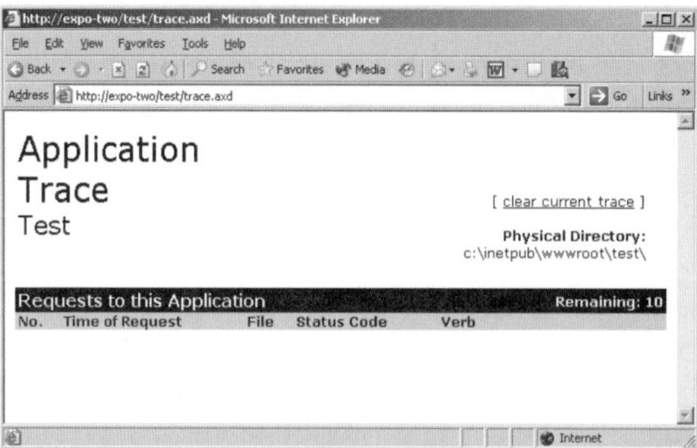

Figure 11-3 The trace viewer in action, activated by the fake *trace.axd* URL

ASP.NET 2.0 has many other AXD resources with a new HTTP handler running behind them. Figure 11-4 shows the list of internal handlers defined in ASP.NET 2.0.

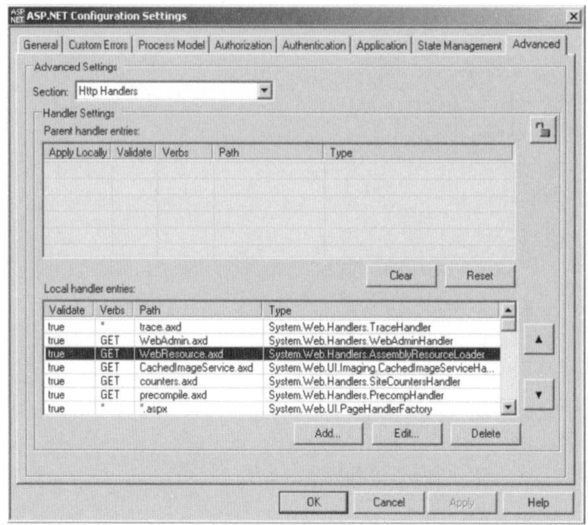

Figure 11-4 The list of ASP.NET 2.0 internal HTTP handlers as it appears in the ASP.NET configuration snap-in

The snap-in component that you see in the figure represents another pleasant addition in ASP.NET 2.0. It is a sort of user interface built around the contents of the machine.config file. It's just one of the features that developers called for loudly in the past months! Let's see what role these new HTTP handlers really play in ASP.NET 2.0.

Table 11-3 lists the ASP.NET 2.0 internal HTTP handlers. All are new but one—the aforementioned trace handler that is mapped to the trace.axd resource.

Table 11-3 ASP.NET 2.0 Internal HTTP Handlers

Resource	Description
CachedImageService.axd	Allows you to retrieve cached copies of dynamically generated images created by the Image Generation service. Requires the *data* parameter, which indicates the storage key.
Counters.axd	Allows you to retrieve information captured by the Site Counter service. In cooperation with controls such as *HyperLink* and *AdRotator*, the service collects counting information and caches it to a database—typically Jet or SQL Server.
Precompile.axd	Precompiles the current application so that any access to application resources doesn't cause delay.
Trace.axd	As in ASP.NET 1.x, traces the application by collecting and showing on demand the trace output generated by the various requests.
WebAdmin.axd	Links to the ASP.NET Web Application Administration tool. The tool enables administrators to manage application security, add personalization, view reports, and select or change the application data sources.

WebResource.axd	Used to insert script code into HTML pages. In ASP.NET 2.0, any script code needed to make the page work (such as the notorious *__doPostBack* Javascript function) is referenced into the source HTML through this handler. Here's a code snippet that brings in the default code for handling Web Forms basics:
	`<script language="javascript"`
	`src="WebResource.axd?r=WebForms.js"`
	`type="text/javascript" />`
	If you want to save a copy of the script code, point your browser to the AXD resource and save the output to disk.

The Web Site Administration tool is also integrated with Visual Web Developer and Visual Studio. Among other things, it allows you to create any database infrastructure for security, membership, and personalization.

New HTTP Modules

The ASP.NET framework defines a number of built-in HTTP modules that implement services to applications. Table 11-4 lists the predefined modules registered in ASP.NET 2.0's machine.config file. Figure 11-5 shows them through the new ASP.NET snap-in.

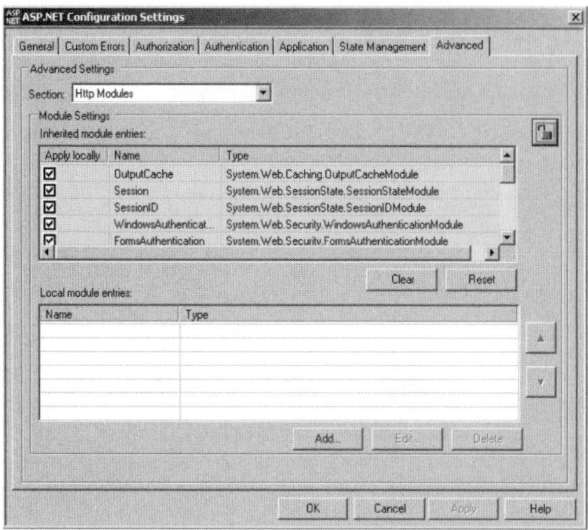

Figure 11-5 The list of the default HTTP modules in ASP.NET 2.0

Some of the modules are a revised version of modules already available in ASP.NET 1.x, while others are specific to ASP.NET 2.0. The modules shown in bold in Table 11-4 are new in version 2.0.

Table 11-4 Default ASP.NET 2.0 HTTP Modules

HTTP Module	Description
AnonymousIdentification	Creates and sets the personalization ID that ASP.NET 2.0 associates with each anonymous user.
ErrorHandlerModule	Installs an event handler for the application's error event so ASP.NET mobile applications can report errors in a sort of automated way.
FileAuthorization	Verifies that the remote user has Windows NT permissions to access the requested resource.
FormsAuthentication	Enables applications to use Forms authentication.
OutputCache	Manages the page output caching.

Table 11-4 Default ASP.NET 2.0 HTTP Modules

HTTP Module	Description
PageCountersModule	Counts successful requests for a page and writes them to the database. Pages served from the cache are still counted, but not pages that return errors.
PassportAuthentication	Provides a wrapper around Passport authentication services.
Personalization	Provides personalization services for an application. It adds a dynamically generated personalization class to *HttpContext*.
RoleManager	Retrieves the list of roles from the role manager cookie on every request and populates the *User* property on *HttpContext*.
SessionState	Provides session-state services for the application.
SessionID	The default implementation of the *ISessionIDModule* interface, which allows to provide your own custom session ID generation, validation, encoding, and decoding.
UrlAuthorization	Provides URL-based authorization services to access specified resources.
WindowsAuthentication	Enables ASP.NET applications to use Windows and IIS-based authentication.

HTTP modules are behind many of the important new features of ASP.NET 2.0 that you've already seen in this book—in particular, the personalization mechanism and anonymous identification. (Anonymous identification is not an oxymoron—it's the built-in implementation of a feature that many developers coded manually in dozens of e-commerce Web sites.)

Page Output Caching

In version 1.x, page output caching was a hot new feature that sped up many applications. Page output caching is the system's ability to store in memory the image of requested pages and serve them up as static resources until something happens to invalidate the cached image. Under the hood, cached pages are stored in the ASP.NET *Cache* and organized in various ways—per header, parameter, name, or duration.

Although page output caching and the *Cache* API are often presented as distinct features, they are simply two sides of the same coin. In both ASP.NET 1.x and ASP.NET 2.0, page output caching is implemented using the *Cache* API, and the overall configuration can be controlled at the page and control level via the *@OutputCache* directive.

The *@OutputCache* Directive

The *@OutputCache* directive declaratively controls the output caching policies of an ASP.NET page or a user control. In ASP.NET 2.0, it supports the attributes listed in Table 11-5.

Table 11-5 Attributes of the *@OutputCache* Directive

Attribute	Description
Duration	A required attribute that indicates the time, in seconds, that the page or user control is maintained in the cache.
Location	Indicates the location of the output cache. Not supported for user controls. The default value is *Any*, which means the page can be cached anywhere—client, proxy server, or original Web server.
Shared	Indicates whether the output of a user control is shared among multiple pages using that control. The default is *false*, which means that each page has its own copy of the control's output. *The attribute is not supported for ASPX pages.*
SqlDependency	Indicates a dependency on the specified table on a given SQL Server database. Whenever the contents of the table changes, the page output is removed from the cache.
VaryByControl	A semicolon-separated list of strings representing fully qualified names of properties on a user control. Valid only for caching user controls; don't use it with ASP.NET pages.
VaryByCustom	Specifies any text that represents custom output caching requirements. If this attribute has a value of *<browser>*, the cache is varied by browser name and major version information. The value can be a custom string, but you must provide the custom logic to determine whether multiple copies of the same page must be created and how.
VaryByHeader	A semicolon-separated list of HTTP headers that's used to vary the output cache. When this attribute is set to multiple headers, the output cache contains a different version of the requested page for each specified header.
VaryByParam	A semicolon-separated list of parameters that's used to vary the output cache. When this attribute is set to multiple strings, the output cache contains a different version of the requested document for each specified parameter.

The *Shared* attribute is new to ASP.NET 2.0. If it is set to *true*, the cached output of user controls across different ASP.NET pages is shared among all pages, thus conserving processing power and memory. In ASP.NET 1.x (and, by default, in ASP.NET 2.0) each page using a given user control maintains a distinct copy of the user control.

The *SqlDependency* Attribute

The *SqlDependency* attribute is the *@OutputCache* directive's interface to the *SqlCacheDependency* class we discussed in Chapter 9. When the *SqlDependency* attribute is set, a SQL Server cache dependency object is created. When the dependency is broken, the page output is invalidated. The *SqlDependency* attribute offers an interesting shortcut to setting up a full dependency via manual code. (See Chapter 9.)

The *SqlDependency* attribute binds the output of the containing page to the state of a particular table in a SQL Server 7.0 or SQL Server 2000 database:

```
<% @OutputCache Duration="15" VaryByParam="none"
                SqlDependency="Northwind:Employees" %>
```

A page containing this code snippet has its output cached for 15 seconds or until a record changes in the Employees table in the Northwind database. Note that the Northwind string here is not the name of a database—it's the name of an entry in the *<caching>* section of the configuration file. That entry contains detailed information about the connection string to use to reach the database. For the mechanism to work, the database and the table must be enabled for change notification, as discussed in Chapter 9.

You can specify multiple dependencies by separating multiple *database:table* pairs with a semicolon in the value of the *SqlDependency* attribute. If you're setting the attribute while using SQL Server Yukon, you must set the attribute's value to the name of a command notification object. The command notification object embeds information about the connection string, the database, and the particular query run. (See Chapter 9 for more details.)

Disk Output Cache

Disk output cache is an optional feature that allows you to store the response of pages on disk instead of in memory. Saving to disk allows caching of more pages while reducing impact on the process working set and enabling cached data to survive application restarts. You enable disk output caching through the *diskCacheable* attribute in the *<outputCacheSettings>* configuration block.

```
<caching>
    <outputCacheSettings diskcacheable="true" />
</caching>
```

By using the *<diskOutputCache>* block at the same level as *<outputCacheSettings>*, you can control the amount of disk that can be used for caching. Not all pages can be cached to disk. Cacheable pages include pages with file dependencies only or absolute expiration. Pages that take advantage of the *VaryByCustom* attribute in *@OutputCache* can't be cached. The same applies to pages that have sliding expirations and have dependencies on other cached items. In addition to system requirements for disk cacheability, you can prevent a page from disk caching programmatically:

```
Response.Cache.SetDiskCacheable(false);
```

A page marked for disk cacheability can fail to persist for a number of reasons, including exceeded quotas or incompatible settings. Because disk output cache is a noninvasive feature, these failures are handled silently and no exception is thrown.

Post-Cache Substitution

Post-cache substitution is a new ASP.NET 2.0 feature designed to optimize the partial caching of pages. In ASP.NET 1.x, developers must resort to user controls to cache portions of a page. Post-cache substitution allows you to cache portions of a page using the opposite approach—the whole page is cached except specific regions. By using this mechanism, you can have an *AdRotator* control serve a different advertisement on each request even if the host page is cached.

To use post-cache substitution, you place a new control—the *<asp:substitution>* control—at the page location where content should be substituted, and you set the *MethodName* property of the control to a callback method:

```
<form runat="server">
  <h2>
     Welcome
     <asp:Substitution runat="server" MethodName="GetUserName" />!
  </h2>
</form>
```

The *MethodName* property must be set to a static method on the control's containing page or user control. Here's an example:

```
<script language="C#" runat="server">
   public static string GetUserName(HttpContext context)
   {
        return context.User.Identity.Name;
   }
</script>
```

The method is a sort of callback that is invoked when the page is being restored from the cache.

The Structure of ASP.NET 2.0 Pages

ASP.NET 2.0 is 100 percent backward compatible, and the source code you need to write for a relatively simple page is nearly identical to that in ASP.NET 1.x. But ASP.NET 2.0 has a bag of new goodies that make the source code of a real-world page look a bit different from a functionally analogous page in ASP.NET 1.x.

A Sample Page

In ASP.NET 2.0, the structure of Web pages is the same as in ASP.NET 1.x. Pages still have three main parts—directives, procedural code, and layout information. However, a few more directives have been defined (such as *@Image* and *@Master*) and a few attributes have been added to the main directive—*@Page*. The code-behind mechanism is still supported, but it obeys different rules because the compilation model has been redesigned. Consider the following relatively simple page:

```
<%@ Page Language="C#" %>

<script runat="server">
void DoSomething(object sender, EventArgs e)
{
   msg.Text = data.Text;
}
</script>

<html>
<body>
<form runat="server">
   <asp:textbox runat="server" id="data" />
   <asp:button runat="server" Text="Click me" onclick="DoSomething" />
   <br />
   <asp:label runat="server" id="msg" />
</form>
</body>
</html>
```

The page displays a text box and a command button. When the button is clicked and the page posts back, the content of the text box is displayed in the body of the page. Figure 11-6 shows the output of the page.

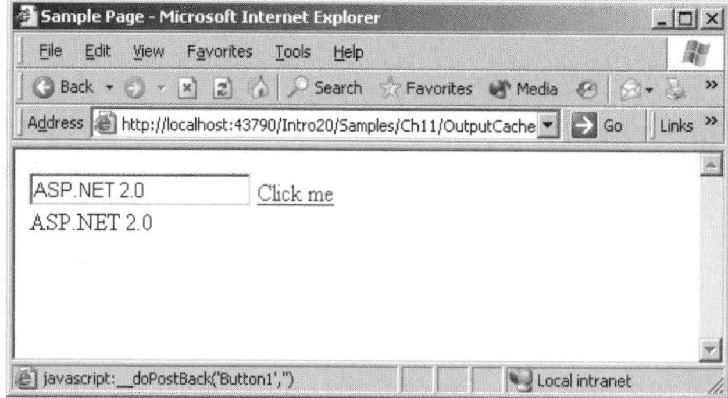

Figure 11-6 The output of the sample page

The page behaves as expected. The single form model is preserved, and the postback mechanism works as before. The page is compiled on the fly the first time it is accessed. The .aspx source code is parsed, and a C# or Visual Basic .NET class is generated and compiled to a dynamic assembly. The assembly is stored in a temporary folder, whose name and location are determined using the same pattern as in previous versions. So is the page processing the same way as in ASP.NET 1.1? Well, not exactly.

A Quick Look at the HTML Source Code

After the first version 2.0 page displays in the browser, look at the HTML source code created for it. Even a quick glance reveals enhancements, particularly to the client-side script code that implements the postback eventing model.

The following is the HTML code generated for the page shown in Figure 11-6:

```
<html>
<body>
<form name="Form1" method="post" action="test1.aspx">
<div style="display:none">
  <input type="hidden" name="__EVENTTARGET" value="" />
  <input type="hidden" name="__EVENTARGUMENT" value="" />
  <input type="hidden" name="__VIEWSTATE" value="... " />
</div>

<script language="javascript" type="text/javascript">
<!--
var theForm = document.forms['Form1'];
function __doPostBack(eventTarget, eventArgument) {
    if (theForm.onsubmit == null || theForm.onsubmit()) {
        theForm.__EVENTTARGET.value = eventTarget;
        theForm.__EVENTARGUMENT.value = eventArgument;
```

```
        theForm.submit();
    }
}
// -->
</script>
<input name="data" type="text" value="ASP.NET 2.0" id="data" />
<a id="Button1" href="javascript:__doPostBack('Button1','')">Click me</a>
<br />
<span id="msg">ASP.NET 2.0</span>
</form>
</body>
</html>
```

In general, ASP.NET 2.0 supports more Web form interaction scenarios that require some script code. For example, you can now designate a default button in the form and catch the user pressing Enter. A built-in piece of Java-Script code then performs the magic of firing the action associated with the default form button. Other script-related features are the long-awaited option of setting the focus programmatically and the ability to execute cross-page posting by programmatically changing the *action* property of the form.

The Compilation Model

Since the first version, ASP.NET has compiled a few file types on the fly—Web pages (.aspx), Web services (.asmx), HTTP handlers (.ashx), and embedded user controls (.ascx). These files are compiled on demand when first required by an application. Any changes made to a dynamically compiled file—or to global.asax and web.config—invalidate all affected resources and are reflected in the displayed page. This mechanism greatly simplifies application development. In fact, developers need only save the file to cause changes to take effect within the application.

Such a dynamic compilation model is extended in ASP.NET 2.0 to account for other file types—typically class files. The new ASP.NET build system removes the need for an explicit precompilation step within the Visual Studio .NET IDE and provides an extensibility model allowing new file types to be added.

Dynamic Compilation

When designing a Web site, many developers group source files and resources in different folders. In most cases, the name of the folder defined to contain certain resources is unimportant, but some folder names are commonly used. For example, virtually any site has an images folder filled with pictures and graphics for the pages. Likewise, a Components folder is often used to group user and custom controls, helper classes, and the like. In ASP.NET 1.x, the xBin folder is for local assemblies that have application scope.

ASP.NET 2.0 has a few new predefined folders, which the build system handles: Code, Resources, and Themes. Their content is managed by ASP.NET, which processes files and generates and links assemblies.

The Code Folder

The Code folder is intended for class files (.vb and .cs files), Web Service description files (.wsdl files), and typed data sets (.xsd files). All files are processed to generate classes and are then compiled to a single assembly. The assembly has application scope and is placed in an internal folder managed by ASP.NET. No dynamic assemblies are ever found in the Bin folder or anywhere else in the application's Web space. Any class defined in a file placed in the Code folder is immediately visible from any page within the application, regardless of the path to the page. You can also create subdirectories below the Code folder to better reflect the logical organization of the files.

Note that all class files in the Code folder must be written in the same language—be it Visual Basic .NET or C#—because they're all compiled to a single assembly and thus must have a matching source language. To use different languages, you must organize your class files in folders and add some entries to the configuration file to tell build system to create distinct assemblies.

Here's an example. Suppose you have two files named source.cs and source.vb. Because they're written in different languages, they can't stay together in the Code folder. You can then create two subfolders—say, Code/VB and Code/CS—and move the files to the subfolder that matches the language. Next you can add the following entries to the web.config file:

```
<configuration>
<system.web>
<compilation>
   <codeSubDirectories>
      <add directoryName="VB" />
      <add directoryName="CS" />
   </codeSubDirectories>
</compilation>
</system.web>
</configuration>
```

Note that the *<codeSubDirectories>* section is valid only if it is set in the web.config file in the application root. Each *<codeSubDirectories>* section instructs the build system to create a distinct assembly. This means that all the files in the specified directory must be written in the same language, but different directories can target different languages.

If WSDL files are placed in the Code folder, the build system creates and compiles a class that represents the proxy to the specified Web service. In ASP.NET 1.x, you have to reference the Web service and generate the proxy explicitly.

A similar pattern is followed for XSD files. An XSD file represents the strongly typed schema of a table of data. In the .NET Framework 1.1, a typed *DataSet* must be manually created using the xsd.exe tool. In ASP.NET 2.0, all you have to do is drop the source XSD file in the Code folder.

The Resources Folder

In the Resources directory, only .resx and .resources file types are considered to be built for the resources assembly. Resource files provide for easy application localization. You create satellite assemblies with application resources (typically, images and text) specific to a culture, and the runtime does the rest, loading and using the right one. In ASP.NET 1.x, the developer had to create satellite assemblies manually. ASP.NET 2.0 parses and compiles resource files in the Resources folders.

A simple naming convention is used to bind a resource file to a particular culture. A single file with no culture defined is the default or neutral resource file (for example, AppResources.resx). All other files that define culture-based resources embed the culture signature in the name. For example, AppResources.en-US.resx represents the American English version, and AppResources.it-IT.resx is for the Italian version.

The Resources directory is compiled before any Code assemblies or ASP.NET assemblies. The resulting resource assembly for the neutral culture has application scope and is therefore referenced from other assemblies generated in the application. Satellite assemblies are generated for the additional cultures. All types defined in the resource assemblies belong to the Resources namespace and are static objects.

The Themes Folder

The application's Themes folder defines one or more themes for controls. A *theme* is a set of skins and associated files such as stylesheets and images that can be used within an application to give a consistent user interface to controls. In the Themes folder, each theme occupies a single subdirectory, which has the same name as the theme. All related files are stored in this directory.

When a theme is loaded, the contents of the theme directory are parsed and compiled into a class that inherits from the *Theme* class. Any theme defined outside the Themes directory structures is ignored by the ASP.NET build system.

Compilation Settings and Life Cycle

The dynamic compilation process is affected by the settings in the *<compilation>* section of the web.config file. Two attributes are of particular importance in this section—*maxBatchSize* and *maxBatchGeneratedSize*. The former indicates the maximum number of pages and classes allowed in a single assembly. The default upper bound is 1000. The latter attribute sets a limit on the size of each generated assembly. The default is 3 MB.

The files in the Resources folder are the first to be compiled. They are followed by the files in the Code folder and any file class file referenced by the application. Next is global.asax and any other resource file outside the Resources folder. Finally, pages and user controls are processed.

> **Note** The ASP.NET 2.0 build system is highly customizable and can be extended to support custom files. The key to this change is the *<buildProviders>* section in the application configuration files. The *<add>* section lets you define a new build provider associated with a file extension and a folder, as in the following example:
>
> ```
> <buildProviders>
>   <add extension="*.my" appliesTo="Web"
>        type="Samples.MyBuildProvider" />
> </buildProviders>
> ```
>
> A build provider object is an object derived from the *BuildProvider* base class. The *appliesTo* attribute indicates one or more folders to which the provider applies. *Web* indicates any Web folder except special folders, such as Code, Resources, or custom folders.

Site Precompilation

As mentioned, dynamically created assemblies are placed in an internal folder managed by the ASP.NET runtime. Unless files are modified, the compilation step occurs only once per page—when the page is first requested. Although in many cases the additional overhead is no big deal, removing it still represents a form of optimization. Site precompilation consists of deploying the whole site functionality through assemblies. A precompiled application is still made up of source files, but all pages and resources are fictitiously accessed before deployment and compiled to assemblies. The dynamically created assemblies are then packaged and installed to the target machine.

Site precompilation was possible in ASP.NET 1.x, but in version 2.0 it has the rank of a system tool, fully supported by the framework. Site precompilation offers two main advantages:

- Requests to the site don't cause any delay because the pages and code are compiled to assemblies.
- Sites can be deployed without any source code, thus preserving and protecting the intellectual property of the solutions implemented.

Precompilation can take two forms: in-place precompilation and deployment precompilation.

In-Place Precompilation

In-place precompilation allows a developer or a site administrator to access each page in the application as if it were being used by end users. This means each page is compiled as if for ordinary use. The site is fully compiled before entering production, and no user will experience a first-hit compilation delay, as in version 1.x. In-place precompilation takes place after the site is deployed, but before it goes public.

Changes and extensions don't strictly require a full stop of the system. Files can be simply added or replaced, and users are served the new version upon next access. To avoid any delay in case of changes, you can precompile just the file that was modified by using the precompile.axd handler:

```
http://www.contoso.com/precompile.axd
```

Note that the compiler skips pages that are up-to-date. Precompilation occurs only on files that have been changed or added or have been affected by changes in file dependencies (such as web.config, global.asax, and files in the Code and Resources directories).

Precompilation is essentially a batch compilation that generates all needed assemblies in the fixed ASP.NET directory on the server machine. If any file fails compilation, precompilation will fail on the application. Once compiled, a site cannot be deployed to another machine. In-place precompilation assumes that the site is running under IIS.

Precompilation for Deployment

Precompilation for deployment generates a manifest of a site made up of assemblies, static files, and configuration files. The manifest is generated on a target machine and can also be packaged and then copied to a production machine. This form of precompilation doesn't require source code to be left on the target machine.

Precompilation for deployment requires the use of the *aspnet_compiler* command-line tool:

```
aspnet_compiler -m metabasePath
                -c virtualPath
                -p physicalPath
                targetPath
```

The role of each parameter is explained in Table 11-6.

Table 11-6 Parameters of the aspnet_compiler Tool

Parameter	Description
metabasePath	An optional parameter that indicates the full IIS metabase path of the application
physicalPath	An optional parameter that indicates the physical path of the application
targetPath	An optional parameter that indicates the destination path for the compiled application
virtualPath	A required parameter that indicates the virtual path of the application

If no target path is specified, the precompilation takes place in the virtual path of the application and source files are therefore preserved. If a different target is specified, only assemblies are copied, and the new application runs with no source file in the production environment. Static files such as images, web.config, and HTML pages are not compiled—they are just copied to the target destination. If you don't want to deploy HTML pages as clear text, rename them to .aspx and compile them. A similar approach can be used for image files. In this case, you expose them through .asix resources. (See Chapter 8.) Note, however, that if you hide images and HTML pages behind ASP.NET extensions, you lose in performance because IIS is used to process static files more efficiently than ASP.NET.

As a final note, consider that packaged sites are not sensitive to file changes unless you deploy them with source code. If you install an assembly-only application, you must separately recompile and redeploy the application for changes to take effect.

Summary

Looking at ASP.NET 2.0 from the perspective of the HTTP runtime might give the misleading impression that upgrading to the new version is no big deal because overall ASP.NET still looks like the same, familiar programming environment. And in spite of the wealth of new features it offers, ASP.NET 2.0 represents an evolution, not a revolution. In this chapter, we first toured the new HTTP runtime hosting model, and then the new compilation model. Both have little visibility at the application level and can pass unnoticed. But this architectural change provides programmers with better performance, scalability, and stability, as well as new features.

ASP.NET 2.0 is better integrated with the .NET Framework and hints at future evolutions of the platform, specifically Indigo. The compilation model is probably the only aspect of the technology that has undergone a true revolution from version 1.x. Now all files of interest can be built by the system, making the just hit save pattern the official way of working within ASP.NET projects. This is definitely an important step toward easier development and greater productivity.

12

ASP.NET Configuration and Instrumentation

The behavior of an ASP.NET application is affected both by system-level settings and by the characteristics of the application itself. When running, the application obtains a map of the current system settings from the system's machine.config file, and then it applies those settings to any changes that the application requires. The machine.config file contains default and machine-specific values for all supported settings. Machine settings are normally controlled by the system administrator, and applications should not be given write access to it. Because the machine.config file is outside the Web space of the application, it cannot be reached even if an attacker succeeds in injecting malicious code into the system.

An application can override most of the default values stored in the machine.config file by creating one or more web.config files. At a minimum, an application creates a web.config file in its root folder. The web.config file is a subset of machine.config, written according to the same XML schema. Although web.config allows you to override some of the default settings, you cannot override all settings defined in machine.config. In particular, the information about the ASP.NET process model can be defined only in a machinewide manner using the machine.config file.

If the application contains child directories, it can define a web.config file for each folder. The scope of each configuration file is determined in a hierarchical, top-down manner. The settings actually applied to an application and thus its Web pages is determined by the sum of the changes that the various web.config files in the hierarchy of the application carry. Along this path, any of those web.config files can extend, restrict, and override any type of settings defined at an upper level, including the machine level, unless the setting is restricted to a certain level (such as process model). If no configuration file exists in an application folder, the settings valid at the upper level are applied.

Changes to the Configuration API

In previous versions of ASP.NET, you can access configuration information by using the *ConfigurationSettings* class. But you can only read the current settings, and only using a weakly typed approach. More important, although in theory you can use the class to read any settings, you can actually use it only for application-specific settings and custom sections. For example, consider the code that would be necessary in ASP.NET 1.1 to read the value of the *EnableVersionHeader* attribute in the *<httpRuntime>* section (which determines whether an ASP.NET-specific header containing version information should be added to all responses):

```
object o = ConfigurationSettings.GetConfig("system.web/httpRuntime");
```

The code returns an object of type *HttpRuntimeConfig*, which is defined in the *System.Web.Configuration* namespace. Unfortunately, though, that class cannot be accessed programmatically because of its protection level. What a shame, because that internal class exposes a property for each attribute and would make programmatic configuration of the application like child's play.

Guess what you find in ASP.NET 2.0? A number of public configuration classes, one per predefined section, that expose through properties and methods the contents of the .config files. ASP.NET 2.0 fills another key gap by supplying tools to programmatically update the .config files (which is allowed when writing privileges have been granted).

Section-Specific Classes

.NET 2.0 ships with a comprehensive management API for reading, editing, and creating web.config file settings. The root class for programmatic access to the configuration infrastructure is *Configuration*. Using the static methods of this class, you can access the machine.config file and any web.config file defined in the context of the application. Table 12-1 lists these static methods.

Table 12-1 Static Methods of the *Configuration* Class

Property	Description
GetExeConfiguration	Returns a *Configuration* object that represents the configuration settings for the current executable. *This method is used by Windows Forms applications only.*
GetMachineConfiguration	Returns a *Configuration* object that represents the contents of the machine.config file for the specified location and server.
GetWebConfiguration	Returns a *Configuration* object that represents the contents of the web.config file for the specified location, server, and path.

Table 12-2 lists the nonstatic properties of the *Configuration* class.

Table 12-2 Properties of the *Configuration* Class

Property	Description
AppSettings	Returns the collection of user-defined application settings, in the form of name/value pairs.
FilePath	Gets the physical path to the configuration file represented by this Configuration object.
HasFile	Indicates whether or not there's a web.config file which applies to this Configuration object.
Locations	Retrieves the collection of the locations (if any) defined in the machine.config file.
Path	Returns the virtual path to the application represented by this Configuration object.
SectionGroups	Retrieves the collection of the section groups defined in the configuration files.
Sections	Retrieves the collection of the sections defined in the configuration files. By using the name of the section as the selector, you can obtain a reference to a class that provides a strongly typed representation of the information.

Each section is mapped to a public class that inherits from *ConfigurationSection*. These classes expose the attributes of the corresponding section as typed properties, making it easy for you to read or edit values. The following listing shows the signature of one of these section classes, *HttpRuntimeSection*:

```
namespace System.Web.Configuration
{
   public sealed class HttpRuntimeSection: ConfigurationSection
   {
      // Constructors
      public HttpRuntimeSection();
      public HttpRuntimeSection(bool allowDefinition, bool allowOverride);

      // Properties
      public int AppRequestQueueLimit             { get; set; }
      public bool Enable                          { get; set; }
      public bool EnableKernelOutputCache         { get; set; }
      public bool EnableVersionHeader             { get; set; }
      public TimeSpan IdleTimeOut                 { get; set; }
      public TimeSpan ExecutionTimeout            { get; set; }
      public int MaxRequestLength                 { get; set; }
      public int MinFreeThreads                   { get; set; }
      public int MinLocalRequestFreeThreads       { get; set; }
      public bool UseFullyQualifiedRedirectUrl    { get; set; }
      public int RequestLengthDiskThreshold       { get; set; }
      ⋮
      // Methods
      public override XmlNode GetRawXml();
      public override void UpdateRawXml(XmlNode xmlNode);
   }
}
```

The two overridable methods are defined in the base class. *GetRawXml* returns an XMLDOM representing the contents of the section. *UpdateRawXml* takes a modified XMLDOM and serializes it to disk in the associated configuration file.

Reading Configuration Settings

Let's look at how to use the configuration API to read a particular setting from a configuration file. Suppose you want to know whether the application is configured to run on a multiprocessor machine in Web garden mode. In the *<processModel>* section, the Boolean *webGarden* attribute tells the ASP.NET runtime about that:

```
Configuration cfg = Configuration.GetWebConfiguration("/");
ProcessModelSection sec = cfg.Sections["ProcessModel"];
bool bWebGarden = sec.WebGarden;
```

The *GetWebConfiguration* method takes the URL of the folder from which you want to read and returns another instance of the *Configuration* class that contains the current snapshot of the settings. Next you navigate to the information required and consume it. As the code shows, the resultant listing is neat and simple to understand.

Writing Configuration Settings

As mentioned earlier, ASP.NET applications should never modify the machine.config file, and you should carefully consider any updates to web.config. Custom settings should be saved to external files. For example, you can use an external XML file linked to the *<appSettings>* section:

```
<configuration>
  <appSettings file="myfile.config" />
</configuration>
```

The custom .config file must have the same schema as standard configuration files. Using an external file offers a number of benefits. First, it simplifies the management of the parameters. Second, you don't need to touch a system file. Notice that any modifications to a .config file cause the affected pages (which might include the whole application) to recompile. If you need to save custom settings, using a distinct file saves you from such side effects.

However, if you must write to a configuration file, how do you do that? Here's an example that overwrites the default value of the *EnableVersionHeader* attribute in the configuration file:

```
Configuration cfg = Configuration.GetWebConfiguration("/");
HttpRuntimeSection sec = (HttpRuntimeSection) cfg.Sections["HttpRuntime"];
bool bEnableVer = sec.EnableVersionHeader;
sec.EnableVersionHeader = !bEnableVer;
cfg.Update();
```

The properties have read/write capabilities, so you can change any value. Notice, though, that simply setting the property doesn't result in a disk update. To persist the changes, you have to call the *Update* method on the *Configuration* class. The update will succeed only if the application has full control of the folder. Notice that, by default, both the ASPNET and the NETWORKSERVICE accounts—those used to run ASP.NET applications in Windows 2000, Windows XP, and Windows 2003 Server—don't have write privileges on any user folder.

The ASP.NET Administrative Tool

In addition to full programmatic access to the configuration settings, ASP.NET 2.0 provides an interactive tool for administering the environment. The tool integrates with the IIS Microsoft Management Console (MMC) snap-in. As a result, a new property page (named ASP.NET) is added to each Web directory node.

The page contains an edit button that, if clicked, provides you with a new set of property pages that together supply an interactive user interface for editing the .config files. The code behind the ASP.NET administrative tool leverages the underlying configuration API. Earlier in this chapter, you saw a few pages from the tool. The page for the HTTP runtime configuration is shown in Figure 12-1.

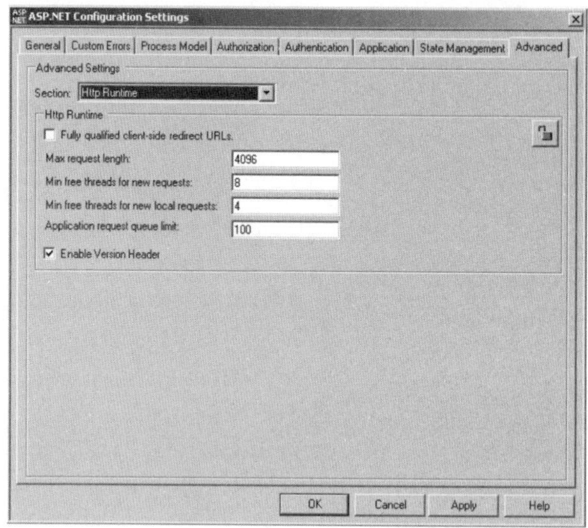

Figure 12-1 The property page for visually editing the *<httpRuntime>* section

Changes to the Configuration Schema

In ASP.NET 2.0, the schema of the configuration files has changed a bit—it includes new sections and modifies some of the existing ones. Let's start with a look at changes to existing sections.

Changed Configuration Sections

Table 12-3 lists the most important configuration sections that have changed between ASP.NET 1.x and ASP.NET 2.0.

Table 12-3 Updated Configuration Sections

Section	Description
<compilation>	Lists default and custom-built providers and sets batch compilation parameters. In this section, you can also control how dynamic assemblies map to source code classes.
<httpHandlers>	Includes new HTTP handlers for precompilation, image caching, counters, and Web resources.
<httpModules>	Includes new HTTP modules such as SessionID, RoleManager, and AnonymousIdentification.
<httpRuntime>	Adds support for automatic shutdown after a specified idle time.
<pages>	Identifies page-specific configuration settings such as import and register directives and master pages settings. This section can be declared at the machine, site, application, and subdirectory levels.
<sessionState>	Now supports custom session stores.

The table is not an exhaustive list of changes to the configuration schema. Other sections, such as *<globalization>*, have minor changes. For more details, refer to the .NET Framework programmer's reference guide.

New Configuration Sections

The long list of new features in ASP.NET 2.0 has directly affected the schema of the configuration files. A number of new sections have been defined in addition to the standard ones supported by ASP.NET 1.1. Table 12-4 lists the major new ones you are likely going to work with.

Table 12-4 New Configuration Sections

Section	Description
<anonymousIdentification>	Configures the built-in mechanism for creating the ID assigned to the anonymous user.
<connectionStrings>	Lists declarative references to connection strings used by applications. Each connection string is given a unique name by which it is referenced.
<healthMonitoring>	Configures the health monitoring API, a set of tools designed to trace the performance of running applications.

Table 12-4 New Configuration Sections

Section	Description
<imageGeneration>	Configures how the Image Generation Service works. Attributes include the type of storage and the cacheability of the images.
<membership>	Configures providers that are registered to store and retrieve membership data (such as user IDs and passwords). Built-in providers store credentials in a local SQL Server database or an Access database.
<profile>	Configures how a user profile is persisted. This section lets you define the schema of the class that represents the user profile. You can also configure the providers that will store personalization data.
<roleManager>	Configures how role information about the current user will be stored (for example, in a cookie) and which providers are enabled to contain the list of supported roles.
<siteCounters>	Configures the built-in service that tracks the Web site usage (for example, links and visits) and the providers to use for storing data.
<siteMap>	Registers the providers supported for storing site layout information. By default, the map is stored in XML files that are read using a particular provider object.. Custom providers of site maps are registered here.
<smtpMail>	Configures the SMTP service by specifying the server name, port, and default values for fields such as From or Subject.
<webSiteAdministrationTool>	Contains information about the location and the structure of the Web Admin tool (WebAdmin.axd). You can use this section to add new toolbar buttons and new features to administer.

We'll conclude the chapter by looking at the new health monitoring API, which is a diagnostic tool for ASP.NET.

The Health Monitoring API

The health monitoring API in ASP.NET 2.0 gives the system administrator and the members of the operational staff of a Web site tools for monitoring the health of the system. The ability to rapidly diagnose failing operations or broken subsystems is crucial to maintaining the performance of a Web site.

The health monitoring API enables real-time tracing of running applications and provides statistics about usage and performance. The API's two main features are customizable analysis and automated notification of problems.

Customizable Event-Level Analysis

To effectively manage ASP.NET applications, administrators need runtime information about the system that is a reliable indicator of the health of the system. More important, this information should be easily consumable using standard tools and techniques. Table 12-5 details the events exposed by the ASP.NET health monitoring facility. The events are registered in the machine.config file.

Table 12-5 Events Exposed by the Health Monitoring API

Event	Description
All Audits	Fired for all audit events caught
All Errors	Fired for any error event caught
All Events	Fired for any event caught
Application Lifetime Event	Contains information about application events, including restart and stop
Failure Audits	Contains information about failure audit events
HeartBeat	Optional periodic event that provides process statistical information
Infrastructure Errors	Contains information about error events that are related to the system configuration or application code (such as compilation errors)
Request Processing Errors	Contains information about errors that occur while servicing a request
Request Processing Event	Contains information about the request and the thread on which it's executing
Success Audits	Contains information about success audit events

By using the web.config file, you can disable some of these events. In addition, you can set a nonnegative integer that indicates (in seconds) how often the HeartBeat event is raised by each AppDomain to update statistics.

The ASP.NET infrastructure provides event information in a variety of modes, including Windows Management Instrumentation (WMI), the Windows event log, and performance counters. How events are delivered depends on which providers are defined in the configuration files and how they are mapped to events.

Automated Notification of Problems

Each event can be associated with a profile and a provider. The profile determines how often the event is fired; the provider indicates the component to which the event is delivered. The links between events, profiles, and providers are established through configuration. Table 12-6 lists supported built-in event stores.

Table 12-6 Event Stores Supported by the Health Monitoring API

Provider	Description
EventLog	Stores events to the specified Windows event log. The default event log is *Application*.
LogFile	Stores events to the specified file on disk.
MailEvent	For each event, sends a notification e-mail to the specified list of e-mail addresses.
SqlEvent	Records events by adding a new row to the specified SQL Server database.
WmiEvent	Reflects generated ASP.NET events as WMI events.

You can configure the settings of these event providers by using the machine.config file.

The profile of an event determines parameters that affect how the event is treated by ASP.NET. For example, the profile establishes the minimum number of occurrences of each event before it's actually fired as well as the threshold after which the event stops being fired. You can also configure the minimum duration between two consecutive events of the same type. Finally, the profile of an event is bound to a comma-separated list of providers that are to be invoked whenever the event is fired. Only those providers receive notification.

Summary

ASP.NET 2.0 is definitely a major upgrade to ASP.NET 1.x. Brand-new features live side by side with improvements and fixes all around the existing infrastructure. In this book, you've discovered what's new and why, and often how it is expected to be implemented in the final version of ASP.NET 2.0. As this final chapter demonstrates, the configuration schema—the schema of the XML file that developers and administrators use to tune up the behavior of an application—has also changed significantly to deal with the new features in ASP.NET 2.0.

The configuration API is now a full-fledged API, not just a collection of utilities for reading settings programmatically. A new suite of classes lets you read and modify the .config files without your having to worry about schema and concurrent access. ASP.NET 2.0 also features new administrative tools, new instrumentation tools for diagnosis, and performance counters to measure the throughput of an application. Ready-to-use system tools and a health monitoring API let you create custom tools that make monitoring ASP.NET 2.0 easier and more effective than ever before.

Index

Symbols

A

B

C

D

E

F

G

H

M

N

O

P

Q

R

S

X

Z

About the Author

Dino Esposito is the Microsoft ASP.NET and ADO.NET expert at Wintellect, a premier training, debugging, and consulting firm.

Dino writes the "Cutting Edge" column for MSDN Magazine and is a regular contributor of .NET Framework articles to Microsoft's ASP.NET and Longhorn DevCenter and other magazines, including asp.netPRO Magazine (*http://www.aspnetpro.com*), CoDe Magazine (*http://www.code-magazine.com*), and the ASP.NET2TheMax newsletter (*http://www.windevnet.com/newsletters*). His books for Microsoft Press include *Programming Microsoft ASP.NET* (2003), *Building Web Solutions with ASP.NET and ADO.NET* (2002), and *Applied XML Programming for Microsoft .NET* (2002). Up-to-date information about his upcoming articles and books can be found in Dino's blog at *http://weblogs.asp.net/despos*.

Dino is a cofounder of VB-2-the-Max (*http://www.vb2themax.com*), a popular Web site full of free technical information for .NET developers, as well as two newer sites, CS-2-the-Max (for C# and C++ developers) and .Net-2-the-Max (for all .NET developers). The 2-the-Max family has a highly selective search engine that lets you search .NET articles and tips published anywhere on the Web by category, language, or keyword.

Before becoming a full-time author, consultant, and trainer, Dino worked for several top consulting companies. Based in Rome, Italy, he pioneered DNA systems in Europe, and in 1994, designed one of the first serious Web applications—an image data bank. These days, you can find Dino at leading conferences such as DevConnections, DevWeek, WinDev, and Microsoft TechEd.

Read more about ASP.NET from Dino Esposito. For free.

Dino is co-founder of the popular **www.vb2themax.com** Web site and the all-new 2-The-Max family of Web sites for developers, which includes **www.cs2themax.com** and **www.dotnet2themax.com**. These sites contain lots of original articles and expose a powerful search engine that lets you quickly locate thousands of the best .NET-related resources anywhere on the Web, by keywords, author, category, publication date, level, and other search criteria.

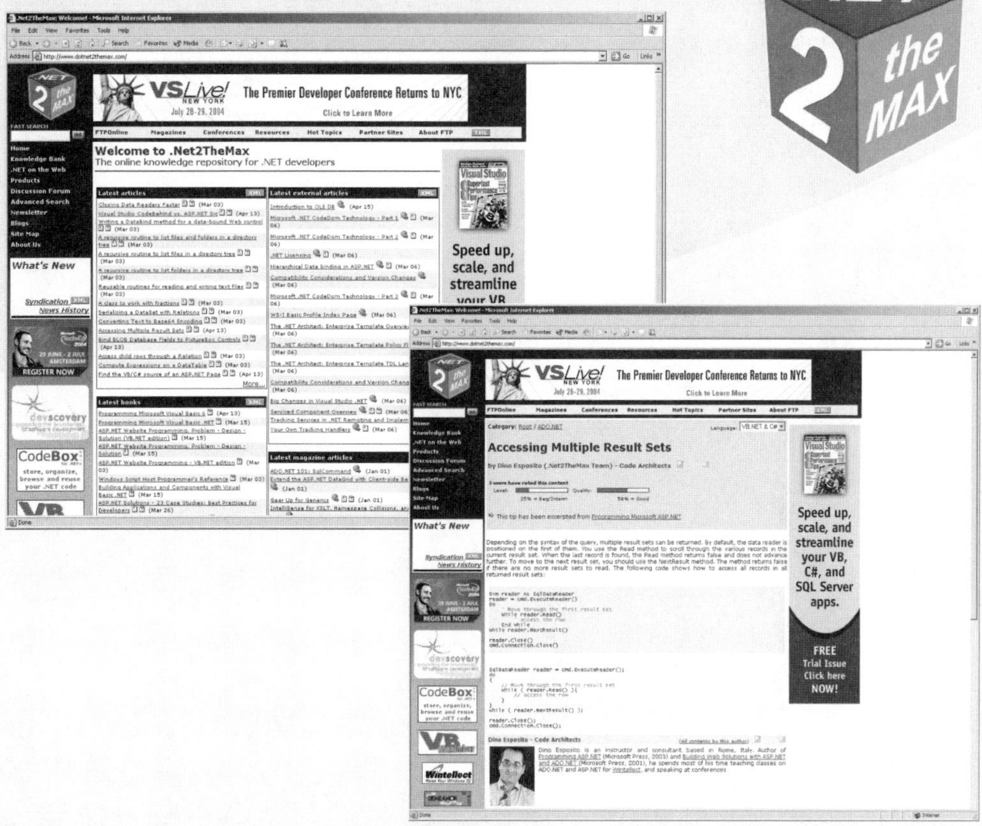

Subscribe to the free newsletter at **http://www.dotnet2themax.com/newsletter/subscribe.aspx**, receive even more tips right in your mailbox, and read about the future of ASP.NET in Dino's column *Whidbey Watcher*.

What do you think of this book?
We want to hear from you!

Do you have a few minutes to participate in a brief online survey? Microsoft is interested in hearing your feedback about this publication so that we can continually improve our books and learning resources for you.

To participate in our survey, please visit:
www.microsoft.com/learning/booksurvey

And enter this book's ISBN, 0-7356-2024-5. As a thank-you to survey participants in the United States and Canada, each month we'll randomly select five respondents to win one of five $100 gift certificates from a leading online merchant.* At the conclusion of the survey, you can enter the drawing by providing your e-mail address, which will be used for prize notification *only*

Thanks in advance for your input. Your opinion counts!

Sincerely,

Microsoft Learning

Learn More. Go Further.

To see special offers on Microsoft Learning products for developers, IT professionals, and home and office users, visit: *www.microsoft.com/learning/booksurvey*

* No purchase necessary. Void where prohibited. Open only to residents of the 50 United States (includes District of Columbia) and Canada (void in Quebec). Sweepstakes ends 6/30/2005. For official rules, see: *www.microsoft.com/learning/booksurvey*